29. 85

Consulting Editor

Edward Keynes
Pennsylvania State University

 Random House   New York

AMERICAN
POLITICS
AND
PUBLIC POLICY

Edited, with Introductions, by Michael P. Smith

Library of Congress Cataloging in Publication Data

Smith, Michael P   comp.
American politics and public policy.

Includes bibliographical references.
1.   United States—Politics and government—1945
—Addresses, essays, lectures. I. Title.
JK271.S583   320.9'73'092   72-10056

Manufactured in the United States of America

Typography by Karin Gurski Batten

First Edition

987654321

Permissions
Acknowledgements

Peter H. Odegard, "The Alienation of Political Science" from Peter H. Odegard, "The Alienation of Political Science," *Governmental Research Center Occasional Papers,* Lawrence, Kansas, University of Kansas, 1967. Reprinted by permission.

Louis Hartz, "The Liberal Tradition in America" from *The Liberal Tradition in America,* copyright © 1955 by Louis Hartz. Reprinted by permission of Harcourt Brace Jovanovich, Inc.

Peter F. Drucker, "A Key to Calhoun's Pluralism" copyright Peter F. Drucker 1948, 1971. Reprinted with permission of the author from *Men, Ideas and Politics* by Peter F. Drucker (New York: Harper & Row, 1971).

George H. Sabine, "The Two American Traditions" from George H. Sabine, "The Two Democratic Traditions," *The Philosophical Review,* LXI (October 1952). Reprinted by permission of the publisher.

Dean Jaros, "Transmitting the Civic Culture: The Teacher and Political Socialization" from Dean Jaros, "Transmitting the Civic Culture: The Teacher and Political Socialization," *Social Science Quarterly,* XLIX (September 1968), pp. 284–295, omitting footnotes. Reprinted by permission of the author and the publisher.

Robert Lane, "Fathers and Sons: Foundations of Political Belief" from Robert Lane, "Fathers and Sons: Foundations of Political Belief," *American Sociological Review,* XXIV (August 1959). Reprinted by permission of the author.

Kenneth Keniston, "Notes on Young Radicals" from Kenneth Keniston, "Notes on Young Radicals," *Change* (November-December 1969), pp. 25–33. Reprinted by permission of the author and the publisher.

Joe McGinniss, "The Selling of the President, 1968" from Joe McGinniss, *The Selling of the President, 1968.* Copyright © 1969 by JoeMac, Inc. Reprinted by permission of Trident Press, a division of Simon & Schuster, Inc.

Nelson W. Polsby, "Policy Analysis and Congress" from Nelson W. Polsby, "Policy Analysis and Congress," *Public Policy,* XVII (Fall 1969), pp. 61–74, omitting footnotes. Reprinted by permission of the publisher.

John F. Manley, "Wilbur D. Mills: A Study in Congressional Influence" from John F. Manley, "Wilbur D. Mills: A Study in Congressional Influence," *American Political Science Review,* LXIII (June 1969), pp. 442–464, omitting footnotes. Reprinted by permission of the author and the publisher.

E. E. Schattschneider, "The Scope and Bias of the Pressure System" from *The Semi-Sovereign People* by E. E. Schattschneider. Copyright © 1960 by E. E. Schattschneider. Reprinted by permission of Holt, Rinehart and Winston, Inc.

FOR PAT

Acknowledgments

Few intellectual endeavors are entirely the fruit of solitary reflection. I am indebted to Denis Sullivan and Richard F. Winters of Dartmouth College and Edward W. Gude of the Adlai Stevenson Institute for providing the stimulating intellectual milieu within which this book was conceived. For his helpful review of the manuscript I wish to thank Marvin Surkin. A special note of thanks is also due all those authors who have consented to my use of their work.

In the course of preparing this volume for publication I have received valuable encouragement and editorial advice from Barry Rossinoff of Random House. He was always accessible and helpful at appropriate moments. I am grateful as well to my manuscript editors Susan Gilbert and James Wittenmyer for their editorial assistance.

For their grant to underwrite the preparation of the manuscript I wish to thank the Faculty Research Committee of Dartmouth College. The comments of my colleague Stephen Sternheimer of Boston University, the efforts of research assistant Mark Pfeiffer, and the secretarial assistance provided by Judy Mazurski, Elizabeth MacBurney, and William M. Clapham are all gratefully acknowledged.

My greatest debt is to my wife Pat, to whom this book is dedicated. Her love, understanding, and assistance have made the preparation of this work enjoyable.

April 1972   M.P.S.
Boston, Massachusetts

Contents

PART EIGHT / DEMOCRACY AND MASS SOCIETY

Introduction

This book attempts to assess American politics and the making of public policy in the context of two alternative theories of democracy—pluralism and majoritarian democracy. Its central thesis is that the American political system can best be understood as an incessant contest between the pluralistic pattern of rule by well-organized private interests and the populistic pattern of demands for public policies that serve the common interest. In contemporary America, "politics as usual" means that politically powerful and well-organized minorities rule. The result is a piecemeal, gradualist approach to the making of public policy, engendered by the political system's responsiveness to organized interests that benefit from the status quo. This approach creates the very conditions that foster appeals to the people for support of a comprehensive redistribution of political power and social values.

Despite the regularity of mass protest movements expressing socioeconomic and political discontent throughout our nation's history, the majority of scholars who study American politics continue to accept mass uprisings as abnormal and self-defeating deviations from the normal pattern —that is, from the resolution of conflict through negotiation and compromise among a multiplicity of organized interest groups. The prevailing theory purporting to explain the dynamics of the American political process is the pluralist or "group" theory, which portrays the American political system as fundamentally stable and moderate. Severe conflict among competing interests is assumed to be checked by America's many levels and agencies of government, which provide "points of access" where groups that are aggrieved may express their demands and receive some measure of satisfaction. In addition, societal cleavages are said to be minimized because many political activists belong to groups whose memberships overlap, and the cross-pressures felt by the members of these overlapping groups render them capable of only moderate political behavior.

Public policies produced by the political system envisaged in the group theory reflect marginal or incremental changes resulting from the balance of forces among contending parties. The pluralists claim that any group of citizens having political grievances can and will express them in the political arena, thereby creating disequilibrium in the current balance of forces, followed by negotiation, followed by the establishment of a new equilibrium that includes the previously aggrieved group. It is only a short step from this conceptualization of the process by which conflict is resolved to the normative conclusion that the "resultant" of the vector of pressures exerted by organized interest groups is equivalent to the "public interest."

The selections in this book are intended to show that the pluralist model, although descriptively accurate in several respects, contains a number of conceptual difficulties that lead to an idealized picture of the role of interest groups in the policy-making process. These images of political reality, if accepted at face value, become key components in an ideology that legitimizes the process of incremental change and political stability. Thus, although the theory is partially useful, it is necessary at the outset to identify its empirical shortcomings and to clarify its ideological biases.

The group theory idealizes the process of group bargaining in the policy-making arena in four ways. First, the term "group" connotes and focuses our consciousness on the Tocquevillian conception of a "voluntary association" of individual citizens closely bound together for common purposes. But the kind of power exercised by the most successful private interest groups in America is bureaucratized power. The most politically viable private interest groups—General Motors, International Telephone and Telegraph, organized labor, and the food-processing industry, for example—are themselves hierarchically organized bureaucracies. They hardly afford their employees, or "members," the opportunities for individual participation and influence that the term "group" suggests.

In public bureaucracies hierarchical authority is constrained by fears of governmental coercion embedded in the American political culture and by numerous constitutional barriers against the exercise of public power. In contrast, there are far fewer cultural and legal checks on the concentration of power in private interest groups and on the hierarchical bureaucratization of authority within such groups. To call a conglomerate such as I. T. & T. a "group" is to evoke romantic and misleading images of individual citizens directly participating in the determination of their political fate. The component of group theory that deserves to be underlined is the term "organized" rather than the term "group," for such an emphasis places the "interest group" concept in a more realistic perspective. Thus, in the selections that follow, meaningful distinctions are made between organized "corporate interest" groups, speaking for industry, labor, and agriculture; organized "public interest" groups, such as Common Cause; unorganized protest movements, articulating broad social goals; emerging protest groups, seeking benefits for heretofore powerless minorities; and the unorganized general public.

The second idealizing conception found in the group theory is the assumption that Americans are a nation of "joiners" who can readily turn their attention to political concerns if they become disenchanted with the content of American public policy. This assumption has been challenged successfully by E. E. Schattschneider* and other political scientists, who have shown that there is an upper-class and business bias among those who

---

* *The Semi-Sovereign People* (New York: Holt, Rinehart, Winston, 1960). For a detailed development of Schattschneider's argument, see Part Three.

participate regularly in the activities of organized interest groups. This class bias extends to other forms of political activity, such as voting and political party activism, that are regarded as legitimate by those who support the group theory. In fact, less than one-third of the American adult populace even belongs to organized interest groups (unless, of course, we use the term "belong" in the sense that a clerk can be said to "belong" to General Motors).

The third conceptual difficulty is the failure to perceive the long-term social consequences of bargaining by organized interest groups. The pluralists tend to be ahistorical—that is, they are concerned with the immediate factors and pressures that account for single policy decisions. By failing to examine the relationship between political processes and their cumulative historical *results,* many advocates of the group theory fail to recognize the status quo biases of pluralistic public policies. The public policies that emerge from what Schattschneider has termed the "pressure system" tend to be conservative in at least three senses. First, because of the bias in political participation, public officials who respond to the demands of organized interest groups are usually responding to the segments of the population that benefit most from the status quo. Thus, the policy changes that organized interest groups espouse are likely to be marginal or incremental in scope. Second, this same bias tends to limit the future political agenda by excluding issues that call for fundamental reexamination of the existing social structure and its dominant institutions. Third, the federal government's policy of recognizing the leaders of a handful of giant, bureaucratic interest groups as the legitimate spokesmen for broad segments of the population is also conservative: it inhibits changes in power and in policy goals within the groups themselves. William Connolly has observed that

By co-opting legitimate interest group elites as the official spokesmen for broad seg-ments of society, the government helps to freeze the status quo, making it difficult for "members" in these . . . [bureaucratic] associations to challenge their leaders without risking legally supported internal sanctions.*

The fourth conceptual pitfall is the pluralists' tendency to treat bargaining as not merely a useful means of resolving conflict, but as a desirable end in itself. The tendency of many American political scientists to accept organized interest-group bargaining not only as a fully adequate explanatory theory of the dynamics of the American political process but also as a desirable political norm derives primarily from their previously mentioned preoccupation with readily observable political *processes* rather than with the *results* of the political system. In raising the question "Who governs,

---

* *The Bias of Pluralism* (New York: Atherton Press, 1969), p. 16.

and by what process?'' political scientists are seeking to explain only the behavior of those who are active in making political decisions. This research question calls attention away from the values, aspirations, and social conditions of those who are *in*active but who are nevertheless potential participants in the policy-making process, be they weak and unorganized minorities or the general public. In effect, the research questions being asked direct our attention to the bargaining process between governmental officials and organized interest groups, which the pluralists tend to treat as the whole of politics. By defining the scope of political inquiry so narrowly, the group theory tends to overlook or misinterpret many historical forces that might explain political phenomena but that lie outside the frame of reference of the active decision makers. For example, many pluralists view the politics of protest as an irrational and cataclysmic deviation from the interest-group bargaining process rather than as a historically predictable by-product of the government's long-term responsiveness to the needs and interests of organized bureaucratic private power. In practice, this view has amounted to a kind of tunnel vision that has important implications.

When an industry, an established trade union, or corporate agriculture has obtained direct access to and influence on a congressional subcommittee, a federal line agency, or an independent regulatory commission, the appropriate bargaining style entails communications that symbolize reasonableness and "give and take." In contrast, expressive rhetoric and occasional threats of direct mass confrontation characterize the style of political protest by loosely organized political movements. Such tactics make the action taken by these movements appear to be unreasonable or even totally irrational when considered only as a "process" or style of politics independent of the substantive grievances being expressed. However, certain questions must be asked: "Who benefits, and who is burdened by the public policy being protested? Are these particular benefits or burdens justified, and if so, on what grounds? What power resources other than direct action are available to the protesters? Once these questions are answered, various forms of direct political action can be regarded as entirely understandable and justifiable in the context of the socioeconomic situation in which they are taken. The boycotts on grapes and lettuce organized by Cesar Chavez are good examples of the kind of situation to which I refer.

Similarly, if one were to focus on the *results* of a bargained decision rather than solely on the *process* by which a conflict is resolved, one might easily conclude that a regulatory agency's bargained decision approving an inflationary rate increase, or a wage package passing along to the consumer the cost of a publicly sanctioned settlement, was an irrational attempt to serve the public interest.

The essays in this book examine the dynamic relationship between American political processes, the public policies they produce, and the long-term political impact of these policies. They were chosen to highlight the political actions and policies that are consequences of the "pressure system." The major national political institutions—Congress, the Presidency, and the Supreme Court, as well as the federal bureaucracy—are treated as regular targets of organized interest groups, as periodic targets of broad- and narrow-purpose protest movements, and as occasional targets of general public expectations. The selections illustrate that the way in which these institutions have evolved has created numerous obstacles to a comprehensive and rational development of public policy. Often it is the public's frustration with the failures of these institutions to respond effectively to felt needs and policy problems that emerges as political protest.

Parts One and Two of this book deal with the overall cultural context within which public policies are developed. Expectations concerning desirable and possible public policies held by organized interest groups, by public officials, by emergent mass movements, and by the general public are shaped by the political culture into which citizens are socialized. In Part One the abstract political values that establish the boundaries of what a culture regards as legitimate political styles and demands are discussed within the context of three political value systems—classical liberalism, pluralism, and populism. Part Two analyzes how various segments of the population are socialized, by agencies of political socialization such as the family, the school, the mass media, and the government, into acceptance or rejection of these abstract values.

Parts Three through Six deal with the institutional and political context within which American public policy is made. Major institutional and political constraints, which impede comprehensive problem-solving and the effective use of public power, are identified and analyzed. These constraints include not only the role of organized private interests, but also the ideologies and perspectives of public officials; the growing size, complexity, and fragmentation of public bureaucracies; the effect of past policies on the making of future policies; and the numerous checks that the political culture and the legal system impose on the exercise of public power.

Parts Seven and Eight deal with several contemporary changes in the social structure that are presently testing the capacity of America's fragmented political structure to direct national priorities. These changes include the growing political consciousness among powerless poor people, the concentration of ownership and control of the mass media, and the ever-increasing growth of massive "private governments." The most politically formidable change in the social structure since the end of World War II has been the emergence of a grand coalition of interests whose shared belief in maintaining persistently high levels of public expenditure for national defense is sapping the nation's capacity to respond to other pressing domestic needs. The meaning and impact of this "military industrial complex," as it has been termed by some, forms the basis for the final selections in this book.

The principal materials chosen to deliver the main themes of this volume are thought-provoking theoretical and research essays by both advocates and critics of the group theory. Each Part concludes with a descriptive case study designed to add some flesh and blood to the bones of democratic political theory. The essay selected to begin this book is the late Peter Odegard's important and neglected article "The Alienation of Political Science." Odegard's analysis of the public policies that are consequences of the growth of private corporate power in American society provides compelling reasons to reexamine the dynamics of American political life and the nature and quality of their results.

The Alienation of Political Science

1

Peter H. Odegard

"The greatest and fairest sort of wisdom by far," said Plato, "is that which is concerned with the ordering of states." Why should this be so—if, indeed, it is so? Is it because, as Aristotle remarked, Politics is not only an architectonic science but antedates and transcends all other sciences? The *record* would seem to indicate that men were concerned with a more or less systematic study of government long before they began to search systematically for the laws which govern the physical universe. Is it not true, as Thomas Hobbes said, that until man had mastered the science or art of government, there could be no other science, "no knowledge of the face of the earth, . . . no account of time, no arts, no letters, no society, and, which is worst of all, continual fear and danger of violent death; and the life of man [was] solitary, poor, nasty, brutish, and short."

But even if all this be true, it is not the only reason for the primacy of politics among the arts and sciences. For among all the institutions which make civilization possible—the family, the church, the school, the economic system, the state—the political system alone has established its claim to the legitimate use of violence against those who deviate from or defy its ordinances. And it is upon this monopoly of violence that peace, security, law and order, depend. When to this one attaches the principle of territoriality to which political systems in a unique way lay claim, it is easy to understand why civilization is properly regarded as a by-product of politics and not the other way around.

If these, then, are some of the root reasons for the primacy of politics, others of which we are more immediately and urgently aware readily come to mind. Problems of population pressures on scarce resources, of crime and delinquency, unemployment, poverty and deprivation, health and welfare, urban sprawl—that witches' cauldron of so many other problems—racial and religious conflict, education, scientific research and cultural growth, national independence and world security, war and peace, are but a small sample of the urgent problems that confront mankind—and every one is primarily a *political* problem crying out for a *political* solution. The physical and biological sciences, engineering and technology, the earth sciences, medicine, and some of the social sciences—notably psychology, sociology, and economics—have provided at least tentative answers to the technical aspects of many of these problems. The laggard in all this is that Queen of all the sciences—the Science of Politics. This most ancient and most honored of the sciences has shown itself but ill-equipped to tell us how this great store of knowledge can be put to its best and most efficient use in solving the problems that beset us.

3

Part of our problem, no doubt, arises from the historic gap between theory and practice, or between so-called pure and applied research. Plutarch tells us that Archimedes was better known for his practical inventions than for his scientific theories. Yet such was his disdain for applied science that "he would not deign to leave behind any commentary or writing on such subjects, but repudiated as sordid and ignoble the whole trade of engineering and every sort of art that lends itself to mere use. . . . He [rather] placed his whole affection and ambition in those purer speculations where there can be no reference to the vulgar needs of life." This gap between pure and applied science still remains in the natural sciences, but it has become progressively narrow. Science and engineering have formed a partnership in which mutual aid and respect have largely replaced ancient antagonism and contempt. The contemporary theoretical physicist knows that without the engineers who build his accelerators and cloud chambers, his own work would be impossible. So, too, does the geneticist, the biochemist, and the astronomer. Without the telescope, both Copernicus and Galileo might well have remained mere stargazers; without the microscope or the electro-microscope, modern biological science might never have advanced beyond taxonomy or gross anatomy. The development of technical instrumentation and equipment has brought vastly greater scope and depth to scientific inquiry and experiment. And the increasing interdependence of science and technology in the laboratory has been matched by a growing interdependence of theory and practice outside the laboratory. The gap between the ideas and experiments of pure science and their application to the practical problems of medical care, mental health, and transportation and communication, including the exploration of outer space, has been accordingly diminished. It is this marriage of pure and applied science that accounts for what we now call the knowledge explosion.

Yet by a kind of paradox the great achievements of the natural sciences and technology have generated political problems of increasing urgency and complexity. They have made the human race a community of neighbors in a shrinking world. But they have also brought traffic congestion and air pollution, nuclear weapons and improved delivery systems that pose a continuous threat of human destruction on a global scale. The biological sciences, medicine, and the healing arts have extended the span of human life but have also generated a population explosion that threatens to engulf mankind in a Malthusian tragedy of unexampled scope and severity. In spite of revolutionary changes in the production and distribution of goods and services, the ancient paradox of Progress and Poverty remains. These are but a few of the problems of our contemporary civilization which cry out for study and solution. Most of them are political problems, since they involve the authoritative allocation of values of both human and natural resources.

To avoid confusion, let me say at once that in its broadest sense, the term "political" has a wider sweep and cuts more deeply into our civilization than is commonly assumed. The allocation of values is a function not alone of the political state but of many other organizations and institutions as well. The family, the school and the church, the corporation, the trade union—indeed, virtually all forms of organized human activity—in one way or another, are engaged in the allocation of values. Wherever the interaction of people, or access to available goods and services, is governed by identifiable rules enforced by sanctions of some kind, we are confronted by what the late Arthur Bentley called the Process of Government or Politics. Such rules may govern activities as simple and direct as the use of the family automobile, and the behavior of players in a game, or as complex as the operations of an economic system, or the allocation, management, and conservation of the natural resources of an empire. How, by whom, by what authority, to what ends, with what effect these rules are made and enforced are the basic questions of political science. Without identifiable rules of this kind, civilization would be impossible. Politics, therefore, the making and enforcement of rules of conduct, serves as the integrative process of any society just as the central nervous system serves to integrate the human mind and body. Perhaps this is why Aristotle described man as a political animal and politics as an essential condition of human life itself.

Seen in this light, the dimensions of political science exceed the span of attention or analysis of any single individual. At one time it may have been possible to explore politics as the integrative process in all the various social organizations embraced within the Greek City State, the medieval manor, or an isolated and autonomous village or town. Plato's *Republic* and Aristotle's *Politics* represent political science of this kind. With the emergence, however, of more extensive and complex societies, the angle of vision of the political scientist changed. It came to focus on the political state. Analysis of the political process in the family, the church, or the economic system was left to the new sciences of sociology, anthropology, and economics. Although these, too, are political institutions engaged in the allocation of resources or values, their jurisdiction is more functional than territorial; and in the enforcement of their rules they are denied the use of physical coercion to which the political state alone lays claim.

As the legitimacy of this claim by the political state to a monopoly of coercive power over all individuals and groups within a given territory was established, it came increasingly to be a synonym for all political power and authority. And when political scientists refer to politics as the authoritative allocation of values in society, it is to the political state that they usually refer. The allocation of values by the family or other so-called private associations is generally regarded as non-authoritative, mainly because they may not legitimately use physical coercion in the process. Political scientists have accordingly distinguished between so-called public and private political systems with the former having an exclusive claim to the legitimate use of coercive power. Because of this claim, men and women as individuals and as members of private groups and associations have been jealous of the scope of power to be vested in the political state. Except for national defense, the administration of justice, internal security, and the protection of property, it was argued, the allocation of values and resources in society should be left to private individuals or associations. The sanctions of the market-place, the laws of supply and demand, it was said, were more efficient regulators of prices, wages, interest rates, and profits than state-imposed rules or regulations enforced by physical coercion. As for the human casualties of this system—the dependent children, the aged and infirm, the indigent, the unemployed—they were to be provided for by their families, friends, and neighbors, the churches, private philanthropy, or, when these proved to be inadequate, by public authority through such measures as the Elizabethan Poor Laws, the Poor Farm, the Orphans' Home, and the County Home for the Aged.

Modern political scientists like John Locke, Adam Smith, John Stuart Mill, Lord Acton, and Herbert Spencer shared many of these ideas. If they were not prepared to say, with the anarchist Proudhon, that (coercive) "governments are the scourge of God," they generally agreed with Lord Acton that "power (i.e., coercive power) tends to corrupt and absolute power corrupts absolutely," and with Lord Macaulay that "political (i.e., authoritative or coercive) means to achieve social ends will destroy liberty and prosperity if not civilization itself." John Stuart Mill, a major political scientist and prophet of modern liberalism, declared that "the sole end for which mankind are warranted, individually and collectively, in interfering with the liberty of action of any of their members is self-protection. . . . His own good, either physical or moral, is not sufficient warrant." And Herbert Spencer, in *Man Versus the State* and *The Coming Slavery,* attacked virtually all forms of state intervention in social and economic affairs.

This denigration of the political state, this hostility to the exercise of public power, was accompanied by a massive increase in the exercise of power by so-called private governments. Giant combines, corporations, and trusts, trade unions and trade associations emerged as centers of private political power, some of which had resources to match or exceed those of the political state itself. At the same time, functional specialization both within and among these private associations created a new interdependent society that cried out for central planning and control. The so-called "natural" controls of the price system—the laws of supply and demand—in a free competitive market proved inadequate. Not only were they unable to provide an equitable allocation of values among individuals and groups, but they were unable to provide that minimum of order and stability essential to the successful operation of the system as a whole. Yet central planning—long recognized as essential in private associations—was either denied or deplored in the political state. At the very time centripetal forces were transforming a diffuse and decentralized agrarian society into an interdependent and integrated one, we continued to operate our public political system as though none of these changes were taking place. We continued to rely on a political philosophy of providential guidance in which competing private interests would, in some mysterious fashion, promote a more perfect union and the general welfare and insure the blessings of liberty to all. In this process the political state was regarded as but another type of group or association whose major role was to serve as umpire among private power systems to insure what was called equilibrium or stability. To be sure, its territorial base and its monopoly of coercive power were recognized as unique. But for this very reason, so ran the argument, its functional jurisdiction must be severely restricted to foreign relations, national defense, and internal order and security. And while decision making and enforcement within the private sector was increasingly centralized, in the public sector it remained—save again for foreign policy and national defense—diffuse and decentralized. Local government, including states' rights, *ad hoc* special districts, and occasionally interstate or regional compacts were in all circumstances to be preferred to centralized planning and control.

Under these circumstances the political state became increasingly preoccupied with foreign relations and national defense in which areas there was great opportunity and little opposition to its expansion. Nor is this surprising. After all, violence was the state's business. Moreover, defense expenditures do not involve adverse intervention in the private power structure to the same extent as government sponsored housing, health services, electric power, or the ownership, management, and conservation of natural resources. ICBM's and bombing planes do not compete in the market with automobiles, washing machines, etc., for the consumer's dollar; but defense expenditures do generate purchasing power to sustain the market for private capital and for consumer goods and services. Public contracts with major industrial concerns for defense hardware and services and for research and development became an almost indispensable feature of the total economy. The fact that they were also inflationary was viewed as a healthy influence in normal times, contributing to an improved rate of economic growth. And when, during war or emergencies, this defense-generated inflation threatened to get out of hand, the proper remedy was to cut expenditures for education, health, welfare, and other so-called non-essential services. One result of this has been an active partnership between private and public power structures that looks with favor upon the expansion of public power as expressed in defense budgets. The pervasive political influence of this military-industrial complex, as President Eisenhower called it, is felt throughout the country and, indeed, throughout the world.

In other respects, however, the political state as an integrative and dynamic force in our society continues to play a minor role. Nor is it well designed to do so. The central government of checks and balances, deliberately designed to limit the use of public power, provides a built-in system of minority vetoes which makes it difficult to translate the demands and expectations of the people into public policy. The Federal System continues to operate within the context of 18th and 19th century concepts, and at the local level the structure is even less well adapted to the complex, highly integrated, and swiftly moving conditions of our own time. Problems of water supply and flood control, transportation and communication, sewage and other waste disposal, air and water pollution, racial and ethnic conflict, crime and delinquency, health and welfare, education and recreation—all are beyond the reach of most local political structures as they now exist.

To be sure, changes in organization and procedure have improved the governmental process. To describe them as first steps toward modernization is not to say they are unimportant or futile. And it is worth noting that these and other reforms owe a great deal to political scientists unafraid of involvement in the living world of government and politics. One thinks in this connection of such men as Frank Goodnow, Woodrow Wilson, Charles Beard, Charles Merriam, Chester Lloyd Jones, Luther Gulick, Richard Childs, and many others. It is obvious, however, that much remains to be done even in this field of governmental organization and management.

To specify or analyze in detail some proposed roads to reform in our public power structure is beyond the scope of this discussion. But even with the most ideal pattern of organization and management we shall fail unless we are prepared to develop public policies better adapted to the actual conditions of contemporary life. Anyone attempting to evaluate public policies in the United States must be impressed with their *ad hoc* character, and the absence of rational planning. Our foreign policies have been mainly panic-induced responses to real or imaginary threats to what we are pleased to call our national interests. But just what these national interests are we do not say. In large measure our policies in Europe, Asia, and Africa and even in this hemisphere have been negativistic and defensive rather than creative or affirmative. Even a generously conceived program of foreign economic aid has been poorly conceived and administered, and an implied relationship of *quid pro quo* has cast a cloud over what should be its larger objectives. Plans to rationalize the foreign aid programs such as those proposed by President Kennedy and, more recently, by Senator Fulbright, have been rejected. Yet in what Walter Lippmann has called a kind of messianic megalomania we have made rhetorical commitments far beyond our resources, seeing ourselves as 20th century inheritors of the White Man's Burden. As a result not a few nations, both old and new, have come to regard us as counter-revolutionary, intent upon upholding "legitimate" governments, however weak, unpopular, or reactionary they may be, so long as they maintain an anti-communistic posture. The result is a kind of neo-isolationism in which we strive to isolate ourselves, if necessary, by military intervention, from the revolutionary forces now sweeping the world.

On the home front public policies display a similar pattern of improvisation with little in the way of long term planning for the realization of stated goals. At home and abroad, policy decisions reflect a response to crisis or panic born of crisis. A nation that can plan and carry into effect a vast program of space exploration and military intervention on a global scale somehow finds itself confused, frustrated, or impotent in dealing with the urgent problems of its own domestic life. Except for token recognition of our housing, medical, educational, economic, and cultural needs and the multiple forces of urban sclerosis and decay, we have barely begun to define the problems in terms of public policy. What we call a war on poverty is in fact little more than a minor skirmish with outmoded weapons derived from Woodrow Wilson's New Freedom and FDR's New Deal. When I sketched the outlines of President Johnson's Great Society to an audience in Hamburg, Germany, they were astounded to hear that measures with which they have been familiar since Bismarck should be regarded as novel or radical in contemporary America. The fact is that public policies in the United States represent not rational plans for the achievement of stated goals but grudging and minimal concessions made by our private power structures to our quasi-democratic political state. I say quasi-democratic because the full force of mass demands for a more perfect union, civil rights, and the general welfare are muted, diluted, and delayed by the complex political process that characterizes decision making in our public power system. It seems to me high time for us to take another look at that system and to search for ways and means by which the exigencies of modern life and the needs and expectations of people may be translated into public policy. So long as we believe that political power corrupts except when it is used to wage war, so long as we regard the political state as our enemy rather than our servant, and so long as we believe with Macaulay that political means to achieve social ends is an abuse of power, we shall fail. We need to learn that political power can be used to protect and promote civil rights as well as to destroy it and to promote human welfare as well as to impair it. We need, in short, to learn that the democratic political state can, in fact, become a major integrative and creative force in modern life.

In achieving all this, contemporary academic political scientists have a special obligation and opportunity. Unfortunately it seems to me they have, instead, become increasingly indifferent to basic problems of government and public policy. They seem increasingly preoccupied with problems of individual motivation, socialization, perception and cognition, with results often remote from the political process as such. Studies of micro-politics (i.e., small groups) or those based on theoretical models or computer simulations often yield brilliant socialized insights but more often than not the results are redundant or trivial or have little or no application to the real world of government and politics. We are told, for example, with great solemnity that "opinions are really formed through the day-to-day exchange of observations and comments which goes on among people," or that "where strong and opposing forces act on an individual the resultant behavior will demonstrate the characteristics of conflict," or that turnout at elections is a function of voter interest. In the field of international relations we learn the not too spectacular fact that political integration is usually a function of social and /or economic integration, or at any rate that they are reciprocals of one another. Much of what is called comparative or cross-polity analysis under the guise of new concepts or systems of classification in fact yields little more than ingenious semantic innovations or what I have called polysyllabic neologisms. Not infrequently the data offered to the computers in these studies are themselves so fuzzy, incomplete, inaccurate, non-comparable, or unavailable, that the variances even when computed to three decimal points are virtually useless. Contemporary studies of voting, administrative, legislative, and judicial behavior lay emphasis on the socio-economic, psychological, cognitive, or ideological factors involved without indicating their relation to actual political behavior. And many of them merely tend to confirm theories of the political process familiar to political scientists since Aristotle.

One has only to read Hamilton's or Madison's analysis of the role of social and economic classes in the fight for ratification of the Constitution; Hancock and Bowdoin's report on social stratification in the gubernatorial vote in Massachusetts in 1789; or John Taylor of Carolina's critical study of the Hamiltonian-Federalist alignment under President Washington to realize that behavioral analysis of political processes has a long history even in this country. To be sure these older statements lacked the elegant methodology and the subtle social and psychological insights of contemporary studies. They were also less addicted to deterministic theories of human behavior, and less given to quantitative statements. They were, however, on the whole more politically orientated and relevant. One would not say of them what V. O. Key once said of the Erie County Study, *The People's Choice,* that they "take the politics out of the study of electoral behavior." And in spite of considerable skepticism concerning mass behavior in general, these early American political scientists looked for and hoped for a larger coefficient of rationality in political behavior than has been the case of contemporary academic political scientists. It may be that increasing emphasis on perception and cognition in the political process indicates a partial retreat from the Hobbesian determinism that has characterized so much behavioral theory. V. O. Key's posthumous volume on *The Responsible Electorate* assigns a much larger place in voting behavior to the voters' conscious policy preferences than has generally been the case. We are a long way from the romantic but never widely held image of the voter as an altogether rational man making political choices upon the basis of marginal utility or cost-benefit analysis. But we seem reluctant to give up the equally romantic pseudo-scientific image of the voter as a non-rational creature of pressures and cross-pressures in his external environment.

It is, however, not my purpose here to present an extended review of the contemporary scene in political science. If one may summarize, it may be said that political science in this generation has been moving from a normative, humanistic, descriptive, or taxonomic discipline to one whose cutting edge has become empirical and analytical. As in other sciences, emphasis on empirical research and analysis has meant not only greater emphasis on quantitative methods, but a progressive narrowing of focus on smaller and smaller components of the total political process. Ancient generalizations and normative judgments about political systems have given way to empirical statements about sub-systems, classes, groups, or interests. These in turn have been reduced to smaller and smaller units or particles. While analysis of this kind has helped to make political science more objective, empirical, and rational, it has also tended to de-emphasize government and the political process as a whole. Micro-politics bids fair to displace macro-politics. In doing so, it also tends to widen the gap between appearance and reality, and between pure and applied political science. As a consequence we have become increasingly indifferent to the pressing problems of public policy and governmental organization and management. Indeed, the more zealous we are in our scientific or methodological posture, the more indifferent or even contemptuous we become of those who continue to ask not only How? but Why? and To What End? We have allowed our zeal for quantitative analysis to dull our interest in qualitative analysis. In a very real sense, much that passes for political science today represents what one critic has described as "the triumph of technique over purpose." Like fanatics, we redouble our effort after having lost our aim.

Contemporary political science has been vastly enriched by an increasing emphasis on interdisciplinary integration, although one often wonders whether it has not been swallowed up in the process. It has also been technically enriched not only by an increased emphasis on quantitative statements but by the availability of survey research centers with incredibly efficient data processing equipment. My concern arises from our reluctance to employ these new insights, methods, and facilities on the urgent problems that contront our contemporary civilization. To say that we must first develop more meaningful concepts and perfect our methods of inquiry is not a sufficient answer. Concepts and methods of inquiry can be tested and improved quite as easily by applying them to real problems as by continued research on minutiae having only a tangential relation to the process of government or by indulging in endless fantasies about pseudo-problems, models, or ideal types. As Sigmund Freud once remarked, "there comes a time when you have to stop cleaning your glasses and take a look through them."

Nor do I believe that to apply our skills and our knowledge of the political process to such mundane problems as crime and delinquency, war and peace, progress and poverty, or to the reconstruction of political institutions, would impair our scientific purity and objectivity. No one, I think, would argue that the biologists' search for the cause and cure of cancer, or the physicists' quest for peaceful uses of atomic energy, has impaired their scientific rigor or integrity. If, as I believe, the so-called knowledge explosion of this century in the natural sciences and technology has been made possible by a marriage of pure and applied research, who can say that political revolutions in the future may be the result not of violent confrontations of conflicting ideologies but a similar partnership between pure and applied political science. If, as I believe, politics is the major integrative factor in civilization, a closer partnership between the natural sciences and technology and what Harold Lasswell has called the Policy Sciences is imperative.

This partnership between what Walter Bagehot called Physics and Politics has already assumed impressive proportions not only through the Patent Office, the Smithsonian Institution, the National Institute of Health, the National Science Foundation, and innumerable research agencies in other departments of the government, but through such dramatic programs as the Manhattan Project, the Atomic Energy Commission, and the Aeronautics and Space Agency. Upwards of 70 percent of all expenditures on scientific research and development in the United States are currently accounted for by agencies of Federal and State Governments. Yet neither political science as a discipline nor political scientists as such seem to have seen the full political implications of this development. Less so in fact than our junior partners among the policy sciences—economics, sociology, psychology, and law. This is bound to be the case so long as political science continues to avoid involvement in what Archimedes described as the "vulgar needs of life" and prefers to take refuge in so-called pure research having only a tangential relation to government and the political process. The hostility of so many political scientists to the political state in favor of a neo-pluralist society where the allocation of values is left to uncontrolled private governments has contributed to the alienation of political science. This alienation becomes increasingly obvious if not onimous as the functional jurisdiction of the political state continues to expand. Wagner's law, according to which state intervention expands as population increases, has proved to be an altogether too modest forecast of what actually occurs. In fact, both the scope and rate of such intervention has vastly increased under pressure of a population explosion complicated by increasing density, mobility, and interdependence. As the problems of this interdependent culture, which transcends the boundaries of private individuals and groups, multiply, the scope and variety of state intervention will increase. Under these circumstances, politics as the integrative factor in civilization will become not only more obvious but more important. If, in this event, political scientists persist in their present trend toward alienation from the political state and its burgeoning problems, they and their discipline, however elegant their theoretical and conceptual formulations, will drift inevitably into sterility and impotence while mankind stands knee-deep in sewage shooting rockets at the moon.

"In my opinion," says Galileo, "the only goal of science is to alleviate the hardships of human existence. If men of science, intimidated by self-seeking rules, are content merely to store up knowledge for the sake of knowledge, science can be crippled and your new machines mean only new oppression. In time you may discover everything that can be discovered and still your progress will be progress away from humanity. The distance between you and them can one day become so great that your joyous cry over some new gain could be answered by a universal shriek of horror. . . . As things are now, the most that one can hope for is a race of inventive pygmies that can be hired for anything."

It was President Kennedy who told the United Nations Assembly that "never before have the nations of the world had so much to lose and so much to gain. Together we shall save our planet or together we shall perish in its flames. Save it we can. Save it we must." Are we, as political scientists, to stand by as spectators, or are we to play an active role as participants in this drama? Our opportunity and our responsibility is very great, for it is still true, as Plato put it two thousand years ago, that "the greatest and fairest sort of wisdom by far is that which is concerned with the ordering of states."

THE AMERICAN POLITICAL TRADITION

PART ONE

The three philosophical schools of thought used to structure and explain the underlying values of the American political tradition are Lockean liberalism, Madisonian pluralism, and American populism. Liberalism focuses on the individual as the basic unit of politics, pluralism on the organized interest group, and populism on the conflict between masses and elites. The aim of this Part is to identify the basic tenets of these political value systems and to sketch their major contemporary political implications.

For different reasons, classical liberalism and pluralism share certain key assumptions about the nature, scope, and limits of political power. They define politics as a process of rational competition that is likely to result in compromise among competing parties. For the Lockean liberal, political man is basically a rational creature who shapes his own destiny through discussion, debate, bargaining, and compromise. The liberal tradition is optimistic in tone. In Lockean thought, "rationality" conveys a special meaning embedded in religious notions of natural law. Reason is a shared natural faculty that can help men to discover good and right political conduct. Since all individuals possess this faculty, liberalism implies that men can generally reach agreement with others on matters of public policy.

Like the liberals, American pluralists—from James Madison and John C. Calhoun to many contemporary political scientists—define politics as the pursuit of rational goals. However, the pluralist definition of political rationality entails less optimistic expectations. Reason denotes calculation or cunning in the pursuit of self-interest. Pluralists believe that men tend to band together in political associations, out of self-interest, to pursue narrow objectives. Thus they contend that stability in the political realm will occur only if interest is made to check interest and ambition is made to frustrate ambition.

From these somewhat disparate beliefs and assumptions emerges a consensus among pluralists and classical liberals concerning the desirability of limited government. According to Locke and his more recent disciples, men are naturally inclined to decide economic and social matters in a rational and harmonious fashion. Thus, strong government is unnecessary. Positive government might also frustrate the mobility and energy of the bourgeois merchants and traders whom the Lockeans sought to liberate from feudal paternalism. Madisonian pluralists also mistrust the positive state. They fear that one dominant faction or interest group might use its political strength and organization to seize the reins of a strong centralized government and might use the power of government for its own narrow ends, to the detriment of other minorities. Accordingly, the liberals and the pluralists seek to fragment political power through such mechanisms as the separation of powers, checks and balances, and federalism.

As a result of the foregoing beliefs, tendencies, and institutional arrangements, both the liberals and the pluralists believe that the American political system affords a high probability for the peaceful adjustment of political differences. Both the liberal and the pluralist traditions are legalistic and gradualist. Both provide numerous institutional mechanisms intervening between the mass public and the political elite. Neither seeks comprehensive social programs from the positive state.

Populism, the third strain in the American political tradition, emerged as a response to the narrow distribution of public benefits fostered by liberalism and pluralism. The original populists eschewed "interest" politics and sought a fundamental redistribution of political power and economic wealth through the positive force of the federal government. The socioeconomic dislocations caused by the Industrial Revolution produced a political movement of the economically marginal classes that was egalitarian in its objectives and apocalyptic in its tone. Perceived historically, in terms of its relationship to the development of American public policy, the recurrent manifestation of populistic protest may be viewed as a catalyst to comprehensive political and social change. Often the populists themselves, and numerous subsequent protest movements, lacking other bargaining resources in the liberal-pluralist political arena, have been forced into direct mass action as a political tactic of last resort. Abolitionism, populism, women's suffrage, labor unrest in the 1930s, and the Black Power movement have all won political benefits through a recurring cycle of direct confrontation, partial acceptance of the movement's demands, and absorption of many of the movement's leaders into the pluralist arena of political bargaining.

The selections in Part One have been chosen to highlight the different aspects of the American political tradition. Louis Hartz's book *The Liberal Tradition in America,* from which the first article is taken, offers an explanation for the fertility of laissez-faire liberalism in colonial America and for its persistence since then. Hartz discusses how the open frontier and the absence of competing European ideologies were important in planting laissez-faire traditions firmly in American theory and practice. Ironically, the absence of a feudal experience in America caused American liberals to overlook the fact that the Lockean state, although limited, was the only association that might legitimately coerce men. Locke, a committed opponent of feudal institutions, mistrusted private corporate power. In contrast, many neo-Lockeans in America worship at its shrine, perceiving the private corporation as an extension of the human desire to acquire and possess private property.

In "A Key to American Politics: Calhoun's Pluralism," Peter F. Drucker discusses the political impact of the pluralistic assumptions in John C. Calhoun's theory of "concurrent majority." For Calhoun, and for many contemporary American pluralists, social tyranny can be prevented if all major groups having a direct interest in matters of public policy are given veto power over policies that immediately affect them. In contemporary American politics, the representation of "state's rights" and the sectional interests of Calhoun's theory have been replaced by the direct representation of functional interests such as the farm industry's direct influence on agricultural policy and the influence of organized labor and of management on the economy.

Drucker argues that pressure-group politics is ill equipped to protect the national interest, to resolve genuine ideological conflicts, and to produce comprehensive national public policies. He traces three major political trends to a desire to overcome the defects of interest-group politics: the development of a strong presidency; the rise of the political role of the Supreme Court; and the growth of a homogeneous, unifying "American

Creed"—a kind of ideological combination of Lockean liberalism, civics-book values, and the Horatio Alger myth. The creed forms a unifying set of assumptions that limits ideological consciousness and provides a receptacle within which interest-group bargaining can take place. These assumptions define the narrow boundaries of legitimate political participation by contending interests.

George Sabine's article "The Two Democratic Traditions" bridges the gap between the American liberal-pluralist tradition and the majoritarian theory of democracy. Sabine's second democratic tradition, developed in the political thought of Rousseau and French Jacobinism, entailed a much more intense rejection of the special privileges afforded by the feudal order than did Locke's bourgeois liberal revolution. Locke accepted a division of labor and status in society as being inevitable, indeed even desirable, insofar as it would advance the industrious middle class to a preeminent place in the social order and displace the indolent feudal nobility. The French revolutionaries, like the American populists, sought to replace caste, status, and interest politics with equal citizenship, direct political participation by the masses, and political rule on behalf of the "general" interest. Both Rousseau and the populists mistrusted intervening parties and interests and legal barriers standing between man and the state. They espoused a positive state, responsive directly to the will of the people. Their ultimate objective was equal respect for all men, regardless of private roles or statuses in society.

Sabine traces some of the possible side effects of the second democratic tradition: social isolation, remote authority, and the vulnerability of the isolated individual to messianic political elites. A life rich in numerous associations with small groups may help to provide the individual with a sense of active participation in his society and to give him a touchstone for his sense of sanity and reality. Nonetheless, the revolt against status and against invidious comparisons among men is a necessary ingredient of a functioning democracy. Sabine concludes that the free exchange of ideas and arguments, which can result in reasonably acceptable public policies, can occur only when society's many and diverse interest groups are able to communicate with each other on an equal footing, on the basis of mutual respect. Thus, both liberty of association and relative equality among contending parties are necessary conditions for a viable democratic political order. Second-class citizenship encourages resentment, resistance, and political violence.

Indeed, much of the history of American political violence is a history of rebellion against elite privilege. This is the message of "Violence in American History," a selection drawn from the findings of the National Commission on the Causes and Prevention of Violence. The commission's report offers a penetrating critique on those who conclude that the impact of Lockeanism has been nothing more than political stability and consensus politics. The recurring pattern of political discontent, protest, and violence in America is rooted in many of the very same forces that many have cited to account for our stabilizing bourgeois liberal ideology—the frontier, affluence, and Anglo-Saxon cultural dominance.

The Liberal
Tradition
in America

2

Louis Hartz

. . .

When we study national variations in political theory, we are led to semantic considerations of a delicate kind, and it is to these, finally, that we must turn if we wish to get at the basic assumption of American thought. We have to consider the peculiar meaning that American life gave to the words of Locke.

There are two sides to the Lockian argument: a defense of the state that is implicit, and a limitation of the state that is explicit. The first is to be found in Locke's basic social norm, the concept of free individuals in a state of nature. This idea untangled men from the myriad associations of class, church, guild, and place, in terms of which feudal society defined their lives; and by doing so, it automatically gave to the state a much higher rank in relation to them than ever before. The state became the only association that might legitimately coerce them at all. That is why the liberals of France in the eighteenth century were able to substitute the concept of absolutism for Locke's conclusions of limited government and to believe that they were still his disciples in the deepest sense. When Locke came to America, however, a change appeared. Because the basic feudal oppressions of Europe had not taken root, the fundamental social norm of Locke ceased in large part to look like a norm and began, of all things, to look like a sober description of fact. The effect was significant enough. When the Americans moved from that concept to the contractual idea of organizing the state, they were not conscious of having already done anything to fortify the state, but were conscious only that they were about to limit it. One side of Locke became virtually the whole of him. Turgot ceased to be a modification of Locke and became, as he was for John Adams, the destruction of his very essence.

It was a remarkable thing—this inversion of perspectives that made the social norms of Europe the factual premises of America. History was on a lark, out to tease men, not by shattering their dreams, but by fulfilling them with a sort of satiric accuracy. In America one not only found a society sufficiently fluid to give a touch of meaning to the individualist norms of Locke, but one also found letter-perfect replicas of the very images he used. There was a frontier that was a veritable state of nature. There were agreements, such as the Mayflower Compact, that were veritable social contracts. There were new communities springing up in *vacuis locis,* clear evidence that men were using their Lockian right of emigration, which Jefferson soberly appealed to as "universal" in his defense of colonial land claims in 1774. A purist could argue, of course, that even these phenomena were not enough to make a reality out of the presocial men that liberalism dreamed of in theory. But surely they came as close to doing so as anything history has ever seen. Locke and Rousseau themselves could not help lapsing into the empirical mood when they looked across the Atlantic. "Thus, in the beginning," Locke once wrote, "all the world was America. . . ."

In such a setting, how could the tremendous, revolutionary social impact that liberalism had in Europe be preserved? The impact was not, of course, missing entirely; for the attack on the vestiges of corporate society in America that began in 1776, the disestablishment of the Anglican church, the abolition of quitrents and primogeniture, the breaking up of the Tory estates, tinged American liberalism with its own peculiar fire. Nor must we therefore assume that the Americans had wider political objectives than the Europeans, since even their new governmental forms were, as Becker once said, little more than the "colonial institutions with the Parliament and king left out." But after these cautions have been taken, the central point is clear. In America the first half of Locke's argument was bound to become less a call to arms than a set of preliminary remarks essential to establishing a final conclusion: that the power of the state must be limited. Observe how it is treated by the Americans in their great debate with England, even by original thinkers like Otis and Wilson. They do not lavish upon it the fascinated inquiry that we find in Rousseau or Priestley. They advance it mechanically, hurry through it, anxious to get on to what is really bothering them: the limits of the British Parliament, the power of taxation. In Europe the idea of social liberty is loaded with dynamite; but in America it becomes, to a remarkable degree, the working base from which argument begins.

Here, then, is the master assumption of American political thought, the assumption from which all of the American attitudes discussed in this essay flow: the reality of atomistic social freedom. It is instinctive to the American mind, as in a sense the concept of the polis was instinctive to Platonic Athens or the concept of the church to the mind of the middle ages. Catastrophes have not been able to destroy it, proletariats have refused to give it up, and even our Progressive tradition, in its agonized clinging to a Jeffersonian world, has helped to keep it alive. There has been only one major group of American thinkers who have dared to challenge it frontally: the Fitzhughs and Holmeses of the pre-Civil War South who, identifying slavery with feudalism, tried to follow the path of the European reaction and of Comte. But American life rode roughshod over them—for the "prejudice" of Burke in America was liberal and the positive reality of Locke in America transformed them into the very metaphysicians they assailed. They were soon forgotten, massive victims of the absolute temper of the American mind, shoved off the scene by Horatio Alger, who gave to the Lockian premise a brilliance that lasted until the crash of 1929. And even the crash did not really shatter it.

A Key to American Politics: Calhoun's Pluralism

3

Peter F. Drucker

The American party system has been under attack almost continuously since it took definite form in the time of Andrew Jackson. The criticism has always been directed at the same point: America's political pluralism, the distinctively American organization of government by compromise of interests, pressure groups and sections. And the aim of the critics from Thaddeus Stevens to Henry Wallace has always been to substitute for this "unprincipled" pluralism a government based as in Europe on "ideologies" and "principles." But never before—at least not since the Civil War years—has the crisis been as acute as in this last decade [the 1940s]; for the political problems which dominate our national life today, foreign policy and industrial policy, are precisely the problems which interest and pressure-group compromise is least equipped to handle. . . .

Yet, there is almost no understanding of the problem—precisely because there is so little understanding of the basic principles of American pluralism. Of course, every politican in this country must be able instinctively to work in terms of sectional and interest compromise; and the voter takes it for granted. But there is practically no awareness of the fact that organization on the basis of sectional and interest compromise is both the distinctly American form of political organization and the cornerstone of practically all major political institutions of the modern U.S.A. As acute an observer as Winston Churchill apparently does not understand that Congress works on a basis entirely different from that of Britain's Parliament; neither do nine out of ten Americans and 999 out of a 1,000 teachers of those courses in "Civics." There is even less understanding that sectional and interest-group pluralism is not just the venal expediency of that stock-villain of American folklore, the "politician," but that it in itself is a basic ideology, a basic principle—and the one which is the very foundation of our free society and government.

[1]

To find an adequate analysis of the principle of government by sectional and interest compromise we have to go back almost a hundred years to John C. Calhoun and to his two political treatises published after his death in 1852. Absurd, you will say, for it is practically an axiom of American history that Calhoun's political theories, subtle, even profound though they may have been, were reduced to absurdity and irrelevance by the Civil War. Yet, this

20

"axiom" is nothing but a partisan vote of the Reconstruction Period. Of course, the specific occasion for which Calhoun formulated his theories, the slavery issue, has been decided; and for the constitutional veto power of the states over national legislation, by means of which Calhoun proposed to formalize the principle of sectional and interest compromise, was substituted in actual practice the much more powerful and much more elastic but extra-constitutional and extra-legal veto power of sections, interests and pressure groups in Congress and within the parties. But *his basic principle itself: that every major interest in the country, whether regional, economic or religious, is to possess a veto power on political decisions directly affecting it,* the principle which Calhoun called—rather obscurely—*"the rule of concurrent majority,"* has become the organizing principle of American politics. And it is precisely this principle that is under fire today.

What makes Calhoun so important as the major key to the understanding of American politics is not just that he saw the importance in American political life of sectional and interest pluralism; other major analysts of our government, Tocqueville, for instance, or Bryce or Wilson, saw that too. But Calhoun, perhaps alone, saw in it more than a rule of expediency, imposed by the country's size and justifiable by results, if at all. He saw in it a basic principle of free government.

Without this *[the rule of concurrent majority based on interests rather than on principles]* there can be . . . no constitution. The assertion is true in reference to all constitutional governments, be their forms what they may: It is, indeed, the negative power which makes the constitution,—and the positive which makes the government. The one is the power of acting;—and the other the power of preventing or arresting action. The two, combined, make constitutional government.

. . . it follows, necessarily, that where the numerical majority has the sole control of the government, there can be no constitution . . . and hence, the numerical, unmixed with the concurrent majority, necessarily forms, in all cases, absolute government.

. . . The principle by which they [governments] are upheld and preserved . . . in constitutional governments is *compromise;*—and in absolute governments is *force.* . . .

And however much the American people may complain in words about the "unprincipled" nature of their political system, by their actions they have always shown that they too believe that without sectional and interest compromises there can be no constitutional government. If this is not grasped, American government and politics must appear not only as cheap to the point of venality, they must appear as utterly irrational and unpredictable.

[2]

Sectional and interest pluralism has molded all American political institutions. It is the method—entirely unofficial and extra-constitutional—through which the organs of government are made to function, through which leaders are selected, policies developed, men and groups organized for the conquest and management of political power. In particular it is the explanation for the most distinctive features of the American political system: the way in which the Congress operates, the way in which major government departments are set up and run, the qualifications for "eligibility" as a candidate for elective office, and the American party structure.

To all foreign observers of Congress two things have always remained mysterious: the distinction between the official party label and the "blocs" which cut across party lines; and the power and function of the congressional committees. And most Americans though less amazed by the phenomena are equally baffled.

The "blocs"—the "Farm Bloc," the "Friends of Labor in the Senate," the "Business Groups," etc.—are simply the expression of the basic tenet of sectional and interest pluralism that major interests have a veto power on legislation directly affecting them. For this reason they must cut across party lines—that is, lines expressing the numerical rather than the "concurrent" majority. And because these blocs have (a) only a negative veto, and (b) only on measures directly affecting them, they cannot in themselves be permanent groupings replacing the parties. They must be loosely organized; and one and the same member of Congress must at different times vote with different blocs. The strength of the "blocs" does not rest on their numbers but on the basic mores of American politics which grant every major interest group a limited self-determination—as expressed graphically in the near-sanctity of a senatorial "filibuster." The power of the "Farm Bloc" for instance, does not rest on the numerical strength of the rural vote—a minority vote even in the Senate with its disproportionate representation of the thinly populated agricultural states—but on its "strategic" strength, that is, on its being the spokesman for a recognized major interest.

Subordination of a major interest is possible; but only in a "temporary emergency." Most of the New Deal measures were, palpably, neither temporary nor emergency measures; yet their sponsors had to present them, and convincingly, as "temporary emergency measures" because they could be enacted only by over-riding the extra-constitutional veto of the business interests.

Once the excuse of the "temporary emergency" had fully lost its plausibility, the major interest could no longer be voted down; and the policy collapsed. By 1946, for instance, labor troubles could be resolved only on a basis acceptable to both labor and employer: higher wages *and* higher prices. (Even if a numerical majority had been available to legislate against either party— and the business group could probably still have been voted down two and a half years ago—the solution had to be acceptable to both parties.)

The principle of sectional and interest compromise leads directly to the congressional committee system—a system to which there is no parallel anywhere in the world. Congress, especially the House, has largely abdicated to its committees because only in the quiet and secrecy of a committee room can sectional compromise be worked out. The discussion on the floor as well as the recorded vote is far too public and therefore largely for the folks back home. But a committee's business is to arrive at an agreement between all major sectional interests affected; which explains the importance of getting a bill before the "right" committee. In any but an American legislature the position of each member, once a bill is introduced, is fixed by the stand of his party which, in turn, is decided on grounds that have little to do with the measure itself but are rather dictated by the balance of power within the government and by party programs. Hence it makes usually little difference which committee discusses a bill or whether it goes before a committee at all. In the United States, however, a bill's assignment to a specific committee decides which interest groups are to be recognized as affected by the measure and therefore entitled to a part in writing it ("who is to have standing before the committee"), for each committee represents a specific constellation of interests. In many cases this first decision therefore decides the fate of a proposed measure, especially as the compromise worked out by the committee is generally accepted once it reaches the floor, especially in the House.

It is not only Congress but every individual member of Congress himself who is expected to operate according to the "rule of concurrent majority." He is considered both a representative of the American people and responsible to the national interest and a delegate of his constituents and responsible to their particular interests. Wherever the immediate interests of his constituents are not in question, he is to be a statesman; wherever their conscience or their pocketbooks are affected, he is to be a business agent. This is in sharp contrast to the theory on which any parliamentary government is based— a theory developed almost two hundred years ago in Edmund Burke's famous speech to the voters at Bristol—according to which a member of Parliament represents the commonweal rather than his constituents. Hence in all parliamentary countries, the representative can be a stranger to his constituency—in the extreme, as it was practiced in Weimar Germany, there is one long national list of candidates who run in all constituencies—whereas the Congressman in this country must be a resident of his constituency. And while an American Senator considers it a compliment and an asset to be called "Cotton Ed Smith," the Speaker of the House of Commons not so long ago severely reprimanded a member for calling another member—an official of the miners' union—a "representative of the coal miners."

The principle of sectional and interest pluralism also explains why this is the only nation where Cabinet members are charged by law with the representation of special interests—labor, agriculture, commerce. In every other country an agency of the government—any agency of the government—is solemnly sworn to guard the public interests against "the interests." In this country the concept of a government department as the representative of a special interest group is carried down to smaller agencies and even to divisions and branches of a department. . . .

The mystery of "eligibility"—the criteria which decide who will make a promising candidate for public office—which has baffled so many foreign and American observers—Bryce for instance—also traces back to the "rule of the concurrent majority." Eligibility simply means that a candidate must not be unacceptable to any major interest, religious or regional group within the electorate; it is primarily a negative qualification. Eligibility operates on all levels and applies to all elective offices. It has been brilliantly analyzed in "Boss" Flynn's *You're the Boss.* His classical example is the selection of Harry Truman as Democratic vice-presidential candidate in 1944. Truman was "eligible" rather than Wallace, Byrnes or Douglas precisely because he was unknown; because he was neither New Deal nor Conservative, etc.; in short because he had no one trait strong enough to offend anybody anywhere.

But the central institution based on sectional pluralism is the American party. Completely extra-constitutional, the wonder and the despair of every foreign observer who cannot fit it into any of his concepts of political life, the American party (rather than the states) has become the instrument to realize Calhoun's "rule of the concurrent majority."

In stark contrast to the parties of Europe, the American party has no program and no purpose except to organize divergent groups for the common pursuit and conquest of power. Its unity is one of action, not of beliefs. Its only rule is to attract—or at least not to repel—the largest possible number of groups. It must, by definition, be acceptable equally to the right and the left, the rich and the poor, the farmer and the worker, the Protestant and the Catholic, the native and the foreign-born. . . .

As soon as it cannot appeal at least to a minority in every major group (as soon, in other words, as it provokes the veto of one section, interest or class), a party is in danger of disintegration. Whenever a party loses its ability to fuse sectional pressures and class interests into one national policy—both parties just before the Civil War, the Republican Party before its reorganization by Mark Hanna, both parties again today—the party system (and with it the American political system altogether) is in crisis.

It is, consequently, not that Calhoun was repudiated by the Civil War which is the key to the understanding of American politics but that he has become triumphant since.

The apparent victors, the "Radical Republicans," Thaddeus Stevens, Seward, Chief Justice Chase, were out to destroy not only slavery and states rights but the "rule of the concurrent majority" itself. And the early Republican Party—before the Civil War and in the Reconstruction Period—was indeed determined to substitute principle for interest as the lodestar of American political life. But in the end it was the political thought of convinced pluralists such as Abraham Lincoln and Andrew Johnson rather than the ideologies of the Free Soilers and Abolitionists which molded the Republican Party. And ever since, the major developments of American politics have been based on Calhoun's principle. To this the United States owes the strength as well as the weaknesses of its political system.

[3]

The weaknesses of sectional and interest compromise are far more obvious than its virtues; they have been hammered home for a hundred years. Francis Lieber, who brought the dominant German political theories of the early nineteenth century to this country, attacked pluralism in Calhoun's own state of South Carolina a century ago. Twenty years later Walter Bagehot contrasted, impressively, General Grant's impotent administration with those of Gladstone and Disraeli to show the superiority of ideological party organization. The most thorough and most uncompromising criticism came from Woodrow Wilson; and every single one of the Professor's points was amply borne out by his later experience as President. Time has not made these weaknesses any less dangerous.

There is, first of all, the inability of a political system based on the "rule of the concurrent majority" to resolve conflicts of principles. All a pluralist system can do is to deny that "ideological" conflicts (as they are called nowadays) do exist. Those conflicts, a pluralist must assert, are fundamentally either struggles for naked power or friction between interest groups which could be solved if only the quarreling parties sat down around a conference table. Perhaps, the most perfect, because most naive, expression of this belief remains the late General Patton's remark that the Nazis were, after all, not so very different from Republicans or Democrats. (Calhoun, while less naive, was just unable to understand the reality of "ideological" conflict in and around the slavery problem.)

In nine cases out of ten the refusal to acknowledge the existence of ideological conflict is beneficial. It prevents fights for power, or clashes of interests, from flaring into religious wars where irreconcilable principles collide (a catastrophe against which Europe's ideological politics have almost no defense). It promotes compromise where compromise is possible. But in a genuine clash of principles—and, whatever the pluralists say, there *are* such clashes—the "rule of concurrent majority" breaks down; it did, in Calhoun's generation, before the profound reality of the slavery issue. A legitimate ideological conflict is actually aggravated by the pluralists' refusal to accept its reality: the compromisers who thought the slavery issue could be settled by the meeting of good intentions, or by the payment of money, may have done more than the Abolitionists to make the Civil War inevitable.

A weakness of sectional and interest pluralism just as serious is that it amounts to a principle of inaction. The popular assertion "it's better to make the wrong decision than to do nothing at all," is, of course, fallacious; but no nation, however unlimited its resources, can have a very effective policy if its government is based on a principle that orders it to do nothing important except unanimously. Moreover, pluralism increases exorbitantly the weight of well organized small interest groups, especially when they lobby *against* a decision. Congress can far too easily be high-pressured into emasculating a bill by the expedient of omitting its pertinent provisions; only with much greater difficulty can Congress be moved to positive action. This explains, to a large extent, the eclipse of Congress during the last hundred years, both in popular respect and in its actual momentum as policy-making organ of government. Congress, which the Founding Fathers had intended to be the central organ of government—a role which it fulfilled up to Andrew Jackson—became the compound representative of sections and interests and, consequently, progressively incapable of national leadership.

Pluralism gives full weight—more than full weight—to sections and interests; but who is to represent the national welfare? Ever since the days of Calhoun, the advocates of pluralism have tried to dodge this question by contending that the national interest is equal to the sum of all particular interests, and that it therefore does not need a special organ of representation. But this most specious argument is contradicted by the most elementary observation. In practice, pluralism tends to resolve sectional and class conflicts at the expense of the national interest which is represented by nobody in particular, by no section and no organization.

These weaknesses had already become painfully obvious while Calhoun was alive and active—during the decade after Andrew Jackson, the first President of pluralism. Within a few years after Calhoun's death, the inability of the new system to comprehend and to resolve an ideological conflict —ultimately its inability to represent and to guard the national interest—had brought catastrophe. For a hundred years and more, American political thought has therefore resolved around attempts to counteract if not to overcome these weaknesses. Three major developments of American constitutional life were the result: the growth of the functions and powers of the President and his emergence as a "leader" rather than as the executive agent of the Congress; the rise of the Supreme Court, with its "rule of law," to the position of arbiter of policy; the development of a unifying ideology—the "American Creed."

Of these the most important—and the least noticed—is the "American Creed." In fact I know of no writer of major importance since Tocqueville who has given much attention to it. Yet even the term "un-American" cannot be translated successfully into any other language, least of all into "English" English. In no other country could the identity of the nation with a certain set of ideas be assumed—at least not under a free government. This unique cohesion on principles shows, for instance, in the refusal of the American voter to accept Socialists and Communists as "normal" parties, simply because both groups refuse to accept the assumption of a common American ideology. It shows, for another example, in the indigenous structure of the American labor movement with its emphasis on interest pressure rather than on a political philosophy. And this is also the only country in which "Civics" could be taught in schools—the only democratic country which believes that a correct social philosophy could or should be part of public education.

In Europe, a universal creed would be considered incompatible with a free society. Before the advent of totalitarianism, no European country had ever known anything comparable to the flag salute of the American school child. For in Europe all political activity is based on ideological factions; consequently, to introduce a uniform ideology in a European country is to stamp out *all* opposition. In the United States ideological homogeneity is the very basis of political diversity. It makes possible the almost unlimited freedom of interest groups, religious groups, pressure groups, etc.; and in this way it is the very fundament of free government. (It also explains why the preservation of civil liberties has been so much more important a problem in this country—as compared to England or France, for instance.) The assumption of ideological unity gives the United States the minimum of cohesion without which its political system simply could not have worked.

. . .

[4]

Yet . . . critics and reformers not only fail to ask themselves whether an ideological system of politics would really be any better equipped to cope with the great problems of today—and neither the foreign nor the industrial policy of England, that most successful of all ideologically organized countries, look any too successful right now; the critics also never stop to consider the unique strength of our traditional system.

Our traditional system makes sure that there is always a legitimate government in the country; and to provide such a government is the first job of any political system—a duty which a great many of the political systems known to man have never discharged.

It minimizes conflicts by utilizing, rather than suppressing, conflicting forces. It makes it almost impossible for the major parties to become entirely irresponsible: neither party can afford to draw strength from the kind of demagogic opposition, without governmental responsibility, which perpetually nurtures Fascist and Communist parties abroad. Hence, while the two national parties are willing to embrace any movement or any group within the country that commands sufficient following, they in turn force every group to bring its demands and programs into agreement with the beliefs, traditions and prejudices of the people.

Above all, our system of sectional and interest compromise is one of the only two ways known to man in which a free government and a free society can survive—and the only one at all adapted to the conditions of American life and acceptable to the American people.

The central problem in a free government is that of factions, as we have known since Plato and Aristotle. Logically, a free government and factions are incompatible. But whatever the cause—vanity and pride, lust for power, virtue or wickedness, greed or the desire to help others—factionalism is inherent in human nature and in human society. For 2,000 years the best minds in politics have tried to devise a factionless society—through education (Plato), through elimination of property (Thomas More), through concentration on the life of the spirit outside of worldly ambition (the political tradition of Lutheranism). The last great attempt to save freedom by abolishing faction was Rousseau's. But to create the factionless free society is as hopeless as to set up perpetual motion. From Plato to Rousseau, political thought has ended up by demanding that factions be suppressed, that is, that freedom, to be preserved, be abolished.

The Anglo-American political tradition alone has succeeded in breaking out of this vicious circle. Going back to Hooker and Locke, building on the rich tradition of free government in the cities of the late middle ages, Anglo-American political realism discovered that if factions cannot be suppressed, they must be utilized to make a free government both freer and stronger. This one basic concept distinguishes Anglo-American political theory and practice from continental European politics, and accounts for the singular success of free and popular governments in both countries. Elsewhere in the western world the choice has always been between extreme factionalism which makes government impotent if not impossible and inevitably leads to civil war, and autocracy which justifies the suppression of liberty with the need for effective and orderly government. . . .

But—and this is the real discovery on which the Anglo-American achievement rests—factions can be used constructively only if they are encompassed within a frame of unity. A free government on the basis of sectional interest groups is possible only when there is no ideological split within the country. This is the American solution. Another conceivable solution is to channel the driving forces, the vectors of society, into ideological factions which obtain their cohesion from a program for the whole of society, and from a creed. But that presupposes an unquestioned ruling class with a common outlook on life, with uniform mores and a traditional, if not inherent, economic security. Given that sort of ruling class, the antagonist in an ideological system can be expected to be a "loyal opposition," that is, to accept the rules of the game and to see himself as a partner rather than as a potential challenger to civil war. But a ruling class accepted by the people as a whole, and feeling itself responsible to the people as a whole, cannot be created by fiat or overnight. In antiquity only Rome, in modern times only England, achieved it. On the Continent, all attempts to create a genuine ruling class have failed dismally.

In this country, the ruling-class solution was envisaged by Alexander Hamilton and seemed close to realization under the Presidents of the "Virginia Dynasty." Hamilton arrived at his concept with inescapable consistency; for he was absorbed by the search for a foreign policy and for the proper organization of an industrial society—precisely the two problems which, as we have seen, pluralism is least equipped to resolve. But even if Hamilton had not made the fatal mistake of identifying wealth with rulership, the American people could not have accepted his thesis. A ruling class was incompatible with mass immigration and with the explosive territorial expansion of nineteenth-century America. It was even more incompatible with the American concept of equality. And there is no reason to believe that contemporary America is any more willing to accept Hamilton's concept, Mr. James Burnham's idea of the managerial elite notwithstanding. This country as a free country has no alternative, it seems, to the "rule of the concurrent majority," no alternative to sectional pluralism as the device through which factions can be made politically effective.

It will be very difficult, indeed, to resolve the problems of foreign and of industrial policy on the pluralist basis and within the interest-group system, though not provably more difficult than these problems would be on another, ideological, basis. It will be all the harder as the two problems are closely inter-related; for the effectiveness of any American foreign policy depends, in the last analysis, on our ability to show the world a successful and working model of an industrial society. But if we succeed at all, it will be with the traditional system, horse-trading, log-rolling and politicking all included. An old saying has it that this country lives simultaneously in a world of Jeffersonian beliefs and in one of Hamiltonian realities. Out of these two, Calhoun's concept of "the rule of the concurrent majority" alone can make one viable whole. The need for a formulated foreign policy and for a national policy of industrial order is real—but not more so than the need for a real understanding of this fundamental American fact: the pluralism of sectional and interest compromise is the warp of America's political fabric —it cannot be plucked out without unravelling the whole.

4

The Two Democratic Traditions

George H. Sabine

Professor Edward Hallett Carr, in his brilliant book, *The Soviet Impact on the Western World*, remarks that the concept of democracy in Western Europe has never been altogether univocal; that, on the contrary, from the time when democracy first became a force in Western politics, there have been two democratic traditions, or at least two strands of thought in the philosophy of democracy, which stressed different ideals and on occasion might seek quite different ends. The one was more characteristic of, and tended to prevail in, Anglo-American thought and practice; the other was more characteristically French or Continental. And though the two were never altogether separable and usually were not distinguished, they were different and in some respects were capable of becoming antagonistic. Professor Carr's diagnosis is at once historically correct and highly suggestive. This article is concerned with two questions: first, the mainly historical question about the contexts of political experience in which the two traditions originated and which were largely responsible for their differences; and second, the mainly philosophical question about the nature of the differences and the relationship between the two traditions. . . .

That the program of democracy might harbor incompatible purposes is of course no new idea. From its very beginning the theory of democracy linked together the two ideals of liberty and equality, and quite early it became apparent that these two would not unite as easily as the democrats of Thomas Jefferson's generation had hoped. Both in Europe and America democratic thought had followed, sometimes tacitly and sometimes explicitly, Aristotle's conception of a middle-class polity, prevailingly agricultural in its economy and politically controlled by a relatively large proportion of landowners who, being neither very rich nor very poor, met on a footing of independence and equality. This conception was hardly more than an episode in the social history of the nineteenth century. Industrialism increased rather than diminished disparities of wealth and power, and in the Gilded Age that followed the Civil War liberty seemed to mean the power of the more able or the more energetic, or merely the more unscrupulous, to gain their advantage at other men's expense. And after De Tocqueville's study of democracy in America equality seemed to mean the tyranny of majorities and the rule of mediocrity. Thus in the accusations of its enemies, both conservative and radical, the democratic argument seemed to be caught in a dilemma: the more liberty the less equality, and the more equality the less liberty. . . .

. . . But liberty and equality are very abstract words and taken out of context are very vague in meaning. When they symbolize realizable ideals they are shorthand for redressing quite definite grievances or bringing about quite definite results. For this reason history, which supplies context, is one of the ways of analyzing and clarifying their meaning; it shows what, concretely, the men who used the words intended to accomplish. . . .

. . . The two democratic traditions . . . had their points of origin respectively in the two great European revolutions which by common consent mark the beginnings of modern European politics: the Puritan Revolution of the mid-seventeenth century, which was consummated in the bloodless English Revolution of 1688, and the French Revolution a century later. As is the habit of revolutions each had its philosopher: in the one case John Locke, in the other Rousseau. These men were the intellectual ancestors of the two democratic traditions. In their political philosophies were crystallized the purposes of the English and French revolutionists, and through them these purposes became a part of the meaning that later generations tried to work out in a realized idea of democracy.

[1]

. . .

. . . What the English Revolution contributed to the democratic tradition was the principle of freedom for minorities, together with a constitutional system both to protect and to regulate that freedom. For the individual it meant freedom of association in accord with his own understanding of his own interests, and for the group it meant freedom to decide for itself its own manner of life within a framework of legally supported and legally limited rights and duties consonant at once with public order and a considerable, but not an unlimited, competence for self-determination. This is a principle that apparently must be acknowledged in some form by any government that is to remain free and constitutional. It is two-sided. It assumes that the area within which a government ought to act is limited, is defined by law, and cannot extend over all the interests and activities of its citizens; a free government cannot be totalitarian. On the other side it assumes that there is a wide range of social and moral and religious practices that can safely be, and ought to be, left to voluntary associations, partly because membership in them is compatible with the performance of all a man's duties as a citizen, partly on the more positive ground that diversity of interest is a genuine contribution to good citizenship. People can and ought to manage most of their affairs for themselves in groups that they organize for themselves and that make their own rules, the function of the state being largely protective and regulative. To no small extent this is what in fact political liberty has meant.

[2]

A generation after the fierce antagonisms and bitter recriminations of the Puritan Revolution had died down, John Locke was able to see quite clearly what had been accomplished and to state it dispassionately in the little pamphlet which, more than any other book, provided for Englishmen and Americans the philosophy of democracy. In simple terms and without its now obsolete technicalities it can be paraphrased in three principal statements.

In the first place, religion is not a matter that directly concerns either the theory or the practice of a political society; what needs to be said about it can be summed up in the single word "toleration." This was indeed a summary disposition of a question that had been bitterly controversial; it accepted as a foregone conclusion a degree of secularism in politics that as a rule neither the Puritans nor their opponents had been able to imagine. . . .

In the second place, men and women, in so far as a political theory needs to consider their nature, are socially and morally adult, in short, reasonable. They acknowledge, and in general they practice, rules of fair dealing, justice, and right in their relations with one another. The validity of these moral rules may therefore be taken for granted; the "law" in this broad sense would be binding even if there were no governments. The state itself, considered as different from society, makes no moral rules at all but only supplements them when impartial judgment and enforcement are needed to give them effect. Its field of operation is limited, and government is in a sense a superficial thing in comparison with the society of which it is, so to speak, the coercive arm. A government may become tyrannous and its subjects may need to rebel against it, to replace it, and to create a new government consonant with their interests, but a society is never dissolved short of complete chaos. Society provides an underlying moral structure that states support but do not create. For this reason they ought to act only by known rules of law and within limits set by constitutional guaranties. The justification for coercion, when it becomes necessary, is that it supports a moral and social order that is not coercive. . . .

In the third place, Locke assumed as a matter of course that society, just as it should permit many churches, will harbor a maze of private relationships and permit a multitude of groups and associations that pursue their own interests and mostly make their own rules, subject only to such control by the state as is needed to protect the public interest and to preserve the inherent social purpose of the group itself. . . . His conception of natural law was thus continuous with that of St. Thomas Aquinas, and ultimately with Aristotle. The fundamental assumption of Aristotle, and indeed of Greek social philosophy in general, was that society depends on division of labor and therefore consists of social classes that perform indispensable social functions. From this point of view there is a close relationship between liberty and social position, because it is presumed that in finding a socially useful work the individual finds also a satisfying expression for his natural capacities. In other words the theory assumes that in principle at least there is no deep disparity between individual aspiration and the existing structure of social classes, with the opportunities that the latter afford. In general Locke probably shared this belief and could therefore suppose that freedom of association, which had resolved antagonisms between religious sects, would also mitigate the most serious compulsions that occur when social position becomes discriminatory and oppressive.

It was this aspect of Locke's political philosophy, and of the democratic tradition that grew most directly from it, that gives rise to the contrast between it and the second democratic tradition now to be considered. Locke's political philosophy was never detached from a theory of society which accepted status as a matter of course and which regarded status as not only compatible with political freedom but even as a condition of it. . . . Certainly England would never have been counted a democracy by anyone who got his connotations of the word from French Jacobinism; Hegel regarded its government as a degenerate form of feudalism. Except in America the democratic tradition that stemmed from Locke implied very little of social equality, and the American version was due to America and not to Locke. The other democratic tradition was widely different, in origin, in context, in purposes, and in philosophy.

[3]

In this other case the historian's formula about abolishing "feudalism" was ready-made; the French Revolution really did abolish feudalism—by resolution of the National Assembly on August 4, 1789. The abolition of feudalism was the myth of the French Revolution, much as restoring the Englishman's birthright was the myth of the Puritan Revolution. In its context the myth had a definite and concrete meaning, even though it had little to do with feudalism as a living political system. Certainly no Frenchman in 1789 would have fought for his birthright because he was not aware of having any. The one political attribute that he had in common with all other Frenchmen was his loyalty and subjection to the king, which the Revolution transformed into loyalty and subjection to the nation. . . .

For the revolutionist of 1789 the abolition of feudalism meant relief from very galling realities of his everyday political experience. Everywhere he found himself confronted by the fact that his legal rights and his political privileges depended not at all on the fact that he was a Frenchman but on his membership in some group to which custom or royal grant assigned a special place in the society and the economy and the government. Affiliations of this sort determined his social standing, his place in the army, his position in the economy, his taxes, and the part in politics that he might hope to play. If he belonged to the nobility, he had substantial privileges but he was debarred by law from engaging in many occupations. If he [was] a professional man, a lawyer for example, his position was fixed by membership in a professional association, and such membership was costly and hard to get, for the association held a monopoly of some branch of practice and membership conveyed the right to take part in the affairs of some municipal corporation. The same was true if he [was] a skilled artisan and [a] member of a guild. And if he [was] a peasant, he shared privileges in common land controlled by his village but he shared also a communal responsibility for taxes and road work. If he [was] an official, his office was likely to be property which he must inherit or buy, and he was irremovable. In 1789, when the government revived the obsolete practice of electing a States General, everyone voted with the group where his station in life placed him, for according to the constitutional theory what was represented was not the individual but the corporations which composed the estates of the realm. French society was a maze of corporate bodies that were at once legal, vocational, and political and that were endowed with privileges and monopolies and duties. . . .

The abolition of feudalism meant that the revolutionist, quite definitely and consciously, intended to sweep away this whole cumbersome and irritating complex of status, which was in truth obsolete for any existing economic or political purpose. For it he meant to substitute a uniform citizenship giving equal political rights and imposing equal political obligations on everyone, and he meant to open all occupations to every qualified person, without regard for social position or membership in any special kind of association. In a profound sense the Revolution was a revolt against status and its ideal was to destroy every status except one—namely, citizenship in the state, which by becoming universal would cease to be invidious. And broadly speaking something of this sort was what the French Revolution in fact accomplished. It put at the center of modern politics the concept of equal national citizenship and as its counterpart the concept of the sovereign national state, supreme over every other form of social organization.

This characterization throws into sharp relief the contrast between the French and the English revolutions. In making the churches into voluntary associations the English Revolution had recognized that a sect or a religious minority is in fact a community devoted to practicing a way of life that is at once communal and individual, and it assumed the value of such associations. The French Revolution, devoted to the ideal of equal citizenship within the single unity of the state, assumed that communities within the state are potentially a threat to the state. So far as it could it abolished religious communities not only Catholic but Jewish, in the latter case often against the will of Jews who preferred their old corporate status to the new equality. Indeed it sought to spread the principle of a radical individualism right across the social structure. It abolished the corporate character of schools, hospitals, charitable foundations, the universities, and the learned academies. It nationalized perhaps a fifth of the land in the country but only for the purpose of transferring it to individual owners. And it forbade every kind of union or trade association, either of workers or employers. . . .

[4]

. . . Rousseau . . . spoke for the French Revolution as authentically as Locke had spoken for the English, though with one great difference in the temper of the statement. Locke had represented the sober second thought of Puritanism a generation after its radical phase; Rousseau wrote down as literal truth the messianic hopes of the French Revolution a generation before it occurred. But he saw quite clearly what was to be the major object of its attack: the intolerable and discriminatory system of status and hierarchy that stood between the citizen and both his private rights and his civic duties. The glorification of citizenship was common to Rousseau and to the Revolution. A free paraphrase of Rousseau, like that of Locke already given, might run as follows.

First, the human individual apart from the state is not at all the adult and reasonable being that Locke had taken him to be. Natively he is a nonrational and a nonmoral animal, guided in his behavior solely by instinct, and his instincts are directed toward his own self-preservation. He achieves morality and reason, and therefore freedom, only when he becomes a citizen, for only then "the voice of duty takes the place of physical impulses and the right of appetite." The rights of man, therefore, are his rights as a citizen, and until he is a citizen he is not a social or a moral being at all.

Second, it follows that the claims which the state can make upon its citizens and the area in which it can rightfully act are by no means limited, as Locke had regarded them. In Rousseau the state and society, which Locke had definitely though inadequately distinguished, are merged; the state overlaps and includes every phase of society. To the state the citizen surrenders totally his private rights and interests. His personal will, when properly understood, is identical with the General Will of the society, and this Will is identical with morality, is infallibly right, and quite exhausts the citizen's will when he has contributed to forming a consensus of the group. If he imagines his interest to be otherwise, he is mistaken, and if he is coerced, he is "forced to be free."

Third, a private association of citizens, merely because it is private, is inimical to the public interest. Deliberation about the public good would always reach the right conclusion if it could be conducted in such a way that "the citizens had no communication one with another." A party is a faction and faction defeats the common good. Corporate bodies, as Hobbes had said, are like "worms in the entrails of a private man." Ideally they ought not to exist and if they exist they must be weak. For every such association absorbs the citizen's loyalty, which ought to be directed solely toward the state; a democratic society should be one in which absolutely nothing stands between man and the state. Nothing points up the difference between Locke and Rousseau more sharply than their differing attitudes toward religious toleration. Both men indeed supported toleration as a policy, but Rousseau's remarkable chapter on "Civil Religion" expressed a degree of hostility toward Christianity that has no counterpart in Locke. Rousseau perceived that the essence of Western Christianity had always been a claim of spiritual freedom, whether in the form of freedom of conscience or of spiritual independence in the church. And for Rousseau this was a radical vice, an incurable source of dissension in every Christian state. If a man were really a Christian he would for that reason be a bad citizen, and there have been good citizens only because most men have been bad Christians. . . .

Rousseau's version of democracy, therefore, is not in any fundamental sense incompatible with absolute government, provided absolutism can claim to speak for "the people." This fact always strikes an Englishman or an American as utterly paradoxical, though it is not really more so than the parallel fact that Locke's version was not fundamentally incompatible with social stratification and a government that was hardly popular at all. . . .

[5]

This account of the two democratic traditions sharpens, perhaps exaggerates, the contrast between them, and the point of the contrast depends on the fact that the evolution of democratic government throughout the nineteenth century continually drew upon both. In England, and indeed wherever democracy prevailed, it tended to level off inherited rank and position: by extending the suffrage until it became practically universal, by making parliamentary constituencies into numerically equal blocks of population, by abolishing legal privileges and disabilities before the law, and by changing the law itself to offset the advantage that power may give to a litigant. Equal citizenship was a concept indispensable to the growth of democratic government. In France, and again wherever democracy prevailed, democratic government depended on freedom of association and the collective power of minorities: by permitting organized agitation by freely formed political parties and pressure groups, in legalizing collective bargaining, and in supporting freedom of thought, publication, and speech, which are in effect the liberties of groups as much as of individuals. The freedom of minorities also was a concept indispensable to the growth of democratic government. Both traditions, then, were authentically democratic. Any viable program of democracy, it seems, depends on finding a way to conserve the values affirmed both in the name of equality and in the name of liberty, and any valid analysis of democracy must relate them . . .

. . . It can . . . be shown that the two democratic traditions had a common ground, which accounts for the fact that liberty and equality were ethical presumptions inherent in both. As was made clear in the historical exposition given above, each tradition was in part dominated by the purpose of redressing a specific and really intolerable grievance, in one case the regimentation of groups associated by a religious interest felt to be personal and private, in the other the repression occasioned by vested interests and legally intrenched privilege. Each constructed its idea of democracy in terms of the grievance it meant to redress, and in so doing each failed to reckon with the mutual dependence between personality, society, and state. . . . A legitimate claim at one point became self-defeating at another which the theory did not envisage. The concluding portion of this article is intended to show how this was so. In general its conclusion will be that the ideal common to both traditions was social and political organization through mutual understanding and agreement, and hence as little coercive as possible, and that liberty and equality were conditions of there being any such understanding.

. . . In general, extension of the suffrage and representation on the basis of numbers did not increase the powers of the legislature, which Locke regarded as the center of power in the state, but tended rather to increase the power of the executive and to restrict the deliberative phases of government. Moreover, the elevation of the state to supremacy over all other forms of social organization did not necessarily diminish social stratification or reduce the power of special interests over government. One rather obvious consequence of wiping out the legal and economic privileges of the estates and corporations was to make property almost the sole index of social position, and in France the middle-class monarchy that followed the Napoleonic Empire made property the qualification for political rights. The competition of property interests for control of government led directly to, and in a large measure tended to justify, Marx's accusation that bourgeois democracy in fact means plutocracy. The individualist radicalism of the Revolution gave place to the class radicalism of the nineteenth century and the present. What the two types of radicalism had in common was a form of individualism that flattened down individuality into mere likeness of kind, in the one case of man in the abstract or citizenship, in the other of membership in a social class. But likeness of kind carries no implication of spontaneous, active, and contributing membership in a social community, which is certainly what the individualist intended that liberty should mean.

. . . A group of human beings associated according to a principle of unadulterated individualism is not a society but a rabble, and a society approaches such a condition only by being demoralized. This sort of disintegration reacts inevitably both on the individuals that compose the society and on government. It can be ruled by a combination of force and mass hysteria and indeed can be ruled in no other way. For its members, crowded into a structureless organization that is merely gregarious, are in effect isolated and powerless, and social isolation is incompatible not only with effective individual action but in the end with clear thinking or responsible judgment. Government tends to become a practice of applied psychiatry designed to produce rather than to cure neurosis. The ruler becomes the messianic or charismatic leader, and the governed become amenable to manipulation by every form of unreasoning indoctrination. The tyranny of the majority, on which the philosophers of the nineteenth century wasted so much anxiety, was mostly a myth. What happens is the tyranny of a minority that can use social demoralization to monopolize terror and propaganda.

. . . Organization both of industry and government on a vast scale with consequent centralization of power, urbanization and high mobility which identify residence merely with the tie of the job, the reduction of the family practically to its biological limit, and the fact that religious congregations have long ceased to be communities all tend to thin out the social medium and to increase the number of persons who in effect are socially isolated. Urbanization and industrialism were feared and disliked by first-generation democrats, but it is ironical that they are a risk to democracy precisely in so far as they produce a state of affairs superficially like what equalitarian individualism held to be desirable. That is to say they level off highly differentiated work groups and neighborhood groups, in which membership may be a genuine personal good, but they bring the normal consequence of remote and impersonal authority.

This conclusion follows, and the conclusion sets an inescapable problem for democracy: in order to be democratic a society has to be a complex structure of lesser societies which are corporately or collectively units because they stand for interests that are at once personal to their members and are shared, and such groups have to provide the conditions for giving their members a justified sense of participation. Collectively they have to be self-governing in the sense that they set the standards of their own performance, gauge their own interests, and in general live their own lives in their own way, and at the same time they have to give their members individually a part in forming the collective decision. This is what liberty means, in so far as it is a personal experience in a social organization. The principle applies to government but obviously has no exclusive reference to it; so far as it affects the individuals concerned, there may be very little difference between public and private organizations. A labor union is not necessarily democratic merely because membership in it is "voluntary," and business in important respects is, to use Beardsley Ruml's expression, "a private government." Society is full of "rules-making institutions," but whether rules are oppressive or not depends very much on how they are made and enforced, and particularly on the attitude engendered in a person who is subject to them. If he genuinely feels that they are *his* rules and are not merely imposed on him, he is quite likely to think of them as the safeguards of his liberty. Liberty is not simply an attribute of an individual; it is a relationship between a person and the complex of societies to which he belongs. The extent to which freedom of association can be generally and effectively achieved, and the extent to which association can preserve individual spontaneity, are the measures of liberty in any society.

From this conception of liberty it follows that the exercise of authority, or the more specifically political aspect of social organization, is consequent on deliberation and only marginally becomes downright coercion. The theory candidly accepts the existence of many and diverse interests and of groups with real power to protect them, and also the certainty that diverse interests in many cases will be antagonistic. Democratic politics is inherently contentious, though not contentious without limit. The theory can lead to a workable policy only if negotiation and mutual adjustment lead to agreements that are at once reasonably acceptable and reasonably stable. Consequently the political institutions of a democratic society are primarily organs for keeping open the channels of communication on which consultation and negotiation depend, or for creating channels of communication where none exist. In point of fact the development of democratic constitutionalism has largely consisted in extending or inventing institutions before which conflicting interests could be made to confront one another under conditions leading to successful negotiation and orderly regulation. . . .

[6]

Such a confrontation of interests, designed to foster free exchange of view and to issue in understanding, requires not only freedom but also equality. This is true in the elementary sense that free bargaining does not in fact take place except between persons or groups with relatively equal power. But it is also true in the more profound sense that full understanding cannot be

reached except on the basis of mutual respect and with a mutual acknowledgment of good faith and the acceptance of the principle that the purpose
of understanding is to protect all valid interests. This condition is not inconsistent with there being differences of position or even of rank, but it is not
met unless such differences themselves count as values that ought to be taken
into account. Consequently a society that is hierarchical simply by assumption, or that depends on use and wont in such a fashion that its ranks and
orders are not themselves subject to criticism and revision, does not offer the
possibility of more than a qualified form of democracy. The historical exposition given above has tried to show that some such assumption, made tacitly
by reason of its failure to make explicit its implicit premises, really was
contained in the form of democratic constitutionalism that stemmed from
Locke.

It was this which was met by the more equalitarian individualism of the
other democratic tradition. This equalitarianism, despite its fallacious suppo-
sition that liberty could be gained by the absorption of personality into
citizenship, was right at least in what it denied, namely, that personality can
be identified with, or exhausted by, social position or status. It was this phase
of Rousseau's thought that Kant summed up in the ethical axiom that persons are to be treated as ends rather than as means. And indeed the ethical
dictum, vague as it is, corresponds to a quite genuine fact of social psychology. It throws into relief an important feature of the kind of relationship
that connects a person with his cultural *milieu*. Every society depends on and
exacts some kind and degree of conformity, and different cultures support
widely different systems of status, but no culture reduces its members to
automata or fails to acknowledge that self-respect is both a genuine good and
a powerful human motive. While it is quite true that no theory of personality, psychological or ethical, can dispense with the conception of social role,
it is a sociological exaggeration to describe a personality as a kind of intersec-
tion at which social relationships meet and cross. The process of internaliza-
tion by which a growing personality takes up interests and values from his
culture is selective and is never wholly a passive acceptance. It does not
foreclose a critical reaction on his society or his station in it, or even his
rebellion against it, and originality, when it occurs, is as dependent on acculturation or socialization as conformity is. . . .

The question about which speculation has sometimes raged, from Rousseau to Freud, whether on the whole civilization liberates or inhibits personality, whether it makes men free or makes them slaves, is utterly fictitious.
It is not fictitious to ask whether a given society imposes too many relationships on too many of its members that they experience as frustrating, or puts
whole classes of them into positions that they feel to be ridiculous or degrad-
ing or humiliating. This is not a matter of social position as such, or of
differing ranks and stations, or even of authority and subordination; these
exist always and everywhere in societies. The question is rather how the
persons concerned experience their position. They may take it as a matter of
course, as something that has always been and that is intrinsically right and
reasonable, and if so they accept their lot in life, even though it may be a
very hard lot, with equanimity and self-respect. It is quite another matter if

they are confronted by differences of rank that seem to them to be senseless, to correspond to no socially useful purpose, and to give power and privilege for no substantial service. In that case they feel themselves to be exploited and coerced, to be burdened with exactions that have no relation to their deserts, and to be placed in a position that is humiliating and menial. An organization may be held together by the loyalty of its members, and that kind of relationship is not a burden but one of the most exhilarating of human experiences. It may be held together by meaningless routines and impositions from which its members will escape if they can. The difference is not altogether describable by the objective nature of the relationship but depends on the way it is experienced. And if the experience is of the latter sort, it is personally stultifying and it calls our resistance and resentment. Obviously it was this kind of experience that lay behind the revolutionary demand for equal citizenship. Equal citizenship meant escape from second-class citizenship.

The demand that men of differing position shall meet on terms of mutual respect and self-respect has been and will continue to be a recurring demand made in the name of democracy. The perpetuation of what is in effect second-class citizenship, one must sorrowfully admit, has been a rather conspicuous failure on the part of Anglo-American democracy. Its society has preserved irrelevant and invidious discriminations against classes of people to whom overtly it gave legal and constitutional equality. We have indeed given to minorities like the Jews and Roman Catholics the right to practice their religions unmolested, but a candid American who recalls occasional ugly outbreaks of religious intolerance in our elections will hardly claim that we have given them effective equality, even on a political level. In the aggregate the minorities thus relegated to a subordinate position add up to no insignificant part of our total population. Asiatics on the Pacific Coast, Americans of Spanish extraction in the Southwest, and negroes both North and South have to be counted in millions. In reality they have neither full political equality, nor equality of opportunity measured by capacity, nor equal access to education, though education figures in this country as a social service offered at public expense ostensibly to all citizens. The issue will not remain domestic; whether we like it or not, the status of the American Negro will be discussed from Moscow to Singapore. For colonialism or imperialism, which are other names for second-class citizenship, is an issue the world over, in India and China and Southeast Asia, and in Iran and Egypt. A candid Englishman will hardly claim that the British Commonwealth dealt successfully with that issue. The root of the matter is not bad government, or imperialist exploitation, or even poverty; it is far more the resentment aroused in persons who feel themselves crowded into a position that is incompatible with self-respect. And it is idle to hope for understanding with people in that frame of mind.

What tied together liberty and equality in democratic thought was the ideal, common to both traditions, of a society and government formed by the willing coalescence of human beings who could be at once spontaneous in their behavior and responsible in their dealings with one another. It was this hope that made "consent" or "contract" the symbols or metaphors by which the ideal was most naturally and simply expressed, for these terms suggest a relationship which is at once free and binding. This conjunction of attributes is obviously an invitation to paradox. Yet the paradox is measurably resolved in any human association where there is a "meeting of minds" based on free communication and mutual understanding. But communication and understanding, in any sense in which a meeting of minds can issue in joint action, have moral as well as semantic presuppositions. It was these which democratic theory in all its forms was mainly concerned to express, and democratic practice has been an experiment in finding institutions which could make actual the moral conditions of understanding. The one democratic tradition was founded on the principle that understanding depends on the freedom of parties at interest to speak their minds without fear of reprisal, and it took for granted that a social and political system that does not allow for agreement by the tolerant device of agreeing to differ, or which equates difference of interest or belief or manner of life with moral delinquency, is not compatible with a workable plan of equality. The other democratic tradition was founded on the principle that there can be no genuine meeting of minds where one party negotiates on an assumption of superiority that the other party regards as gratuitous, and it took for granted that a social and political system in which status is virtually hereditary and which sets up discriminations that are practically impassible bars to opportunity is not compatible with a workable plan of liberty. And indeed a democratic philosophy can hardly avoid making both these assumptions. Equality does depend on liberty and liberty on equality, because each expresses a phase of the kind of human relationship that democracy hopes measurably to realize. If, as continually happens in the democratic experiment, an attempt to advance one puts an obstacle in the way of the other, the simple device of rejecting one is not a live option. Ideals that have been imbedded for centuries in a culture are not discarded with impunity, but neither do they carry with them a blueprint for their realization.

Violence in American History

5

The National Commission on the Causes and Prevention of Violence

Because we believe that the past has much to tell us about the present and the future, this Commission has studied the history of violence in America. We wanted to know whether Americans are more violent today than they have been in the past. We studied historical events which parallel current events in hopes of finding basic principles that might guide us toward solutions. Most of all, however, we sought the broad perspective which would help us and our fellow citizens to understand better the nature, the character, and the dilemma of contemporary America.

This study of history has illuminated for us the causes of violence in this nation and some of the ways to reduce it:

1. America has always been a relatively violent nation. Considering the tumultuous historical forces that have shaped the United States, it would be astonishing were it otherwise.
2. Since rapid social change in America has produced different forms of violence with widely varying patterns of motivation, aggression, and victimization, violence in America has waxed and waned with the social tides. The decade just ending, for example, has been one of our most violent eras—although probably not the most violent.
3. Exclusive emphasis in a society on law enforcement rather than on a sensible balance of remedial action and enforcement tends to lead to a decaying cycle in which resistance grows and becomes ever more violent.
4. For remedial social change to be an effective moderator of violence, the changes must command a wide measure of support throughout the community. Official efforts to impose change that is resisted by a dominant majority frequently prompt counter-violence.
5. Finally, Americans have been, paradoxically, . . . a turbulent people but have enjoyed a relatively stable republic. Our liberal and pluralistic system has historically both generated and accommodated itself to a high level of unrest, and our turmoil has reflected far more demonstration and protest than conspiracy and revolution.

These are a few of the conclusions we have drawn from our study of American history. It is a source of partial consolation and reassurance that our present pattern of violence falls largely within that tradition and that traditionally violence has subsided as political and social institutions gradually responded to the underlying social dislocations and injustices that caused it. But it is a source of great concern that the very velocity of historical change itself has been vastly accelerated by modern technology. Technological progress causes enormous dislocation and demands for social change; our techniques of instant communications intensify these demands manyfold. Whether our political and social institutions can respond as rapidly as new demands arise will largely determine how much violence we are about to experience.

If we are wise—if we listen carefully and watch closely—we will realize that violence is a social bellwether: dramatic rises in its level and modifications in its form (as is the case today) tell us that something important is happening in our political and social systems.

1 Historical Roots of the American Consensus

Our current eruption of violence must appear paradoxical to a generation of Americans who witnessed the emergence from depression to unparalleled affluence of a nation they regarded as the world's moral leader in defense of freedom. Only a decade ago America's historians and behavioral scientists were celebrating the emergence of a unique society, one sustained by a burgeoning prosperity and solidly grounded in a broad political consensus. This "consensus" school of America's scholars, and particularly of her historians, was reacting against an older view that had pictured America as a crucible of conflict—colonials against the British, Jeffersonians against the Federalists, Jacksonians against the Bank, North against South, East against West, capital against labor, Republican against Democrat. While regarded as morally as well as materially superior to Europe, America in this older discordant view nonetheless functioned according to a common Western dynamic of class and ideological warfare.

Not so, said the consensus scholars of the 1950s. Rather, America had evolved as a truly unique society in which class, party and sectional divisions only served superficially to blind us to a far greater and distinctive commonality. We were told—and the implications were reassuring—that our uniqueness was derived from a progression of fundamental historical experiences which, mutually reinforcing one another, had joined to propel us toward a manifestly benevolent destiny.

We were, first, a nation of immigrants, culturally enriched by the variety of mankind. From America's melting-pot would emerge a new and superior synthesis of mankind—what Hector St. John de Crèvecoeur called "the American, this new man." It is hard, from the perspective of the latter third of the 20th century, to recapture the grandeur of this noble dream—as did Emma Lazarus, writing a century earlier in "The New Colossus":

> Give me your tired, your poor,
> Your huddled masses yearning to breathe free,
> The wretched refuse of your teeming shore,

Send these, the homeless, tempest-tossed, to me:
I lift my lamp beside the golden door.

In the introduction to his Pulitzer Prize-winning book on American immigrants, *The Uprooted,* Oscar Handlin wrote: "Once I thought to write a
history of the immigrants in America. Then I discovered that the immigrants
were American history."

What did these millions of immigrants encounter upon their arrival in the
New World? They found a vast and rich continent, thinly populated by
native "Indians" who were themselves Asian immigrants from millennia
past. In the extraordinary three-century process of exploring and settling this
fertile wilderness, the American immigrants and their progeny were themselves transformed into the unique American democrat. The frontier, in the
view of its most celebrated historian, Frederick Jackson Turner, lured the
discontented and the dispossessed, the restive and the ambitious. This second formative influence encouraged ingenuity, demanded self-reliance,
broke down class distinctions, nurtured opposition to governmental coercion, reinforced the sanctity of private property and contract, and fostered
political individualism. Though many were illiterate, America's immigrants
insisted upon universal education as a prerequisite for an informed and
productive citizenry. Universal education profoundly shaped the American
character, thus contributing to America's uniqueness, power, and creative
enterprise.

These distinctive traits, the American democratic ethos, were probably
more reflected in than molded by the third historical source of our unique
commonality: the American Revolution. We were told by the consensus
historians that our revolution was essentially a *conservative* revolution, in that
it achieved independence, through a surgical separation from Britain, for a
"nation" that had already evolved its liberal ethos and lacked only the acute
self-awareness that anti-colonial revolution inevitably brings.

Hence the new Federal Constitution and government forged by the founding fathers rested squarely upon a common ideology of Lockean-Jeffersonian
liberalism, our fourth historic well-spring of American uniqueness. This
liberal creed was shared by virtually all Americans, whether self-consciously
or not—whether Federalist, Whig, Democrat or Republican—for a reveal-
ingly *negative* reason: America lacked a feudal past. In the Old World, encumbered as it was by an ancient feudal tradition, the fires of social
revolution raged in societies deeply cleft by divisions of class and ideology.
Hence, in Europe, the ideological spectrum would remain broad, and legions
on the far left and the far right would make socialism and communism and
fascism possible. But in pragmatic and non-feudal America, ideological loyalties remained tightly clustered around the liberal center and extremist
politics could find no sizeable constituency.

This celebration of the American liberal consensus must be qualified historically by acknowledging the prominent exception of the "reactionary
enlightenment" of the southern slavocracy. But every schoolboy knows that
this near-fatal flaw was purged by the Civil War, and that this cancerous

contradiction between the Declaration of Independence and the Constitution was at last resolved in favor of the former by the addition to the latter of the 13th, 14th, and 15th Amendments. During Reconstruction the South also was committed to provide free public education to all citizens, thereby belatedly embracing the crucial American doctrine that democracy depends upon a literate and informed as well as a free electorate.

Hence, also when the next major historical transformation swept America, the urban-industrial revolution, America accomplished it with turbulence but without Marx. Whereas labor in Europe, given the Old World's feudal legacy of acute class consciousness, had rather automatically gone socialist, American workers virtually ignored socialism and produced instead the solidly capitalist AF of L and CIO. Given "Americanism," who needed socialism —or any other "ism"? American workers did not hate Andrew Carnegie; they wanted to *become* an Andrew Carnegie. And, uniquely in rags-to-riches America, that seemed possible, for America was clearly destined to become the richest nation in the world.

Affluence, then, was perhaps the climactic historical source of American uniqueness. According to the foremost historian of the American national character, David M. Potter, Americans have been most characteristically a "people of plenty." American abundance was perhaps the keystone of the unique American arch. It made viable the pressure-relieving, rags-to-riches dream of upward mobility. It made the two-party system stable and workable by guaranteeing that transitions in power—between two parties that did not differ ideologically very much anyway—would also make relatively small difference in the distribution of property. (Abundance thereby afforded America the luxury of apathetic voters.) Indeed, abundance probably made democracy itself possible, by cushioning the abrasions inherent in an aggressive society bent on maximizing both the exercise of rights and the accumulation of property. The system was admittedly imperfect; for liberal, pluralistic societies inherently tolerate a measure of inequity as the price exacted by equality of opportunity. But the established system had produced in the aggregate a democratic nation unmatched in longevity of Constitution and currency, two-party stability, exercise of civil liberties, and standard of living.

It was a just and proud legacy, one which seemed to make sense in the relatively tranquil 1950s. America could still vividly remember then that even when the Great Depression had devastated the Western world and so much of Europe had turned in desperation to extreme ideologies of the left and right, America had simply once again switched leaders and parties. Turning her back, as ever, on red flags and brown shirts, she had shored up her rickety capitalism by reforming it through the New Deal. Changes were wrought which legitimized the power of government to shape economic forces in the interests of the general welfare, reduced the power of the capitalist elite, and broadened the popular base of participation in the economic system. Concurrently, America muddled through until World War II brought both recovery and—characteristically for America—victory. Indeed, the consensus view of the American past seemed ideally constructed to ratify the present: locked in a Cold War with totalitarian communism, the United States represented not only the powerful and self-acknowledged leader of the free world, but also a politically stable and democratic model society that the rest of the world might seek to emulate.

2 The Roots of American Discontent

With the 1960s came shock and frustration. It was a decade against itself: the students of affluence were marching in the streets; the nation that had never lost a war to any power was mired in a seemingly endless, unpopular, and possibly unwinnable land war in Asia; the national consciousness was shocked by savage assassinations; and Negro Americans were responding to ostensible victories in civil rights and to their collectively unprecedented prosperity with a paradoxical venting of outrage. It seemed as if America, so long especially blessed by the fates, had suddenly been cheated. Emerging victorious from the world war against fascism, she faced not a century of Pax Americana (as had her British counterparts faced a century of Pax Britannica) but, instead, frustrating cold and hot war abroad and turmoil at home. How could the violent 1960s be explained in the light of our past?

Historical analysis of our national experience and character would suggest that the seeds of our contemporary discontent were to a large extent deeply embedded in those same ostensibly benevolent forces which had contributed to our uniqueness. First, we are indeed a nation of immigrants, but one in which the original dominant immigrant group, the so-called Anglo-Saxons, effectively preempted the crucial levers of economic and political power in government, commerce, and the professions. This elite group has consistently resisted—though by no means with uniform success—the upward strivings of successive "ethnic" immigrant waves. The resultant competitive hierarchy of immigrants has always been highly conducive to violence, but this violence has taken different forms. The Anglo-Americans used their access to the levers of power to maintain their dominance, using legal force surrounded by an aura of legitimacy for such ends as economic exploitation; the restriction of immigration by a national-origin quota system which clearly branded later immigrants from southern and eastern Europe and from Asia as culturally undesirable; the confinement of the original Indian immigrants largely to barren reservations; and the restriction of blacks first to slavery, then to a degraded caste. Periodically in times of national crisis, dominant Anglo-Americans rallied to "nativist" movements that directed violence toward "ethnic" scapegoats: in the 1790s with the Alien and Sedition Acts; in the 1850s with sectional split; in the decade 1886-96 with unrestricted immigration and labor and racial unrest; in World War I with the Red Scare; in World War II with the Nisei.

But the system was also conducive to violence among competing racial and ethnic groups themselves. The massive New York draft riots of 1863 prompted thousands of poor Irish, who felt the brunt of an inequitable conscription that allowed wealthy men to purchase substitutes, to vent their wrath upon New York's Negroes. Much of the inter-ethnic hostility has flowed from genuine economic competition among lower-class Americans, and this source of ethnic antagonism has historically been exacerbated by the tendency of American industrialists to combat union organizers by employing black "scabs" and strikebreakers. This practice most clearly linked two mutually supportive sources of social anxiety: economic threat and status frustration. Given America's unprecedented ethnic pluralism, simply being born American conferred no automatic and equal citizenship in the eyes of the larger society. In the face of such reservations, ethnic minorities had constantly to affirm their Americanism through a kind of patriotic ritual which intensified the ethnic competition for status and invited severe and abiding conflict.

The second major formative historical experience was America's prolonged encounter with the frontier. While the frontier experience indubitably strengthened the mettle of the American character, it also witnessed the brutal and brutalizing ousting of the Indians and the forceful incorporation of Mexican and other original inhabitants, and fastened into the American character a tenacious habit of wastefully exploiting our natural resources. Further, it concomitantly created an environment in which, owing to the paucity of law enforcement agencies, a tradition of vigilante "justice" was legitimized. Originally prompted by frontier lawlessness and inspired—or at least rationalized—by the doctrines of self-preservation, the right of revolution, popular sovereignty and the Higher Law, American vigilantism has historically enjoyed powerful ideological support. Vigilantism has persisted as a socially malleable instrument long after the disappearance of the frontier environment that gave it birth, and it has proved quite congenial to an urban setting. The longevity of the Ku Klux Klan and the vitality both of contemporary urban rioting and of the stiffening resistance to it owe much to this tradition.

Third, the revolutionary doctrine that our Declaration of Independence proudly proclaims is mistakenly cited as a model for legitimate violence by contemporary groups such as militant Negroes and radical students who confront a system of both public and private government that they regard as contemptuous of their consent. Entranced by the resurgence of revolution in the underdeveloped world and of international university unrest, radical students and blacks seize upon our early doctrine of the inherent right of revolution and self-determination to justify their rebellion. That their analogies are fatefully problematical in no way dilutes the majesty of our own proud Declaration.

The fourth historic legacy, our consensual political philosophy of Lockean-Jeffersonian liberalism, was premised upon a pervasive fear of governmental power and has reinforced the tendency to define freedom negatively as freedom *from*. As a consequence, conservatives have been able paradoxically to invoke the doctrines of Jefferson in resistance to legislative reforms, and the Sumnerian imperative that "stateways cannot change folkways" has historically enjoyed a wide and not altogether unjustified allegiance in the public eye. Its implicit corollary has been that forceful and, if necessary,

violent local and state resistance to unpopular federal stateways is a legitimate response; both Calhoun and Wallace could confidently repair to a strict
construction of the same document invoked by Lincoln and the Warren
court.

This ability of the American liberal consensus to encompass widely divergent social views within a common framework of constitutionalism was
clearly demonstrated by the failure of Reconstruction following the Civil
War. While the taut prohibition of the 13th Amendment permitted no am-
biguity concerning slavery, the conservative Supreme Court of the post-war
years consistently demonstrated the extraordinary flexibility of judicial construction in largely eviscerating the substance and perverting the purpose of
the 14th and 15th Amendments and the social reform of Reconstruction law.
The resultant hypocrisy for generations made a mockery of liberal rhetoric
and fueled the fires of alienation. Black education became separate and
manifestly unequal, yet for a century the local bias of Jeffersonian liberalism
effectively blocked federal assistance or intervention. The massive expansion
of public education in recent years, together with the social reform of the
Second Reconstruction, has to some extent bolstered public faith in the
contemporary efficacy and relevance of the American liberal tradition and
particularly its commitment to free public education. But this proud commitment has too often been advanced as a panacea wherein America's schools
are expected somehow to solve her most deeply-rooted social problems.

The next historic source both of our modern society and our current plight,
following Civil War and Reconstruction, has been our industrial revolution
and the great internal migration from the countryside to the city. Yet the
process occurred with such astonishing rapidity that it produced widespread
socioeconomic dislocation in an environment in which the internal controls
of the American social structure were loose and the external controls were
weak. Urban historian Richard Wade has observed . . .

> The cities inherited no system of police control adequate to the number or to the
> rapid increase of the urban centers. The modern police force is the creation of the 20th
> century; the establishment of genuinely professional systems is historically a very
> recent thing. Throughout the 18th and 19th century, the force was small, untrained,
> poorly paid, and part of the political system. In case of any sizeable disorder, it was
> hopelessly inadequate; and rioters sometimes routed the constabulary in the first
> confrontation.

Organized labor's protracted and bloody battles for recognition and power
occurred during these years of minimal control and maximal social upheaval.
The violence of workers' confrontation with their employers was partly the
result of a lack of consensus on the legitimacy of workers' protests, partly
the result of the lack of means of social control. Workers used force to press
their grievances, employers organized violent resistance, and repeatedly state
or federal troops had to be summoned to restore order.

The final distinctive characteristic—in many ways perhaps our most distinctive—has been our unmatched prosperity. Ranked celestially with life
and liberty in the sacrosanct Lockean trilogy, property has generated a quest

and prompted a devotion in the American character that has matched our devotion to equality and, in a fundamental sense, has transformed the idea of equality from the radical leveling of the European democratic tradition into a typically American insistence upon equality of *opportunity*. In an acquisitive society of individuals with unequal talents and groups with unequal advantages, this had resulted in an unequal distribution of the rapid accumulation of abundance that, especially since World War II, has promised widespread participation in the affluent society to a degree unprecedented in history. Central to the notion of "revolutions of rising expectations" is the assumption that improved economic rewards can coincide with and often obscure a degree of *relative* deprivation that generates frustration and can prompt men toward violent protest despite measurable gains. Revolutions have not historically occurred in stagnant and utterly destitute nations; rather, they have occurred in nations in which rising but uneven prosperity at once inspired hope and intensified frustations and impatience with the old order.

3 Violence in the American Tradition

Our historical evolution, then, has given our national character a dual nature: we strive for both liberty and equality, which can be—and often in practice are—quite contradictory goals. This is not to suggest that American society is grounded in a fatal contradiction. For all the conflict inherent in a simultaneous quest for liberty and equality, American history is replete with dramatic instances of the successful adjustment of "the system" to the demands of disparate protesting groups. An historical appraisal of these genuine achievements should give pause to contemporary Cassandras who bemoan in self-flagellation how hopelessly wretched we all are. To be sure, these radically disillusioned social critics can find abundant evil in our historical legacy: centuries of Negro slavery, the cultural deracination and near extinction of the Indians, our initiation of atomic destruction—*ad infinitum*. But these radical new social critics in their overcompensations tend to distort the American experience in much the same fashion, although in an opposite direction, as have the more familiar superpatriotic celebrants of American virtuosity. Even so, a careful and honest historical appraisal should remind us that violence has been far more intrinsic to our past than we should like to think.

Although violence has been a disagreeably persistent characteristic of American social life, this recurrent theme of violence has taken different forms in response to America's rapidly changing social context. Historical analysis suggests that while much of the American violence was prompted by environmental conditions that no longer exist, many of the social tensions that produced violence are recurrent and remain of contemporary relevance.

Perhaps the historically violent American episode that is least relevant to our contemporary concerns is the family feud. The famous and colorful clan feuding of Hatfields versus McCoys and Suttons versus Taylors seems to have been triggered by the Civil War in border areas where loyalties were sharply divided and where the large extended family of the 19th century provided both a focus for intense loyalties and a ready instrument of aggression. But this tradition has waned with the fading of the peculiar circumstances that conditioned its birth. It is arguable, however, that the brutalizing traditions associated with the Indian wars have left their callous imprint on our national character long after the estimated 850,000 to one million American Indians had been ruthlessly reduced by 1950 to 400,000. Similarly, the violence associated with the American Revolution, the Civil War, and the two Reconstructions has surely reinforced the ancient notion that the end justifies the means.

[That] the long association with violence of agrarian uprising and the labor movement has permanently faded with changing modern circumstances is fervently to be hoped, but by no means certain. Employer acceptance of unions during and after the New Deal suggests that that long and bloody conflict is largely behind us. But the growing guild-like defensiveness and exclusiveness of especially those unions threatened by automation, together with the persistent reality that the majority of American laborers—especially black workers—remain outside the unions, invited a resurgence of intramural labor unrest. Also, the stubborn persistence of rural poverty constitutes a latent invitation to a resurgence of latter-day populism.

Two other sordid American traditions that have largely waned but that recently have shown some signs of revival are vigilantism and lynching. If vigilantism is defined broadly to include regional and even national movements as well as local organizations, then America's preeminent vigilante movement has been the Ku Klux Klan—or rather, the Ku Klux Klans, for there have essentially been three of them. The original Klan arose in the South in response to radical Reconstruction and, through terror and intimidation, was instrumental in the "redemption" of the southern state governments by white conservatives. The second Klan, by far the largest, was resurrected in Atlanta in 1915 and boomed nationally in the 1920s. Strong in the Midwest and Far West as well as in the South, and making inroads even in the cities, the Klan of the 1920s—despite its traditional racist and xenophobic rhetoric—focused its chastisement less upon Negroes, Catholics, and Jews than upon white Protestants who were adjudged guilty of violating smalltown America's Victorian moral code. The third Klan represented a proliferation of competing Klans in the South in response to the civil rights movement of the 1950s. Generally lacking the prestige and organizational strength of the earlier Klans, these groups of lower-class whites engaged in a period of unrestrained terrorism in the rural and smalltown Black Belt South in the 1950s and early 1960s, but have belatedly been brought under greater control.

Lynching, vigilantism's supreme instrument of terror and summary "justice," has been widely practiced in America since the Revolution era, when miscreant Tories were tarred and feathered, and worse. Although lynching is popularly associated with racial mob murder, this pattern is historically a relatively recent one, for prior to the late 19th century, white Americans perforce lynched one another—Negro slaves being far too valuable to squander at the stake. But lynching became predominantly racial from 1882 to 1903, when 1,985 Negroes were murdered in the tragic but successful effort of those years to forge a rigid system of biracial caste, most brutal and explicit in the South but generally reflective of national attitudes. Once the point that this was a white man's country was made, lynching gradually declined. Its recent resurgence in response to the civil rights movement is notorious, but it nowhere approximates its scale at the turn of the century.

The contemporary relevance of political assassination and freelance multiple murder needs no documentation to a nation that has so recently witnessed the murders of John and Robert Kennedy, Dr. Martin Luther King, and, on television, Lee Harvey Oswald—in addition to the chilling mass slaughtering sprees of Charles Whitman in Austin and Richard Speck in Chicago. Historically, political assassination has become a recurrent feature of the American political system only in the South during (the first) Reconstruction and in the New Mexico Territory. Although four American Presidents have been assassinated since 1865, prominent politicians and civil servants occupying the myriad lesser levels of government have been largely immune. Whether the current spate of public murder is an endemic symptom of a new social malaise is a crucial question that history cannot yet answer, other than to observe that precedents in our past are minimal.

Similarly, historical precedents are few regarding massive student and anti-war protests. American students have historically engaged in food riots and succumbed to the annual spring throes of the panty-raid syndrome, but the current wave of campus confrontations is essentially an unprecedented phenomenon—as is the massive and prolonged opposition to the war in Vietnam. But the size of and sophistication of the contemporary college student body are also unprecedented. Now outnumbering America's farmers by almost three million, America's seven million college students confront, largely without votes, a society that nags the conscience of the best of them by sending younger non-college students off to an unpopular war in Asia, and threatens their security and careers by greeting them with the same grim summons upon graduation. We have lived with these harsh realities before —unpopular wars, inequitable conscription, threatened young men—but never in such potent combination. Unfortunately, in this regard, the past does not have much to tell us; we will have to make our history along uncharted and frightening ways.

But the past has much to tell us about the rioting and crime that have gripped our cities. Urban mobs are as old as the city itself. Colonial seaports frequently were rocked for days by roving mobs—groups of unruly and often drunken men whose energies were shrewdly put to political purpose as Liberty Boys in the American Revolution. Indeed, our two principal instruments of physical control evolved directly in response to 19th-century urban turmoil. The professional city police system replaced the inadequate constabulary and watch-and-ward in response to the urban rioting of the 1840s and 1850s, largely in the Northeast. Similarly, the national guard was organized in order to control the labor violence—or more appropriately, the anti-labor violence—of the 1880s and 1890s.

4 Conclusion

Probably all nations are given to a kind of historical amnesia or selective recollection that masks unpleasant traumas of the past. Certainly, Americans since the Puritans have historically regarded themselves as a latter-day "Chosen People" sent on a holy errand to the wilderness, there to create a New Jerusalem. One beneficent side effect of our current turmoil may be to force a harder and more candid look at our past.

Violence has usually been the lava flowing from the top of a volcano fed by deeper fires of social dislocation and injustice; it has not been stopped solely by capping the top, but has usually subsided when our political and social institutions have managed to make the adjustments necessary to cool the fires below. If our future is to be more just, less violent, less crime-ridden, and free of fear, we obviously must do much better than we are now doing to speed social reform and simultaneously improve the effectiveness of the entire law enforcement system of the nation. Only in an orderly society can we achieve the advances which militants and moderates alike know are required.

POLITICAL SOCIALIZATION

PART TWO

How the public at large and various political subgroups evaluate the legitimacy of political appeals and public policies is shaped by their encounters with various agencies of political socialization. These agencies include the school, the family, peer groups, political institutions, and the mass media. The purpose of Part Two is to examine the ways in which the various values and symbols of the American political culture that were discussed in Part One are transmitted to the individual citizen.

Much past research dealing with the agencies of political socialization has selectively focused on system-maintaining values transmitted by social institutions. It has failed to give appropriate attention to conflict and to change-oriented socialization experiences. Many empirical theorists have tended to treat as processes of political socialization only the messages that reinforce prevailing community values, encourage obedience to the existing regime, and hence promote political stability. Socialization into change-oriented attitudes and behavior tends to be treated as a failure to socialize rather than as an alternative form of political socialization that reflects existing subcultural cleavages in the social system. The difficulty with this narrow usage of the concept is that it allows the user to conclude prematurely that political protest behavior is by definition a manifestation of individual maladjustment or disacculturation, not to be taken seriously as a symptom of deficiencies in existing institutions. It constitutes an a priori linkage between individual pathology and active political protest, which is not born out by tangible evidence.

The selections that follow were chosen to avoid this conceptual pitfall. They focus on four major agencies of socialization—the school, the family, political candidates, and the mass media—and call attention to the widely divergent patterns of political socialization to be found in contemporary America.

In "Transmitting the Civic Culture: The Teacher and Political Socialization," Dean Jaros sheds light on how adolescents learn political values in school. Formal instructional content is less important than the personal impact that the teacher has on his students. Jaros focuses on the modes by which teachers are induced to communicate system-oriented political norms such as a sense of personal efficacy, a sense of obligation to participate in politics, and a belief in the desirability of political party activity. In effect, he is asking to what extent and by what mechanisms teachers are persuaded to stress the pluralist's confidence in political participation through organized group activity and deemphasize the populist's mistrust of self-interested politics. The teachers from central Kentucky whom he questioned strongly supported the value of citizen participation in politics, but they only moderately supported the value of organized partisan activity in achieving political objectives. When confronted in later life with the realities of such activity, the students of these teachers might suffer disillusionment and political alienation. On balance, however, the values transmitted by teachers are institutionally conservative, system-supporting values. Jaros devotes much of his article to explaining how teachers come to hold the values they espouse in the classroom.

Robert Lane's "Fathers and Sons: Foundations of Political Belief" traces the socialization process to its earliest stages: the relationship between father and son. In the late 1950s Lane intensively interviewed fifteen men employed in working-class and clerical occupations who today might be termed "forgotten Americans." He found that their rebellion against parental authority in adolescence did not take the form of protest or political radicalism because politics was not particularly important to their fathers. Given the fathers' Lockean values of privatism, faith in education, and upward mobility, those adolescents who did rebel chose to hurt their families by quitting school. Nonetheless, damaged father-son relationships did produce political alienation. In the case of four of the men, the personal preoccupation caused by the damaged filial relationships tended to produce low levels of political interest and information, fears of expressing hostility toward authority figures, feelings of political powerlessness, and a generally cynical view of the political process. The overall response was a turning inward of aggressive drives. Self-alienation led to passive estrangement from politics rather than to active protest.

According to Albert Camus, "every act of rebellion expresses a nostalgia for innocence and an appeal to the essence of being." Camus' point is that the rebel has overcome his despair. The rebel believes that there are some human values worth fighting to preserve. Hope, rather than nihilism, is at the heart of much political protest. Nihilism, if it does find political expression, is likely to manifest itself in episodic and wasteful ejaculations of rage and in extreme acts of violence.

In his essay "Notes on Young Radicals," Kenneth Keniston develops this distinction between idealism and nihilism to refute the thesis, advanced by Lewis Feuer and others, that radical protest by students is merely a manifestation of generational rebellion. Hostile rebellion against parents of the same sex is associated not with student activism but with political withdrawal and quietism.

Keniston's essay also includes a particularly perceptive critique of the status quo bias of the theoretical concepts traditionally used in political socialization literature. His own research treats student radicalism as an alternative type of socialization process rather than as "desocialization" or "disacculturation"—terms that incorrectly connote isolation and barbarism.

The final selection in Part Two is a case study drawn from Joe McGinniss' book *The Selling of the President, 1968.* It demonstrates the extent to which media campaigns, such as Richard Nixon's 1968 run for the presidency, are designed to identify the candidate with what social psychologists have called "condensation symbols." Such symbols condense a wide range of deeply felt emotional attachments into abstract words and expressions that often have no reference to objective things or situations in the world outside the mind. For example, campaign language contains such symbols or code words as "law and order," "great nation," and "bring our country back,'' designed to arouse a mass response of support for the candidate by stimulating the voters' emotional hopes and fears. The fact that Richard Nixon's campaign advisors changed the vocabulary of the campaign rhetoric to appeal to special audiences indicates their awareness of the widely divergent pattern to political socialization processes in America as a result of race, class, regional, ethnic, and life-style differences in the population.

Transmitting the Civic Culture: The Teacher and Political Socialization

6

Dean Jaros

It is a common assertion that all regimes seek to insure their continued survival by indoctrinating their citizens with values that are tolerant of basic government practices and productive of stable patterns of political behavior. Such values are typically acquired—and firm commitments to them developed—during childhood and youth. It is thus reasonable to think that the schools, which are at least in part formally charged with maintaining a flow of supportive values, would be instrumental in this process. Indeed, philosophers, statesmen, educators and active citizens have for centuries discussed the great role of formal education processes in the political indoctrination of the young. But, in some contrast to expectations, modern empirical scholarship has largely failed to demonstrate the efficacy of school-mediated experiences in the development of political orientations. Political scientists have not yet devoted much attention to this agent, but what results they have produced suggest an extremely limited school influence. Their studies tend to concentrate on courses or curricula as the effective variables. Good reason exists, however, to believe that the critical variables in any school learning experience are mediated by teachers *per se* and that formal instructional content is a secondary consideration.

Research by educators about the learning experience, on the other hand, is voluminous. Much of it focuses on what appears to be important teacher-related variables. But the educators' success in assessing the school as an agent of political socialization has been, perhaps, even more limited than that of the political scientists. This is in part due to failure to consider the proper dependent variables. To the educator, citizen training may simply mean teaching children not to perform acts disruptive of the regular routine of the school nor otherwise to interfere with extant patterns of human relationships. Though such learning doubtless could be transferred to political objects as children mature, there is little evidence as to how this transfer would take place. "Civics," on the other hand, does concern the relationship of the child to the political world, but research on the topic is often disappointing. Commentary on important variables such as partisan activity or "subject" participation is scant. Either teaching about such topics does not go on in the schools or it is poorly researched.

There are, thus, great gaps in the knowledge which is needed not only to develop adequate theories about political stability and change—certainly a task of cardinal importance to the political scientist—but also more effec-

58

tively to manipulate and administer civic education programs in the schools. What political values do various community agencies urge upon schools? How do they influence the schools to enunciate them to children? To what extent and by what processes are these communications effectively received by the children in the schools? The questions are manifold.

This paper reports on a preliminary investigation—part of a larger study designed to approach most of the questions specified above—of the modes by which teachers are induced to communicate certain political norms to children. In question are the participatory norms of the "civic culture" as discussed by Almond and Verba. There is little doubt that the persistence of stable, democratic regimes requires the widespread sharing of basic attitudes toward involvement in governmental affairs. This attitudinal base upon which democracy supposedly is built includes feelings of *civic competence* (the sense of ability to mobilize citizen influence to affect aspects of public policy); feelings of *subject competence* (belief that one can receive responsible treatment in the administration of already determined public policy); belief in the desirability of *party activity* as a device for citizen influence upon government; and a sense of *obligation* to participate in at least electoral input to the polity.

Three Modes of Transmission

There are several ways by which regimes could employ teachers in this process of induction of the young. We shall investigate three of the more obvious and direct possibilities. (1) Persons of particular social backgrounds could be brought to the teaching profession through a process of selective recruitment. Having already been "properly" socialized within their background contexts, such persons could be counted upon to teach preferred values. (2) Teacher training could be conducted in such a manner that the values expected to be taught are made clear to new recruits. If training is a sufficiently momentous experience, these expectations would be acted upon. (3) Induction to the norms of the profession or of the local community may occur after the teacher has begun work. Such norms may include the teaching of political values particularly "appropriate" to given locales.

It is probable that all of these modes plus others are simultaneously operative. The problem is not so much to decide which is effective, but to specify relative influences and to describe how they interact. Given the fact that teachers are exposed to the posited three categories of independent variables in a definite sequence, we feel that there are important changes in the relative significances of these modes with length of time in the teaching profession.

Though the behavioral consequences of social background are many, we do not feel that possibility #1 is greatly important in determining the political value output of the schools. There is relatively little evidence that teachers of divergent class or community origins teach notably different values. Though the notion that middle-class values are communicated through the schools because teachers (themselves of the middle class) are representative of those values is venerable in educational sociology, its validity is severely undermined by the observation that the value output of American schools has not notably changed with the recent recruitment of large numbers of relatively lower-class males to the teaching profession. But on the other hand, it would be foolish to discount entirely the effect of background on political teaching. We posit the existence of a moderate effect, but one which is eroded as the teacher is socialized into his profession.

Given the findings of such research on teacher education and training, possibility #2 seems more likely to be an efficacious instrument of society's political norms. Many kinds of teacher behavior have been asserted to depend upon both kind and amount of training. It appears that like other occupations, the profession of teaching involves heavy doses of induction into particular attitudes. This induction process begins, apparently, with formal education. Indeed, teachers' norms about political expression also appear to be dependent upon college major and kind of degree. It is thus but a short extension to suggest that the particular political value content which is enunciated by teachers is a function of the teacher-training experience. Specifically, we expect that much political teaching will be profoundly influenced by perceptions of values held by instructors of education. We further suggest that this influence will decline, though not be eliminated, as the teacher grows older and is socialized by other professional agencies and by community sources.

It follows that we expect possibility #3 to operate as a social transmission device through more experienced personnel. There is considerable ground for believing that teachers, once they perceive the realities of their immediate positions, will regard the imperatives of earlier experience as less compelling. As a group, teachers are known to be compliant, non-competitive, and deferential. Accordingly, if strong expectations on the part of immediately important persons are perceived, it is quite likely that these expectations will produce conformity. Teachers realize that their supposed access to the minds of children makes deviant ideas, especially deviant political ideas, the objects of widespread hostility. "Inappropriate" behavior and associated sanctions are easily identifiable. But, interestingly, most of the inducements to conformity are seen as emanating from within the professional milieu rather than directly from the community. Teachers fear sanctions for deviant political behavior from their supervisors and peers more than from most external community agencies. Thus we expect that in teachers who have had time to become aware of expectations surrounding their particular positions, political teaching behavior will be less related to background and educational influences and more related to perceived values of school administrators and other teachers.

However, it is known that political teaching behavior varies importantly with local community characteristics. Values attendant upon community variation are somehow reflected in what is taught. It is felt that this is in part due to direct perception of community expectations. There should be a modest relationship between teaching behavior and perceived values of local elites.

Method

A complete enumeration of social studies teachers in grades seven through twelve in seven central Kentucky counties provided research subjects for the present study. These grades and courses were chosen because they represent the time and place in the educational process at which discrete classes are addressed toward political subjects and at which teachers with specifically differentiated political studies responsibilities can be identified. If any teachers are likely to be oriented toward the civic culture or to communicate it, these are the ones. . . .

Each teacher was interviewed at length and asked to respond to an instrument which was partially structured and partially of the free response type. Several topics were under investigation so that the items of concern to this paper were interspersed with many others. Any pattern to our inquiry was not immediately evident to respondents.

Dependent variables, the teaching of the four participatory values of the civic culture, were measured by inferring from free responses to each of four hypothetical student queries which were put to the subjects. For example, in the area of subject competence, each respondent was asked to imagine a student in his class who asks about an appeal to obtain redress for an unsatisfactory property tax assessment. The questions were so worded as to permit, but not require, a normative response. If the teacher without probing approved of the activity in question, he was regarded as a strong communicator of that value. If, after specific probing, a favorable normative response was rendered, the respondent was regarded as a moderate communicator of that value. If, even after probing, there was no normative response, or if the activity was disapproved, the subject was regarded as a non-communicator of the value. . . .

The teachers' perceptions of the civic culture values of various socializing agencies, such as college instructors of education or community leaders, were assessed in a simple and straightforward way: single statements either extolling or rejecting . . . each of the four values were read to the respondents who were then asked to adjudge the position of "most" of the members of the appropriate socializing agencies as to their degree of agreement. Respondents were scored as to whether they perceived (1) a strong supportive position on the value, (2) a supportive position that was not strong, or (3) a neutral or rejective position on the part of the agents. As an example, the following statement was used to elicit information on perceived values about the obligation to participate:

"Many Americans feel that in some elections, it really doesn't make any difference who wins. If they feel this way, they should not bother to vote." How do you think most school administrators around here feel [on this matter]?

Strongly agree   agree   neutral   disagree   strongly disagree

Two background variables, respondents' class origins and size of community in which respondents grew up, were measured. The former was gauged by classifying fathers' reported occupations according to Warner's seven-rank scheme, while the latter was determined by a single query as to whether respondents grew up on a farm, in a town, in a small city, or in a large city.

. . .

Table 1 Distribution of Support for Civic Culture Participatory Values in Teaching (in percentages)

	Civic Competence (N = 174)	Subject Competence (N = 174)	Party Activity (N = 174)	Obligation (N = 174)
Strongly Support	29	30	28	67
Moderately Support	51	56	29	25
Do Not Support	19	14	32	7
No Response	1	0	11	1
	100	100	100	100

Findings

The civic culture is at least moderately communicated in central Kentucky junior and senior high schools. Table 1 describes the distribution of teaching postures with respect to the four participatory variables. Patterns which have been found in other studies of political education are repeated in the heavy emphasis on obligation and in the at least partial rejection of partisan activity. These results encourage us in our belief that our respondents are not grossly atypical of American teachers. Though it is difficult to attach any absolute significance to these values, they merit at least passing comment. One wonders whether there is not some disparity between the heavy emphasis on teaching an obligation to participate and the relatively moderate support for teaching effective modes of bringing influence to bear on government. Perhaps this represents a concealment of the realities of political life from pupils. Subsequent exposure of these realities might lead to cynicism in later life.

Table 2 Relationships* between Teaching of Values and Size of Respondents' Community of Origin

Civic Competence	.07
Subject Competence	−.11
Party Activity	−.04
Obligation	−.01

*All correlation coefficients in this and subsequent tables are Goodman and Kruskal gammas.

Regardless of the "adequacy" or effects of these teaching behaviors, it remains to be asked how teachers are induced to transmit these regime-supportive values. Our suggestion that background variables would be relatively unimportant in explaining what is taught is confirmed by these central Kentucky data. Table 2 indicates the relationship between the size of the respondents' communities of origin and their teaching of each of the four civic culture values. The general lack of association is complemented by a similar array of data on social-class origins and teaching. Given the importance of status to sociological research, it is perhaps surprising to find that class and the transmission of the civic culture are totally unrelated, with average absolute values of gamma = .03.

. . .

These results indicate that society most certainly does not communicate civic culture norms through selective recruitment. Background influences on teaching do not survive. The notion of the middle-class teacher communicating middle-class values, a favorite form of this hypothesis, is dealt a double blow, for there were no teaching differences by class of origin, even among the most inexperienced teachers.

Table 3 Relationships between Teaching of Values and Respondents' Perceptions of Values fo College Education Instructors

Civic Competence	−.09
Subject Competence	.24
Party Activity	−.24
Obligation	.12

Though their influence might also erode with time, we expected that the values of education instructors would have a somewhat more pervasive impact on the teaching of civic culture values. A look at Table 3 only partially substantiates that expectation. Two teaching variables seem indeed to be associated with perceptions of college instructors' values, but one is quite unexpectedly negatively related! In teaching values about party participation, teachers seem specifically to reject what they take to be the college educators' values.

Though this pattern is initially puzzling, imposition of a control for length of time in the profession resolves many difficulties. It also confirms that education of teachers is a more powerful determinant of behavior than is background (Table 4). Strangely, teachers are provided with no cues about civic competence during their formal training. Either college instructors say nothing about organizing for application of political influence, or else communicate meaningless platitudes. It is likely that the whole question is de-emphasized in favor of stressing formal voting participation. The massive dependence of new teachers' instruction about obligation to vote upon perceived values of the college educators suggests this to be the case. Though new recruits are clearly greatly moved by their instructors, the effect is short lived, for their more experienced counterparts' teaching of obligation clearly depends on other antecedents. A more dramatic example of the erosion of early influences on behavior can hardly be imagined.

Table 4 Relationships between Teaching of Values and Respondents' Perceptions of Values of College Education Instructors, by Length of Time Teaching

	Less Than Two Years	Two-Five Years	More Than Five Years
Civic Competence	−.02	−.08	−.15
Subject Competence	.33	.16	.17
Party Activity	−.37	.42	.49
Obligation	.81	−.09	−.20

The impact of college instructors' values on the teaching of subject competence is maintained across all levels of experience. Perhaps these early teaching patterns are not challenged by later socialization agencies. They may even be reinforced.

The anomaly of party participation at first appears compounded with the imposition of the control. Initially rejected, college instructors' values appear to have increasing influence with increasing experience in teaching. This is the diametric opposite of eroding influence. . . . Perhaps we are witnessing a retrospective acceptance of professorial wisdom.

We are prepared to assert that one of the modes by which the regime seeks to transmit the civic culture to younger generations is through the training of teachers. Perceived college education instructors' values do influence teacher behavior, though not with respect to all four variables nor in exactly the pattern originally suggested. Erosion does not necessarily occur; influence may be maintained or even increased as the teacher progresses through his career. Possibility #2, however, is indeed operative.

Despite this, a great deal of teaching behavior—particularly that of older teachers—remains unexplained. It is interesting to note that in the teaching of obligation and citizen competence, more experienced respondents, if anything, *reject* their backgrounds and their educations. On what basis do they reject them? Various socialization agencies surrounding the job—some professional and some community-oriented—are likely providers of cues. Table 5 demonstrates, however, that the over-all impact of the variables posited for possibility #3 is modest indeed. Given the acknowledged importance of induction to occupational norms, we might have expected somewhat larger relationships between perceived values of administrators and other teachers on the one hand and the teaching of the civic culture on the other. Though indeed professional sources—school administrators and teachers—have more influence that the external agent—community elites—the implications for the political indoctrination of youth are small.

Table 5 Relationships between Teaching of Values and Respondents' Perceptions of Values of Job-Related Agents

	Community Leaders	School Administrators	Other Teachers
Civic Competence	−.01	−.13	−.04
Subject Competence	.07	.11	.10
Party Activity	.12	.13	.08
Obligation	.08	−.18	.19

Of course, any impact of such agents should be concentrated in older teachers. However, imposing a control for length of service upon these relationships only very marginally confirms our expectations.

. . .

It seems safe to conclude that the regime only minimally transmits the civic culture to its youth through professional or community socialization of its teachers. Even if there were a great many older teachers in a system, their long exposure to such later socializing influences appears to produce only modest effects upon teaching behavior. This small impact on only two variables suggests that the regime which relied solely upon possibility #3 to inculcate its youth would be seriously deficient.

Conclusion

If regimes employ teachers to communicate supportive political orientations to upcoming generations, how do they insure that the educators will communicate particular values? We suggested three modes by which the teaching of democratic participatory norms might be induced. Indeed, they were found partially to explain teacher behavior. The impact of background variables is primarily among young teachers. It is limited, however, to only some aspects of the civic culture, and, as expected, it rapidly erodes. The perceived values of college education instructors are somewhat more important. Though certainly not pervasive, they affect the teaching of several values. Despite the early occurrence of these influences in the teachers' career patterns, they do not generally decline with experience. The perceived values of job-related agents, especially professional rather than community-oriented ones, have a modest role in supplanting earlier influences. Though they have virtually no effect upon young teachers, an independent, if rather limited, impact upon older personnel is present.

Despite these observations, there is much observed teaching for which no antecedent variables have been found. This is especially true for the norm of civic competence. Variance on this teaching dimension is almost totally unaccounted for. Similarly unexplained is the teaching by more experienced educators of the obligation to participate. Factors influential early in the career appear to be rejected, but the basis for rejection remains unknown.

Though the over-all picture is one in which professional socialization appears to be most responsible for teachers' transmission of participatory values, we must acknowledge that it is a highly incomplete picture. But it is not bleak, for though it is obvious that additional explanatory processes must be found, this preliminary investigation contains enough hints of potentially interesting relationships to serve as at least a partial guide in more extensive studies of how the civic culture gets learned.

Fathers And Sons: Foundations of Political Belief

7

Robert Lane

Loosely speaking, there are three ways in which a father lays the foundations for his son's political beliefs. He may do this, first, through indoctrination, both overt and covert as a model for imitation, so that the son picks up the loyalties, beliefs, and values of the old man. Second, he places the child in a social context, giving him an ethnicity, class position, and community or regional environment. And, he helps to shape political beliefs by his personal relations with his son and by the way he molds the personality which must sustain and develop a social orientation. The combination of these three processes produces the "Mendelian law" of politics: the inheritance of political loyalties and beliefs. But while imitation and common social stakes tend to enforce this law, the socialization process may work to repeal it. It is the socialization process, the way in which fathers and sons get along with each other, that we examine in this paper.

Some perspective is gained by noting a number of possible models of the way fathers through their rearing practices may affect their sons' social outlook. The German model of the stern father who emphasizes masculine "hardness" and "fitness" in the son, and who monopolizes the opportunity for conversation at the dinner table, is one that has been explored at length. The Japanese father, partially deified like his ancestors, strictly attentive to protocol and detail in the home, is another. The Russian father image—the gruff, indulgent, somewhat undisciplined but spontaneous and warm individual—is a third. And the American father is said to be more of a brother than a father, joined with his son under the same female yoke, uninspired but certainly not frightening. Here is an image to compare with others and, as with the other models, its caricaturistic exaggeration nevertheless represents an identifiable likeness.

The father-son relationship may be explored with the help of data on the lives and politics of fifteen men interviewed recently at considerable length. These men represent a random sample drawn from the voting list of 220 citizens living in a moderate income housing development in an Eastern industrial city. Out of fifteen asked, fifteen (prompted by a modest stipend) agreed to be interviewed, even though these interviews ranged from ten to fifteen hours, administered in from four to seven installments. The characteristics of the sample were as follows:

There were all white, married, fathers, urban, and Eastern.
Their incomes ranged from 2,400 to 6,300 dollars (with one exception: his income was about 10,000 dollars in 1957).

Ten had working class occupations such as painter, plumber, policeman, railroad fireman, and machine operator. Five had white collar occupations such as salesman, bookkeeper, and supply clerk.
Their ages ranged from 25 to 54 years—most of them were in their thirties.
Twelve were Catholic, two Protestant, and one was Jewish.
All were native-born; their nationality backgrounds included: six Italian, five Irish, one Polish, one Swedish, one Russian (Jewish), and one Yankee.
All were employed at the time of the interviews.
Three concluded their schooling after grammar school and eight after some high school; two finished high school, one had some college training, and one went to graduate school.

The interviews were taped, with the permission of the interviewees, and transcribed for analysis. There was an agenda of topics and questions but the interviews were not closely structured, being conducted with probes and follow-up questions in a conversational style. The topics included: (1) current social questions, such as foreign policy, unions, taxes, and desegregation; (2) political parties; (3) political leaders and leadership; (4) social groups and group memberships; (5) ideological orientation toward "democracy," "freedom," "equality," and "government"; (6) personal values and philosophies of life; (7) personality dimensions—partially explored through standard tests; (8) life histories, including attitudes toward parents, brothers and sisters, school, and so forth.

In addition to the interviews, a group of tests were administered on anxiety, authoritarianism, anomie, information, and certain social attitudes.

The characteristics of the sample, as in any study, affect the relationships discovered. It should be stressed that this is a sample of men who, by and large, are well adjusted to society: they are married and have children, hold steady jobs, they are voters. This probably implies that any warping of personality which may have taken place in childhood was marginal. We are, then, dealing with the relationships of childhood experiences and political expression in a moderately "normal" group. We are not involved with the extremes of personality damage, or the bottom rung of the social ladder, or a highly socially alienated group. Unlike the studies of American Communists or of nativist agitators, this paper is concerned with middle and normal America, with more or less adjusted people. This is an important point because our findings differ in certain respects from those of other studies, but they do not necessarily conflict with them.

The Unfought War of Independence

The influence of the son's rebellious attitudes toward his father has often been said to be important in explaining radical movements, particularly "youth movements." The son's basic position is one of growing from complete dependence to independence. During the later stages of this growth he and his father each must make a rather drastic adjustment to the changing relationship called forth by the son's maturation. Under certain circumstances the son may rebel against the family and particularly against the father. Is this the typical American pattern—as Erikson denies? Unlike German youth, he argues, American youngsters do not rebel, although willing and able to do so, because the paternal discipline is not something to rebel against.

We explored the question of rebellion, particularly in its political aspects, with our fifteen men and found that there was indeed very little evidence of the kind of relationship that Erikson describes in the German situation. Apparently, only rarely did a family-shattering clash of wills occur when the son thought himself old enough to behave as a man. The father-son opposition took relatively minor forms: the question of what hour to come in at night, the use of the family car, the son's conduct in school. Concerning the political expression of such rebellious feelings, there were strong indications that this subject remained on the periphery of the men's world of experience.

Although the major evidence comes from the biographical material, answers to a question on youthful rebellion or radicalism are revealing. Rapuano, an auto parts supply man with a rather undisciplined tendency to vent his aggression on social targets (Communists and doctors), responds in bewilderment and finally denies any such tendency. O'Hara, an oiler in a large factory and one of the more class-conscious interviewees, is confused and takes the question to mean rebellion against his brothers and sisters. Woodside, a policeman who rejected his father with venom, responds to an inquiry about his own youthful rebellion or radicalism:

I do remember through the depression that my folks mentioned that it seems as though more could have been done—that the parties should have made more means of work so that the poverty wouldn't be existing so much around you—and, not only around you—but with you yourself.

He turns the question of his own rebellion and radicalism into a family matter: the family was more or less disgruntled. Only one man, better educated than others, speaks of his own moderate radicalism in a way which could be interpreted as a search for independence from or opposition to his parents.

There are several reasons why political expression of youthful defiance failed to come off. One is the low salience of politics for the parents. Few of the men could remember many political discussions in the home and some were uncertain whether their parents were Democrats or Republicans. If the old man cared so little about politics, there was little reason to challenge him in this area. Another reason is that when there is a need to assert independence there are ways of doing it which come closer to the paternal (and generally American) value scheme. One of these is to quit school. Four or five men sought independence and the economic foundations for a life no longer dependent on paternal pleasure by leaving school shortly before they were ready to graduate—thus striking directly at the interests of parents determined to see their children "get ahead in the world." Of course this act had compensations for parents in need of money, but there seems to have been more of a genuine conflict of wills in this area than in any other. Quitting school, in some ways, is the American youth's equivalent of his European opposite of conservative parentage joining a socialist or facist party.

Two reasons then for the apolitical quality of youthful revolt are the low salience of politics in the American home and the opportunity for rebellion in other ways. A third reason may be—to use a hyperbole—the relatively low salience of the father in the American scheme. We asked our men, "Who made the important decisions in your parents' household?" One replied that they were jointly made, two that their fathers made the important decisions, and twelve testified that mother was boss. . . . Now it may be that from a child's perspective Mother is usually boss. But the near unanimity on this point is convincing, all the more so because the accompanying comments generally show no overlord in the background. Even in this immigrant and second generation population Mom had taken over. Why, then, rebel against Father?

There is a fourth reason for the generally low rate of political rebellion. In the American home a child is given considerable latitude. "Permissiveness" is the term used currently to express this idea and although the term and idea are in bad odor among some critics, it is clear that the prevailing standards of child care even twenty years ago allowed a degree of freedom in school, neighborhood, and home not generally prevalent in Europe or Asia. To a large extent, the boy is on his own. This is Erikson's point, but we can illustrate it in detail. Thus Farrel, a man from a working class background whose schooling included graduate study, reports on his tendency to political radicalism in his youth: "I think there must also be the adolescent revolt aspect, which was never acute with me. . . . There was, as far as I was concerned, no necessity for it to be acute. I didn't feel hemmed in by my parents." Rapuano talks of his "reckless" youth in which he ran free with other boys, and some of the men speak of their parents' preoccupations that gave them opportunity to live a "free life." Many of the boys had earned money for their own as well as their families' use by selling papers, working in grocery stores, or cleaning up the school. Nor was this freedom attributable to parental indifference. When Rapuano was struck by a school teacher, his mother (not his father) visited the school to beat the teacher with a stick. A free child assured of supportive parental assistance when in need does not need to rebel.

A minority of four or five of these children, however, had suffered under controls which seem strict by most American standards.

Four Men Whose Fathers Failed Them

Although it is true that the symptoms of *rebellion* are rather slight and that its political expression is minuscule, it does not follow that the American son, particularly the son of immigrants, identifies with his father—introjects the parental ideal, as the psychoanalysts might say—and accepts the male role as it has been played on the home stage. At least four of our fifteen men probably had experienced seriously damaged relations with their fathers and even in the roseate glow of remembered childhood do not like the old man. Interpretation of this situation must be circumspect, since people are supposed to love their parents and are even commanded to honor them. During the interviews, however, interstitial comments, reportorial selection of incidents, and graphic silences, as well as the explicit expressions of like and dislike, present a clear picture of father-son relations.

There are, of course, many varieties of both bad and good father-son relations. In these four cases of damaged relations we note two patterns. One is *identification without affection,* represented by only one case. The other, the *rejection pattern,* is illustrated by three cases. This section briefly pictures the father-son relationships of these four men. In the following sections their political expression is explored.

Identification without affection.   The American youth, as we have noted, typically does not invest much emotional energy in a father rebellion on the European scale. But of course the latter does occur. And sometimes the process resembles the German pattern where the youth identifies with his father, struggles for his approval, gradually asserts himself against him as though assaulting a fortress, departs, and returns to be like him—another paternal fortress against his own son.

Sullivan, a railroad fireman and former semi-professional boxer, follows this tradition. Now, at the age of 25, he stresses his respect for his father, but his report shows little affection. . . . When asked about his father's good points he responds in the same terms as though everything else were blotted out: "Well . . . (long pause) . . . his good points were that he knew when to be strict and when to be lenient." Except on the question of sports (where the father gave instruction, but nothing is said of a good time), there is little joy in this relationship.

Yet there is identification. The son has adopted his father's strict manner. Sullivan had left his family because his wife would not follow his orders about the management of the home; he now sees that the children should, properly, give instant obedience. His rebellion—and he did rebel—is over. . . .

Rejection of the father.   Unlike Sullivan, three others, Woodside, Dempsey, and DeAngelo, reject their fathers outright. There is no effort to cover over their feelings, to take back the criticism, undo the damage, unsay the words. Something within them is quite clear and solid on this matter and they are not shaken by fear or guilt at the thought of such rejection.

DeAngelo is a factory machine operative, whose father and mother separated when he was an infant; he subsequently acquired a step-father. Of his father, who lives in the same town, laconically he says: "I don't bother with him." Of his step-father:

He was a good guy when he was sober, but he was bad when he was drunk. I never had too much respect for him. . . . When he was drunk he wanted to argue, you know. But my mother was bigger than him—didn't have too much trouble taking care of him. After a while my mother left him, you know, and we were on our own. . . .

Woodside, a policeman with a conscience, remembers his childhood with horror because of the irresponsible drunken behavior of his father and particularly his father's "outside interests," women. He says, quite simply: "At one time I felt I'd hate my father—that if anything ever happened to him it would be a wonderful thing." But today he plays checkers with the pathetic old man and helps him when he's in trouble. He hated his father in the past for the beatings he gave his mother, the humiliation he brought on the household, and the physical suffering to the children: "It's a pretty gruesome thing to tell anybody that a father could neglect his kids so much. Believe me, a good many days I've seen where I had just water, and I was lucky to have water—for a meal for the whole day."

Dempsey is an older man who married a widow when he himself was 40, having previously lived with his mother and, until they were married, with his brothers. In comparison with DeAngelo and Woodside, his reactions to his father are more veiled and he identifies somewhat more with him. He thinks of him as "a hard working man, the same as I am now, and couldn't get much further than I probably will . . . although my hopes are probably a little bit higher." But through the veil we see more granite than flesh and blood:

"Did your father have a sense of humor?"—Well, that I couldn't say. As I say, we were never too chummy with him. He never was a fellow to be chummy with us children. . . . He was one of them guys—it had to be it, or there was no way out of it. . . .

The Politics of Filial Alienation

Having examined a modal American pattern of father-son relationships and isolated four deviant cases, we turn to an inquiry into the politics of these latter four men.

Low information and social interest. The question of political information is considered first, partly because it indicates the degree of interest in the social world outside oneself. Our measure of political information is made up of questions on local, national, and international institutions and events. The local events, in particular, are not usually learned in school, since they include such items as "Who is the local boss of New Haven?" and "How would you go about getting a traffic light put on your corner?" It is therefore especially significant that these four men, concerning political information, rank as the four lowest of the fifteen cases.

There are several reasons for this. The loss or lack of a secure parental model encouraged each of these four to frame his own life style and to engage in the lifelong business of self-discovery. Each man is his own Pygmalion. More importantly, the development of a personal sense of security, of being a loved and wanted and respected person, which is a bulwark against psychic conflict, is lacking. This lack seems to be borne out by the evidence of severe anxiety in all four cases. Dempsey and DeAngelo rank among the four highest scorers on the "neurotic anxiety" scale. Sullivan ranks third on a social anxiety scale and shows evidence of severe sex-tension, as indicated by his top score in this area (and his marriage is breaking up). DeAngelo ranks fourth on this sex-tension scale. Woodside, while less troubled by sexual problems and not "neurotically" anxious, ties for first place on the scale of social anxiety; he is, by his own account and other evidence, a worrier, a searcher for all-around "security," and has somatic difficulties.

Anxiety can lead into politics as well as away from politics. People can defend themselves against anxiety by knowing more than others—or people may succumb to the demands of anxiety by knowing less. Generally in the American apolitical culture the anxious man does not employ politics as a defense against his conflicts. One of the little-appreciated benefits of such a culture is the low premium on politics for the anxious and neurotic.

Authoritarianism.   Three of the four men score strongly on authoritarianism: DeAngelo has the highest score in the group, and Sullivan and Woodside tie for fourth; only Dempsey's ranking is moderate. The genesis of authoritarianism and its close connection with father-son relations are well known. Here it is sufficient to note that in order to believe that people can live and work as cooperative equals or at least as trusting partners, a person must have experienced such a relationship. In their relations with their fathers, these men had no such experience.

Speak no evil of the political leader.   There is a third area of political outlook which seems to be shared by these four men with damaged father relations, a quality which in some measure sets them apart from the others. Although political lore would have it otherwise, people generally prefer to speak well of political leaders than to speak ill of them. But the average citizen can criticize such leaders, designate those he dislikes, and weigh the good and bad points of each on occasion. Our four deviant cases found such criticism or even objectivity more difficult than the others.

Sullivan admires Monroe, Lincoln, Truman, and Eisenhower. He defends Truman against those who believe that his attack on the music critic was out of order. He defends Ike for the vacations he takes. When asked about political leaders he dislikes: "Well, from what I learned in history, Grant seemed to be pretty useless . . . [pause]. He didn't seem to do too much [mentions that he was a drunkard]. And [pause] I mean I don't dislike him, either, but—I don't dislike any of them." Question: "How about living leaders, or recent leaders, which of these would you say you had the least respect for?" Answer, after a pause: "Well [long pause], none that I could think of."

Dempsey likes Washington and Lincoln, and, when probed, Wilson and Truman, for whom he voted. Asked about "any particular feelings about Dewey," he says, "No, I wouldn't say that." Roosevelt was "a very good man." Eisenhower is also a "very good man, doing everything he possibly can." He can think of no mistakes he has made.

DeAngelo says he doesn't particularly admire any political leaders. But: "I like them. I mean I didn't think anything bad about them, y'know." . . .

Woodside's views are a little different. He likes Eisenhower but is more willing to discuss his weaknesses (particularly his signing of an order to execute a deserter). He likes MacArthur as a "big man" and mentions Lincoln favorably. Asked about his dislikes and those he thinks did a poor job, he mentions others' criticisms of Roosevelt but then rushes to his defense, except to say that he thinks Eisenhower is "a little bit more mannish" than Roosevelt. The only political leader he mentions unfavorably is Adlai Stevenson, who strikes him as a man who could say "yes" when he means "no."

With the possible exception of this last comment, these remarks convey three themes: (1) Conventional leaders like Washington, Lincoln, and Monroe are admired. (2) The independent leader who doesn't let outsiders tell him what to do is admired—Truman would stand for no nonsense (Sullivan), Stevenson is too much influenced by his advisors (Woodside). (3) Authority figures are not to be criticized—an especially important point.

These four men are not notably deficient in their general ability to criticize or to express hostility. Why, then, do these four, whose relations with their fathers are strained, find it so hard to criticize political leaders in a whole-hearted way?

In answering this question, Sullivan's case should be distinguished from the others. Sullivan feels guilty about his negative feelings toward the original political authority in the family. He cannot bring himself to express his hostility without quickly withdrawing his remarks and saying something of a positive nature. The expression of hostility to authority figures is painful and Sullivan simply avoids this pain.

The other three men express outright hostility toward or unrelieved criticism of their fathers. Why not also of political authority? In the first place, there is a carryover of fear from the childhood situation which has not been obliterated by the adult emancipation. Men do not easily forget those childhood moments of terror when the old man comes home drunk, abuses the mother, or gets out the strap to deal with the child in anger unalloyed with love. Secondly a combined worship and envy of strength exists, which father-hatred fosters in a child, for it is the father's strength in the family that penetrates the childish consciousness. Finally, there is the persistent belief in the futility and danger of countering and rebelling against authority. Although DeAngelo was a rebel in high school and was expelled and Woodside stood up to his father threatening him with a log behind the wood shed, both are successful now partly because they have curtailed these anti-authority impulses that threatened to bring disaster once before. Their consciences are composed of anti-rebellion controls; this is why, in part, they can be good citizens.

Utopia and conservatism. The basis for a hopeful view of the world lies in the self; the world is ambiguous on this point. In the self, the notion that we can move toward a more perfect society is supported by the belief that people are kindly by nature and considerate of one another. Moreover, when the idea of a better social order is developed even a little, the mind quickly turns to the nature of authority in such a society. Is there a kind of authority which is strong and directive, yet at the same time solicitous and supportive of the weak in their infirmities—in short, paternal?

We asked our subjects about the nature of their vision of a more perfect society (with results which must await detailed analysis). At the end of the discussion we inquired whether or not there is evidence that we are moving closer to such a society. Although the men were not asked if the world was possibly moving in the opposite direction, some volunteered this answer. Our fifteen men answered the questions on an ideal society as follows:

	Damaged Father-Son Relations	Others
We are moving closer to ideal society	0	8
We are not moving closer to ideal society	3	2
(volunteered) We are moving away from ideal society	1	1

The pattern is clear. . . .

. . .

Fathers and Sons—And History

The state is "man writ large"; the family is a microcosm of society. The history of a nation may, in considerable measure, reflect the changes in the ways children and parents, sons and fathers, struggle to get along with one another. Some of the characteristics of a nation's politics may rest on the resolution of these struggles. With this point in mind, we turn to certain aspects of American and foreign politics.

To recapitulate, in American society: (1) "good" father-son relations are the norm; (2) of those youth with rebellious feelings against their fathers there are few for whom the rebellion takes political form; and (3) there is a tendency for moderately damaged father-son relations to be associated with relatively low levels of hope, interest, and capacity to criticize political leaders. These tendencies are revealed in what may be called the American political "style" in the following ways:

1. American politics is often said to embody a kind of consensualism in which both sides tend to come together, rather than a bipolarization or radicalism. At the same time, campaigns become quite heated with highly critical comments passed between the partisans of one candidate and those of another. This situation parallels the qualities we find associated with sons of strong but nurturant fathers: lack of alienation but a capacity for outspoken criticism.

2. Compared with the citizens of other nations, the American citizen is reported to be relatively well informed about current events and civic matters. On the other hand, his intensity of concern is relatively low. He can exchange blows during campaigns and then accept the victory of the opposition without much trouble. This pattern (a considerable cultural achievement) is difficult, as we have seen, for the poorly socialized and again suggests an important family component in American democracy.

3. It is often noted that a strain of idealism exists in American international politics which distinguishes it from the hard-boiled realism of the

Continent. Wilson's Fourteen points, Roosevelt's Four Freedoms, and Truman's Point Four illustrate the character of this idealism, an idealism nourished by the hope that we can do away with war and establish a peaceful world order. Behind these beliefs and supporting them in their many expressions lies that quality of hope and trust which is forged in boyhood, when the son is apprenticed to a protective and loving father.

Summary: Some Hypotheses

With a humility based on an appreciation of the great variety of experience that goes into the making of political man, we suggest the following hypotheses.

1. Compared with other Western cultures, American culture discourages youthful rebellion against the father. It further discourages political expression of whatever rebellious impulses are generated. This is because: (a) There is less need to rebel in a permissive culture. (b) Rebellious impulses are less likely to be expressed against the father because of his relatively less dominant position in the family. (c) The low salience of politics for the father means that rebellion against him is less likely to be channeled into politics or political ideology. (d) The high salience of the father's ambition for the son (and the resulting independence) means that rebellion against the father is more likely to be expressed by quitting school and going to work, or by delinquent conduct.

2. Damaged father-son relations tend to produce low political information and political cathexis. This is because, *inter alia:* (a) Without an adult model the youth must give relatively greater attention to the process of self-discovery and expend greater energy in managing his own life problems. (b) Failure of father-son relationships creates anxiety which is often (not always) so preoccupying that more distant social problems become excluded from attention.

3. Damaged father-son relations tend to develop an authoritarian orientation.

4. Damaged father-son relations tend to inhibit critical attitudes toward political leaders because: (a) The damaged relations encourage an enduring fear of expressing hostility toward authority figures. (b) They stimulate a reverence for power over other values. (c) In children they provoke the belief that it may be useless to rebel or petition authority.

5. Damaged father-son relations discourage a hopeful view of the future of the social order because: (a) The damaged relations often give rise to a less favorable view of human nature. (b) They help to create skepticism about the possibility of kindly and supportive political authority. (c) They encourage a cynical view of the political process: it is seen in terms of corrupt men seeking their own ends.

6. The history, political style, and future development of a political community reflect the quality of the relationship between fathers and sons. The permissive yet supportive character of model father-son relationships in the United States contributes to the following features of the American political

style: (a) a relatively high consensualism combined with a capacity for direct and uninhibited criticism; (b) a relatively large amount of interest and political information combined with relatively low emotional commitment; and (c) a relatively strong idealism in foreign affairs (and in general social outlook).

Notes on
Young Radicals

8

Kenneth Keniston

In the summer of 1967, I studied a small group of anti-war radical student leaders. The study, clinical and exploratory, was published in May 1968. Even by that time, the radical scene had changed so drastically that many of my comments were already outdated. Now, two years later, still more needs to be said about the changes of the last two years, about how they alter earlier generalizations about the psycho-social origins of student radicalism, and about the lessons to be learned from recent studies of youthful activists.

I should state at the outset that I continue to see student activism as an essentially constructive force in American life. I am far more worried about police riots and American military violence than I am about "student violence," and I consider the radicalism of a minority of today's college students a largely appropriate, reasonable and measured response to blatant injustices in our foreign policies, our domestic policies and practices, and our university structure and policies. I do deplore (as a tendency) that special self-righteousness of a minority of today's student radicals, the nobility of whose purposes is not matched by an equal awareness of their own ambivalence or potential for corruption, a lack that sometimes allows them to treat their opponents as less-than-human—as pigs, for example. But in any case, the study of the psychology of radicals should never be equated with the study of the causes of radicalism, much less with its merits.

There was clearly something about the Civil Rights Movement—its style, its mood, the character of its members and its target—that won the sympathy of American liberals. (Many Southerners, of course, found the tactics and goals of the movement nihilistic, communistic, violent or, at the very least, provocative.) The tactic of militant non-violence—whether adopted as a Gandhian first principle or as a useful tactic—seemed an altogether worthy and admirable principle. To be sure, the sit-in was essentially disruptive and confrontational. To the restaurant owner whose floor was covered by demonstrating civil rights workers, a sit-in seemed a violation of his property rights and an obstruction of his business. But to the greater part of the liberal American public, the disruptive and obstructive element in these tactics seemed justified, a relatively mild way of expressing opposition to unjust and discriminatory policies.

But as the student movement has journeyed from the South to the North, from the ghetto to the campus, new reactions have come to prevail. There is a new tendency to try to separate the "good guys" who remain non-violent, constructive and idealistic from the "bad guys" who are nihilistic, violent, destructive and anarchistic. This distinction pervades political rhetoric and has found its way into scholarly publications as well. In several recent discussions, for example, I have been asked to contrast the "constructive and idealistic" young radicals I studied two years ago with the "nihilistic and violent" radicals who have purportedly replaced them today.

I believe there has been a change toward militancy, anger and dogmatism in the white student movement, but that it has been greatly exaggerated. At least part of the distance between sitting in at a Southern segregationist lunch counter (thereby preventing its owner from doing business) and occupying a Northern administration building (thereby "bringing the machine to a halt") is a difference in target, not tactics. In both cases, individuals use their bodies to obstruct, disrupt or prevent the orderly conduct of business as usual. To be sure, there are other differences, too; but the one central difference is in our attitude toward Southern segregationists and Northern college presidents. Part of the distance the student movement has traveled is the distance from Selma to Morningside Heights, from Bull Connor to Nathan Pusey.

Yet the mood, temper and rhetoric of the student movement *has* drastically changed. In place of a non-violent willingness to endure the punishments decreed by law for violations of local ordinances, we instead see an often angry and militant demand for amnesty. (It should be recalled, of course, that in the early days of the Civil Rights Movement, a demand for anmesty would have been quixotic: civil rights workers had no choice but to accept the punishment that was inflicted upon them. Today, in contrast, *de facto* amnesty is often a real possibility, in practice if not in principle.)

More important, the often religiously Christian or Gandhian non-violent mood of the Civil Rights Movement has been replaced by a more defiant, more angry, more politically revolutionary stance among today's student radicals. The influence of Mao Tse-tung, mediated through the Progressive Labor Party and Worker-Student Alliance, is only one of many new influences. The writings of Fanon, Debray and other apostles of armed revolution have had their effect; the model of revolutionary leaders like Castro, Guevara and Ho Chi Minh has become more important; and Marxist and neo-Marxist concepts increasingly dominate the political rhetoric of radicals. In addition, the rising militancy of portions of the black community has had its impact upon white students, now effectively excluded even from campus alliances with blacks. There often ensues something analogous to a game of "chicken": black militants and white radicals vie with each other to up the ante, each demonstrating to the other that they are more truly revolutionary.

How do we account for this shift in mood, tone and rhetoric in the student movement? Is the New Left recruiting new members who are more violent, more uncontrolled, more nihilistic and destructive than the "gentle" civil rights workers of the past? Has there been an influx of what within the student movement are called Crazies? Or is essentially the same group (in personality terms) reacting differently because of a different political situation? Can we distinguish in any useful way within the student movement between the "nihilistic" and "idealistic" activists?

At this point, anyone who like myself is essentially a clinician must remind himself of what we all know but frequently forget: the essential ambivalence of human nature. Even the most cursory reading of the history of the Russian revolutionary student movement shows that some of its most able and devoted leaders began as populist idealists of the highest principle but moved on to become members of the terrorist or "nihilist" movement, forever thereafter named after them. It seems unlikely that their basic characters, ideals and personalities changed in any fundamental way. Instead, we must posit "learning from experience," situational reactions to harassment, defeat and Czarist repression which led to the surfacing of aspects of personality that were previously controlled, suppressed or repressed. Introspection should further convince us that ambivalence is not confined to student activists, nor indeed to students; psychologists and educators, among others, exhibit the same mixture of feelings. The point is obvious: The same person, depending on circumstances, is invariably both an idealist and a nihilist.

Some people, though, are more nihilistic or idealistic than others, and recent research has pointed to the existence, within the student movement, of two distinct personality types, which can be loosely associated with the nihilistic-idealistic distinction. Robert Liebert, a New York psychoanalyst, after intensive interviewing of a large group of white and black participants and non-participants in the Columbia "liberation" of last year, found that students in the occupied buildings fell along a continuum of idealistic and constructive to nihilistic and destructive. He hypothesized different developmental patterns in each group, and noted their different style and approach to political action. But he found that the "great majority" of students in the buildings at Columbia were idealists, and argued plausibly that most nihilists in his sense are never admitted to college (or at least not to Columbia). So while the distinction between nihilists and idealists can be made, the empirical conclusion nevertheless emphasizes the predominance of idealists even among the purportedly obscene, destructive and nihilistic students involved in the Columbia disruption.

Similar conclusions emerge from far-reaching research conducted at the University of California at Berkeley and San Francisco State College by Brewster Smith, Jeanne Block and Norma Haan. Their research is especially conclusive in its analysis of the relationship between moral development and participation in student protest activities. Their study is built on the research into moral development by Lawrence Kohlberg, who, in essence, distinguishes three major stages in moral reasoning: *pre-conventional* (the individual egocentrically defines right and wrong in terms of what is good or pleasurable for him); *conventional* (the individual identifies right and wrong either with being a "good boy" or a "good girl," or with a more general concept of law and order—that is, with the existing community standards); and *post-conventional* (a stage which most individuals never reach, in which right and wrong are identified with the long-range good of the community or with such abstract personal principles as the sanctity of life, the categorical imperative or the Golden Rule). In the post-conventional stage, the individual may, of course, find himself in sharp conflict with existing community standards; for example, with concepts of law and order.

Comparing large numbers of students who participated in protest activities at San Francisco State and Berkeley with students who had not, the Smith research group found massive differences. They found that 56 percent of the protesters were at the post-conventional stage of moral development as compared with 12 percent of the non-protesters, while 85 percent of the non-protesters were at the conventional stage as compared with 34 percent of the protesters. No other researcher, studying any other variable, has shown such massive differences between activists and non-activists. The Smith research thus supports what many commentators have also suggested —namely, that moral issues are at the heart of student revolt.

Smith and his colleagues, though, also found disproportionate numbers of "pre-conventionals" (egocentrics) among the protesters. In their sample, the pre-conventionals constituted 10 percent of the protest group, but only 3 percent of the non-protesters. The work of Smith and Kohlberg suggests that such young men and women are in a state of temporary moral regression, which often accompanies an individual's development from the conventional to the post-conventional stage. Kohlberg aptly terms this moral regression the "Raskolnikoff Syndrome." It might also be called the "Trobriand Island Syndrome," inasmuch as the moral reasoning that accompanies it is, "If they do it in the Trobriand Islands, why shouldn't I do it, too?"

Finally, Jeanne Block makes an important distinction between what she terms "parental continuity" and "parental discontinuity" groups among activists and protesters. The parental continuity group was extremely critical of American society, but its members evidenced strong continuity with their parents and their parents' values. The parental discontinuity group was critical of *both* American society *and* their parents. Contrasting these two groups, both active politically, Block found that they differed in a variety of respects: members of the discontinuity group (the "rebellion" group) adopted more of a hippie life-style, seemed more profoundly alienated from American society and were less conventionally "responsible" in their other activities. Members of the continuity group (the "chips-off-the-old-block") were less expressive, less irresponsible and less affected by personal conflicts.

These studies thus suggest the viability of a rough distinction between nihilistic and idealistic radical activism. Indeed, research on the relation between moral development and activism points to what may be a bipolar grouping within the activist camp. For Smith and his colleagues find that both extremes—the "post-conventionals" and the "pre-conventionals"—are overrepresented in the protesting group. But again there is the question of ambivalence. For even the pre-conventional (egocentric) student is, we know from other evidence, likely to be in a temporary and usually partial state of regression to earlier concepts of morality, all as a part of a long-range trajectory toward post-conventional ethical thinking. Which potential is activated in him—pre-conventional or post-conventional, egocentric or ethical—depends much upon the fate of his causes and the company he keeps. In short, if the distinction between nihilists and idealists among today's student radicals holds water, it is with the essential qualification that everyone is always a little of both.

Two years ago, in discussing the personality development of radicals, I contrasted two hypotheses. The first, the "Oedipal rebel" hypothesis, rests on the notion of strong Oedipally-based rebellion against the father "acted out" symbolically during late adolescence and youth in attacks on authority figures like college presidents, generals, the Establishment, and government policies and leaders. The second theory, the "red diaper baby" theory, posits that today's student radicals are the children of yesterday's radicals (raised in red diapers). Yet neither of these views adequately accounted for the feelings that male radicals reported about their fathers—a combination of genuine affection and determination to act more resolutely in the service of principle. This pattern contrasted sharply with the more truly rebellious pattern I had previously observed in a study of alienated students, none of whom were politically active and most of whom today would probably have been hippies rather than political radicals.

In the last two years, the Oedipal rebellion thesis has received widespread publicity. Lewis Feuer, in his brilliant but tendentious book, *The Conflict of Generations,* makes Oedipal rebellion the basis for his explanation of the psychodynamics of student radicalism. Bruno Bettelheim has offered Oedipal rebellion, among other explanations, as one of the causes of student revolt. Ben Rubenstein and Morton Levitt have analyzed the psychodynamics of the student movement in terms of "totem and taboo." And Joseph Alsop, in a recent article in *Newsweek,* lumped me together with Feuer and Bettelheim as one of those who "takes seriously" the Oedipal rebellion hypothesis.

I take it seriously enough to argue that it is incorrect. So, too, it should be noted, does virtually every other investigator who has done empirical research on the subject. Seymour Martin Lipset, the Harvard sociologist, hardly a hero of or apologist for today's student radicals, concludes a recent summary of research on student activism by noting that the central finding on politically active left-wing students, not only in America but elsewhere in the world, is that they come from liberal and politically active families. This is hardly evidence of Oedipal rebellion. Despite the great variety of personality types and motivations that enter into radicalism, empirical studies find continuity with parental values to be the rule and discontinuity the exception. Within any group of activist protesters, it is possible, as the new research shows, to distinguish two subgroups, one of which consists of chips-off-the-old-block, the other rebels. But even then the evidence suggests that the chips-off-the-old-block are more numerous and that unequivocal rebellion against the same-sex parent is more likely to lead to a withdrawn posture of dissent, to a hippie quietism.

Yet in considering relationships with parents, as with the whole question of gererational continuity, one must again recall the central fact of ambivalence in human development. Even in working with students who present themselves as unqualifiedly hating their parents, we frequently find that beneath hatred, defiance and rebellion lie love and dependency, all the more intense because they have been so strongly repudiated. Similarly, *The Authoritarian Personality* and a series of later studies have shown that many individuals who portray their parents as virtually perfect turn out to possess at a less conscious level a contrasting and opposite view of harsh, tyrannical and hated parents. It would be contrary to everything we know about human development and generational relations were we not to find mixed feelings about parents in any group. What is impressive, then, in the studies of student radicals is the *relative* predominance of positive feelings, positive identification and basic value continuity.

Another thesis commonly advanced, especially in popular discussions of today's student radicalism, is that today's student activists behave as they do because of the Spockian permissiveness of their upbringing. "Permissiveness" is used as a bad word, and the explanation usually goes on to note that students have not learned self-restraint, have never experienced the force or coercion they desperately needed in order to develop inner controls, and have no respect for limits, older people, etc. This view has been advanced not only by such critics of the student movement as Bruno Bettelheim, but also, a number of years ago (in modified form), by Richard Flacks, a founder of SDS and now a distinguished researcher on student activism. Flacks found that the parents of activists, compared with those of non-activists, would be less distressed were their children to drop out of college or to live (unmarried) with a member of the opposite sex; he also found that activist students less often reported that their parents were strict. In his initial writings, he interpreted this as evidence of parental permissiveness, one factor in what he termed the "deviant socialization" of student radicals.

Three recent studies, however, discredit the permissiveness hypothesis. One, an unpublished PH.D. thesis by Lamar Thomas, a student of Flacks, compares the children of politically active parents of both the Right and the Left. It finds generally higher levels of political activity among the children of left-wing parents, but *no* relationship in either group between activism and permissiveness. A second study, by Norma Haan and Jeanne Block, concludes (on the basis of data on almost one thousand students) that permissiveness is not a determining variable of activism. And William Cowdry at Yale found no relationship between permissiveness and anti-war activism among college seniors.

But even if permissiveness is not the issue, recent studies suggest that methods of discipline and family values *are* important. In my study two years ago, my radical subjects emphasized the subtle yet pervasive power of parental principle in their upbringing. They had been brought up in families with a moral atmosphere that was largely implicit but nonetheless powerful. The methods of discipline used in these families generally avoided physical punishment, direct coercion, even ostracism. Instead, reasoning and the transmission of high expectations were the favored methods of inculcating family values. Parental expectations were communicated by the promotion of independence, by the assumption that the child would accept responsibility and control himself, and by the use of such indirect (but powerful) sanctions as the expression of disappointment in the child when he misbehaved.

Empirical research has in general confirmed these findings. Flacks' study, which involved intensive interviewing of the parents of activists and non-activists, found important distinctions in the value emphases of activist and non-activist families. In activist families, he found a greater emphasis on the importance of ideas (intellectualism), on the expression of feelings (romanticism), and on serving others (humanitarianism)—and a lesser emphasis on strict control of impulse (low moralism). Approaching the same questions differently, the Smith research group found, in general, that the socialization experiences reported by protesters emphasized training for independence by parents who themselves had strong independent interests not involving their children. These studies are consistent with the hypothesis that the dominant socialization pattern for today's student activists involves not permissiveness but a highly principled family culture which is transmitted to children through the use of reasoning and persuasion, and the encouragement of independence in thought and action.

As for the critical question of social versus psychological determinants of political attitude and behavior, most researchers have found consistent demographic and socioeconomic correlates of political activism. In general, these point to a relationship between activism and high socioeconomic status, high parental education and high parental involvement in professional and, in particular, "helping" vocations. (Flacks finds that higher levels of education characterize even the grandparents of activists.)

But as Lipset points out, many sociodemographic characteristics have known psychological concomitants. The use of reasoning and persuasion in bringing up children, for example, is more common in upper-middle-class than in working-class families. Similarly, religion has been shown to be associated with activism: a disproportionate number of students from Jewish families are involved in radical protest activities. The theoretical problem these findings raise can be seen in an example. Suppose we find that the mothers of political activists show a distinctive concern for the nurture of their children. We still do not know how to interpret this finding. Does it indicate a causal relationship between maternal nurturance and filial activism? Or does it merely reflect the accidental fact that more radicals, being Jewish, have nurturant Jewish mothers? According to the second interpretation, radicalism might be "caused" by other factors directly connected with Jewishness (for example, familiarity with or enjoyment of the position of an out-group member). Or it might be related to still other factors indirectly connected with Jewishness (for example, great stress on acting in the service of one's beliefs). Without further studies that control for these factors, we do not know whether psychological or sociological variables are more important.

Several recent studies permit us to approach this question, however, at least in a preliminary way. Flacks' research controlled for type of college attended, area of residence and class in college. It thus provided at least an informal control on socioeconomic status, and the fact that Flacks found distinctive differences between the families of activists and non-activists is consistent with the view that "family culture" variables are critical in political activism. Haan and Block, moreover, have recently responded directly to Lipset's challenge by re-analyzing their data with religion controlled. Analyzing family socialization variables independently for two groups, Jews and non-Jews, they found that within each of these groups the same socialization variables continued to be associated with political activism. And Cowdry, studying a highly homogeneous Yale College senior class, found many socialization variables, but no social, religious or demographic factors, associated with activism.

Still, the issue cannot be settled with only the evidence at hand. In all probability, several interacting factors are involved. On the one hand, it seems clear that *if* children are brought up in upper-middle-class professional families with humanitarian, expressive and intellectual values, and *if* the techniques of discipline emphasize independence and reasoning, and *if* the parents are themselves politically liberal and politically active, then the chances of the child's being an activist are greatly increased, regardless of factors like religion. But it is also clear that these conditions are fulfilled most often in Jewish families. And there may be still other factors associated with social class and religion that independently promote activism; for example, being in a Jewish minority group that has preserved its culture in the face of opposing community pressures for centuries may in some way prepare or permit the individual to take controversial positions as a student.

Another question left unanswered by most research on student activism is whether we have been studying the determinants of radical beliefs, of action in general, or of the interaction between a particular set of radical beliefs and a particular type of radical action. The typical study of student activists selects for intensive investigation a group defined by *behavioral* criteria: Were they or were they not arrested for disruption at Dartmouth in 1969? Did they or did they not take part in Mississippi Summer? Such "activists" then are typically compared with a "control group"—usually a random sample of the college population. The extremely consistent differences routinely found in such research provide the current portrait of the activist.

But how should the differences be interpreted? Do they reflect radical *beliefs?* If so, then occupying a building or participating in an anti-war protest presumably reflects the intensity of the beliefs: We suppose there is a direct connection between the strength of one's beliefs and the probability of acting on them. But it is equally possible that by contrasting activists defined by behavioral criteria with others in the college population, we are studying something besides beliefs—namely, a tendency to take action in the name of one's convictions. This factor of "consistency" between beliefs and behavior may, in fact, turn out to have determinants other than those of beliefs alone.

In his recent research on this issue, Cowdry, then a Yale College senior, studied a random sample of the Yale class of 1968. He was initially interested in examining how attitudes toward the war in Vietnam were related to plans concerning military service. But in the course of his study, a strongly-worded anti-war resolution was distributed, with wide publicity, to the entire senior class. Since two-thirds of the class said they opposed the war but only one-third signed the resolution, Cowdry was able to compare two groups with equally strong anti-war sentiments: the group which signed the resolution and the one which did not. His findings support the view that *with* anti-war attitudes held constant, the determinants of beliefs are different from the determinants of action (signing the resolution). Indeed, his study suggests that many of the characteristics of activists reported in previous studies may be related not as much to having radical beliefs as to behavior-belief "consistency." For the two groups that were "consistent" (the anti-war signers and the pro-war non-signers) were in many respects more like each other than either group was like the "inconsistent" group (the anti-war non-signers). One question raised by this finding is whether the observed characteristics of behaviorally-defined activists—especially the socialization variables associated with activism—have any necessary relation to left-wing (as opposed to right-wing) views, or whether they are concomitants of taking action consistent with one's beliefs—regardless of where these beliefs fall on the political spectrum.

One further finding of interest emerged from Cowdry's study. He found that anti-war beliefs were associated with a set of characteristic self-descriptions: The anti-war students described themselves as more expressive, more aesthetic, more idealistic than did the pro-war students. At the same time, Cowdry found that virtually these same characterizations were applied to their fathers by "consistent" students (anti-war signers), but *not* by "inconsistents" (anti-war non-signers). This suggests that the student most likely to hold radical beliefs *and* act on them is identified with a humanitarian, idealistic and expressive father. Conversely, the student most likely to hold radical beliefs but not act upon them is one who sees *himself* as humanitarian, idealistic and expressive, but has developed this self-characterization in rebellion against his father.

Several points, based on the voluminous body of research on student radicals, can be made:—Student radicals are an elite group, and not the "rabble of rejects" they have been termed. There is an impressive uniformity in the finding of a great variety of studies conducted by different researchers using different methods with different populations: Free Speech Movement students at Berkeley, activists at San Francisco State, Mississippi Summer Volunteers, Columbia radicals, Michigan State and Penn State SDS members, Dartmouth College arrestees, and so on. These similarities can be summarized, perhaps oversimplified, in a sentence: The activist group is, compared to the student population from which it is drawn, an "elite" group in virtually every respect.

—Moral issues are central to student radicalism. The most impressive differences found between activists and non-activists have been in the area of moral development. There are many other statistically significant differences, but the moral differences observed are so overwhelming that they suggest that Smith and his co-workers are close to the heart of the matter. To be sure, the determinants of levels of moral development are themselves extremely complex, and not perfectly correlated with activism. Nevertheless, recent research strongly indicates that a central factor in radical political activism is level of moral development.

—There are several routes to radicalism. With regard to male radicals, for example, at least two pathways to radical beliefs can be distinguished. The first is the pathway of identification. Both father and son are described as expressive, humanitarian, and idealistic. The son identifies with his father, although the son is usually more radical. Such sons are very likely to be radicals in action as well as beliefs. They generally fall into the "idealistic radical" group. There is, however, clearly a second pathway to radical beliefs, though less often to radical actions: the pathway of rejection of identification. Such students describe themselves as expressive, idealistic, and humanitarian, but describe their fathers as distinctively *not* any of these things. They are rather less likely to be politically active, more likely to adopt an apolitical or "hippie" style of dissent, and, if they become involved in political action, more likely to fall within the "nihilist" group.

—A great many students with vehemently radical beliefs do not implement their beliefs in action. Most psychological research has so far emphasized the enduring states and characteristics of those who act. But for every activist, there are many others who share his beliefs but do not act. In our democratic society, it is commonly asserted that citizens with strong convictions should be willing to express them and work to implement them. If we assume that "consistency" between beliefs and action is desirable, we need to know better what produces it, regardless of political convictions. As yet, little is known about the psychological and social processes by which individuals are activated, by which a community is politicized, and by which potential activists find and activate each other. Nor do we know anything about short-term and long-term consequences to the individual of implementing—or not implementing—his beliefs.

—Psychological explanations alone are not adequate to understand today's student radicals. Student radicalism has developed within a social, cultural and, above all, a political context. High levels of moral development, for example, did not begin with the Civil Rights Movement; nor can we interpret the recent changes in mood, tone, rhetoric, ideology and style of the student movement primarily in terms of the changing personality composition of radical groups. More to the point, we must study the evolution and rationale of the student movement itself. For example, even such minimal goals of student activists as an end to the war in Vietnam, a major attack on racism and poverty, and a "restructuring" of the university have not been attained. Given this fact, it probably does not take complex psychological explanations to explain the rise in militancy, anger and dogmatism that we see.

—Most important, the study of student radicalism exposes the ideological bias and theoretical inadequacy of many of the concepts by which we have attempted to understand the relationship of men to politics and society. Until recently, the most widely-used concepts have focused largely upon processes that lead to stasis and stability in society and politics. The study of socialization has focused upon how children adapt their personalities to the social roles, norms and institutions of their society. The study of acculturation has emphasized how values and symbol systems are internalized so that they become part of the individual. And into many such analyses there has crept a covertly evaluative element: Viable societies are assumed to be those which "effectively socialize" the young into their available roles; valid cultures are those which inspire the greatest consensus and loyalty to their symbols and values. The evaluative weight of the concepts of "socialization" and "acculturation" becomes apparent when we reverse the terms: "de-socialization" connotes misanthropy, anomie and possibly psychiatric illness, while "disacculturation" connotes a collapse of values into barbarity or nihilism.

The study of student radicals indicates that these connotations are often incorrect, and that the study of socialization and acculturation must be complemented by the study of de-socialization and dis-acculturation as the psychological correlates and, to some extent, the causes of social and political change. Indeed, some purportedly "socializing" environments (like liberal arts colleges and universities) do anything but neatly "socialize" or "integrate" all their charges into available social roles, existing social institutions, traditional values and conventional symbol systems. On the contrary, we witness today, both in America and in other nations, a phenomenon that can be called *youthful de-socialization*. Traditional roles, institutions, values and symbols are critically scrutinized and often rejected, while new roles, institutions, values and symbols more adequate to the modern world are desperately sought.

Research on student activism points to the enormous complexity of youthful de-socialization. On the one hand, this research finds underlying value continuity between most activists and their families. But on the other hand, it also reveals discontinuity, innovation and change: rejection by the children of liberal parents of many liberal assumptions in favor of more radical political beliefs, the emergence of new political tactics, efforts to find new political procedures, roles, institutions and methods for change. Youthful de-socialization, then, is always *partial*, but it may still be far-reaching and politically decisive. The tumult, controversy and criticism that pervades higher education today, then, should remind us that if we are to understand change, innovation, reform and revolution, we cannot do so solely with concepts designed to explain stability and equilibrium. In addition, we must attempt to understand the forces that lead intelligent, talented and idealistic men and women (both young and old) to refuse, challenge or revitalize the conventional wisdom.

9
From The Selling
of the President, 1968

Joe McGinniss

Fred LaRue was getting bald and he smoked cigars. He was from Atlanta, Georgia. His job was to persuade people in the South not to vote for George Wallace, but he had to do it in a way that would not upset people in the rest of the country.

In early October, it did not look as if he had done this job very well. South of Baltimore, Wallace seemed immense.

In fact, on the morning of the day I saw Fred LaRue, I said to Harry Treleaven, "I'm going up to headquarters this afternoon to learn about the southern strategy." And Treleaven laughed and said, "If you find out what it is, please tell me."

Fred LaRue did not talk very colorfully but he wrote memos. There was one he wrote on September 7 in which he summed up what he was going to do in the South.

"The anti-Wallace message will be indirect—'between the lines' and in 'regional code words,'" he wrote. He, like the rest of them, was afraid of being obvious. It was all right to chase the Wallace vote but not all right to get caught.

"One example of the propaganda innovations to be employed," LaRue wrote, "is a special ballad-type song in the current 'country and western' music style, by which nationally famous artists will 'sing' the message via the radio and TV. The multi-stanza ballad will allow issues to be included or excluded as the local situation indicates. The song's technical aspects will be such that 'local talent' as well as a variety of 'stars' can render it effectively. . . ."

The name of the song was "Bring Our Country Back":

> *How far down the road has our country gone,*
> *In this time of trouble and strife?*
> *How can we bring our country back*
> *To the good and decent life?*
>
> *Have we gone so far that we can't return?*
> *Have we lost our place in the sun?*
> *Yes, we can bring our country back,*
> *But it's up to everyone!*
>
> *This time, this time, your precious vote will get the big job done,*
> *This time, this time, your vote can bring a change in Washington.*

(Alternate verses and chorus changes)

Tell me where's there a man . . . in this fair land
Who can get us back on the track?
Dick Nixon is a decent man
Who can bring our country back.

Our votes can bring our country back
But it's up to everyone!

This time, this time, with leadership from Richard M. Nixon.

"But let me tell you something," Fred LaRue said. "You could spend a million dollars on songs like that and it's wasted money unless you get them played in the right spots. You got to get that on or adjacent to country and western programs. Either that or wrestling. That's a special kind of audience. The people that watch country and western and wrestling. What you do for those people would not appeal to other kinds of people and vice versa. Now you take Orlando, Florida, for instance. There is no country and western show in town there, so we go to wrestling instead."

Then Fred LaRue went into his desk and pulled out a list of the radio programs on which "Bring Our Country Back" was being played. There were the singing shows of such people as Bill Anderson, Buck Owens, Ernest Tubb, and the Wilburn Brothers, and such specials as the Wally Fowler Gospel Hour and Chattahoochee RFD.

The problem was in finding country and western singers to do the song. Most were backing Wallace. Finally Fred LaRue went back to the 1940s and '50s and found Roy Acuff and Tex Ritter and Stuart Hamblen.

Then he explained about the other southern commercials. These had been provided by the Thurmond Speaks Committee of South Carolina. A lot of them had Thurmond himself talking about crime and busing and the Supreme Court. They were used, LaRue said, "very selectively," which meant they would never be heard in New York.

LaRue, in fact, had a map of the South on the wall of his office. Little green and red and yellow pins were stuck all through it. The red and yellow pins represented areas in which the Thurmond commercials were being used, while the green pins represented those locations to which Senator Thurmond had personally carried the campaign.

All this was advertising which Harry Treleaven had nothing to do with. He did not even see it. He was considered Madison Avenue, and it was felt that Madison Avenue did not understand the South.

Kevin Phillips, the "ethnic specialist," was twenty-seven years old, pale and dour. He worked at a desk in a hallway because by the time he had been hired all the offices at headquarters had been filled.

"It took awhile to get programed," he said, "but I've been effectively plugged in since late August."

This was how he always talked. Len Garment called him "The Computer." Roger Ailes swore he was stuffed with sawdust.

"Essentially what I do is determine what blocs can be moved in what states by what approach," he said. " 'Group susceptibility' I call it.

"For instance, in Wisconsin you have Germans and you have Scandinavians, and the two groups respond to very different things. First, we determine where the groups are and then we decide how to reach them. What radio station each listens to, and so forth. I started too late to do it properly this year, but by 'seventy-two I should have it broken down county by county across the whole country so we'll be able to zero in on a much more refined target."

Kevin Phillips had graduated from Colgate and the Harvard Law School and had been administrative assistant to Paul Fino, a congressman from New York City. Besides working for Nixon, he was writing a book about American voting patterns which the Conservative Book Club was going to publish.

He was convinced that a Conservative revolution was sweeping America. He kept saying things like, "The Democratic party will not carry Oklahoma again for the rest of this century." Then he would go into a desk drawer and pull out the results of surveys made among sixth-graders in St. Louis and the Bronx which proved that they were far more conservative than their parents.

"It's happening," he would say. "It is really coming to pass. But no one sees it. No one knows."

He said he was very highly respected at headquarters. When he had first come to work, there had been a real computer doing his job. Some people from MIT were running it. He disposed of them immediately.

"The first time I checked their stuff I took them apart so badly that I never saw them or heard from them again. Now, I'm plugged in absolutely. Any memorandum I write gets to the top of the heap in five minutes."

One of his big jobs was to help Fred LaRue with the South. "When a northerner designs anti-Wallace stuff, it's bad stuff," he said. "It's tricky, smoothie, smacks of the Establishment. This doesn't work. You don't mock this guy. You don't talk about his wife being a clerk in a five-and-ten-cent store. A lot of people are clerks in five-and-ten-cent stores and they have cousins all over Alabama."

Phillips would take the reports of people like John Maddox, the Semantic Differential man, and analyze them and make specific strategy suggestions.

For instance, Maddox recently had written, "Billy Graham is the second most revered man in the South among adult voters." It was not made clear whether Wallace or Christ ranked first, but the message was plain: Be pals with Billy Graham and publicize the friendship.

The same Maddox report said, "the simple folksy manner of John Wayne can be effective with the target group." And that, Kevin Phillips said, was an insight.

"Wayne might sound bad to people in New York, but he sounds great to the schmucks we're trying to reach through John Wayne. The people down there along the Yahoo Belt. If I had the time I'd check to see in what areas *The Green Berets* was held over and I'd play a special series of John Wayne spots wherever it was."

Another thing Kevin Phillips did was evaluate the Gene Jones commercials and make recommendations as to how they should be used.

He wrote things like: "*Great Nation:* This is fine for national use, but viz local emphasis it strikes me as best suited to the South and heartland. They will like the great nation self-help, fields of waving wheat stuff and the general thrust of Protestant ethic imagery."

And: "*Order:* Entirely suitable for national use, emphasis on cities which have had riots (Cal., Ill., Ohio, Mich., Pa., N.J.) . . . and in the South to reinforce RN's hardline image."

Beyond this, Phillips made suggestions for future Gene Jones spots.

"We need a red-hot military music, land of pride and glory special for the South and Border. I think that this is very important. Secondarily, we need more concern for the countryside, its values and farmers welfare spot, complete with threshing threshers, siloes, Aberdeen Angus herds, et al.

"Look," he said, "I have no interest in how many voters can fit on the head of a pin. All I care about is how many we can get out there by hook or by crook who will vote for us."

THE
CONGRESS,
REPRESENTATION,
AND
CALHOUN'S
PLURALISM

PART THREE

Political power in Congress is decentralized and fragmented. Congress was deliberately designed by the framers of the American Constitution to fulfill the liberal-pluralist rather than the majoritarian definition of a democratic political order. Part Three will explore the congressional policy-making process, the receptivity of Congress to pressures from organized interest groups, and some of the key policy consequences of its decentralized decision-making structures.

The original Constitution provided for a bicameral legislature to provide points of access and representation for different political interests. Short-range local and popular interests were to be the focal point of the House of Representatives. Long-range state and sectional interests were to be represented in the Senate. Over the years, Congress has evolved along lines that reversed the responsiveness of the two Houses to short-term popular pressures. Nevertheless, various formal and informal rules for the conduct of congressional business in both Houses have added numerous stages to the process of policy making. These developments have fragmented political power in Congress and have thereby provided numerous opportunities for the exercise of influence by intense and well-organized interest groups seeking to delay legislation.

Proponents of innovative public policies must obtain influence at all stages of the legislative process. They must first mobilize winning coalitions within the substantive committees that have jurisdiction over the policy. Next they must confront the conservative House Rules Committee, which determines what bills will reach the floor of the House. If their measure is approved on the floor of both Houses, it can still be altered within the Conference Committee, which was established to iron out differences between the House and Senate versions of bills. Opponents can veto legislation by controlling any of these stages. Failing this, they can still limit the scope of a new program by influencing the appropriations process. This elaborate procedure is specifically designed to give influential minority interests a veto over public policies that most directly affect them. Other aspects of Congress, such as the specialized committee system for developing public policies, the extensive powers of committee chairmen, and the tendency of Congress to defer to the judgment of its committee decisions, add to the leverage of organized interest groups that have succeeded in obtaining influence through a congressional committee or its chairman.

The selections in Part Three were written by both supporters and opponents of political pluralism. They illustrate disagreement as to which kinds of interest groups are likely to gain access to congressional committee subsystems and whether or not innovative and rational solutions to national problems can regularly emerge from congressional decision making.

Nelson W. Polsby, a leading political pluralist, sees a "hidden rationality" in the process of congressional policy making. In "Policy Analysis and Congress," Polsby argues that the elaborate decentralized division of labor in the House, which maximizes political considerations in policy deliberation, allows House members to master the technical details of legislation that is initiated by the bureaucracy. Floor debates and committee investigations in the Senate constitute rituals that are depicted as contributing to the formulation of larger national debate over issues and to "the incubation of new policy proposals that may at some future time" become legislation. Through what Polsby terms the "hidden hand" of the Senators' desire for publicity, issues gradually reach the level of public consciousness necessary to move Congress and the President. Polsby contends that the many congressional points of access cut two ways. Sympathetic Congressmen are free to lend an ear to outside interest groups proposing innovations, to keep alive temporarily defeated proposals, to modify executive proposals, and to monitor complaints about existing legislation from those whom it affects. Despite these potential long-range possibilities, the institutional structure of Congress makes the legislative process uniquely insensitive to immediate and pressing policy needs. Polsby fails to deal with the prospect that the long-term nature of the incubation process might result in programs that are inadequate for solving problems such as pollution, poverty, and urban decay, which continue to grow while proposed policy solutions incubate.

Because of the highly decentralized nature and extensive formal powers of the committee system in the House of Representatives, the political influence of individual committee chairmen is great. John F. Manley's "Wilbur D. Mills: A Study in Congressional Influence" traces the personal influence resources that Representative Mills has added to his formal powers to make him one of the most influential men in the contemporary American political system. Mills combines hard work, the avoidance of firm positions on issues, and extensive bargaining skills in ways that encourage the members of the House Ways and Means Committee to defer to his particular brand of "leadership through followership." Decisions emerge from a collegial process. Mills waits for consensus within his committee before sending any tax or social security measures to the floor of Congress. This informal norm of committee consensus has given Mills an extraordinarily high batting average on the floor. It has also ensured that legislation will emerge slowly, through an evolutionary process of consensus building. Manley's study also illustrates the extent to which Congressmen's interpersonal relationships give shape and direction to the formulation of legislative policy.

E. E. Schattschneider was one of the leading critics of the modern pluralist theory of democracy, which shifted attention away from the role of the mass public in the political system and attempted to explain all of American politics in terms of interest-group activity. In "The Scope and Bias of the Pressure System," Schattschneider does not deny that organized interest groups often play a decisive role in determining the distribution of benefits and burdens by government. Rather, he argues that meaningful distinctions can be made between public interest groups and special-interest groups and between organized and unorganized interest groups. Such distinctions allow one to assess the democratic legitimacy of various competing interests rather than lump together spokesmen for civil rights, General Motors, corporate agriculture, and consumer protection.

Schattschneider demonstrates the distinct business and upper-class bias that permeates the "pressure system"—that is, the system of competition among organized special-interest groups. This bias in political participation has important policy consequences. Not all interests are organized into the pressure system. Less than one-third of the adult American populace belongs to organized political groups pursuing private objectives. This means that Congress's proclivity to respond to the blandishments of special-interest groups provides direct representation for a biased sample of the population. But Congress does not always simply comply with the wishes of this biased sample. It is always possible to expand the scope of the conflict, to increase the number of "interested" parties in order to tip the balance of influence in favor of ever wider coalitions of interests. In this way even a majority of the normally unorganized mass public may be drawn into a conflict and may change the probable outcome. An assumption in Schattschneider's theory of conflict expansion is that the most powerful parties in a dispute will resist outside intervention—either by public opinion or by public authority; the weak appeal for government intervention just as the small boy in the schoolyard appeals to the teacher to stop the bully.

Theodore Lowi's "How the Farmers Get What They Want" provides an interesting footnote to Schattschneider's theory. Corporate agriculture represents a formerly weak interest that succeeded in obtaining legislative and administrative support. Once various sectors of the farm industry were able to establish a firm toehold in the development of national agricultural policy, they sought insulation from intervention by nonagricultural groups in what they defined as "strictly agricultural affairs." As a result of the low visibility of the policy-making process, leading farm interests have succeeded in establishing a host of largely self-governing feudal baronies. They represent probably the most extreme example of the tension between maximum representation and coordinated policy planning. Lowi's study also implicitly illustrates that maximum representation for the powerless at one period in history may preclude representation of other weak interests in subsequent generations. The wheat, cotton, and soybean industries are represented in the self-governing agricultural establishment, but small farmers and migrant workers are given short shrift. The triangular influence pattern between local farmer committees, congressional subcommittees, and central agency personnel encourages a mutual commitment to maximizing the productivity and profits of the leading farm interests. This pro-industry perspective leaves little room for outside spokesmen seeking consumer representation. It also frustrates the development of a system for the distribution of surplus food that can be tied more closely to the needs of the poor and less to agricultural market conditions. "Strictly agricultural affairs" appear to have far-reaching consequences for which the pluralist theory of functional representation does not adequately provide.

The case study that concludes Part Three, "The Subcommittee Chairman: Politics of Fear," vividly describes the extent to which the feudalized system of decision making discussed by Lowi can systematically undermine attempts to cope with major national problems such as hunger. Nick Kotz's portrait of Jamie Whitten, Chairman of the House Appropriations Subcommittee on Agriculture, illustrates how one arch-reactionary Congressman, with a great deal of seniority and a cooperative subcommittee membership, can use the power of the purse and the norm of deference to subcommittee specialization to intimidate a Secretary of Agriculture and to kill virtually any reform designed to feed the hungry.

Policy Analysis and Congress

10

Nelson W. Polsby

One of the functions of the United States Congress is to act as a machine for making decisions about public policy. In what sense does Congress engage in analytic activity in the process of decision-making? How can Congressional decision-making be made more receptive to the kinds of policy analysis that are carried on elsewhere, both within the government and outside it?

The fact that Congress is organized differently from conventional bureaucracies leads many observers to assert overhastily that Congressional decision-making is inefficient, cumbersome, and in need of instant reform. Consider, for example, the fact that Cabinet officers are asked to justify certain aspects of their programs in much the same language before authorization and appropriation committees in both houses, adding up to four presentations in all—clearly an inefficient use of a busy executive's time, according to the busy executive and his friends. Yet this same busy executive insists as a matter of course that programs coming up the line to his office be justified repeatedly to program review committees, bureau chiefs, department level staff, and departmental budget officers, and he would think nothing of justifying the program again to other interested executive branch departments, the President and the budget bureau. Cabinet-level officers quite commonly make presentations, formal and informal, justifying their programs to the general public, to interest groups, to newspapermen. Why, then, does alleged inconvenience to an executive officer of the government provide an excuse for the recommendation that Congress change its structure if the same reasoning does not lead (for example) to an outcry to consolidate those three well-known extra-constitutional entities, "Face the Nation," "Meet the Press," and "Issues and Answers"?

This is one of the little mysteries of Washington politics, wrapped inside the bigger enigma that the organizational structure of Congress presents to most of the outside world. As an outsider myself I cannot pretend to know all the ins and outs of Congressional decision-making, but I believe nevertheless that some attempt has to be made to comprehend the unique qualities of the two houses in order to capture a sense of why they interact as they do with one another, with the executive branch, and with the rest of their environment.

The structure of an organization, after all, maps the topography of its economizing devices. So in viewing the structures of the House of Representatives and the Senate whole and from a distance, it may be easier to see how rational calculation enters into the wiring diagram of Congressional decision-making, how Congress does research, how "politics" aids and deters rational calculation, and how increased professionalization in policy analysis can improve the political position of generalist politicians.

[1]

As institutions, the House and the Senate differ markedly in their essential character. The House is a highly specialized instrument for processing legislation. Its great strength lies in its firmly structured division of labor. This division of labor provides the House with a toehold in the policy-making process by virtue of its capacity to farm out and hence, in some collective sense, to master technical details. House members are frequently better prepared than senators in conferences, and usually have the better grasp of the peculiarities of the executive agencies they supervise. This is an artifact of the strong division of labor that the House maintains: Members are generally assigned to one or two committees only; and floor debate is generally limited to participation by committee members. There is an expectation that members will concentrate their energies, rather than range widely over the full spectrum of public policy. Patterns of news coverage encourage specialization; general pronouncements by House members are normally not widely reported. Senators, because they are fewer, more socially prominent, and serve longer terms (hence are around long enough for newsmen to cultivate), and allegedly serve "larger" districts, can draw attention to themselves by well-timed press releases almost regardless of their content.

The coordination of an organism like the House is difficult because it cannot entail excessive centralization of power. Decentralization is necessary for the House to maintain its capacity to cope with the outside world (that is, through its complex and specialized division of labor). And this in turn produces the House's major career incentive, namely the opportunity accorded a tenth to a fifth of its members to possess the substance of power in the form of a committee or subcommittee chairmanship or membership on a key committee. At present seniority acts as a bulwark of this incentive system, by guaranteeing a form of job security at least within the division of labor of the organization.

Thus, as I once observed in another connection:

To that large fraction of members for whom the House is a career and a vocation, the longevity of members above them in the many hierarchies of the House—not the entirely predictable congressional election returns in their home districts—is the key to the political future.

The essence of the Senate is that it is a great forum, an echo chamber, a publicity machine. Thus "passing bills," which is central to the life of the House, is peripheral to the Senate. In the Senate the three central activities are (1) the cultivation of national constituencies (that is, beyond state lines) by political leaders; (2) the formulation of questions for debate and discussion on a national scale (especially in opposition to the President); and (3) the incubation of new policy proposals that may at some future time find their way into legislation.

This conception of the Senate is, in some respects, novel, since it focuses on an aspect of Senate life that is much deplored by aficionados of the "inner club" conception of the institution, who often defend the curious thesis that the persons anointed by the mysterious chemistry of Senate popularity are the very elite that keeps this nation from the mob scene in *The Day of the Locust.*

I think, however, that there is considerable use in a democratic republic for an organization that encourages—as the Senate currently does—the generation of publicity on issues of public importance. One must grant there have been abuses in the pursuit of publicity by senators; but Senate "great debates," investigations, and hearings have also performed considerable public service.

Where the House of Representatives is a large, impersonal, and highly specialized machine for processing bills and overseeing the executive branch, the Senate is, in a way, a theater where dramas—comedies and tragedies, soap operas and horse operas—are staged to enhance the careers of its members and to influence public policy by means of debate and public investigation.

In both the House and the Senate the first commandment to newcomers is "Specialize." But this means vastly different things in the two houses. "Specialize" to a representative means "tend to your knitting": Work hard on the committee to which you are assigned, pursue the interests of your state and region. In the Senate everyone has several committee assignments. Boundaries between committees are not strictly observed: Occasionally a senator who is not a committee member will sit in on a hearing if a subject interests him. On the floor, quite unlike the House, virtually any senator may speak for any length of time about anything. Thus the institution itself gives few cues and no compulsions to new senators wondering what they should specialize in. For the Senate, specialization seems to mean finding a subject matter and a nation-wide constituency interested in the subject that have not already been pre-empted by some more senior senator.

It is a cliché of academic political science that in legislative matters, it is the President who initiates policy, and Congress which responds, amplifying and modifying and rearranging elements which are essentially originated in the executive branch. Not much work has been done, however, on following this river of bills-becoming-and-not-becoming-laws back to its sources. Where do innovations in policy come from *before* the President "initiates" them?

Old Washington hands know the answer. There is very little new under the sun. A great many newly enacted policies have "been around," "in the air" for quite a while. In the heat of a presidential campaign or when a newly inaugurated President wants a "new" program, desk drawers fly open all over Washington. Pet schemes are fished out, dusted off, and tried out on the new political leaders.

There is often a hiatus of years—sometimes decades—between the first proposal of a policy innovation and its appearance as a presidential "initiative"—much less as a law. Commentators have greatly underestimated the role of the Senate in gestating these ideas, by providing a forum for speeches, hearings, and the introduction of bills going nowhere for the moment. This process of gestation accomplishes a number of things. It maintains a sense of community among far-flung interest groups that favor the innovation, by giving them occasional opportunities to come in and testify. It provides an incentive for persons favoring the innovation to keep up to date information on its prospective benefits and technical feasibility. And it accustoms the uncommitted to a new idea.

Thus the Senate is in some respects at a crucial nerve-end of the polity. It articulates, formulates, shapes, and publicizes demands, and can serve as a hothouse for significant policy innovation.

Hence proposals to increase the structuredness of the Senate, to force germaneness in debate, to tighten committee assignment procedures, and to reduce the number of assignments per senator misunderstand the nature of the Senate and the contribution it can uniquely make to the political system. What is needed in the Senate is as little structure as possible; its organizational flexibility enables it to incubate policy innovations, to advocate, to respond, to launch its great debates, in short to pursue the continuous renovation of American public policy through the hidden hand of the self-promotion of its members.

[2]

What has this to do with analysis in policy-making? It suggests that the analytic roles that Congress plays in the process are somewhat more varied than the customary "President proposes, Congress disposes" overview would suggest. Let us decompose the policy-making process into stages.

1. *Initiation.* How are policies initiated in the American political system? The process is by no means uniform, or clear. It is certainly not generally true that policy innovation begins with a presidential message to Congress. For behind each presidential message lurk months of man-hours of work and sometimes years of advocacy and controversy. The two great fountainheads of policy seem to be: (1) sudden demands upon government that spur bureaucrats to ad-hoc problem solving that ultimately has to be codified or rationalized as "policy"; and (2) a longer range build-up in the society of some demand upon the government where the formulation of a "solution" may first be made by a professor, or by technical support personnel attached to an interest group, or by a government "expert." On rare occasions, experts attached to a Congressional committee will initiate a policy. More often, I think, Congress is in on the beginning of a policy innovation because it provides the first sympathetic ear for an innovation concocted by outside experts.

2. *Incubation.* Many of our most important policy innovations take years from initiation to enactment. Surely the idea of medicare, to take an obvious

example, was not "initiated" by the Johnson administration in the 89th Congress when proposals incorporating its main features had been part of the landscape since the early Truman administration. Medicare, like other great policy innovations, required *incubation*—a process in which men of Congress often play very significant roles. Incubation entails keeping a proposal alive while the problem to which it is addressed grows. Senators and (to a lesser extent) representatives contribute to incubation by proposing bills that they know will not pass, making speeches, making demands for data and for support . . . from interest groups favoring the proposal. Sometimes a sympathetic committee chairman can be persuaded to allow hearings on such a proposal. Hearings focus public attention, mobilize interest groups for and against, and provide an occasion for the airing of a proposal's technical justifications.

3. *Formulation.* When, finally, a proposal moves toward enactment it is usually the executive branch that focuses the energy sufficient to overcome inertia. A presidential priority is a tremendous advantage in clearing away obstacles, but the President's support is usually purchased at a price: The proposal becomes his. This is not merely a matter of credit, although who gets credit is no trivial matter. The executive branch begins the process of bargaining by including some features of the proposal and dropping others, adding bait here and padding there. In some cases (e.g., foreign aid, civil rights) executive branch control over bargaining is tight and continues right through the legislative mill. In others (e.g., surtax, medicare) influential members of Congress establish which provisions will survive and which will be sacrificed. Sometimes (e.g., the HUD bill in the Kennedy administration) the most significant battle is precisely over who will control the bill.

4. *Modification.* The legislative gauntlet is too well known to require discussion here. The analytical questions at the focus of attention during this part of the policy-making process are: Who wants the proposal? Who wants it to fail? How resourceful and well mobilized are they? By what means (invocation of party loyalty, promises of future help, log-rolling, the sacrificing of certain provisions, etc.) are coalitions for and against the proposal built? In addition, committee staffs generally assemble competent justifications on the merits for legislation. Often these reports reflect work done by the downtown bureaucracies. Hearings provide additional evidence on the merits, as do interest group representatives on a more informal basis.

5. *Appraisal.* After a bill is enacted it goes into effect. Presumably this has an impact upon members of the general public, who in turn communicate with their Congressmen about this and myriad other topics. By monitoring the tides of complaint and appeals for assistance from constituents, Congress keeps track of the activity of the entire federal government. Congressmen learn quickly enough which agencies are throwing off benefits to their constituents, which cause the people back home grief, which preoccupy them, which they ignore.

This appraisal process operates day and night on a piecemeal basis, and separately from the more formally organized oversight activities of the Congress: investigative hearings, budgetary hearings, confirmation hearings, on-site inspections of physical plant, informal briefings, conferences, and so on.

[3]

In short, Congress in the normal course of events gathers great amounts of information, processes this information according to reasonably well-known criteria, and matches what it learns against goals. That is, it conducts a tremendous amount of policy analysis. This simple fact is generally somewhat obscured by two important conditions under which policy analysis takes place on Capitol Hill. Much Congressional policy analysis takes place under adversary circumstances. Thus Congressional decision-makers ordinarily cannot enjoy the luxury of examining alternative means to stipulated ends. In an adversary process ends are not stipulated but contested. Agreement on means is often sought as a substitute for agreement on ends. Ends are often scaled down, pulled out of shape, or otherwise transformed. In short, from the standpoint of an outside observer whose focus is as often as not on some pressing problem in society, the Congressional process of policy analysis looks chaotic at best, perversely insensitive at worst.

Insensitivity in Congressional policy analysis is not altogether curable. It can come about because the strength of a demand in society as it is felt by an observer has no counterpart equally strong within the Congressional process itself. Sometimes Congress does not reflect "needs" as defined in the society at large because Congress itself is malapportioned, or because the "wrong" sorts of people dominate the relevant committee. Thus a wave of short-run, intense demands may break futilely across the superstructure of any institution. Given the stately metabolism decreed for it by the founding fathers, Congress could hardly be expected to operate efficiently with respect to short-run demands in the best of circumstances.

The second basic condition under which Congress conducts policy analysis is inexplicitness and fragmentation. All knowledge on a particular topic is rarely collected in a single spot or systematically marshalled. Nevertheless, the executive branch does impose some order, principally because the Congressional division of labor is organized according to executive agencies so as to provide oversight. Thus jurisdictional anomalies in the executive are echoed in the legislature. Fragmentation can be spatial—as when a bill's best friends and worst enemies are not members of the relevant committee—or temporal, when excellent analytic work is done in the incubation process but is not picked up in the formulation or enactment stages. There are often structural as well as coincidental reasons for this phenomenon when it occurs —jurisdictional jealousies between committees may prevent efficient communication, for example.

All this suggests that the analytic activity undertaken by Congress, while formidable in amount, is inexplicit with respect to some matters regarded as crucial outside and systematically skewed toward the reduction of the sorts of uncertainty about which most members of society are indifferent. Yet Congressmen, as elected officials, *must* ask who will get the credit—or the blame. They must know who is for what and how strongly, because these matters affect not only their own future efficacy but also their present chances of assembling a coalition "on the merits."

Is there a practical alternative to policy analysis in which alternative policies are put to such tests? The alternative, for a legislature, is total passivity. Legislative arenas, as contrasted with legislative institutions having transformative effects (and therefore "insensitivities"), can faithfully reflect the balance of forces as they are generally arrayed in society, and they can if they like commission policy analysis. But they are powerless to incorporate such analysis into their deliberations because legislative arenas do not deliberate, they merely transmit. The sponsorship of research by parliamentary bodies that are principally "electoral colleges" is at best a means of lobbying the cabinet or the prime minister.

[4]

Under the circumstances, is there any use in considering the improvement of explicit policy analysis by Congress? I believe the answer is yes, principally because most substantive policy that Congress is concerned with affords nearly complete freedom from constituent knowledge, much less pressure. The adversary process may be muted or perfunctory, or capable of drastic modification by the infusion of detailed technical knowledge. Thus explicit policy analysis, although it comprises only a fraction of the policy analysis actually going on at any one time in Congress, is well worth improving.

Where does Congress get technical knowledge? Principally from committee staff personnel, who virtually monopolize the activity of explicit policy analysis in most subject matter areas. But while the executive branch has systematically been engaged in professionalizing its search for technical detail over the past decade or more, Congress on the whole has not done so. It is romantic for Congressmen to think of themselves as not in need of expert and detailed explicit analysis because they are "generalists." Generalism is too often a genteel name for ignorance. Like all other modern institutions, Congress can only preserve its autonomy and effectiveness by reducing ignorance.

Are there means by which Congress can do so? Two such come readily to mind. Both seek to apply to Congressional committee staffs lessons from the executive branch, where the professionalization of economic forecasting and defense procurement led to tremendous increases in the power of political decision-makers to identify options and choose among them. This is precisely the battle many Congressmen feel they are losing. Yet if they choose to do so, they can professionalize their own committee staffs, thereby increasing the efficiency of their explicit analytical activities and enhancing their own knowledge and power.

To "professionalize" implies continuous contact with a community outside the world of Capitol Hill. Professional economists, operations researchers, psychologists, and so on, maintain standards of performance by participating in professional communities through meetings, scholarly journals, and similar specialized communications media. Typically, nowadays, the top economists of the executive branch—the men who formulate fiscal policy, anti-trust policy, international trade policy, and so forth—are first and foremost professional economists. The primacy of loyalty to professional craft standards on the part of executive technical personnel vastly increases the probability that the options presented to political executives will be feasible and technically sound.

Typically, Congressional committees are staffed by an older, less effective process of patronage. This produces loyal service, and by the standards of an earlier day, highly competent service. But unswerving loyalty to the chairman is seldom enough to produce technically advanced criticism of executive proposals, sophisticated insight into alternatives, or sensitive awareness of emerging problems in the world. Yet these are what Congress needs. Hence, here are two modest proposals, both of which have already been tried out in small ways on Capitol Hill. Committees should be encouraged to constitute outside advisory groups to advise the chairman on the technical competence of the work they are receiving from their staffs. Secondly, exchanges for one-year or two-year hitches of service should be instituted between Congressional committee staffs and staff persons in the executive branch, private business, labor unions, social service organizations, and universities.

The purpose of these proposals is to bring to bear upon explicit policy analysis on Capitol Hill some of the standards—and the considerations—that are commonly employed in policy analysis within the executive branch and elsewhere in society. It is not contemplated that steps such as these will necessarily bring Congress into harmony with the executive branch in areas where they now disagree, since there is no reason to suppose that a large number of disagreements over national policy are *based* upon ignorance— although some may be. These disagreements should be resolved. Other disagreements may rear their heads, if Congress chooses to equip itself with more professional analytic personnel, since not all executive branch proposals are free from controversy even when they are grounded in thorough professional knowledge. Thus more professionalism in explicit analysis can assist Congress in finding disagreements and weak spots in executive branch recommendations and can increase the probability that Congress itself can initiate policy. These proposals, therefore, genuinely attempt to strengthen Congress rather than the opposite—as is the case with so many proposals for Congressional reform.

Many of these proposals, in my opinion, make a fundamental mistake: They attempt to force Congress into an organizational format that mimics the hierarchical arrangement of the executive branch. For example, PPBS (Planning-Programing-Budgeting System), where it has been used successfully in the executive branch, is in part a political device for forcing decisions upward in the hierarchy. There is a point, however, beyond which this technique cannot go. PPBS is a technique for comparing alternative and substitutable methods of achieving specific goals. But it is not and cannot be a device for selecting desirable goals. In rare cases, where costs differ greatly, PPBS can help decision-makers identify goals as more or less achievable given limited resources, but in the end political and not technical decisions are the outcome of PPBS analyses.

Thus Congress is at present satisfactorily organized to assess the results of PPBS analysis in each of the sectors to which it can be or has been applied. The Armed Services Committees have for some time received the benefit of detailed discussion of cost-benefit analysis by Pentagon planners. There is no reason to assume that the same sort of information would not be forthcoming from other agencies that succeed in using PPBS techniques, and presented to the appropriate committees of Congress.

Some observers may assume that because on the executive side an aggregation process takes place in the Bureau of the Budget and the Executive Office of the President that establishes priorities in the funding of programs, some similar explicitly synoptic act of aggregation ought to be instituted on the legislative side. This is a mistake. It assumes that the act of establishing priorities is a technical, not a political, matter in the Executive Office Building, when in fact judgments are being made about items that are incommensurable and nonsubstitutable by technical criteria. Secondly, it ignores the fact that just as the executive branch employs a method of aggregation suitable to its organizational design, so too does Congress. Decomposition of budgetary and program proposals by subject-matter specialties and the assembling of successive majorities around specific proposals is a process of setting priorities and aggregating preferences no more political than the analogous activities in the top of the executive branch. It merely entails politics appropriately responsive to the relatively decentralized character of a complex legislative institution.

Unlike the Supreme Court, the legitimacy of Congress does not rest even in small measure upon the intellectual excellence of its work. Congress legitimizes policy because it embodies the will of the people by giving voice to the collective judgment of their duly elected representatives. Technical competence and intellectual excellence in one phase of policy analysis are therefore not strictly necessary for Congress to be important in the American system of government. But sound and sophisticated explicit policy analysis can increase the capacity of Congress to contribute to the solution of the problems besetting America. Since Congressmen must choose among solutions, they may as well equip themselves as best they can for the task. This aim does not require the revamping of Congress itself, but rather greater attention to unused resources currently well within the power of Congress to command.

Wilbur D. Mills: A Study in Congressional Influence

11

John F. Manley

All leaders are also led; in innumerable cases, the master is the slave of his slaves. Said one of the greatest German party leaders referring to his followers: "I am their leader, therefore I must follow them."
—Georg Simmel

Political scientists studying Congress have shown the same disinclination for the study of individual leaders as that of the profession as a whole. Whatever the reasons for avoiding an analysis of social and political processes from the perspective of an individual—and there are several good ones—it is difficult to ignore, if not discount, the extreme emphasis placed on personalities by experienced participants and observers of the congressional process. One may decide, with Fenno, to underplay references to specific individuals in an effort "to show how much generalization is possible short of a heavy reliance on personality data." But the fact remains that those closest to the legislative process do see it in terms of individuals and personalities; more important, much can be learned, as evidenced by Huitt's work, by focusing on individual legislators and the contexts within which they function. Whether it is Lyndon Johnson as Senate Majority Leader searching for the man who is the "key" to a particular bill, the differences between a Rayburn and a McCormack, or the skill of a Judge Smith, the individual looms large on Capitol Hill.

Among the reasons why political scientists have shied away from individual or personality-centered studies of Congress are, first, the extreme variability of personalities, which stands as a barrier to generalization; and, second, the fact that it is hard to say how much of the legislative process is due to individuals and how much is due to the situational factors that confront them. Faced by these old problems, there is an understandable tendency to downplay individuals and personalities, and, implicitly or explicitly, to treat the situation and the group as the primary determinants of behavior. Before taking this step, however, it might be wise to consider a warning made by Homans apropos of Durkheim's social mold theory (which overemphasized the impact of society on individuals): "Intellectually the descent into hell is easy. One false step, and logic will do the rest."

Durkheim erred, according to Homans, because he thought of the individual-society dichotomy in terms of cause and effect and not in terms of mutual dependence. Norms, for example, are the result of human interaction but they may also be the cause of such interaction if, once established, they govern future behavior. The same kind of mutual dependence exists between individual leaders and the group. "Neither individual character structure nor the contextual configuration alone," Edinger writes, "can explain a leader's behavior, but careful analysis of their interaction—in as many instances as possible, may reveal certain patterns and facilitate understanding."

Thus, for certain analytical purposes, one may take either a group-socio-logical or an individual-personality approach to the study of Congress, but the two approaches may also be treated as complementary. Indeed, in the case of the Ways and Means Committee, Chairman Wilbur D. Mills stands out as one of the most influential committee chairmen in recent years, if not in history, and, like all leaders, he also follows. The paradox of leadership is that it always involves followmanship; and, as a leading House liberal once said of Mills, "He's an expert in followmanship." The group that forms the base of his influence in the House and that he is most likely to follow is the Committee.

Mills's leadership is here conceived not solely in terms of the traits he possesses which enable him to lead others, a view of leadership which has been rejected for many years, but as a function of his relationship to his colleagues on the Committee. "There can be no leadership," as Gibb says, "in isolation, it is distinctly a quality of a group situation." We will be concerned with Mills as he interacts with the Committee, a concern which tends to stress the group-sociological side of leadership. A balance is sought between Mills as an individual leader and the nature of the group he leads, but the approach to the former is primarily through the ways in which Mills is seen by the rest of the Committee: their perceptions of his leadership, what they like and dislike about the way he runs the Committee, the scope and limitations of his leadership as they see it, why they respond to him in certain ways, and how it is that he is allowed to exert influence on them. . . .

. . .

1. Mills as Instrumental and Affective Leader

Studies of small groups, as is well-known, commonly report a tendency for two types of leaders to function in groups: the instrumental or task-oriented leader, and the socio-emotional or affective leader. Instrumental leaders are primarily concerned with realizing the goals of the group and directing the group toward the completion of its tasks. Task-oriented direction may give rise, however, to intra-group conflict and disintegrative pressures, creating a need for some way to relieve tension. The affective leader helps to cool internal tensions and to stimulate a harmonious working atmosphere. Theoretically, the activities of the two leaders complement each other and the stable group achieves a state of equilibrium internally and in relation to its environment. Experiments with small groups have found that one man may perform both task and maintenance functions, but by and large the opposing requirements of these functions lead to a division of labor within the group.

The author's initial research on the Ways and Means Committee led to no

evidence that the task and affective leadership functions were separated in
the Committee; in fact, Mills appeared responsible for guiding the Committee's task efforts and his leadership seemed to be the main reason that the
affective tone of the Committee was high. In order to test this hunch, the
members of the Committee were asked two questions:

1.   When you come to particularly difficult problems, does any member of
     the Committee stand out as being the one who most often comes up with
     a way out?
2.   During the course of discussing legislation things can get rather tense
     from time to time. I know that this happens even in Ways and Means
     at times. Does anyone stand out as the peacemaker in these situations?

Table 1 categorizes the responses to these questions by party. The results
on the task leadership question show a greater tendency among Democrats
to assign this function to Mills than the Republicans. For the Republicans,
Mills and the ranking Republican, John Byrnes (Wis.), together and in that
order, are the instrumental leaders in the sense posed by the question. The
results on the affective leadership question are more mixed but again Mills
is most often seen as the man who stands out in this regard, for Republicans
and Democrats alike. Although the data are more suggestive than conclusive,
it is interesting to note that the Republicans were more inclined to cite Mills
as the affective leader by himself, while they linked Mills and Byrnes as the
instrumental leaders.

Table 1 Task and Socio-Emotional Leadership in the Ways and Means Committee

| | Task Leadership | | | |
	Mills	Mills and Byrnes	No One Stands Out	Other and No Response
Democrats	9	2	2	0
Republicans	1	4	2	0
	Socio-Emotional Leadership			
Democrats	6	2	1	3
Republicans	4	1	1	1

. . .

What is not shown in the table is that although the members named Mills
as the task and affective leader of the Committee, many members qualified
their answers with the comment that Mills and Byrnes are the dominant
figures on the Committee but any member is free to participate and contribute if he so desires. Leadership is . . . more diffuse in the Committee than the
task-affective dichotomy implies, and there is a relationship between affective relations in the Committee and the way Mills performs the taskmaster
function. Task leadership, in short, is more collegial in the members' eyes

than the conspicuousness of Mills in the public eye might lead one to expect, and because this is true Mills also rates high as the affective leader of the Committee.

Such a finding should not be altogether unexpected. Simply because leadership functions are separated in some groups is no reason why they cannot be joined in others. There is no reason why a skillful leader cannot operate in such a way that although he is the primary instrumental leader of the group he guides the group in performing its tasks so that he is the main reason why the job gets done, and without much tension. . . . Mills is a democratic committee chairman par excellence. In this way, he guides the Committee on tasks and maintains good affective relations in the process.

Seen in this light, one familiar observation on Mills's style of leadership, i.e., that he is a consensus-seeker, an observation made by almost everyone who has ever looked at the contemporary Committee, is of great interest. Mills's search for a consensus in the Committee is another way of saying that he is a democratic chairman of the Committee, a task leader who encourages the members to influence one another, who shares the quest for solutions to problems with the members even though at the end of the process he may articulate and legitimate the conclusion they reach together, a leader who directs the members along lines he may favor but who does not attempt to force his predilections on others. Mills's task leadership of the Committee, subtle and indirect, is an important source of the high esteem in which he is held by the members and a major factor in explaining why the members like the Committee as well as they do.

. . .

To reach a consensus in the Committee Chairman Mills will compromise, bargain, cajole, swap, bend, plead, amend, coax, and unite until as much of the controversy as possible is drained from the bill, and as many members of the Committee as possible support it. "Mills, although he may feel strongly about things, is not by nature an uncompromising man, you know, even on some principles he may have. . . . He likes to be a leader, to be in front of the troops, and if he sees that the troops are ahead of him then he'll circle around and make sure that he gets out in front again." Other Republicans say that if Mills "finds out my backers have a lot of votes, he'll give in, he'll compromise," "he encourages you to participate and the first 95 percent of the approach is nonpartisan," "our committee is a little unique in that we have a chairman who doesn't let the political dominate," and

If we had a partisan chairman the Committee would become partisan overnight. In some ways, for political purposes, it might be better to have a partisan chairman. This would unite the minority, we could come out with our political position, and perhaps get some votes in the next election. But I don't think on our committee it should be like that.

Republican appreciation for the way Mills runs the Committee is probably heightened by their awareness that there is no absolute necessity for Mills to treat them well. In fact, a few of them commented on this point. "Some committee chairmen just use their authority and ram things through. Wilbur won't do this." A second Republican refuted an erroneous popular image of the Chairman which he felt was propagated by the newspapers,

Although consensus is a bad term since Johnson screwed it up, he is a consensus seeker. He never pushes things to votes, we reach a compromise. Nothing bothers me more than to read, as you do in the newspapers, that he's an authoritarian—the "little authoritarian from Kensett, Arkansas." That's not it, he's no authoritarian. The reason the tax bill is not going through is because they have to cut expenditures. . . . It's not that Mills is a dictator, the newspapers are all wrong.

A third Republican put the matter strongly, but well, "Anyone who has ever been on another committee appreciates the way Mills conducts Ways and Means. There's almost a reverence among the members about him because they know how it is on other committees."

Democratic members of Ways and Means are no less unanimous in their agreement on Mills's fairness, the considerate way he treats all members, and that, above all, he directs the Committee's task operations with consensus uppermost in mind. Few members of either party would disagree with the Democrat who said, "He's evasive, aloof, coy and he's not a stern oak that stands in the wind and splits rather than bends. He'll bend in the wind." . . . Questions about Mills drew the inevitable comparison, "Now you take Education and Labor, they never try for a consensus, they battle it out. But on Ways and Means we try to reach a consensus. . . . He always seeks a consensus and he's a genius at getting one on complex problems."

If, as one Democrat said, "Mills loves harmony," and will sometimes "abandon his position" to get it, it is also true, as another Democrat said, that the search for harmony is not the easiest way to proceed. "It's long, hard, tedious work, but he seeks a consensus." In the course of this work the Chairman guides but does not continually dominate the Committee's discussion. He does participate more than other members but much of his participation involves commenting on the comments of others, raising searching questions if not objections about various ideas, and, most important, stepping in to legitimize a position which the active members have arrived at under his guidance, not under his urging. This kind of leadership requires a flexible approach to controversies, and an inclination to accommodate the opposing views of the members. In this regard, the comment of an HEW official is instructive,

Mills is an eminently successful opportunist. He does not announce his position and force it through. He sits and listens to the members and knows what will go. I'd say 80 percent of it is consensus, 20 percent Mills, but certainly not 50 percent Mills.

It could be argued, of course, that this is not real leadership, that all Mills does is sense what the members will accept, fix his position accordingly, and take a firm stand in favor of a sure thing. But this interpretation—which is sometimes made—seriously distorts a complex form of leadership because it does not conform to one aspect of leadership: getting other people to accept one's position. Leadership, as Simmel says, always involves a certain amount of followmanship. . . .

. . .

By stepping in at the right time and suggesting that a particular line of action may be acceptable to the members, and thereby resolving whatever tensions arise, he is seen by the members as "powerful," "smart," "expert," "clever," and a "good synthesizer," qualities that are associated with instrumental leadership, and as "fair," "considerate," "pleasant," "patient," and the "peacemaker," qualities that go with affective leadership.

In concluding this initial look at the way in which Mills runs Ways and Means it is well to remember that in some ways the Committee is jointly directed. Mills and Byrnes together, not just Mills alone, are responsible for the way the Committee goes about its business. Although Mills is the most salient member of the Committee a great many of the policy decisions taken by the Committee (e.g., excise tax reduction and the scope of medicare in 1965) can be traced to Mills and Byrnes. If Mills and Byrnes disagreed over the way the Committee should function the amount of conflict in the Committee would be appreciably higher than it is. As implied, the Chairman and the ranking Republican are agreed on the nature of the Committee's job and how it should be done, if not on all major policy questions.

It is difficult to exaggerate the importance of the Mills-Byrnes relationship to Ways and Means. The Democrats were more inclined to reserve Committee leadership to Mills than the Republicans, but the fact that the Republicans feel that Mills and Byrnes together are the leaders of the Committee helps explain the nature of partisanship in the Committee. Far from being cut off from influence in the Committee the Republicans feel that because of Mills and Byrnes they have as much if not more say than the Democrats. One Republican observed that the Committee under Byrnes would be about the same as it is under Mills. Asked why, he said, "Because we Republicans get so much in now."

. . .

Mills's Perception of His Job

Up to now the analysis of Mills has been based on how the members of the Committee see and respond to his leadership in the Committee. Little has been said about the way Mills himself sees the Committee and its tasks. As expected, there is a close fit between the way Mills sees the Committee's job and defines his role as chairman and the perceptions of the other members of the Committee. To put the matter briefly, Mills thinks that the Committee, in addition to reporting technically sound bills, should report bills which can pass the House, and the best means of insuring passage in the House is through compromise in the Committee. His reputation and that of his committee are at stake every time a Ways and Means bill comes before the House, and if there is one thing Mills tries hard to avoid it is defeat in the House.

Mills believes that part of the Committee's job is to examine carefully all of the policy proposals it actively considers. Given the complexity of tax law and fiscal policy, and the need to protect the actuarial soundness of the social security sytem, he makes sure that the Committee is painstakingly thorough in the mark up stage of the legislative process, that it studies the alternatives before reaching conclusions, and that it proceeds cautiously so as to lessen the chances of adversely affecting the economic status of the country, corporations, or individuals. It is up to the Committee to perfect bills before sending them to the House for final approval, and he sees no sense in spending two or three days on the House floor amending Ways and Means bills. Hence the argument that bills reported by the Way and Means Committee are so "intricate" and "complex," reported only after weeks of concentrated study, that no floor amendments should even be considered unless they are first approved by the Committee.

A workmanlike job on the legislation, however, is only half the task. The other half is to get enough votes in the Committee and in the House to pass the Committee's product. "As I see it," Mills has said, "our job is to work over a bill until our technical staff tells us it is ready and until I have reason to believe that it is going to get enough support to pass. Many of our bills must be brought out under a closed rule, and to get and keep a closed rule you must have a widely acceptable bill. It's as simple as that."

. . .

Because Mills is the chairman of an enormously important committee, and because he has acquired a position of legitimate leadership to go with his formal status, many people in the Washington community enjoy trying to explain why Mills leads the Committee as he does. Some dismiss him as a man who has a built-in aversion to taking chances, others see him as a man who does not have strong feelings about any policy in particular and so is willing to hold back until the feelings of others make victory certain if policy is formulated according to the least common denominator. Mills's admirers —most notably all the members of the Committee save one—see him as "the most capable man in the House of Representatives." His detractors, like one House liberal, explain his influence in the House as a "myth that he always has his Committee under control," and argue that even if he does it is because he has no real competition for leadership in the Committee.

Amidst the conflicting opinions of Mills and the reasons which ostensibly explain why he is influential, none is more common than the observation that he will do practically anything to avoid losing a bill on the floor of the House. Several members of the Committee noted that Mills lost one of the first major bills he brought to the floor and this loss is supposed to have had a permanent effect on the Chairman. It made him cautious.

But this explanation ignores the possibility that Mills might have expected —indeed planned—his first defeat. Mills claims that his first so-called defeat was in fact part of the strategy he used to pass a controversial unemployment compensation bill. By bringing a two-part bill to the floor Mills contends that he was willing to sacrifice one part in order to get the other passed. The controversial matter thus acted as a lightning rod, drawing criticism away from the other section which, on its own, would have had trouble in the House. A recommittal motion extracted the controversial title and the bill itself was passed. If this is true Mills's humiliating loss was in truth a clever —if little-known—victory.

It would be naive not to admit the possibility that Mills's explanation of his first defeat might be a post hoc rationalization (at least one reporter who was on the scene in 1958 thinks it is), but whether it is fact or fiction is, for our purposes, irrelevant. Even if the Chairman's first loss had no lasting impact on him, as it probably did not, his behavior since 1958, and his view that policy disputes should be resolved in the Committee, make it highly probable that the tenuousness of power in the House, which is less often stressed than the concentration of power in the committee chairman, is an important constraint on how he conducts the Committee. Mills is probably well aware that underneath the "cocoon of good feeling" which envelops House members the House is sentimental, even maudlin, about everything but who has power. His reputation in the House is on the line every time he commits himself to the passage of a bill and, although one defeat is not necessarily disastrous, a few defeats and it rapidly becomes known that he has lost his grip. To guard against this Mills tries for support from both sides of the Committee table. Although he can win with just the 15 Democrats behind him it is much more comfortable to have bipartisan support. In any event, his leadership is conducive to the maintenance of harmony in the Committee and to the completion of a quality job on the complex legislation considered by the Committee. When rough spots appear in the interaction of members he tries to soothe them just as he tries to iron out rough spots in the bills. Whether Mills is conscious of it or not, this is what he does and this is why his leadership is effective.

2. Mills: Influence and Exchange

Influence, not power, is the concept to use in thinking about the leadership of individuals such as Chairman Mills. Power means many different things to many people but intuitively it conjures up the notion that individual A who "has" power can, through the expression of his will, activate obligations on the part of B which stimulate B to do something he would not otherwise do. Despite the general agreement that power is a relational or transactional concept, of some presumed utility for describing and analyzing political relations, the tendency to speak of it as a commodity which some persons have and others do not will not die. So too with influence, another relational concept, which for purposes of shorthand is spoken of in commodity terms when, in fact, it refers to relationships among people. Thus it should be kept in mind that in using the term influence in connection with Mills all that is meant is a relationship between him and the other members of the Committee, not something he has and they do not. This, of course, is in keeping with the notion of leadership used in Part I.

The reason why influence is a better concept to use in analyzing Mills than power is not that it has fewer theoretical problems. Nor is it that it is easier to devise an operational definition of influence, and measure it, than of power. The main reason is that the theoretical and empirical meaning of influence is much closer to the kind of relationship between Mills and the Committee than the meaning usually given to power. Influence, as Parsons points out, may be distinguished form power in the sense that influence is, in essence, a means of *persuasion* which involves giving reasons or justifications for doing certain things and avoiding others, whereas power may be taken to mean the communication of decisions which activate obligations. Power has a much more direct connotation than influence. When one thinks about power between A and B there is a tendency to view the relationship as unidirectional, A$\longrightarrow$B; with influence, the relationship is more apt to be seen as a mutual process of stimulation, A$\longrightarrow$B. The essence of a consensus-seeking form of leadership, the kind practiced by Mills, is mutual dependence, a relationship between Mills and the Committee which involves the flow of influence from the Committee to Mills just as much as the flow from Mills to the Committee.

. . .

. . . Focusing on, in Coleman's words, "the investments that a person makes in another which permits the other to have influence on him," draws attention away from the influencer to the influenced, and with this focus we will discuss five bases of Mills's influence. The five bases of influence are adapted from French and Raven's useful classification of the bases of power, as follows:

1. *Expertise:* based on Mills's knowledge of the subject matter.
2. *Legitimacy:* based on Mills's rights as the formal leader of the Committee.
3. *Rewards:* based on what Mills can do for the members in a positive way.
4. *Reference:* based on the identification of others with Mills.
5. *Sanctions:* based on what Mills can do, in a negative way, to promote compliance with his objectives.

1. *Expertise.*   As befits a leader whose style is that of persuasion—giving "facts" from which others can draw their own conclusions—Mills, as he is seen by the members, has great expertise in the abstruse areas considered by the Committee. When asked to explain Mills's influence in the Committee no reason was given as often as the Chairman's knowledge of the subject matter, and its only serious rival in importance was his fairness. The evidence gathered from the members illustrates perfectly Blau's comment that "A person whose demands on others are fair and modest relative to the great contribution he makes to their welfare . . . earns their approval."

Mills has earned the approval of the Committee members on his hard work and his mastery of the subjects coming before the Committee. Moreover, by becoming an expert Mills has reduced the cost of Committee membership to others. Those members who are unsure of the answers to complex questions can rely on his judgment, safe in the feeling that he knows what he is talking about, and those members who do not care to immerse themselves in technical complexities can let him do it, confident that he knows what he is doing. By acquiring some degree of expertise the Chairman has allowed other members "to perform rewarding activities with less effort, less anxiety, or in less time—in general, at lower cost." And by lowering costs to others Mills has raised his own influence.

. . .

2. *Legitimacy.*   Committee chairmen are not ipso facto leaders in Congress, but they can become leaders if they have certain kinds of skills, and certain kinds of followers. The kinds of men on Ways and Means are men oriented toward bargaining, accommodation, peaceful settlement of disputes, and the subordination of specific policy objectives to the maintenance of the power and prestige of their Committee. They are men who actively strive for legislation but who operate on the principle that the legislative process makes one fundamental demand, patience. The question now before us is, what does it take to exert influence in a decision-making system composed of men who are, in theory, peers, and who must make important decisions while they are engaged in close, long-term relationships with one another?

Seniority is one answer the members of Congress have given to this question. Seniority is nothing more than a norm which organizes the decision-making process, giving to the senior members the right to make certain decisions which structure the legislative process. The list is familiar: control of the legislative agenda, appointment of junior members to subcommittees, organizational questions such as whether or not to have subcommittees, how many subcommittees there should be, management of the committee staff, the right of recognition of members who desire to speak, and general leadership in the shepherding of bills through the House. But none of these rights guarantees influence to the senior leaders. They are resources to be used in meeting the demands of the members or in reducing the costs of committee membership to them, and only if they are used in this way will there be a relationship between seniority and influence.

Homans, in discussing the successful leader, illuminates the basic qualification that must be placed on the formal prerogatives of senior leaders in the House: "If his chief external job is to be successful, his chief internal one is to be just. 'He's fair,' are the words in the mouths of his followers from which all other praises spring." The successful committee chairman in the House is the just chairman in the committee, justice meaning in this case distributive justice, a favorable balance between rewards and costs (inducements and contributions) for the members resulting from the actions of the chairman. If the chairman so uses his prerogatives he enhances his influence with the members. If, however, the costs of the way he performs his leadership functions exceed the benefits to the members he may be able to implement his will for a time but his influence with the members will decrease, and if it decreases to a certain point the members, as they have done in some committees, may strip him of all but the gavel.

Put baldly, the argument applied to the Ways and Means Committee is that the rights granted to Mills because he is chairman are sources of influence because he exercises them in such a way that the members approve of his leadership. By so doing Mills is seen by the members as a chairman who makes important contributions to their welfare and, in Blau's words, "their common approval of his fairness, reinforced by their consensus concerning the respect his abilities deserve, generate group pressures that enforce compliance with his directives."

"He has the ability and he's very fair," was the judgment on Mills by one Republican, and no one interviewed for this study disagreed. Even the one member who was highly critical of Mills said, "He is considerate of the fellow members, no one is more considerate. Don't get me wrong—I have to say his good points. He knows his stuff." A Democrat declared, "He is fair. He doesn't ride roughshod over anyone, although it has happened—it's been known to happen. But it's rare that he's roughshod." . . .

. . .

Viewed from this perspective, the contribution of his legitimate prerogatives to Mills's influence is not that he has certain rights but that he uses them to win approval from the members. The question of the staff is a good example. As one of the more perceptive members put it, "Sure all the members have the staff but they are his men first—the Chairman's men. *And the reason they are is that he does the work."* The staff gives Mills's needs precedence over other members' needs but they are available to the other members and most of the members are quite satisfied with the staff. A few think the Committee could use more staff but there is no widespread demand for more and, if there were, the Chairman would probably be receptive to hiring more poeple. The point is that an expert staff in the hands of an inexpert chairman can be a liability instead of an asset, and the reason the staff professionals are seen as the "Chairman's men" on Ways and Means is not that he is chairman but that he is the kind of chairman he is. The other members do not begrudge him the staff because they know that he puts more into the Committee than they do and consequently has more need of the staff.

Another good example is the Chairman's decision not to use subcommittees for legislative purposes. Committee members prefer to work without subcommittees but it is no doubt true that the absence of subcommittees makes for a highly centralized operation in the Committee, an operation centered around Mills. As a Democrat said, "This means that he is there with five or six members who would normally be a subcommittee and he is chairman of all the subcommittees." But the main significance of conducting the Committee's legislative business in plenary session is that although it makes for high centralization the members do not mind. In fact, with Mills as the center they prefer it to the normal subcommittee arrangement. No doubt the members realize that this style of operation increases the opportunities for the Chairman to influence their decisions but the Chairman's influence is precisely what they like about the Committee. "If we had a new chairman we might have subcommittees," a Democrat commented, "someone who wanted to delegate. But as long as Mills wants all the responsibility we're willing to let him have it. We don't have white hats as I told you. A lot of the bills are tough." . . .

In considering legitimacy as a base of influence for the Chairman it is important to remember that many of the mundane functions of the Chairman which may increase his ability to persuade the members on certain questions fall within what Barnard calls the "zone of indifference." For a member like Thomas B. Curtis (who left the Committee in 1968) the zone was very narrow and he constantly supervised Mills to make sure that the Committee was, by his standards, well run, an oversight function which on occasion irritated the Chairman. For other members, however, the zone of indifference is comparatively large and may include everything but how to cast votes in the final stages of the Committee process. On many questions the members are content to rely on Mills. Ranking the tedious Committee meetings low on their list of priorities, these members open up a wide area in which Mills can make decisions in a relatively unrestrained way. Mills, characteristically, has a good feel for the boundaries of his autonomous zone and when he receives requests from members which fall within it, such as having someone in particular testify before the Committee, he accedes and thus insures the continuation of his general control over such matters. It is conceivable, indeed likely, that decisions such as allowing executive department representatives to participate in the executive sessions of the Committee affect the decisions of the Committee, and may affect them in ways desired by Mills, but few members care deeply about such matters. For the most part, the members are willing to let Mills run the Committee because on many questions of procedure he consults them and on nearly everything he runs the Committee, with or without consultations, to their satisfaction. By so doing, Mills maximizes the influence potential of his formal powers while minimizing the complaints that are sometimes heard about other committee chairmen in the House. Thus he is considered by one member (and nearly all) as "the best damn chairman in the House, best I've seen in all my years in the legislature."

3. *Rewards.*   Bargaining, regardless of what form it takes (logrolling, side payments, splitting the difference), is peculiarly suited to a decision-making system in which every man has some influence, no man and no group of men has undivided control over important resources of influence, and in which men who are in a formal sense equals must bring a common interest out of a diversity and conflict of interests. Such a system is built for bargaining, as those who built it—with their concern over factions—no doubt realized. And such a system, if it is to function smoothly, requires agreement on one fundamental norm: the duty to reciprocate assistance or rewards received from others.

Most of the exchanges that take place in Congress are subtle exchanges to which political scientists and others have given inelegant names: logrolling, *quid pro quo,* and back-scratching. Normally there is little need for the members to spell out what is expected when one gives or receives assistance. "He keeps his word" is high praise in Congress but the word, if the relationship is good, need not be spoken. Most of the bargaining in Congress is, in short, implicit.

To become an influential leader in such a system requires much more than seniority. Influence in Congress is earned, not bestowed. Those men whose influence transcends their own vote have made use of whatever limited formal advantages they are given plus—and this is the vital factor—their skill at exchanging benefits with their colleagues. No one, neither the Speaker nor the most influential committee chairman, commands; he negotiates.

Compared with leaders of many organizations, committee chairmen have few material incentives or rewards with which to negotiate. A committee member's salary, for example, is not dependent upon how well he performs in the committee, his attendance record at committee meetings, or the number of hours he spends each week on committee business. Nor does the chairman have control over other common rewards, such as stock options, insurance plans, paid vacations, and the like. He may, of course, allocate committee funds so some members can travel to boring conferences in exciting places but in the case of the Ways and Means Committee the Chairman is notoriously frugal on such matters. How, then, does Mills, by using the limited rewards and favors at his disposal, induce the members to make contributions to the Committee's work and to his own objectives?

Before discussing Mills's use of rewards it should be noted that by constantly guarding the Committee's reputation in the House he is in effect protecting one of the most significant rewards the members have. Like leaders of all groups the Chairman relates the organization to others and this function is particularly important in the House where the tendency is strong for committees to be equated with and judged in terms of the chairman. If the Ways and Means Committee ranks high in the House it is partly because of Mills and his leadership.

To some people decision-making through bargaining and exchange of favors has pejorative connotations. It contrasts with making decisions according to a normative "rational" model: Step 1: problem; Step 2: weigh pros and cons of alternatives; Step 3: study merits; Step 4: make decision. Congressmen are no less sensitive to the pejorative aspects of exchange than other decision-makers; indeed, given the persistence of the rumor that legislatures are bastions of logrolling, congressmen are probably more likely than others to deny or discount the importance of the exchanges that occur. This makes gathering of evidence on exchange in Congress difficult. Bargaining is an intensely personal relationship among the members, one they are reluctant to discuss with outsiders.

It is true, nonetheless, that bargains, implicit or explicit, are made in Congress, and that exchanges of rewards and favors are inevitably associated with the decision-making process.

But going beyond the assertion that men such as Mills use rewards and favors to build good relationships with other members, though necessary, is not easy. With the difficulties clearly in mind, it was decided to attack the problem by asking the members of the Committee, point-blank, how they stood with Mills on the exchange of rewards and favors. It was clear that Mills was the source of at least some rewards for the members, in addition to the rewarding aspects of his leadership discussed above, and it was felt that Mills probably did more for the members than he requested of them. If true, this is another reason why the members are inclined to respond favorably to his leads and, though not the only reason for his influence, is a reason.

Accordingly, 18 members of the Committee (ten Democrats and eight Republicans) were asked the following question:

In the normal course of passing legislation Mills has the opportunity of doing a number of things for the members. He also calls on members to do things for him occasionally. In your relations with Mills how do you stand: would you say you have done more for him, he has done more for you, or are you about even?

. . .

Table 2 presents the responses. As expected, most of the members replied that in their opinion Mills has done more for them than they have for him, a close second was the response that it does not work that way in the Committee, four members felt they are about even with the Chairman, and only one man felt the balance favored Mills. As we shall see, this man's reply was one of the most interesting received.

Table 2 Members' Estimates of Their Bargaining Position with the Chairman

Responses	Democrats	Republicans
1. Mills has done more for me.	2	5
2. It doesn't work that way.	4	2
3. We are about even.	3	1
4. I've done more for him.	1	0

As was not expected, but perhaps should have been, the Republican members of the Committee feel more in Mills's debt than the Democrats, a finding which supports the rather common Republican observation that Mills tends to take the Committee Democrats for granted while he pays relatively more attention to the minority members. More than half of the Republicans who were asked the question, and fully half of the ten Republicans on the Committee, said that Mills has done more for them than vice versa. Only two of the ten Democrats replied in kind.

Two Republicans who said Mills has done *much* more for them than they have reciprocated revealed how they felt about Mills in the process, and why it is that on some questions they are likely to be influenced by him. The first Republican stressed Mills's loyalty to the members of the Committee, regardless of party affiliation. "If I want a letter any time for my campaign, support for reelection, he'll give it. A picture with him—any time. He's loyal with his members and I appreciate this." He also discounted his ability to repay the Chairman: "He's a hundred thousand watts and I can't light that candle." When asked if he ever used a letter from Mills in his campaign he

said no, but that he has used a picture of himself with the Chairman. Moreover, he thinks the picture has helped him,

I think it helps you that the Chairman hasn't put you in the isolation box. I'd love to
have him come out to my district and give a speech. Not an endorsement, just a speech.
I'd love to show him to my businessmen. Why, he'd draw a crowd twice as big as I
do. I think he's the top fiscal brain in the country.

The second Republican has had Mills out to his district for a speech. Some
local people contacted him about inviting Mills and he took the matter up
with the Chairman. His approach to Mills was impersonal: he told the Chairman that he knew how busy he was and would understand if he could not
take time to make the trip, but that these people did want him to come, so,
if possible, it would be a nice thing to do for them. Mills made the request
very personal by asking the man, "Do *you* want me to do it?" The member,
a bit reluctantly, said yes. Mills did him the favor.

But this is not the end of the exchange between Mills and the Republican,
it is the beginning. The Republican member and Mills both know, undoubtedly, that repayment of the favor will not involve defecting from the Republican side on a major party issue. It may not involve anything specific at all
for, as the member said, "Wilbur Mills is not the kind to ask you on spe-
cifics." It is important to understand that the second step in the exchange is
implicit, vague, and if Mills ever directly asks the man for assistance on
something neither one will have to recall the Chairman's trip. All the trip did
was lay the foundation for future exchanges and, since Mills did the first
favor, its value may never be completely exhausted.

. . .

A final subtlety that came out of the interviews with the Republican
members is that Mills is so cooperative and helpful with the members that
they impose their own limits on what they ask of him. The Chairman's
willingness to do favors for them is its own control on what they request.
"In fact," said one Republican, "he's so cooperative and agreeable that you,
I do at any rate, hold off on taking advantage, don't want to ask too much.
If it's something big but not quite right yet I'll hold back; something small,
I'll go to him and he'll say remind me to bring that up." Like others, this man
has received praise from Mills which he has used in his campaign for reelec-
tion.

Democratic responses to the reward question, as indicated, were much
more in the direction of discounting the importance of favors than the
Republicans. Two of the Democrats, however, did say that Mills has given
them more than he has received. One of them cited three bills which were
passed with Mills's help and, he felt, because of Mills's help. The other said,
"He's never refused me on anything—any reasonable request I've had—*and
I've never asked for anything unreasonable.*" He feels that he has repaid Mills
by, among other things, speaking for Committee bills on the floor where his
reputation as a conservative Democrat might help get some southern votes,
but in the light of the Chairman's own influence among the southerners he
feels that his efforts may be a little redundant.

One important point needs to be made about the Democratic responses: although it is true that the Democrats are less apt to say that Mills has done more for them, they feel that (a) he has done a lot for them; and/or (b) if they ever need his help he will very likely give it. Five of the seven Democrats whose answers fell in categories two and three made one or the other comment, or both. . . .

. . .

At one end of the continuum Mills may do no more for a member than agree to spend a few minutes listening to someone who has asked a member to set up a meeting with him. This costs Mills time if not agreement with the supplicant's proposals but it allows the member who acts as the middleman to impress those who have access to him, and it makes him indebted to the Chairman. Mills listens patiently to the interest group representative and the representative, informed beforehand by the Committee member not to expect Mills to give any unequivocal reaction, leaves content with having had the opportunity to state his case where it counts. To the uninitiated lobbyist this can be a disconcerting experience. One former lobbyist found Mills "always cooperative, courteous, but you could never get Wilbur Mills to take a stand. If you didn't know him well you could go out of his office thinking he agreed with you and then realize later that he didn't really say that after all." But, at the very least, the interested party has had a hearing, and a memo to a client which begins with, "Today I had a chat with Chairman Mills . . .," is an accomplishment. At election time, when he is confronted by the congressman with, "Remember that chat you had with Wilbur . . .," he is likely to respond. In between these events, the chances are good that Mills has put his arm around the member's shoulder and without reference to past favors asked if he couldn't possibly see his way clear to doing this or that, thus closing the circle of exchanges which makes up a large part of congressional life.

At the other end of the continuum, Mills may commit himself to the inclusion of some member's proposal in a Ways and Means bill and expend a great deal of energy in getting it enacted into law. The members know that because of his influence in the Committee his backing or at least his benevolent neutrality [is] important for them to implement their ideas. Mills rewards the members every time he actively supports and makes his own one of their suggestions.

The Chairman's reward base is not confined solely to assisting members meet the substantive demands of their constituents and friends. As the occupant of the formal position of leadership on the Committee he can make decisions which determine how the Committee functions, discussed above as his legitimate power, but he can also use his formal powers as rewards for the members. Too much should not be made of the little favors the Chairman does for members, but they should not be dismissed as irrelevant either. As a Democrat said, with some exaggeration, "Members have bills they want passed, members they want to get on committees, provisions they want enacted, hearings they want held—these are the little intangibles that make him powerful."

. . .

4. *Reference.* A fourth source of influence for the Chairman, one which probably stems from the above three, is that most of the members of the Committee, if not all, identify with him. The members feel a sense of oneness with him, they like being closely associated with him, they care about their relationship with him, and they are influenced by him. The Chairman, by treating the members with respect, by being fair, by being knowledgeable in the subject matter, and by being receptive to their demands and needs, has ingratiated himself with them. Consequently, when a member disagrees with Mills he does it in such a way that the disagreement does not strain their relationship and, if possible, he prefers to agree with the Chairman more often than not.

. . .

5. *Sanctions.* "You talk about a chairman who uses his power ruthlessly, you're not talking about Wilbur Mills." This comment, by a Democrat, illustrates what is by now abundantly clear: the influence of Mills in the legislative process is not based on the sanctions that he, as the Committee Chairman, could use. Sanctions are defined as actions designed to bring about results through non-physical coercion or force and hence, in contrast to rewards, generate negative effect on the part of other members of a group.

The mark of Mills's leadership is that in doing the job as he defines it he relies on rewards, favors, expertise, persuasion, negotiation, and bargaining, not on coercing the members by using the sanctions that are available to him.

Unlike some committee chairmen, such as Graham Barden of North Carolina who chaired the Education and Labor Committee for eight years, Mills has not used his authority as chairman in such a way as to provoke extreme hostility—mixed with grudging respect—from the members. Mills's objective has been to get legislation out of his Committee with enough support behind it to pass in the House. Barden's objective was to kill and, failing that, delay as long as possible federal aid to education, and his behavior as chairman reflected his perception of the Education and Labor Committee's job.

With fundamentally different objectives Mills and Barden typify fundamentally different styles of leadership in the House. To marshal a majority Mills allows members and witnesses to speak at length; to prevent a majority from coalescing Barden permitted and encouraged the filibuster. To mark up legislation Mills holds the Committee to a stiff regimen; to thwart legislation Barden called meetings irregularly and established ad hoc subcommittees which he controlled. To proceed with speed Mills actively seeks a quorum; to procrastinate Barden banged the gavel and adjourned when a quorum was not immediately present. To ease the burdens of formulating legislation Mills surrounds the Committee with expert help; to heighten these burdens Barden kept the staff weak. To promote a workmanlike atmosphere in the Committee Mills seeks consensus; to promote confusion Barden sowed dissensus. And, finally, to pass the bill Mills carefully maps the House terrain; to defeat the bill Barden allocated disproportionate time to opponents and once, near the end of the proceedings, threw the House into a frenzy by resigning as floor manager.

. . .

Thus Mills, in seeking a consensus, relies on four of the five bases of influence: expertise, legitimacy, rewards, and reference. In the Committee's deliberations he will, if possible, stay in the background by letting the active members, with some coaxing, hit upon the compromise through their own efforts but, since the Quakerlike sense of the meeting may evade them, he will often articulate it and when he does the Committee has made a "decision," always tentative depending upon further developments. The low amount of negative effect expressed toward the Chairman indicates that his style of leadership is approved of by the members, and their agreement on the way he influences them through four of the five bases of influence helps explain why, when he intervenes in the discussion, his suggestions often constitute a Committee decision.

3. Mills: The Swing Vote

When Mills persuades the members of the Committee to make certain decisions it may be on the basis of his expertise, or his influence may be based on the way he has handled interpersonal relations in the Committee, or it may be because the members are indifferent on the outcomes. But then again it may be none of these. It may be a simple matter of arithmetical influence: he, for all the reasons discussed above, has the votes. The Chairman's influence in the Committee is on some issues closely related to his position as the crucial swing vote between the coalitions that appear most often on Ways and Means issues. If the parties split cleanly Mills and the 14 Democrats beat the Republicans 15–10. If an issue divides the Committee along liberal-conservative lines Mills and 12 Democrats can beat the Republicans and two conservative Democrats 13–12; or, in some cases, Mills and two conservative Democrats plus the Republicans can defeat the 12 Democrats 13–12. Mills, as a moderate on policy questions, straddles the coalitions in Ways and Means and, because he does, it is a rare coalition that sees him on the losing side. For many years two conservative Democrats, A. Sydney Herlong of Florida (who left the Committee in 1968) and John Watts of Kentucky, played leading roles in the coalition make-up of the Committee. Both men were close to Mills and if the other Democrats on the Committee banded together into a 12-vote bloc they still lost 13–12 without the Chairman. With the Chairman, the 12 Democrats won by the same margin. The pivot was the Chairman.

. . .

Forty record votes in the Committee have been collected since Mills became chairman in 1958, and the results confirm the dominant position of the Chairman in the Committee. These votes are not comprehensive because more votes were taken in the Committee than were reported. It must be noted, too, that many important issues never come to a vote in the Committee. For example, in 1964 Cecil King did not force medicare to a vote because he knew it would lose.

Of the 40 votes, the Chairman has been on the losing side only seven times: a 1959 bill dealing with interest rates, a 1961 bill regarding tax treatment of the self-employed, a 1962 vote on unemployment insurance, two votes during the consideration of the tax reduction bill in 1963, a social security vote in 1964, and a 1966 vote on providing federal standards for unemployment compensation programs. Based on available data, therefore, Mills's reputation as a winner in the Committee is deserved.

. . .

4. Conclusion

An intensive look has been taken at the Chairman of Ways and Means because, in the eyes of the members and in the eyes of those associated with the Committee, he is the central figure around whom much of the Committee's life revolves. Contrary to the impression one sometimes receives from newspaper stories about the "all-powerful" Chairman Mills, he is perhaps as responsive to the Committee as the Committee is to him. Great influence with the members he no doubt has, but it is influence earned by the way he approaches his job and develops its potential. Ways and Means is highly centralized under Mills but the Committee's policy decisions emerge from an exhaustive—and collegial—process. The decisions of the Committee are shaped and articulated by Mills, but if his word comes close to being law in the Committee it is because he has listened well to the words of others, particularly to the ranking Republican, John Byrnes. The fact that Mills legitimates Committee decisions in no way lessens his leadership of the Committee, but it is a particular kind of leadership, a kind very likely to be effective given the nature of the group he leads.

Mills's influence in the Committee is also attributable to his pivotal position in the blocs that form on policy questions in the Committee. The Chairman, known as a leader who keeps his position, if he has one, to himself, has good reason to be cautious on the controversies surrounding Ways and Means. By letting others commit themselves before he does he follows a winning strategy which has paid rich dividends: he never loses, except once in a while. And because he leads the members as he does he can sometimes persuade enough of them to help him win by voting present, by voting with him, or by not voting at all.

It remains to be seen whether the analytical framework used in studying the leadership of Mills, the variables which are important in understanding him, and the five bases of influence discussed in connection with his influence will be useful in future research on leadership in Congress. Yet it appears clear than an understanding of the legislative process—including the outputs of that process—requires attention to individual leaders, their followers, and how the two interact. This study is intended as a step in that direction.

12

The Scope and Bias of the Pressure System

E. E. Schattschneider

The scope of conflict is an aspect of the scale of political organization and the extent of political competition. The size of the constituencies being mobilized, the inclusiveness or exclusiveness of the conflicts people expect to develop have a bearing on all theories about how politics is or should be organized. In other words, nearly all theories about politics have something to do with the question of who can get into the fight and who is to be excluded.

Every regime is a testing ground for theories of this sort. More than any other system American politics provides the raw materials for testing the organizational assumptions of two contrasting kinds of politics, *pressure politics* and *party politics*. The concepts that underlie these forms of politics constitute the raw stuff of a general theory of political action. The basic issue between the two patterns of organization is one of size and scope of conflict; pressure groups are small-scale organizations while political parties are very large-scale organizations. One need not be surprised, therefore, that the partisans of large-scale and small-scale organizations differ passionately, because the outcome of the political game depends on the scale on which it is played.

To understand the controversy about the scale of political organization it is necessary first to take a look at some theories about interest-group politics. Pressure groups have played a remarkable role in American politics, but they have played an even more remarkable role in American political theory. Considering the political condition of the country in the first third of the twentieth century, it was probably inevitable that the discussion of special-interest pressure groups should lead to development of "group" theories of politics in which an attempt is made to explain everything in terms of group activity, i.e., an attempt to formulate a universal group theory. Since one of the best ways to test an idea is to ride it into the ground, political theory has unquestionably been improved by the heroic attempt to create a political universe revolving about the group. Now that we have a number of drastic statements of the group theory of politics pushed to a great extreme, we ought to be able to see what the limitations of the idea are.

Political conditions in the first third of the present century were extremely hospitable to the idea. The role of business in the strongly sectional Republican system from 1896 to 1932 made the dictatorship of business seem to be a part of the eternal order of things. Moreover, the regime as a whole seemed to be so stable that questions about the survival of the American community did not arise. The general interests of the community were easily overlooked under these circumstances.

Nevertheless, in spite of the excellent and provocative scholarly work done by Beard, Latham, Truman, Leiserson, Dahl, Lindblom, Laski and others, the group theory of politics is beset with difficulties. The difficulties are theoretical, growing in part out of sheer overstatements of the idea and in part out of some confusion about the nature of modern government.

One difficulty running through the literature of the subject results from the attempt to explain *everything* in terms of the group theory. On general grounds it would be remarkable indeed if a single hypothesis explained everything about so complex a subject as American politics. Other difficulties have grown out of the fact that group concepts have been stated in terms so universal that the subject seems to have no shape or form.

The question is: Are pressure groups the universal basic ingredient of all political situations, and do they explain everything? To answer this question it is necessary to review a bit of rudimentary political theory.

Two modest reservations might be made merely to test the group dogma. We might clarify our ideas if (1) we explore more fully the possibility of making a distinction between public-interest groups and special-interest groups and (2) if we distinguish between organized and unorganized groups. These reservations do not disturb the main body of group theory, but they may be useful when we attempt to define general propositions more precisely. If both of these distinctions can be validated, we may get hold of something that has scope and limits and is capable of being defined. The awkwardness of a discussion of political phenomena in terms of universals is that the subject has no beginning or end; it is impossible to distinguish one subject from another or to detect the bias of the forces involved because scope and bias are aspects of the limitations of the subject. It cannot really be said that we have seen a subject until we have seen its outer limits and thus are able to draw a line between one subject and another.

We might begin to break the problem into its component parts by exploring the distinction between public and private interests. If we can validate this distinction, we shall have established one of the boundaries of the subject.

As a matter of fact, the distinction between *public* and *private* interests is a thoroughly respectable one; it is one of the oldest known to political theory. In the literature of the subject the public interest refers to general or common interests shared by all or by substantially all members of the community. Presumably no community exists unless there is some kind of community of interests, just as there is no nation without some notion of national interests. If it is really impossible to distinguish between private and public interests the group theorists have produced a revolution in political thought so great that it is impossible to foresee its consequences. For this reason the distinction ought to be explored with great care.

. . .

In contrast with the common interests are the special interests. The implication of this term is that these are interests shared by only a few people or a fraction of the community; they *exclude* others and may be *adverse* to them. A special interest is exclusive in about the same way as private property is exclusive. In a complex society it is not surprising that there are some interests that are shared by all or substantially all members of the community and some interests that are not shared so widely. The distinction is useful precisely because conflicting claims are made by people about the nature of their interests in controversial matters.

. . .

The distinction between public and special interests is an indispensable tool for the study of politics. To abolish the distinction is to make a shambles of political science by treating things that are different as if they were alike. The kind of distinction made here is a commonplace of all literature dealing with human society, but *if we accept it we have established one of the outer limits of the subject;* we have split the world of interests in half and have taken one step toward defining the scope of this kind of political conflict.

We can now examine the second distinction, the distinction between organized and unorganized groups. The question here is not whether the distinction can be made but whether or not it is worth making. Organization has been described as "merely a stage or degree of interaction" in the development of a group.

The proposition is a good one, but what conclusions do we draw from it? We do not dispose of the matter by calling the distinction between organized and unorganized groups a "mere" difference of degree because some of the greatest differences in the world are differences of degree. As far as special-interest politics is concerned the implication to be avoided is that a few workmen who habitually stop at a corner saloon for a glass of beer are essentially the same as the United States Army because the difference between them is merely one of degree. At this point we have a distinction that makes a difference. The distinction between organized and unorganized groups is worth making because it ought to alert us against an analysis which begins as a general group theory of politics but ends with a defense of pressure politics as inherent, universal, permanent and inevitable. This kind of confusion comes from the loosening of categories involved in the universalization of group concepts.

Since the beginning of intellectual history, scholars have sought to make progress in their work by distinguishing between things that are unlike and by dividing their subject matter into categories to examine them more intelligently. It is something of a novelty, therefore, when group theorists reverse this process by discussing their subject in terms so universal that they wipe out all categories, because this is the dimension in which it is least possible to understand anything.

If we are able, therefore, to distinguish between public and private interests and between organized and unorganized groups we have marked out the major boundaries of the subject; *we have given the subject shape and scope.* We are now in a position to attempt to define the area we want to explore. Having cut the pie into four pieces, we can now appropriate the piece we want and leave the rest to someone else. For a multitude of reasons *the most likely field of study is that of the organized, special-interest groups.* The advantage of concentrating on organized groups is that they are known, identifiable and recognizable. The advantage of concentrating on special-interest groups is that they have one important characteristic in common: they are all exclusive. This piece of the pie (the organized special-interest groups) we shall call the *pressure system.* The pressure system has boundaries we can define; we can fix its scope and make an attempt to estimate its bias.

. . .

By the time a group has developed the kind of interest that leads it to organize it may be assumed that it has also developed some kind of political bias because *organization is itself a mobilization of bias in preparation for action.* Since these groups can be identified and since they have memberships (i.e., they include and exclude people), it is possible to think of the *scope* of the system.

. . .

The business or upper-class bias of the pressure system shows up everywhere. Businessmen are four or five times as likely to write to their congressmen as manual laborers are. College graduates are far more apt to write to their congressmen than people in the lowest educational category are.

. . .

. . . The obverse side of the coin is that large areas of the population appear to be wholly outside of the system of private organization. A study made by Ira Reid of a Philadelphia area showed that in a sample of 963 persons, 85 per cent belonged to no civic or charitable organization and 74 per cent belonged to no occupational, business, or professional associations, while another Philadelphia study of 1,154 women showed that 55 per cent belonged to no associations of any kind.

. . .

The class bias of associational activity gives meaning to the limited scope of the pressure system, because *scope and bias are aspects of the same tendency.* The data raise a serious question about the validity of the proposition that special-interest groups are a universal form of political organization reflecting *all* interests. As a matter of fact, to suppose that everyone participates in pressure-group activity and that all interests get themselves organized in the pressure system is to destroy the meaning of this form of politics. The pressure system makes sense only as the political instrument of a segment of the community. It gets results by being selective and biased; *if everybody got into the act the unique advantages of this form of organization would be destroyed, for it is possible that if all interests could be mobilized the result would be a stalemate.*

Special-interest organizations are most easily formed when they deal with small numbers of individuals who are acutely aware of their exclusive interests. To describe the conditions of pressure-group organization in this way is, however, to say that it is primarily a business phenomenon. Aside from a few very large organizations (the churches, organized labor, farm organizations, and veterans' organizations) the residue is a small segment of the population. *Pressure politics is essentially the politics of small groups.*

The vice of the groupist theory is that it conceals the most significant aspects of the system. The flaw in the pluralist heaven is that the heavenly chorus sings with a strong upper-class accent. Probably about 90 per cent of the people cannot get into the pressure system.

. . .

A Critique of Group Theories of Politics

It is extremely unlikely that the vogue of group theories of politics would have attained its present status if its basic assumptions had not been first established by some concept of economic determinism. The economic interpretation of politics has always appealed to those political philosophers who have sought a single prime mover, a sort of philosopher's stone of political science around which to organize their ideas. The search for a single, ultimate cause has something to do with the attempt to explain *everything* about politics in terms of group concepts. The logic of economic determinism is to *identify the origins of conflict and to assume the conclusion.* This kind of thought has some of the earmarks of an illusion. The somnambulatory quality of thinking in this field appears also in the tendency of research to deal only with successful pressure campaigns or the willingness of scholars to be satisfied with having placed pressure groups on the scene of the crime without following through to see if the effect can really be attributed to the cause. What makes this kind of thinking remarkable is the fact that in political contests there are as many failures as there are successes. Where in the literature of pressure politics are the failures?

Students of special-interest politics need a more sophisticated set of intellectual tools than they have developed thus far. The theoretical problem involved in the search for a single cause is that all power relations in a democracy are reciprocal. Trying to find the original cause is like trying to find the first wave of the ocean.

. . .

The very expression "pressure politics" invites us to misconceive the role of special-interest groups in politics. The word "pressure" implies the use of some kind of force, a form of intimidation, something other than reason and information, to induce public authorities to act against their own best judgment. In Latham's famous statement . . . the legislature is described as a "referee" who "ratifies" and "records" the "balance of power" among the contending groups.

It is hard to imagine a more effective way of saying that Congress has no mind or force of its own or that Congress is unable to invoke new forces that might alter the equation.

Actually the outcome of political conflict is not like the "resultant" of opposing forces in physics. To assume that the forces in a political situation could be diagrammed as a physicist might diagram the resultant of opposing physical forces is to wipe the slate clean of all remote, general and public considerations for the protection of which civil societies have been instituted.

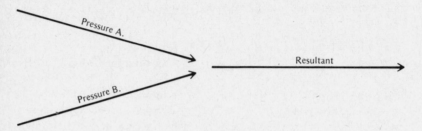

Moreover, the notion of "pressure" distorts the image of the power relations involved. *Private conflicts are taken into the public arena precisely because someone wants to make certain that the power ratio among the private interests most immediately involved shall not prevail.* To treat a conflict as a mere test of the strength of the private interests is to leave out the most significant factors. This is so true that it might indeed be said that the only way to preserve private power ratios is to keep conflicts out of the public arena.

The assumption that it is only the "interested" who count ought to be re-examined in view of the foregoing discussion. The tendency of the literature of pressure politics has been to neglect the low-tension force of large numbers because it *assumes that the equation of forces is fixed at the outset.*

Given the assumptions made by the group theorists, the attack on the idea of the majority is completely logical. The assumption is that conflict is monopolized narrowly by the parties immediately concerned. There is no room for a majority when conflict is defined so narrowly. It is a great deficiency of the group theory that it has found no place in the political system for the majority. The force of the majority is of an entirely different order of magnitude, something not to be measured by pressure-group standards.

Instead of attempting to exterminate all political forms, organizations and alignments that do not qualify as pressure groups, would it not be better to attempt to make a synthesis, covering the whole political system and finding a place for all kinds of political life?

One possible synthesis of pressure politics and party politics might be produced by *describing politics as the socialization of conflict.* That is to say, the political process is a sequence: conflicts are initiated by highly motivated, high-tension groups so directly and immediately involved that it is difficult for them to see the justice of competing claims. As long as the conflicts of these groups remain *private* (carried on in terms of economic competition, reciprocal denial of goods and services, private negotiations and bargaining, struggles for corporate control or competition for membership), no political process is initiated. Conflicts become political only when an attempt is made to involve the wider public. Pressure politics might be described as a stage in the socialization of conflict. This analysis makes pressure politics an integral part of all politics, including party politics.

One of the characteristic points of origin of pressure politics is a break-down of the discipline of the business community. The flight to government is perpetual. Something like this is likely to happen wherever there is a point of contact between competing power systems. It is the *losers in intrabusiness conflict who seek redress from the public authority. The dominant business interests resist appeals to the government.* The role of the government as the patron of the defeated private interest sheds light on its function as the critic of private power relations.

Since the contestants in private conflicts are apt to be unequal in strength, it follows that *the most powerful special interests want private settlements* because they are able to dictate the outcome as long as the conflict remains private. If A is a hundred times as strong as B he does not welcome the intervention of a third party because he expects to impose his own terms on B; he wants to isolate B. He is especially opposed to the intervention of public authority, because public authority represents the most overwhelming form of outside intervention. Thus, if A/B = 100/1, it is obviously not to A's advantage to involve a third party a million times as strong as A and B combined. There-fore, it is the weak, not the strong, who appeal to public authority for relief. It is the weak who want to socialize conflict, i.e., to involve more and more people in the conflict until the balance of forces is changed. In the school yard it is not the bully but the defenseless smaller boys who "tell the teacher." When the teacher intervenes the balance of power in the school yard is apt to change drastically. It is the function of public authority to *modify private power relations by enlarging the scope of conflict.* Nothing could be more mis-taken than to suppose that public authority merely registers the dominance of the strong over the weak. The mere existence of public order has already ruled out a great variety of forms of private pressure. Nothing could be more confusing than to suppose that the refugees from the business community who come to Congress for relief and protection *force* Congress to do their bidding.

Evidence of the truth of this analysis may be seen in the fact that the big private interests do not necessarily win if they are involved in public conflicts with petty interests. The image of the lobbyists as primarily the agents of big business is not easy to support on the face of the record of congressional hearings, for example. The biggest corporations in the country tend to avoid the arena in which pressure groups and lobbyists fight it out before congres-sional committees. To describe this process exclusively in terms of an effort of business to intimidate congressmen is to misconceive what is actually going on.

It is probably a mistake to assume that pressure politics is the typical or even the most important relation between government and business. The pressure group is by no means the perfect instrument of the business com-munity. What does big business want? The *winners* in intrabusiness strife want (1) to be let alone (they want autonomy) and (2) to preserve the solidarity of the business community. For these purposes pressure politics is not a wholly satisfactory device. The most elementary considerations of strategy call for the business community to develop some kind of common policy more broadly based than any special-interest group is likely to be.

The political influence of business depends on the kind of solidarity that, on the one hand, leads all business to rally to the support of *any* businessman in trouble with the government, and on the other hand, keeps internal business disputes out of the public arena. In this system businessmen resist the impulse to attack each other in public and discourage the efforts of individual members of the business community to take intrabusiness conflicts into politics.

The attempt to mobilize a united front of the whole business community does not resemble the classical concept of pressure politics. The logic of business politics is to keep peace within the business community by supporting as far as possible all claims that business groups make for themselves. The tendency is to support all businessmen who have conflicts with the government and support all businessmen in conflict with labor. In this way *special-interest politics can be converted into party policy.* The search is for a broad base of political mobilization grounded on the strategic need for political organization on a wider scale than is possible in the case of the historical pressure group. Once the business community begins to think in terms of a larger scale of political organization the Republican party looms large in business politics.

It is a great achievement of American democracy that business has been forced to form a political organization designed to win elections, i.e., has been forced to compete for power in the widest arena in the political system. On the other hand, *the power of the Republican party to make terms with business rests on the fact that business cannot afford to be isolated.*

The Republican party has played a major role in *the political organization of the business community,* a far greater role than many students of politics seem to have realized. The influence of business in the Republican party is great, but it is never absolute because business is remarkably dependent on the party. The business community is too small, it arouses too much antagonism, and its aims are too narrow to win the support of a popular majority. The political education of business is a function of the Republican party that can never be done so well by anyone else.

In the management of the political relations of the business community, the Republican party is much more important than any combination of pressure groups ever could be. The success of special interests in Congress is due less to the "pressure" exerted by these groups than it is due to the fact that Republican members of Congress are committed in advance to a general probusiness attitude. The notion that business groups coerce Republican congressmen into voting for their bills underestimates the whole Republican posture in American politics.

It is not easy to manage the political interests of the business community because there is a perpetual stream of losers in intrabusiness conflicts who go to the government for relief and protection. It has not been possible therfore to maintain perfect solidarity, and when solidarity is breached the government is involved almost automatically. The fact that business has not become hopelessly divided and that it has retained great influence in American politics has been due chiefly to the over-all mediating role played by the Republican party. There has never been a pressure group or a combination of pressure groups capable of performing this function.

13

How the Farmers Get What They Want

Theodore J. Lowi

In his Farm Message of January 31, President Johnson proposed that Congress establish a bipartisan commission to investigate the concentration of power in the food industry. In the same message the President called for new legislation to strengthen farmer co-operatives, to encourage their expansion through merger and acquisition, and to provide them with further exemptions from the anti-trust laws.

This was the beginning of the "Johnson round" in agriculture. It is part of a familiar pattern. An attack on the food industry's market power, coupled with proposals for expanded and stronger farm co-operatives, is obviously not an attack on concentration itself. Rather it is an attack on the intervention of nonagricultural groups into strictly agricultural affairs.

That agricultural affairs should be handled strictly within the agricultural community is a basic political principle established before the turn of the century and maintained since then without serious re-examination. As a result, agriculture has become neither public nor private enterprise. It is a system of self-government in which each leading farm interest controls a segment of agriculture through a delegation of national sovereignty. Agriculture has emerged as a largely self-governing federal estate within the Federal structure of the United States.

President Johnson recognized these facts within three weeks of his accession when he summoned a conference of agricultural leaders to formulate a program by which agriculture should be served and regulated. The most recent concession to agriculture's self-government was the wheat-cotton bill. Because cotton supports were too high, the cotton interests wrote a bill providing for a subsidy of six to eight cents a pound to mills in order to keep them competitive with foreign cotton and domestic rayon without touching the price supports. On the other hand, wheat supports were too low because wheat farmers last year in referendum overwhelmingly rejected President Kennedy's plan to provide some Federal regulation along with supports. The wheat section of the new act calls for a program whereby wheat farmers may voluntarily comply with acreage reduction for subsidies of up to seventy cents a bushel but without the Federal supply regulations. The press called this a major legislative victory for Mr. Johnson, but the credit is not his. That the press could see this as a victory for anyone but organized cotton and wheat is a testimonial to the total acceptance by President, press, and public of the principle that private agricultural interests alone govern agriculture and should do so.

The reasons for agriculture's self-government are deep-rooted, and the lessons to be drawn are important to the future of American politics. For a century agriculture has been out of step with American economic development. Occasional fat years have only created unreal expectations, to be undercut by the more typical lean years.

Quite early, farmers discovered the value of politics as a counterweight to industry's growth and concentration. Land-grant and homesteading acts were followed by governmental services in research and education. Continuing distress led to bolder demands. First there were efforts to effect a redistribution of wealth in favor of agriculture. As a debtor class, farmers saw inflation as the solution, and Bryan was their spokesman for cheaper money and cheaper credit. The monopolies, the railroads, the grain merchants and other processors, the banks, and the brokers were to be deprived of power over the market by dissolution or by severe restraints. Next, farmers sought solutions by emulating the business system: the co-operative to restrain domestic trade and international dumping over high tariff walls to restrain international trade. Yet all these mechanisms either were not enacted or did not live up to expectations.

With the coming of the New Deal and with its help, organized agriculture turned to self-regulation. The system created during the 1930's has endured to this day, and with only a few marginal additions and alterations is accepted almost unanimously by farm leaders. Self-regulation might have taken several forms, the most likely one being a national system of farm-leader representation within a farmers' NRA. Instead, a more complicated system of highly decentralized and highly autonomous subgovernments developed, largely for Constitutional reasons. Agriculture was the most "local" of the manufacturing groups the Federal government was trying to reach. The appearance if not the reality of decentralizing Federal programs through farmer-elected local committees helped avoid strains on the interstate commerce clause of the Constitution. But this avoidance of Constitutional troubles created very special political difficulties.

The Local Committees

The Federal Extension Service shows how the system works. It is "co-operative" in that it shares the job of farm improvement with the states, the land-grant colleges, the county governments, and the local associations of farmers. The county agent is actually employed by the local associations. In the formative years, the aid of local chambers of commerce was enlisted, the local association being the "farm bureau" of the chamber. In order to coordinate local activities and to make more effective claims for additional outside assistance, these farm bureaus were organized into state farm bureau federations. The American Farm Bureau Federation, formed at the Agriculture College of Cornell University in 1919, was used as a further step toward amalgamation. To this day there is a close relationship between the farm bureaus, the land-grant colleges, and the Extension Service. This tranformation of an administrative arrangement into a political system has been repeated in nearly all the agricultural programs during recent decades. The Extension Service exercises few controls from the top. There are cries of "Federal encroachment" at the mere suggestion in Washington that the Department of Agriculture should increase its supervision of the extension programs or coordinate them with other Federal activities.

As the financial stakes grow larger, the pattern of local self-government remains the same. Price support—the "parity program"—is run by the thousands of farmer-elected county committees that function alongside but quite independently of the other local committees. Acreage allotments to bring supply down and prices up are apportioned among the states by the Agricultural Stabilization and Conservation Service. State committees of farmers apportion the allotment among the counties. The farmer-elected county Stabilization and Conservation Committees receive the county allotment.

These committees made the original acreage allotments among individual farmers back in the 1930's; today, they make new allotments, work out adjustments and review complaints regarding allotments, determine whether quotas have been complied with, inspect and approve storage facilities, and perform as the court of original jurisdiction on violations of price-support rules and on eligibility for parity payments. The committees are also vitally important in the campaigns for the two-thirds vote required to fix high price supports. Congress determines the general level of supports, and the Secretary of Agriculture proclaims the national acreage quotas for adjusting the supply to the guaranteed price. But the locally elected committees stand between the farmer and Washington.

Most other agricultural programs have evolved similarly. Each is independent of the others, and any conflicts or overlapping mandates have been treated as nonexistent or beyond the jurisdiction of any one agency. The Soil Conservation Service operates through its independent soil-conservation districts, of which there were 2,936 in 1963, involving ninety-six per cent of the nation's farms. Each district's farmer-elected committee is considered a unit of local government. The Farmer Co-operative Service operates through the member-elected boards of directors of the farm co-ops. In agricultural credit, local self-government is found in even greater complexity. The Farm Credit Administration exists outside the Department of Agriculture and is made up of not one but three separate bodies politic, a triangular system mostly farmer-owned and totally farmer-controlled.

Ten Systems and Politics

The ten principal self-governing systems in agriculture, in fiscal 1962, disposed of $5.6 billion of the total of $6.7 billion in expenditures passing through the Department of Agriculture. During the calendar year 1962, $5.8 billion in loans was handled similarly. This combined amount represents a large portion of the total of Federal activity outside national defense.

Each of the ten systems has become a powerful political instrumentality. The self-governing local units become one important force in a system that administers a program and maintains the autonomy of that program against political forces emanating from other agricultural programs, from antagonistic farm and nonfarm interests, from Congress, from the Secretary of Agriculture, and from the President. To many a farmer, the local outpost of one or another of these systems *is* the government.

The politics within each system is built upon a triangular trading pattern involving the central agency, a Congressional committee or subcommittee, and the local district farmer committees (usually federated in some national or regional organization). Each side of the triangle complements and supports the other two.

The Extension Service, for example, is one side of the triangle completed by the long-tenure "farm bureau" members of the Agriculture Committees in Congress and, at the local level, the American Farm Bureau Federation with its local committees. Further group support is provided by two intimately related groups, the Association of Land Grant Colleges and Universities and the National Association of County Agricultural Agents.

Another such triangle unites the Soil Conservation Service, the Agriculture subcommittee of the House Appropriations Committee, and the local districts organized in the energetic National Association of Soil Conservation Districts. Further support comes from the Soil Conservation Society of America (mainly professionals) and the former Friends of the Land, now the Izaak Walton League of America.

Probably the most complex of the systems embraces the parity program. It connects the Agricultural Stabilization and Conservation Service with the eight (formerly ten) commodity subcommittees of the House Agriculture Committee and the dozens of separately organized groups representing the various commodities. (Examples: National Cotton Council, American Wool Growers Association, American Cranberry Growers Association.) These groups and congressmen draw support from the local price-support committees wherever a particular commodity is grown.

The Farmer Had His Way

These systems have a vigorous capacity to maintain themselves and to resist encroachment. They have such institutional legitimacy that they have become practically insulated from the three central sources of democratic political responsibility. Thus, within the Executive branch, they are autonomous. Secretaries of Agriculture have tried and failed to consolidate or even to co-ordinate related programs. Within Congress, they are sufficiently powerful to be able to exercise an effective veto or create a stalemate. And they are almost totally removed from the view, not to mention the control, of the general public. (Throughout the 1950's, Victor Anfuso of Brooklyn was the only member of the House Agriculture Committee from a nonfarm constituency.)

Important cases illustrate their power:

¶ In 1947, Secretary of Agriculture Clinton P. Anderson proposed a consolidation of all soil-conservation, price-support, and FHA programs into one committee system with a direct line from the committees to the Secretary.

Bills were prepared providing for consolidation within the price-support committees. Contrary bills provided for consolidation under soil conservation districts. The result: stalemate. In 1948, a leading farm senator proposed consolidation of the programs under the local associations of the Extension Service. Immediately a House farm leader introduced a contrary bill. The result: continuing stalemate.

¶ In Waco, Texas, on October 14, 1952, Presidential candidate Eisenhower said: "I would like to see in every county all Federal farm agencies under the same roof." Pursuant to this promise, Secretary Ezra Taft Benson issued a series of orders during early 1953 attempting to bring about consolidation of local units as well as unification at the top. Finally, amid cries of "sneak attack" and "agricrat," Benson proclaimed that "any work on the further consolidation of county and state offices . . . shall be suspended."

¶ From the very beginning, Secretary Benson sought to abandon rigid price supports and bring actual supports closer to market prices. In 1954, as he was beginning to succeed, Congress enacted a "commodity set-aside" by which $2.5 billion of surplus commodities already held by the government were declared to be a "frozen reserve" for national defense. Since the Secretary's power to cut price supports depends heavily upon the amount of government-owned surplus carried over from previous years, the commodity set-aside was a way of freezing parity as well as reserves. Benson eventually succeeded in reducing supports on the few commodities over which he had authority. But thanks to the set-aside, Congress, between fiscal 1952 and 1957, helped increase the value of commodities held by the government from $1.1 billion to $5.3 billion. What appeared, therefore, to be a real Republican-policy shift amounted to no more than giving back with one hand what had been taken away by the other.

¶ President Eisenhower's first budget sought to abolish farm home-building and improvement loans by eliminating the budgetary request and by further requesting that the 1949 authorization law be allowed to expire. Congress overrode his request in 1953 and each succeeding year, and the President answered Congress with a year-by-year refusal to implement the farm housing program. In 1956, when the President asked again explicitly for elimination of the program, he was rebuffed. The Housing subcommittee of the House Banking and Currency Committee added to the President's omnibus housing bill a renewal of the farm housing program, plus an authorization for $500 million in loans over a five-year period, and the bill passed with a Congressional mandate to use the funds. They were used thereafter at a rate of about $75 million a year.

¶ On March 16, 1961, President Kennedy produced a "radically different" farm program in a special message to Congress. For the first time in the history of price supports, the bill called for surplus control through quotas placed on bushels, tons, or other units, rather than on acreage. An acreage allotment allows the farmer to produce as much as he can on the reduced acreage in cultivation. For example, in the first ten years or so of acreage control, acreage under cultivation dropped by about four per cent, while actual production rose by fifteen per cent. The Kennedy proposal called for national committees of farmers to be elected to work out the actual program.

This more stringent type of control was eliminated from the omnibus bill in the Agriculture Committees of both chambers and there were no attempts to restore them during floor debate. Last-minute efforts by Secretary Orville L. Freeman to up the ante, offering to raise wheat supports from $1.79 to $2.00, were useless. Persistence by the administration led eventually to rejection by wheat farmers in 1963 of all high price supports and acreage controls.

The politics of this rejected referendum is of general significance. Despite all the blandishments and inducements of the administration, the farmer had his way. The local price-support committees usually campaign in these referendums for the Department of Agriculture, but this time they did not. And thousands of small farmers, eligible to vote for the first time, joined with the local leadership to help defeat the referendum. It is not so odd that wheat farmers would reject a proposal that aims to regulate them more strictly than before. What is odd is that only wheat farmers are allowed to decide the matter. It seems that in agriculture, as in many other fields, the regulators are powerless without the consent of the regulated.

Agriculture is the field where the distinction between public and private has been almost completely eliminated, not by public expropriation of private domain but by private expropriation of public domain. For more than a generation, Americans have succeeded in expanding the public sphere without giving thought to the essential democratic question of how each expansion is to be effected. The creation of private governments has profoundly limited the capacity of the public government to govern responsibly and flexibly.

14
The Subcommittee Chairman: Politics of Fear

Nick Kotz

With the sensitive instincts of a successful career bureaucrat, Dr. George Irving scanned the list of states scheduled for the National Nutrition Survey. Halfway down the column his glance froze, and he quickly dialed Congressman Jamie Whitten, the man known in Washington as the "permanent secretary of agriculture."

"Mr. Chairman, they've got Mississippi on that malnutrition study list, and I thought you'd want to know about it," dutifully reported Irving, director of the Agriculture Department's Research Service.

For the better part of 18 years as chairman of the House Appropriations Subcommittee on Agriculture, dapper Jamie L. Whitten has held an iron hand over the Department of Agriculture's budget. The entire 107,000-man department is tuned in to the Mississippi legislator's every whim.

"George, we're not going to have another smear campaign against Mississippi, are we," declared Whitten to his informant. "You boys should be thinking about a *national* survey—and do some studies in Watts and Hough and Harlem!"

Dr. Irving alerted the government's food aid network. "Mr. Whitten wants Mississippi taken off that list," he told Department of Agriculture food administrator Rodney Leonard.

Leonard, in turn, called Dr. George Silver, a Deputy Assistant Secretary of Health, Education, and Welfare, who was responsible for the joint USDA-HEW malnutrition survey.

"Jamie Whitten's found out Mississippi is on the list and is raising hell. I think we'd better drop it," Leonard said.

Silver, recalling HEW Secretary Wilbur Cohen's order to "avoid unnecessary political friction" in choosing the sample states for the hunger survey, called Dr. Arnold Schaefer, the project chief.

"Mississippi's out—politics!" Silver said curtly.

Back at the Department of Agriculture, food administrator Leonard snapped at Jamie Whitten's informant, "You couldn't have killed the project any better if you had planned it!"

141

Thus, in August 1967, the Johnson Administration's first meaningful attempt to ascertain the facts about hunger in Mississippi was stopped cold by an executive department's fear of one congressman. This kind of bureaucratic-congressional maneuvering, exercised between the lines of law, is little understood, seldom given public scrutiny, and far too infrequently challenged. In the quiet process of hidden power, a bureaucrat in the Agriculture Department reacts more quickly to a raised eyebrow from Jamie Whitten than to a direct order from the Secretary himself. Time after time, a few words from Jamie Whitten can harden into gospel at the Department of Agriculture. Indeed, a casual Whitten statement may be so magnified as it is whispered from official to official that the response is more subservient than even the congressman had in mind.

The stocky, 59-year-old congressman is not shy about his meteroric rise from a country store in Tallahatchie County to a key position in the nation's capital. And his record is impressive—trial lawyer and state legislator at 21, district attorney for five counties at 23, U.S. congressman at 31 (in 1941), and Chairman of the Appropriations Subcommittee at 36. His steely self-confidence, studied informality, and carefully conservative clothes suggest anything but the stereotype of country-lawyer-come-to-Washington. Only the beginning of a paunch detracts from a physical sense of strength and energy that radiates from Jamie Whitten.

For all his dynamic presence, Whitten has a way of confounding a listener —or potential critic—with silky southern rhetoric. It is a test of mental agility to remember the original course of conversation, as one high USDA official noted: "When you check on things with him, Whitten can go all around the barn with you. Oftentimes you don't fully understand what he meant. So you latch onto the most obvious point you can find and act on that."

With his implicit power, Whitten doesn't *have* to threaten or be specific. In fact, as Agriculture research official George Irving pointed out about his conversation with the congressmen that led to dropping Mississippi from the national hunger survey, "He wasn't saying 'don't go to Mississippi,' he was just suggesting that we think about other places."

Bureaucratic officials who are familiar with Whitten's oblique way of expressing his ideas know also that the Mississippian can rattle off complicated economic statistics and arguments with precise logic and organized thought.

Whitten legally holds the power of the purse, and he excercises it shrewdly. His Appropriations Subcommittee doles out funds for every item in the department's seven billion dollar budget, and it does not take long for Washington bureaucrats to realize that the chairman's wrath can destroy precious projects and throw hundreds of people out of jobs.

"He's got the most phenomenal information and total recall," one Agriculture official says of Whitten. "Once you fully understand his do's and don'ts and establish rapport with him, life is a whole lot easier!"

Jamie Whitten's considerable power is enhanced by his scholarship. He is a conscientious student of every line of the Agriculture budget, and his hawk-eye is legendary among department officials. They, in turn, anticipate his scrutiny by checking planned moves with him, thus extending to him a virtual veto on the most minute details. "A suggestion, that's all you have to have in this business," admitted Rodney Leonard.

The key to this phenomenal power—which goes beyond that of budget control—lies in Whitten's network of informants within the department, and his skill in directing their activities and operations. Executive branch officials learn to protect their own jobs, adjusting their loyalties to the legislative branch in a way the Founding Fathers may not have envisioned when they devised their splendid system of checks and balances. Bureaucratic allies of a particular congressman may be able to inject that congressman's political views (or their own) into laws or programs sponsored by an administration without the consent, or even the knowledge, of the department head. Secretaries of Agriculture may come and go, but Jamie Whitten remains, a product of Mississippi's political oligarchy and the seniority system in Congress.

Even the Secretary himself feels he must bend to the power of the "permanent Secretary." When a delegation headed by Richard Boone of the Citizens' Crusade Against Poverty had asked Orville Freeman to provide free stamps and commodities to help the hungry in Mississippi, the Secretary told them: "I've got to get along with two people in Washington—the President and Jamie Whitten. How can you help me with Whitten?"

In theory, an appropriations subcommittee only considers requests for funds to finance programs already approved by Congress. In actuality, a skillful chairman such as Whitten can control policy, alter the original authorizing legislation, and wind up virtually controlling the administration of a department.

In addition to Chairman Whitten, the Agriculture Appropriations Subcommittee has seven members: Democrats William H. Natcher of Kentucky, W. R. Hull, Jr., of Missouri, George Shipley of Illinois, and Frank Evans of Colorado; and Republicans Odin Langen of Minnesota, Robert H. Michael of Illinois, and Jack Edwards of Alabama. Because a majority of these members share Whitten's outlook on agriculture and his arch-conservative view of social action, the chairman's will becomes the subcommittee's will. As chairman, he also has a hold over staff appointments.

Much of Whitten's power derives from the system within the House of Representatives. Once a subcommittee makes a decision, the full House Appropriations Committee almost always backs it up. This is particularly true with agriculture appropriations, because House Appropriations Chairman George Mahon of Texas shares Whitten's views of farm policy, welfare spending, and racial issues. For years, Whitten has been in absolute control of all bills before his subcommittee, from the first markup session to the final House vote. "The lines in my face would be deeper except for you," Mahon inscribed his own portrait in the Mississippian's office.

The House at large rarely has challenged Agriculture budgets because most nonfarm bloc members find the subject too complex or dull, and rarely take the trouble to inform themselves about it. If some members, or the public, are roused to the point where a challenge develops, the House's committee chairmen generally pull together to defeat the move. Committee members follow to insure that they will have the chairman's support for their own pet bills—and to keep sacrosanct the whole system of mutual support and protection.

If a challenge happens to get out of hand, the first commandment of a subcommittee chairman is, "Never let yourself in for a battle on the House floor if there is any chance for defeat." Part of the power of a chairman stems from his apparent invincibility—and the image must be preserved! (Therefore, Whitten went along with the Nixon Administration's full budget request for food aid in 1969, knowing there was sufficient pressure for a much bigger appropriation. Whitten responded here only to the politics of the issue, not the substance, for he still complained to Senator George McGovern that hunger was not a problem, that "Nigras won't work" if you give them free food, and that McGovern was promoting revolution by continuing to seek free food stamps for the poorest Americans.)

Where agriculture legislation is concerned, Whitten must share power to some measure with Senator Spessard Holland, a Florida Democrat who chairs the Senate Appropriations Subcommittee on Agriculture. Holland is a blunt man who insists that Section 32 funds—food dollars from customs receipts —should be held in reserve to be used at the proper time to boost the prices of his state's citrus, vegetable, and beef industries. Thus, when Whitten and Holland act in unison—as they often do—the results are predictable. After the School Lunch Act was liberalized in 1964, they managed to refuse funding free school lunches for more than two years. The Johnson Administration had sought only two or three million dollars to help some of the estimated five million poor children who got no benefits from the lunch program, but all the funds were held back in committee until Senator Philip Hart of Michigan threatened to take the fight to the floor.

Jamie Whitten's power is greater than Holland's, however, not only because appropriations usually originate in the House, but also because in the smaller body of the Senate (contrary to its reputation, the Senate is now the more liberal, flexible body), there is less hesitation to overturn subcommittee decisions than in the tradition-bound House of Representatives. The House system, therefore, assures more *inherent* power for its subcommittee chairmen, and Jamie Whitten has been vigorous and skillful in pursuing it.

Just back from their discovery of hunger in Mississippi in April 1967, Dr. Robert Coles and the three other Field Foundation doctors found out about Whitten's influence when they appealed to Orville Freeman. They walked into the Secretary's office feeling that they would be welcomed as helpful, authoritative reporters of the facts, and they left feeling that they had been tagged as troublemakers.

"We were told that we and all the hungry children we had examined and all the other hungry Americans . . . would have to reckon with Mr. Jamie L. Whitten, as indeed must the Secretary of Agriculture, whose funds come to him through the kindness of the same Mr. Whitten. We were told of the problems that the Agriculture Department has with Congress, and we left feeling we ought to weigh those problems as somehow of the same order as the problems we had met in the South—and that we know from our work elsewhere existed all over the country," recalled Coles.

When Senator Jacob Javits asked Agriculture Secretary Freeman, "What are you afraid of in Mississippi?" (at the July 1967 hearing on hunger in Mississippi) the New York liberal wanted to know why Freeman would not modify the food program to reach more of the hungry in Mississippi and elsewhere. The only response he got was ex-Marine Freeman's outthrust jaw and a growl that he was not afraid of anyone and would not be intimidated.

Nevertheless, faced with Jamie Whitten's power over his department, and fed information by a Whitten-conscious bureaucracy, Freeman had failed for two years to take measures to feed more of the hungry poor in America. Moreover, the Secretary had stubbornly refused to acknowledge the chasm between his department's efforts and the real needs of the hungry.

From Freeman on down, every Agriculture Department official knew that hunger spelled "hound dog" to Jamie Whitten.

"You've got to understand how Jamie feels about 'hound dog' projects," a career official explained. (In southern country jargon, a "hound dog" is always hanging around, useless, waiting to be thrown scraps.) Years before, the chairman had killed a small pilot project to teach unemployed southern Negroes how to drive tractors. "Now, that's a 'hound dog' project, and I don't want to see any more of them," he had said.

Whitten's opposition to any program resembling social welfare—or aid to Negroes—contributed to the failure of War on Poverty programs for rural America. When President Johnson signed an executive order giving the Agriculture Department responsibility for coordinating the rural war on poverty, Secretary Freeman created a Rural Development Service to give the Department a focal point for helping the poor. It was designed to coordinate programs meeting all the needs of the rural poor—housing, education, water, food—not only within the Agriculture Department, but throughout the federal government.

Within a year, the Rural Community Development Service was dead. "Whitten thought the Service smacked of social experimentation and civil rights," a Department of Agriculture official said. In addition, Whitten's brother-in-law, one of many cronies who have filled Agriculture jobs over the years, had clashed with Robert G. Lewis, the idealistic Wisconsin progressive who headed the program. Whitten simply cut off the funds, and pigeonholed the coordinating powers of RCDS by placing the responsibility with the docile, conservative Farmers Home Administration. Freeman never fought the issue. There were too many other essential matters, other appropriations, that were more important to him, so the embryonic effort to coordinate rural poverty programs through the Department of Agriculture ended as little more than a passing idea.

(By assigning the broad rural poverty responsibility to the Department of Agriculture, President Johnson, like President Nixon after him, indicated either a great naïveté about the Department or a lack of seriousness in his proposals. The four congressional committees with which the Department of Agriculture must deal undoubtedly are the least receptive of any in Congress to provide meaningful help to the hardcore rural poor.)

Jamie Whitten has wielded that kind of influence since the mid-1940s, when he killed an emerging Agriculture Department study which tried to anticipate the social and economic problems of Negro GI's returning from World War II to the feudal cotton South. At that time, the Mississippi congressman was the youngest chairman of an appropriations subcommittee. By opposing all studies exploring the effects of a changing agriculture upon people, Whitten helped insure that Agriculture Department farm policy would never seriously include consideration of the effects of its programs on sharecroppers or farm workers. Whitten and the other equally powerful southern congressmen who share his views insured that the Department of Agriculture would focus only on the cotton planter and his crop. As a result, farm policies which have consistently ignored their toll on millions of black poor have contributed to a rural-urban migration, to a civil rights revolution, and to the ruin of many Americans.

With his wily ability to juggle figures and cloud ideas, Whitten has convinced officials unfamiliar with his technique (and lacking intimate knowledge of the facts) that he is quite a reasonable man—especially when the conversation turns to hunger and the food programs. As he tells it, he was a pioneer on the nutrition issue.

In 1950, he fought for a Department of Agriculture cook book, and he warned the House it had better concern itself with human as well as animal health. To this day, Whitten insists that the Agriculture Department keep the book in print; he sends a free copy to newlyweds in his district.

The Subcommittee Chairman also denies that he paralyzed Freeman on the hunger issue: "I *helped* the Secretary by making two points with him," Whitten insists. "I told him he had to charge people what they were accustomed to paying for food stamps because that's what the law says. . . . And I pointed out to him that the law forbids selling food stamps and distributing commodities in the same counties." By making these two helpful points, Whitten blocked the most feasible emergency measures.

"Why, I gave him more money for those food programs than he could spend!" said Whitten.

Actually, the hopelessly inadequate $45 million for food programs Whitten "gave" to Freeman were fought, bought, and paid for by the administration and congressional liberals; this was what was left after Whitten and Holland whittled down the original $100 million, three-year authorization won by liberals on the House floor.

Whitten's explanations of food programs may have appeared perfectly reasonable to Freeman, Sargent Shriver, and many members of Congress, but their total impact was to stop any reform that would get food to the hungry. His own strongly held view is that the food programs should serve the farm programs, not vice versa, and his actions over the years have halted any kind of aid the Agriculture Department might have directed toward the poor. In the early 1960s, when the Kennedy Administration was momentarily concerned for the poor of Appalachia, the Department of Agriculture found a way to provide housing grants to aid the hardest-core poor, but once Whitten discovered the grant program in operation, he killed all further appropriations for it.

A few years later, a new cotton program provided advance payments to cotton farmers for withdrawing some of their acreage from production.

Sharecroppers, who provided most of the cotton labor force, were supposed to receive their "share" of government payments for idle land. With Whitten's inspiration or blessing, the Department of Agriculture adopted a regulation permitting the plantation owner to deduct from the sharecropper's government payments the amount he claimed was owned for the sharecropper's rent, farming expenses, etc. Under the feudal system, however, the sharecropper *never* had any legal guarantee that he would receive his fair share of profit for the crop he produced. Blacks who declined to turn over their checks were kicked off hundreds of plantations. The Agriculture Department did not halt the practice.

One of Whitten's sharecropper constituents, trying desperately to find food for her family, gave her own intuitive view of her congressman's attitudes: "He's probably with the bossman's side, don't you know. He's with them. No one's with us but ourselves, and no matter how many of us there are, we don't have what they have."

Although much of the legislation he favors has enriched American agriculture business with government funds, Whitten's stock answer to any liberalization of the Department of Agriculture food programs is that they are "food programs, not welfare programs." He is adamant about suggestions that food programs be moved to the more liberal Department of Health, Education, and Welfare. "Who'll see to it that [funds for food] don't go for frivolity and wine?" he asks.

Whitten's views on welfare, so strongly felt through the Department of Agriculture, are shared by many Americans. Yet when viewed against the background of Tallahatchie County and its social history, these views, and their interpretations through Agriculture Department programs, take on a different meaning. Since hunger means poverty, and poverty, in Mississippi, usually means black, any expanded aid to the hungry means one more threat to the socioeconomic order in which the black worker has always been held in absolute dependency upon crumbs from the plantation owner.

The 100,000 or more black Mississippi farm workers who suddenly found themselves with nothing to hold onto in the winter of 1967 were little concerned with frivolity and wine. They had lost their sole supply of food, as Mississippi counties switched over from the inadequate but free surplus commodities to a food stamp program the poor could not afford. "No work, no money, and now, no food," was their outcry, and they desperately sought a reduction in the price of stamps at the very moment when Jamie Whitten was starting his annual review of the Department of Agriculture's budget, with its accompanying discourse on the nature of the poor man. He had heard, the Chairman said, that "organized groups" sought to make food stamps free to the poor.

"This is one of the things you always run into," he said to Secretary Freeman. "You make stamps available at 30 percent discount; then they want them at 50, then 75. Now, I have heard reports that some of the organized minority groups are insisting they be provided free of charge. . . . When you start giving people something for nothing, just giving them all they want for nothing, I wonder if you don't destroy character more than you might improve nutrition. I think more and more American people are coming to that conclusion."

They built a lot of character in Mississippi that winter, where the disruption caused by the abrupt changeover to food stamps contributed to the kind of wholesale destitution not seen in this country since the Great Depression.

But the Chairman did not seem to think his black constituents were learning the character lesson well enough when it came to the school lunch and new school breakfast programs. Out of work and out of money, few Mississippi Negroes could afford to give their children 25 cents a day for a school lunch, and few schools provided the free lunches which the law technically required for the poor. Department of Agriculture officials virtually begged that the special school lunch assistance budget be raised from two million to ten million dollars annually to give meals to an added 360,000 children in poor areas. Whitten expressed concern only about the impact of civil rights sanctions as he slashed the request by two-thirds.

When another project—a requested million dollars for a pilot school breakfast program to help the neediest youngsters—came up, Whitten's patience wore thin. "Do you contemplate having a pilot dinner program— evening meals—called supper where I grew up?" Whitten asked sarcastically.

When Agriculture Department officials explained that "a hungry child in the morning is not able to take full advantage of the schooling that is offered," Whitten wanted to know why the government should be supplying what the family should have supplied before they left home.

"We all recognize that the type of home from which some children come affects them in many, many ways, but there is a problem always as to whether the federal government should start doing everything for the citizens. You may end up with a certain class of people doing nothing to help themselves. To strike a happy medium is always a real problem."

In this case, Whitten struck it by cutting all $6.5 million requested for breakfast funds from the budget.

Each time a group of doctors, team of reporters, or other investigation produced firsthand reports of hunger in the South, Whitten launched his own "investigation" and announced that parental neglect is largely responsible for any problems. In 1968, when the drive for a bigger food program began to gather steam nationally, Whitten sent out the FBI to disprove the existence of the problem.

The Mississippi congressman demands that the poor, if they are to get any benefits, must prove they are hungry on a case-by-case basis. "These doctors . . . have not submitted any names . . .," he wrote one concerned northern lady, assuring her that he would be "most sympathetic and helpful in trying to work this matter out."

Time after time, Whitten has requested names and addresses of the poor who complain of ill-treatment in his home state. Yet in Jamie Whitten's home county the thought of having their names known strikes terror among those who have had dealing with the local officials.

A news team from television's Public Broadcast Laboratory, interviewing a black housewife in Whitten's home town of Charleston, felt the danger involved in "naming names." As Mrs. Metcalf began to explain why the food stamp and school lunch programs were not helping her family, a task force of sedans and panel trucks began to cruise back and forth on the U.S. highway about 50 yards from her plantation shack. Suddenly the trucks lunged off the highway into the shack's front yard, surrounding the television crew's two station wagons. A rifle or shotgun was mounted in the rear window of each truck.

"You're trespassing. Git!" growled the plantation manager as he pushed his way past the TV reporter and ordered Mrs. Metcalf to get outside the shack if she knew what was good for her.

"You were trespassing when you crossed the Mississippi state line," shouted Deputy Sheriff Buck Shaw as he ordered the PBL crew to clear out.

In an attempt to insure Mrs. Metcalf's safety from the local "law," the reporter phoned Congressman Whitten in Washington.

"You remember when Martin Luther King went through my town?" the congressman answered. "You read the *Wall Street Journal?* It said that he went through there and everybody turned out to look at him. And as soon as he left, they just turned over and went back to sleep. . . . I just know, I live down there and I know. . . . Good God, Chicago, Washington, Detroit . . . every one of them would give any amount of money if they could go to sleep feeling as safe—both races—as my folks will!"

It wasn't so peaceful about three o'clock that afternoon with those hard-eyed men threatening Mrs. Metcalf, the reporter explained.

"I suspect Deputy Shaw's like I am," Whitten snapped. "They recognized when you crossed that state line you had no good intention in your mind. I'm no kingfish. I just know my people and my people get along. Unfortunately, you folks and the folks up here don't know how to get along. . . . I bet you money if I ran tomorrow, and nobody voted except the colored people, I'd get the majority. I grew up where five or six of my closest neighbors were Negroes. We played together as kids. We swapped vegetables. Why, I grew up hugging my Momma, and my Momma hugging them."

There were as many Negroes as whites at his father's funeral, Whitten asserts—and he keeps on his desk a yellowed 1936 newspaper editorial that praised District Attorney Jamie Whitten for successfully prosecuting the white man who burned some Mississippi Negroes to death.

Against Whitten's statements about how he is respected by Negroes and would get their vote, about how close his relationship and understanding with Negroes has been, about how quiet and peaceful life is in Charleston, another point of view appeared, as one of his black constituents spoke on the same subject—rambling much as Jamie Whitten does. An eloquent, middle-aged woman told Dr. Robert Coles about the plantation owner for whom her husband works, about his wife, about food, and about life in America:

"He [the plantation owner] doesn't want us trying to vote and like that —and first I'd like to feed my kids, before I go trying to vote.

"His wife—the boss man's—she'll come over here sometimes give me some extra grits and once or twice in the year some good bacon. She tells me we get along fine down here and I says 'yes' to her. What else would I be saying, I ask you?

"But it's no good. The kids aren't eating enough, and you'd have to be wrong in the head, pure crazy to say they are. Sometimes we talk of leaving; but you know it's just no good up there either, we hear. They eat better, but they have bad things up there I hear, rats as big as raccoons, I hear, and they bit my sister's kid real bad.

"It's no kind of country to be proud of, with all this going on—the colored people still having it so bad, and the kids being sick and there's nothing you can do about it."

Whitten's affection for black constituents like this woman does not extend to federal measures to assist their lot in life. Of the 24,081 residents of Tallahatchie County, 18,000 have family incomes less than $3,000 a year, and 15,197 make less than $2,000. Of these thousands legally defined as poor, only 2,367 qualify for public assistance, and 6,710 receive food stamps. Only a few blocks from Whitten's own white frame house, Negroes live in shacks without toilets, running water, electricity—or food.

Whitten and his fellow white Mississippians point with great pride to the economic progress their state has made in recent years. Improved farming methods, conversion of marginal cropland to timber and other uses, and a strong soil bank program have greatly enriched the commercial farmer in Mississippi. Other government programs, including state tax inducements, have promoted wide industrialization, and rural white workers have found new affluence in the hundreds of factories and small shops that have sprung up.

But the new farming has eliminated thousands of jobs for Negro plantation workers while the segregated social system denies them factory jobs. The able-bodied usually head north, leaving the very young, the very old, and the unskilled to cope with progress. The rural black does not share in the new prosperity of Mississippi, and some Negroes are "worse off" than at any time since the Depression. Indeed, in many parts of the Deep South the black man is literally being starved out by the new prosperity.

Perhaps the white southern politician is no more to blame than are whites anywhere. But the white in the South could not afford to see the truth of the Negro's suffering because to feel that truth would have shattered a whole way of life.

Jamie Whitten truly believes in his own fairness, his idea of good works, and the imagined affection he receives from Negroes back home. For 59 years, he has anesthetized his soul to the human misery and indignity only a few yards from his own home, and has refused to believe that the responsibility for that indignity lies on his white shoulders. His belief in the basic laziness, indifference, and unworthiness of the black poor is as strong as his belief in the virtues of a way of life that for three centuries has denied these same black poor any avenues of pursuing ambition, self-respect, or a better future for their children.

That Jamie Whitten should suffer from blindness to human need is one thing. But that he can use his blindness as an excuse to limit the destiny of millions of Americans is another matter, one which should concern anyone who believes in the basic strengths of this country's constitutional guarantees. The checks and balances of a reasonable democratic republic have gone

completely awry when a huge bureaucracy and the top officials of an administration base their actions concerning deepest human need on their fearful
perception of what one rather limited man seems to want.

The system of seniority and temerity that gives a man such as Jamie
Whitten such awesome power must come under more serious public scrutiny
if the American system of government is ever to establish itself on the basis
of moral concern about the individual human being.

THE BUREAUCRACY: PLANNING, POLITICS, AND THE PUBLIC INTEREST

According to some critics, the chief weakness of the federal bureaucracy is that it cannot plan. The purpose of Part Four is to assess the capacity of American bureaucracy to plan rationally in order to cope with pressing social problems. The selections are designed to illustrate the political obstacles to comprehensive policy planning that prevent administrators from carrying out their public mandates. They examine three related phenomena: the ad hoc nature of the bureaucratic planning process, the tendency of regulatory agencies to become captives of the industries they are supposed to regulate, and the conservative and incremental policy changes encouraged by the political limits on administrative rationality.

In Part Three we saw that a single Congressman could sabotage administrative attempts to carry out congressionally authorized and presidentially endorsed hunger programs. Critics of the present administrative policy-making process argue that the very development of the federal bureaucracy was designed to grant access to a wide variety of political interests by adding agencies piecemeal in response to ad hoc political pressures. Thus, the federal bureaucracy functions well as an institution for representing organized interests but is ill suited to serve the needs of the general public. Moreover, the growth process itself places severe limits on rational planning and public accountability. With the addition of each new agency overall coordination among agencies becomes more difficult. With the growth in size of existing agencies, control over administrative discretion within each agency becomes less possible. With the increase in the number of invisible administrative decisions, the opportunities for accountability to the public are diminished.

Despite these developments, the "ideal type" bureaucracy first defined by Max Weber still forms the basis for popular stereotypes about the formal and mechanical nature of administrative decision making. The Weberian bureaucracy is characterized by primacy of technical knowledge, elimination of personalism, and strict adherence to formal rules and procedures. In the abstract model, hierarchy eliminates administrative discretion, technical expertise replaces charismatic authority, and administration displaces politics. Each of the following selections illustrates the inadequacy of the Weberian model as a guide to the political realities of the American administrative system.

In his article "Ends and Means in Planning," Edward C. Banfield sets forth conditions for systematic administrative decision making that take into account all the probable future consequences of policy choices. These include a careful elaboration of the ends desired, a thorough analysis of all the means available, a design for alternative plans of action, and a comparative evaluation of the probable intended and unintended consequences of each plan. Using his study of the Chicago Housing Authority as a point of departure, Banfield discusses numerous practical obstacles to the realization of rational planning by organizations. Because the future is always uncertain, the goals of an organization may change over time. For example, the goal of slum clearance may come into conflict with the goal of maintaining neighborhood community and the latter with the goal of ending racial segregation. Furthermore, organization members often prefer present to future accomplishments. In all organizations, the desire to survive makes administrators highly vulnerable to political pressures. Both of these factors encourage a short-run perspective and discourage long-term planning. Other constraints on rational planning include staff biases and the confining impact of past decisions on future choices. Despite his feeling that bureaucracies are not especially disposed toward purposive adaptation of means to ends, Banfield concludes that practical limitations are no reason to give up the norm of rational decision making as embodied in his ideal model.

Banfield's conclusion is challenged by the pluralist economist Charles Lindblom in "The Science of 'Muddling Through.' " In contrast to Banfield's "scientific" decision-making procedure, Lindblom discusses the informal rules by which public officials generally do make policy. Means and ends are seldom sharply separated. Values are not clearly delineated. A few intuitively reasonable alternatives are considered, and comparisons are severely limited to marginal assessments of future proposals against the experience of past policies. The critical test of a policy is not whether it effectively maximizes desired political values, but simply whether it can be agreed upon by contending parties. Lindblom sees this "common sense" approach to decision making as imperfect but acceptable in view of the "superhuman comprehensiveness" required to achieve perfect administrative rationality.

Critics of Lindblom's administrative "incrementalism" have argued that tying future policy too closely to past policy tends to favor already established interest groups and to weaken the political influence of new and emerging groups. Lindblom's ideal solution would be to expand Calhoun's pluralism rather than to reform it—that is, to ensure that each important value or interest in society become a major concern of at least one administrative agency. The virtue of this approach would be its guarantee that every important value or interest would have its own watchdog. Its chief limitation would be that no political analyst has yet come up with a suitable set of criteria for distinguishing important from unimportant interests and political values. In the absence of such criteria, political decision makers are likely to use an interest group's power as a measure of its importance.

Some of the political problems engendered by the influence of organized interests in the bureaucratic regulatory process are analyzed by Murray Edelman in the selection drawn from his book *The Symbolic Uses of Politics*. His point is simple: Independent regulatory agencies are not always what they seem. By a process of "mutual role-taking," administrators often come to share the perspective of the industries they are supposed to be regulating in the public interest. Nonetheless, the abstract rhetoric of vigilant regulation is strictly adhered to in order to symbolically reassure the public that decisions emerging from the regulatory arena are taken with a fairly precise view of the common interest in mind. Ironically, the very participation of the administrative agency in decisions to increase rates, authorize industrial mergers, or ratify collective bargaining agreements symbolizes to the public the grandeur and beneficence of the state. Anomalous as the situation may seem, the regulated groups themselves become highly supportive of the continued existence of regulatory agencies. Without this governmental presence their decisions might seem like rapacious raids on the Gross National Product. Thus, regulator and regulated become mutually interdependent. If the agency is abolished, the regulated group is vulnerable to public attack. If the regulated group becomes too weak, the need for the agency diminishes. As one grows and prospers so does the other. Mutual role taking becomes symbiosis. Making rational decisions in the public interest becomes a remote ideal. As each component of the administrative system seeks feudal autonomy, competing claims on the treasury and the economy are seldom considered simultaneously. The only arena where budgetary review takes place regularly is in deliberations over congressional appropriations, in a setting "guaranteeing minimal weighing of the comparative values of alternatives . . . by the committee members, let alone the uninvolved public." Edelman's analysis suggests that the limits on rationality in the administrative arena are not neutral instruments; they entail policy directions advantageous to the already powerful and inhibit the consideration of the consumer's needs and interests.

The nature of budgetary deliberations within the Bureau of the Budget and before the House and Senate Appropriations committees is another example of the uncoordinated and evolutionary fashion by which national policy priorities are established. Aaron Wildavsky's *The Politics of the Budgetary Process* analyzes the piecemeal advocacy of national programs and program expenditures by interest groups and administrative agencies. In "The Budgetary Process," drawn from this study, Wildavsky discusses the experiential but nonetheless systematic "aids to calculation" that Congressmen and budget officials use to guide them in their budgetary choices. These guides—past experience, simplification, lowering expectations, and piecemeal adjustment of previous budgets—systematically affect the outcomes of American public policy. They ensure that problems and interests that have already succeeded in acquiring political legitimacy will probably continue to obtain an incrementally increasing share of public expenditures to the detriment of public spending on behalf of new interests and problems. This tendency is compounded by the lack of technical expertise in Congress. In addition, the complexity of modern life and uncertainty about the future encourage caution and gradualism. The infrequency with which administrative performance is comprehensively reviewed is one reason why so many political battles are fought to obtain or prevent the establishment of new administrative agencies. Once established, agencies may not always grow, but they usually are able to maintain a claim on a fairly stable share of the federal budget.

"Rebuke at HEW" is an account of public criticism by Robert Finch, then Secretary of Health, Education and Welfare, of Dr. Jacqueline Verrett, one of his department's research scientists, for revealing to a national television audience her findings concerning the potential health hazards of cyclamates. Morton Mintz's analysis of this public rebuke underlines the inadequacy of the system of internal communication at HEW. Ironically, in the case of cyclamates an irrationality in the system inadvertently served the public interest by freeing Dr. Verrett to publicize the potential danger of cyclamates before Secretary Finch and other high-level administrators concerned with the political ramifications of her scientific conclusions could weaken the thrust of her analysis. Her actions illustrate that, in a bureaucracy, technical knowledge and administrative authority may work at cross purposes instead of reinforcing each other, as Max Weber expected. The case also shows that neither of these sources of influence is sufficient to remove politics from administration.

15

Ends and Means in Planning

Edward C. Banfield

The word 'planning' is given a bewildering variety of meanings. To some it means socialism. To others the layout and design of cities. To still others regional development schemes like TVA, measures to control the business cycle, or 'scientific management' in industry. It would be easy to over-emphasize what these activities have in common; their differences are certainly more striking than their similarities. Nevertheless, it may be that there is a method of making decisions which is to some extent common to all these fields and to others as well and that the logical structure of this method can usefully be elaborated as a theory of planning.

Such an attempt leads at once to the determining frame of reference, for action, establishing the means-ends schema, and the usual model of rational choices. An actor (who may be a person or an organization) is considered as being oriented towards the attainment of ends. Planning is the process by which he selects a course of action (a set of means) for the attainment of his ends. It is 'good' planning if these means are likely to attain the ends or maximize the chances of their attainment. It is by the process of rational choice that the best adaptation of means to ends is likely to be achieved.

In this article we propose first to develop sufficiently these common conceptions to provide a simple theory of planning, one which is essentially a definition. It will be descriptive in conception and will deal with how planning would have to be done in order to achieve the fullest attainment of the ends sought, not how it actually is done (this latter would be a theory of the sociology of planning). We shall then discuss the argument that the procedures of organizations do not in fact even roughly approximate to those described in the theoretical model; this argument will be illustrated with brief reference to a particular case which the author and a colleague have described elsewhere. We shall then consider the question of why it is that organizations do so little planning and rational decision making.

[1]

The concept of rational choice has been expounded with great rigour and subtlety. Here a much simplified approach will suffice; a rational decision is one made in the following manner: (a) the decision maker lists all the opportunities for action open to him; (b) he identifies all the consequences which would follow from the adoption of each of the possible actions; and (c) he selects the action which would be followed by the preferred set of consequences. According to this definition, no choice can ever be perfectly rational, for there are usually a very great—perhaps an infinite—number of possible actions open to the actor and the consequences of any one of them would ramify *ad infinitum*. No decision maker could have the knowledge (or the time!) to evaluate even a small fraction of the actions open to him. It is possible, however, to be more or less systematic in the canvass of alternatives and probable consequences, so that the conception is not an entirely useless one. For practical purposes, a rational decision is one in which alternatives and consequences are considered as fully as the decision maker, given the time and other resources available to him, can afford to consider them.

A plan (unless we depart very far from customary usage) is a decision with regard to a course of action. A course of action is a sequence of acts which are mutually related as means and are therefore viewed as a unit; it is the unit which is the plan. Planning, then, as defined here, is to be distinguished from what we may call 'opportunistic decision making,' which is choosing (rationally or not) actions that are not mutually related as a single means. The rational selection of a course of action, i.e. the making of a rational plan, involves essentially the same procedure as any rational choice: every possible course of action must be listed, all the consequences which would follow from each course must be identified, and that course selected the consequences of which are preferred.

The process by which a plan is rationally made may conveniently be described under four main headings:

1. *Analysis of the situation.* The planner must lay down in prospect every possible course of action which would lead to the attainment of the ends sought. His task is to imagine how the actor may get from where he is to where he wants to be, but his imagination must work within certain conditions which are fixed by the situation, especially by the resources at his disposal (not merely possessions, of course, but legal and other authority, information, time, executive skill, and so on) and by the obstacles in his way. His opportunity area consists of the courses of action 'really' open to him: i.e. those which he is not precluded from taking by some limiting condition. It may be, of course, that he has no opportunity area at all—that there is absolutely no way by which the ends sought may be achieved—or that the opportunity area is a very restricted one.

2. *End reduction and elaboration.* An end is an image of a future state of affairs towards which action is oriented. The formulation of the end may be extremely vague and diffuse. If so it may have to be reduced to specific or 'operational' terms before it can serve as a criterion of choice in the concrete circumstances. The formulation of the end may be elliptical; in this case the planner must clearly explain the meaning in full. An end may be thought of as having both active and contextual elements. The active elements are those features of the future situation which are actively sought; the contextual are those which, while not actively sought, nevertheless cannot be sacrificed without loss. (The man who burned down his house in order to get the rats out of the cellar ignored

a contextual end in his effort to achieve an active one.) The planner's task is to identify and clarify the contextual as well as the active components of the ends. If they are not fully consistent, he must also 'order' them, i.e. he must discover the relative value to be attached to each under the various concrete circumstances envisaged in the course of action or, as an economist would say, prepare an 'indifference map'.

3. *The design of courses of action.* Courses of action may have a more or less general character. At the most general level, a developing course of action implies a description of the 'key' actions to be taken or the commitments to be made. These constitute the premises upon which any less general course of action is based, e.g. at the 'programme' or 'operations' levels. In other words, decisions of a less general character represent choices from among those alternatives which are not precluded by the more general decisions already taken. A developing course of action may be chosen arbitrarily or capriciously and a programmed course of action based upon it may then be selected with elaborate consideration of alternatives and consequences: in such a case there is 'functional rationality' but 'substantive irrationality'.

4. *The comparative evaluation of consequences.* If the plan is to be rational, all consequences—not merely those intended by the planner—must be taken into account. To a large extent, then, good planning is a search for unintended consequences which may be a component of the active or contextual ends. The planner cannot pick and choose among the consequences of a given course of action: he must take them all, the unwanted along with the wanted, as a set. Their evaluation therefore must be in terms of the net value attached to each set. If all values could be expressed in terms of a common numerical index (e.g. prices) this would raise no great difficulties. In practice, however, the planner must somehow strike a balance between essentially unlike intangibles. He must decide, for example, whether x amount of damage to a beautiful view is justified by y amount of increase in driving safety.

[2]

So far the discussion has been intended to make reasonably clear what is meant by 'rational planning'. If we now take this definition as a yardstick and apply it to organizational behaviour in the real world we are struck at once by two facts: there is very little planning, and there is even less rationality.

In general organizations engage in opportunistic decision making rather than in planning: rather than laying out a course of action which will lead all the way to the attainment of their ends, they extemporize, meeting each crisis as it arises. In the United States even the largest industries do not look forward more than five or ten years. In government, the American planning horizon is usually even less distant. Moreover, such plans as are made are not the outcome of a careful consideration of alternative courses of action and their probable consequences. As a rule the most important decisions— those constituting the developing course of action—are the result of accident rather than design; they are the unintended outcome of a social process rather than the conscious product of deliberation and calculation. If there is an element of rationality it is 'functional' rather than 'substantive'.

A few years ago the writer and a colleague set out to describe how decisions were made by a large and progressive public body, the Chicago Housing Authority. We knew that the housing agency was one of the best administered in the United States (my colleague, a professor of planning on leave from a university, was in fact its director of planning) and we therefore assumed that if we observed closely enough we could see how a large organization lays out alternative courses of action, evaluates their probable consequences, and so arrives at what is, in the circumstances, a rational decision. We did not expect to find that the model described above was being followed consciously or in detail, of course, but we did suppose that the course followed would roughly approximate to it.

What we found was entirely different from what we anticipated. The authority might conceivably have sought to attain its ends by one of various courses of action. (It might, for example, have given rental subsidies to enable people with low incomes to buy or rent housing in the market. Or it might have built small housing projects for eventual sale. Or again, following the example of the United Kingdom, it might have built new towns in the hinterland beyond the metropolis.) No major alternative to what it was doing was considered. The developing course of action—to build large slum clearance projects—was treated as fixed; this course of action had been arrived at cumulatively, so to speak, from a number of unrelated sources: Congress had made certain decisions, the Illinois legislature certain others, the City Council certain others, and so on. Unless the housing authority was to embark upon the unpromising task of persuading all these bodies to change their minds, the development 'plan' had to be taken as settled—settled on the basis of decisions made without regard to each other. 'The process by which a housing programme for Chicago was formulated', my colleague and I wrote, 'resembled somewhat the parlour game in which each player adds a word to a sentence which is passed around the circle of players: the player acts as if the words that are handed to him express some intention (i.e. as if the sentence that comes to him were planned) and he does his part to sustain the illusion.'

The idea of planning, or of rational decision making, assumes a clear and consistent set of ends. The housing authority, we found, had nothing of the kind. The law expressed the objectives of housing policy in terms so general as to be virtually meaningless and the five unpaid commissioners who exercised supervision over the 'general policy' of the organization never asked themselves exactly what they were trying to accomplish. Had they done so they would doubtless have been perplexed, for the law said nothing about where, or in what manner, they were to discover which ends, or whose ends, the agency was to serve.

The agency had an end-system of a kind, but its ends were, for the most part, vague, implicit and fragmentary. Each of the commissioners—the Catholic, the Jew, the Negro, the businessman, the labour leader—had his own idea of them, or of some of them, and the professional staff had still another idea. There were a good many contradictions among such ends as were generally agreed upon. Some of these contradictions went deep into fundamental questions. For example, the authority wanted to build as much housing as possible for people with low incomes; but it also wanted to avoid furthering the spread of racial segregation. These two objectives were in conflict and there was no way of telling which should be subordinated or to what extent.

Most of the considerations which finally governed the selection of sites and of the type of projects were 'political' rather than 'technical'. A site could not be considered for a project unless it was large enough, unless suitable foundations for high-rise construction could be sunk, and so on. But, once these minimal technical conditions were met, for the most part the remaining considerations were of a very different kind: was the site in the ward of an alderman who would support the project or oppose it?

[3]

Unfortunately there does not exist a body of case studies which permits of the comparisons that would be interesting—comparisons, say, between large organizations and small, public and private, single-purpose and multi-purpose, American and other. Despite this lack, some general observations are possible. While the Chicago Housing Authority may be a rather extreme case, there are compelling reasons which militate against planning and rationality on the part of all organizations.

1. Organizations do not lay out courses of action because the future is highly uncertain. There are very few matters about which reliable predictions can be made for more than five years ahead. City planners, for example, can know very little about certain key variables with which they must deal: how many children, for example, will require schools or playgrounds ten years hence? Recent experience has shown how little even demographic predictions can be trusted. The Chicago Housing Authority could not possibly have anticipated before the war the problems it would have to face after it. Some people, knowing that they cannot anticipate the future but feeling that they ought to try, resolve the conflict by making plans and storing them away where they will be forgotten.

Not only do the conditions within which the planner works change rapidly, but so also do the ends for which he is planning. A public housing programme which is begun for slum clearance may, before the buildings are occupied, be primarily an instrument for the reform of race relations. It need hardly be said that the means most appropriate to one end are not likely to be most appropriate to the other.

When an organization is engaged in a game of strategy with an opponent the element of change is likely to be of special importance. The opponent tries to force change upon the organization; the organization's actions must then be a series of counter-measures. In the nature of the case these cannot be planned. To a considerable extent all organizations—and not especially those engaged in 'competitive' business—are constantly responding to change which others are endeavouring to impose upon them.

2. When it is possible to decide upon a course of action well in advance it is likely to be imprudent to do so, or at least to do so publicly (as, of course,

a public agency ordinarily must). For to advertise in advance the actions that are to be taken is to invite opposition to them and to give the opposition a great advantage. This is a principle which many city planners have learned to their cost.

3. Organizations, especially public ones, do not consider fundamental alternatives because usually there are circumstances which preclude them, at least in the short run, from doing anything very different from what they are already doing. Some of these circumstances may be the result of choices which the organization has already made; others may be externally imposed. The housing authority, for example, could not cease building its own housing projects and begin giving cash subsidies to private builders: public opinion favoured projects rather than subsidies and the agency had recruited and trained a staff which was project minded and not subsidy minded. The organization's commitments, and often other obstacles as well, may be liquidated over time and a new course of action initiated. But the liquidation is expensive: it may be cheaper to retain for a while an obsolescent course of action than to incur the costs of instituting a new one. If the organization could see far enough into the future it might liquidate its commitments gradually, thus making an economical transition to a new course of action. As a rule, however, it cannot anticipate very clearly or surely what it will want to do a few years hence. Moreover, if it acknowledges its doubt about the wisdom of what it is presently doing it risks giving aid and comfort to its enemies and damaging its own morale.

4. Organizations have a decided preference for present rather than future effects. One might think that public organizations, at least, would be more willing than are persons to postpone satisfactions—that, in the language of economics, they would discount the future less heavily. They do not seem to, however, and this is another reason why they do not plan ahead.

5. The reason they discount the future so heavily is, perhaps, that they must continually be preoccupied with the present necessity of maintaining what Barnard has called the 'economy of incentives'. That is to say, the heads of the organization are constantly under the necessity of devising a scheme of incentives by means of which they can elicit the contributions of activity required to keep it going. Any scheme of incentives is inherently unstable. It must be continually rebuilt according to the needs of the moment. 'Indeed, it is so delicate and complex', says Barnard, 'that rarely, if ever, is the scheme of incentives determinable in advance of application.'

6. The end of organizational maintenance—of keeping the organization going for the sake of keeping it going—is usually more important than any substantive end. The salmon perishes in order to give birth to its young. Organizations, however, are not like salmon; they much prefer sterility to death. Given the supremacy of the end of organizational maintenance, opportunistic decision making rather than planning is called for. Indeed, from the standpoint of maintenance the organization may do well to make as few long-term commitments as possible. Advantage may lie in flexibility.

7. The end-system of an organization is rarely, if ever, a clear and coherent picture of a desirable future towards which action is to be directed. Usually it is a set of vague platitudes and pious cant the function of which

is to justify the existence of the organization in the eyes of its members and of outsiders. The stated ends are propaganda, not criteria to guide action. What John Dewey said in *Human Nature and Conduct* of a person applies as well to an organization: it does not shoot in order to hit a target; it sets up a target in order to facilitate the act of shooting.

8. It follows that serious reflection on the ends of the organization, and especially any attempt to state ends in precise and realistic terms, is likely to be destructive to the organization. To unify and to stir the spirit they must be stated in vague and high-sounding terms. When they are reduced to their real content they lose their magic and, worse, they become controversial. Had it attempted to formulate a set of ends relating to racial policy the Chicago Housing Authority would certainly have destroyed itself at once.

9. It follows also that organizations do not as a rule attempt to maximize the attainment of their ends or (to say the same thing in different words) to use resources efficiently. If the ultimate end is the maintenance of the organization, how indeed is 'maximization' possible? The organization may endeavour to store up the largest possible quantity of reserves of a kind which may be used for its maintenance at a later time (e.g. to accumulate 'good will', or the wherewithal to procure it, in advance of need). In this case there is a quantity—utility—which is being maximized. But if substantive ends are regarded, Herbert A. Simon is right in saying that organizations 'satisfice' (i.e. look for a course of action that is satisfactory or good enough) rather than maximize.

10. Laying out courses of action, clarifying ends, and evaluating alternatives are costly procedures which take time and money and cannot be carried out without the active participation of the chief executives. However great may be the resulting gain to the organization, full attention to the present crisis—assuming the supreme importance of organizational maintenance—is likely to result in far greater gain. Paradoxical as it may seem, if all costs are taken into account it may be rational to devote very little attention to alternatives and their consequences.

11. Rationality, as defined above, is less likely to be found in public than in private organizations. One reason for this is that the public agency's ends often reflect compromise among essentially incompatible interests. This is not an accidental or occasional feature of public organization in a democracy. Where conflict exists and every conflicting element has to be given its due, it is almost inevitable that there be an end-system which 'rides madly off in all directions'.

12. Whether or not conflict is built into the end-system, the end-systems of public organizations are vastly more complex than those of private ones. Contextual ends, in particular, are far more numerous. A private builder, for example, does not concern himself with the effect of high speed construction on birth rates and family life, but a public one must. The more complex the end-system of the organization, the harder to devise courses of action, the more consequences must be evaluated, and the greater the likelihood that some ends will be sacrificed in the endeavour to attain others. That rationality, in the sense of the definition, becomes more difficult to achieve is of

course not an argument against public enterprise: perhaps private enterprise does not take enough ends into consideration.

[4]

The reader may by now have come to the conclusion that since organizations are so little given to the rational adaptation of means to ends nothing is to be gained from constructing such a model of planning as that set forth above.

Certainly this would be the case if one's interest were mainly sociological. For the study of how organizations actually behave an altogether different conceptual scheme would probably be most rewarding.

But if the interest is normative—if it is in describing how organizations would have to act in order to be in some sense more effective or efficient— it is hard to see how reference to such a model can be avoided or, indeed, why its lack of realism should be considered a defect. And students of administration are, after all, chiefly interested in describing organization only so that they may improve it. Their problem, then, is to find a theoretical model which, without being so far removed from reality as to be a mere plaything, is yet far enough removed to suggest how organizations may be made to function better.

It would be a contribution to the development of a suitable theory if there were a body of detailed case studies, all of them built on a common conceptual scheme so as to allow of significant analytical comparisons. It would be particularly helpful to have a full account of the workings of an organization which is so placed as to be able to encourage the fullest development of planning and rational choice: one, let us say, with a few clearly defined purposes, free of political and other conflict, blessed with a large opportunity area, and headed by persons who make a realistic attempt to be rational. How fully and clearly would such an organization explain and define its ends? How often and how elaborately would it consider alternative courses of action at the various levels of generality? How exhaustively would it inquire into probable consequences, the unintended as well as the intended? Would it perhaps carry planning and rationality beyond the point where marginal cost equals marginal return? And would it 'maximize' or, to use Herbert Simon's terms, would it 'satisfice'?

16

The Science of "Muddling Through"

Charles E. Lindblom

Suppose an administrator is given responsibility for formulating policy with respect to inflation. He might start by trying to list all related values in order of importance, e.g., full employment, reasonable business profit, protection of small savings, prevention of a stock market crash. Then all possible policy outcomes could be rated as more or less efficient in attaining a maximum of these values. This would of course require a prodigious inquiry into values held by members of society and an equally prodigious set of calculations on how much of each value is equal to how much of each other value. He could then proceed to outline all possible policy alternatives. In a third step, he would undertake systematic comparison of his multitude of alternatives to determine which attains the greatest amount of values.

In comparing policies, he would take advantage of any theory available that generalized about classes of policies. In considering inflation, for example, he would compare all policies in the light of the theory of prices. Since no alternatives are beyond his investigation, he would consider strict central control and the abolition of all prices and markets on the one hand and elimination of all public controls with reliance completely on the free market on the other, both in the light of whatever theoretical generalizations he could find on such hypothetical economies.

Finally, he would try to make the choice that would in fact maximize his values.

An alternative line of attack would be to set as his principal objective, either explicitly or without conscious thought, the relatively simple goal of keeping prices level. This objective might be compromised or complicated by only a few other goals, such as full employment. He would in fact disregard most other social values as beyond his present interest, and he would for the moment not even attempt to rank the few values that he regarded as immediately relevant. Were he pressed, he would quickly admit that he was ignoring many related values and many possible important consequences of his policies.

As a second step, he would outline those relatively few policy alternatives that occurred to him. He would then compare them. In comparing his limited number of alternatives, most of them familiar from past controversies, he would not ordinarily find a body of theory precise enough to carry him through a comparison of their respective consequences. Instead he would rely heavily on the record of past experience with small policy steps to predict the consequences of similar steps extended into the future.

Moreover, he would find that the policy alternatives combined objectives or values in different ways. For example, one policy might offer price level stability at the cost of some risk of unemployment; another might offer less

167

price stability but also less risk of unemployment. Hence, the next step in his approach—the final selection—would combine into one the choice among values and the choice among instruments for reaching values. It would not, as in the first method of policy-making, approximate a more mechanical process of choosing the means that best satisfied goals that were previously clarified and ranked. Because practitioners of the second approach expect to achieve their goals only partially, they would expect to repeat endlessly the sequence just described, as conditions and aspirations changed and as accuracy of prediction improved.

By Root or by Branch

For complex problems, the first of these two approaches is of course impossible. Although such an approach can be described, it cannot be practiced except for relatively simple problems and even then only in a somewhat modified form. It assumes intellectual capacities and sources of information that men simply do not possess, and it is even more absurd as an approach to policy when the time and money that can be allocated to a policy problem are limited, as is always the case. Of particular importance to public administrators is the fact that public agencies are in effect usually instructed not to practice the first method. That is to say, their prescribed functions and constraints—the politically or legally possible—restrict their attention to relatively few values and relatively few alternative policies among the countless alternatives that might be imagined. It is the second method that is practiced.

. . .

. . . I propose in this paper to clarify and formalize the second method, much neglected in the literature. This might be described as the method of *successive limited comparisons.* I will contrast it with the first approach, which might be called the rational-comprehensive method. More impressionistically and briefly—and therefore generally used in this article—they could be characterized as the branch method and root method, the former continually building out from the current situation, step-by-step and by small degrees; the latter starting from fundamentals anew each time, building on the past only as experience is embodied in a theory, and always prepared to start completely from the ground up.

Let us put the characteristics of the two methods side by side in simplest terms.

Rational-Comprehensive (Root)	Successive Limited Comparisons (Branch)
1a. Clarification of values or objectives distinct from and usually prerequisite to empirical analysis of alternative policies.	1b. Selection of value goals and empirical analysis of the needed action are not distinct from one another but are closely intertwined.

2a. Policy-formulation is therefore approached through means-ends analysis: First the ends are isolated, then the means to achieve them are sought.

2b. Since means and ends are not distinct, means-ends analysis is often inappropriate or limited.

3a. The test of a "good" policy is that it can be shown to be the most appropriate means to desired ends.

3b. The test of a "good" policy is typically that various analysts find themselves directly agreeing on a policy (without their agreeing that it is the most appropriate means to an agreed objective).

4a. Analysis is comprehensive; every important relevant factor is taken into account.

4b. Analysis is drastically limited:
   i) Important possible outcomes are neglected.
   ii) Important alternative potential policies are neglected.
   iii) Important affected values are neglected.

5a. Theory is often heavily relied upon.

5b. A succession of comparisons greatly reduces or eliminates reliance on theory.

Assuming that the root method is familiar and understandable, we proceed directly to clarification of its alternative by contrast. In explaining the second, we shall be describing how most administrators do in fact approach complex questions, for the root method, the "best" way as a blueprint or model, is in fact not workable for complex policy questions, and administrators are forced to use the method of successive limited comparisons.

Intertwining Evaluation and Empirical Analysis (1b)

The quickest way to understand how values are handled in the method of successive limited comparisons is to see how the root method often breaks down in *its* handling of values or objectives. The idea that values should be clarified, and in advance of the examination of alternative policies, is appealing. But what happens when we attempt it for complex social problems? The first difficulty is that on many critical values or objectives, citizens disagree, congressmen disagree, and public administrators disagree. Even where a fairly specific objective is prescribed for the administrator, there remains considerable room for disagreement on sub-objectives. Consider, for example, the conflict with respect to locating public housing, described in Meyerson and Banfield's study of the Chicago Housing Authority—disagreement which occurred despite the clear objective of providing a certain number of public housing units in the city. Similarly conflicting are objectives in highway location, traffic control, minimum wage administration, development of tourist facilities in national parks, or insect control.

Administrators cannot escape these conflicts by ascertaining the majority's preference, for preferences have not been registered on most issues; indeed, there often *are* no preferences in the absence of public discussion sufficient to bring an issue to the attention of the electorate. Furthermore, there is a question of whether intensity of feeling should be considered as well as the number of persons preferring each alternative. By the impossibility of doing otherwise, administrators often are reduced to deciding policy without clarifying objectives first.

Even when an administrator resolves to follow his own values as a criterion for decisions, he often will not know how to rank them when they conflict with one another, as they usually do. Suppose, for example, that an administrator must relocate tenants living in tenements scheduled for destruction. One objective is to empty the buildings fairly promptly, another is to find suitable accommodation for persons displaced, another is to avoid friction with residents in other areas in which a large influx would be unwelcome, another is to deal with all concerned through persuasion if possible, and so on.

How does one state even to himself the relative importance of these partially conflicting values? A simple ranking of them is not enough; one needs ideally to know how much of one value is worth sacrificing for some of another value. The answer is that typically the administrator chooses—and must choose—directly among policies in which these values are combined in different ways. He cannot first clarify his values and then choose among policies.

A more subtle third point underlies both the first two. Social objectives do not always have the same relative values. One objective may be highly prized in one circumstance, another in another circumstance. If, for example, an administrator values highly both the dispatch with which his agency can carry through its projects *and* good public relations, it matters little which of the two possibly conflicting values he favors in some abstract or general sense. Policy questions arise in forms which put to administrators such a question as: Given the degree to which we are or are not already achieving the values of dispatch and the values of good public relations, is it worth sacrificing a little speed for a happier clientele, or is it better to risk offending the clientele so that we can get on with our work? The answer to such a question varies with circumstances.

The value problem is, as the example shows, always a problem of adjustments at a margin. But there is no practicable way to state marginal objectives or values except in terms of particular policies. That one value is preferred to another in one decision situation does not mean that it will be preferred in another decision situation in which it can be had only at great sacrifice of another value. Attempts to rank or order values in general and abstract terms so that they do not shift from decision to decision end up by ignoring the relevant marginal preferences. The significance of this third point thus goes very far. Even if all administrators had at hand an agreed set of values, objectives, and constraints, and an agreed ranking of these values, objectives, and constraints, their marginal values in actual choice situations would be impossible to formulate.

Unable consequently to formulate the relevant values first and then choose among policies to achieve them, administrators must choose directly among alternative policies that offer different marginal combinations of values. Somewhat paradoxically, the only practicable way to disclose one's relevant marginal values even to oneself is to describe the policy one chooses to achieve them. Except roughly and vaguely, I know of no way to describe —or even to understand—what my relative evaluations are for, say, freedom and security, speed and accuracy in governmental decisions, or low taxes and better schools than to describe my preferences among specific policy choices that might be made between the alternatives in each of the pairs.

In summary, two aspects of the process by which values are actually handled can be distinguished. The first is clear: evaluation and empirical analysis are intertwined; that is, one chooses among values and among policies at one and the same time. Put a little more elaborately, one simultaneously chooses a policy to attain certain objectives and chooses the objectives themselves. The second aspect is related but distinct: the administrator focuses his attention on marginal or incremental values. Whether he is aware of it or not, he does not find general formulations of objectives very helpful and in fact makes specific marginal or incremental comparisons. Two policies, X and Y, confront him. Both promise the same degree of attainment of objectives a, b, c, d, and e. But X promises him somewhat more of f than does Y, while Y promises him somewhat more of g than does X. In choosing between them, he is in fact offered the alternative of a marginal or incremental amount of f at the expense of a marginal or incremental amount of g. The only values that are relevant to his choice are these increments by which the two policies differ; and, when he finally chooses between the two marginal values, he does so by making a choice between policies.

. . .

Relations Between Means and Ends (2b)

Decision-making is ordinarily formalized as a means-ends relationship: means are conceived to be evaluated and chosen in the light of ends finally selected independently of and prior to the choice of means. This is the means-ends relationship of the root method. But it follows from all that has just been said that such a means-ends relationship is possible only to the extent that values are agreed upon, are reconcilable, and are stable at the margin. Typically, therefore, such a means-ends relationship is absent from the branch method, where means and ends are simultaneously chosen.

Yet any departure from the means-ends relationship of the root method will strike some readers as inconceivable. For it will appear to them that only in such a relationship is it possible to determine whether one policy choice is better or worse than another. How can an administrator know whether he has made a wise or foolish decision if he is without prior values or objectives by which to judge his decisions? The answer to this question calls up the third distinctive difference between root and branch methods: how to decide the best policy.

The Test of "Good" Policy (3b)

In the root method, a decision is "correct," "good," or "rational" if it can be shown to attain some specified objective, where the objective can be specified without simply describing the decision itself. Where objectives are defined only through the marginal or incremental approach to values described above, it is still sometimes possible to test whether a policy does in fact attain the desired objectives; but a precise statement of the objectives takes the form of a description of the policy chosen or some alternative to it. To show that a policy is mistaken one cannot offer an abstract argument that important objectives are not achieved; one must instead argue that another policy is more to be preferred.

So far, the departure from customary ways of looking at problem-solving is not troublesome, for many administrators will be quick to agree that the most effective discussion of the correctness of policy does take the form of comparison with other policies that might have been chosen. But what of the situation in which administrators cannot agree on values or objectives, either abstractly or in marginal terms? What then is the test of "good" policy? For the root method, there is no test. Agreement on objectives failing, there is no standard of "correctness." For the method of successive limited comparisons, the test is agreement on policy itself, which remains possible even when agreement on values is not.

It has been suggested that continuing agreement in Congress on the desirability of extending old age insurance stems from liberal desires to strengthen the welfare programs of the federal government and from conservative desires to reduce union demands for private pension plans. If so, this is an excellent demonstration of the ease with which individuals of different ideologies often can agree on concrete policy. Labor mediators report a similar phenomenon: the contestants cannot agree on criteria for settling their disputes but can agree on specific proposals. Similarly, when one administrator's objective turns out to be another's means, they often can agree on policy.

Agreement on policy thus becomes the only practicable test of the policy's correctness. And for one administrator to seek to win the other over to agreement on ends as well would accomplish nothing and create quite unnecessary controversy.

. . .

Non-Comprehensive Analysis (4b)

Ideally, rational-comprehensive analysis leaves out nothing important. But it is impossible to take everything important into consideration unless "important" is so narrowly defined that analysis is in fact quite limited. Limits on human intellectual capacities and on available information set definite limits to man's capacity to be comprehensive. In actual fact, therefore, no one can practice the rational-comprehensive method for really complex problems, and every administrator faced with a sufficiently complex problem must find ways drastically to simplify.

An administrator assisting in the formulation of agricultural economic policy cannot in the first place be competent on all possible policies. He cannot even comprehend one policy entirely. In planning a soil bank program, he cannot successfully anticipate the impact of higher or lower farm income on, say, urbanization—the possible consequent loosening of family ties, possible consequent eventual need for revisions in social security and further implications for tax problems arising out of new federal responsibilities for social security and municipal responsibilities for urban services. . . .

In the method of successive limited comparisons, simplification is systematically achieved in two principal ways. First, it is achieved through limitation of policy comparisons to those policies that differ in relatively small degree from policies presently in effect. Such a limitation immediately reduces the number of alternatives to be investigated and also drastically simplifies the character of the investigation of each. For it is not necessary to undertake fundamental inquiry into an alternative and its consequences; it is necessary only to study those respects in which the proposed alternative and its consequences differ from the status quo. The empirical comparison of marginal differences among alternative policies that differ only marginally is, of course, a counterpart to the incremental or marginal comparison of values discussed above.

Relevance as Well as Realism

It is a matter of common observation that in Western democracies public administrators and policy analysts in general do largely limit their analyses to incremental or marginal differences in policies that are chosen to differ only incrementally. They do not do so, however, solely because they desperately need some way to simplify their problems; they also do so in order to be relevant. Democracies change their policies almost entirely through incremental adjustments. Policy does not move in leaps and bounds.

The incremental character of political change in the United States has often been remarked. The two major political parties agree on fundamentals; they offer alternative policies to the voters only on relatively small points of difference. Both parties favor full employment, but they define it somewhat differently; both favor the development of water power resources, but in slightly different ways; and both favor unemployment compensation, but not the same level of benefits. Similarly, shifts of policy within a party take place largely through a series of relatively small changes, as can be seen in their only gradual acceptance of the idea of governmental responsibility for support of the unemployed, a change in party positions beginning in the early 30's and culminating in a sense in the Employment Act of 1946.

Party behavior is in turn rooted in public attitudes, and political theorists cannot conceive of democracy's surviving in the United States in the absence of fundamental agreement on potentially disruptive issues, with consequent limitation of policy debates to relatively small differences in policy.

Since the policies ignored by the administrator are politically impossible and so irrelevant, the simplification of analysis achieved by concentrating on policies that differ only incrementally is not a capricious kind of simplification. In addition, it can be argued that, given the limits on knowledge within which policy-makers are confined, simplifying by limiting the focus to small variations from present policy makes the most of available knowledge. Because policies being considered are like present and past policies, the administrator can obtain information and claim some insight. Non-incremental policy proposals are therefore typically not only politically irrelevant but also unpredictable in their consequences.

The second method of simplification of analysis is the practice of ignoring important possible consequences of possible policies, as well as the values attached to the neglected consequences. If this appears to disclose a shocking shortcoming of successive limited comparisons, it can be replied that, even if the exclusions are random, policies may nevertheless be more intelligently formulated than through futile attempts to achieve a comprehensiveness beyond human capacity. Actually, however, the exclusions, seeming arbitrary or random from one point of view, need be neither.

Achieving a Degree of Comprehensiveness

Suppose that each value neglected by one policy-making agency were a major concern of at least one other agency. In that case, a helpful division of labor would be achieved, and no agency need find its task beyond its capacities. The shortcomings of such a system would be that one agency might destroy a value either before another agency could be activated to safeguard it or in spite of another agency's efforts. But the possibility that important values may be lost is present in any form of organization, even where agencies attempt to comprehend in planning more than is humanly possible.

The virtue of such a hypothetical division of labor is that every important interest or value has its watchdog. And these watchdogs can protect the interests in their jurisdiction in two quite different ways: first, by redressing damages done by other agencies; and, second, by anticipating and heading off injury before it occurs.

In a society like that of the United States in which individuals are free to combine to pursue almost any possible common interest they might have and in which government agencies are sensitive to the pressures of these groups, the system described is approximated. Almost every interest has its watchdog. Without claiming that every interest has a sufficiently powerful watchdog, it can be argued that our system often can assure a more comprehensive regard for the values of the whole society than any attempt at intellectual comprehensiveness.

In the United States, for example, no part of government attempts a comprehensive overview of policy on income distribution. A policy nevertheless evolves, and one responding to a wide variety of interests. A process of mutual adjustment among farm groups, labor unions, municipalities and school boards, tax authorities, and government agencies with responsibilities in the fields of housing, health, highways, national parks, fire, and police accomplishes a distribution of income in which particular income problems neglected at one point in the decision processes become central at another point.

Mutual adjustment is more pervasive than the explicit forms it takes in negotiation between groups; it persists through the mutual impacts of groups upon each other even where they are not in communication. For all the imperfections and latent dangers in this ubiquitous process of mutual adjustment, it will often accomplish an adaptation of policies to a wider range of interests than could be done by one group centrally.

Note, too, how the incremental pattern of policy-making fits with the multiple pressure pattern. For when decisions are only incremental—closely related to known policies—it is easier for one group to anticipate the kind of moves another might make and easier too for it to make correction for injury already accomplished.

Even partisanship and narrowness, to use pejorative terms, will sometimes be assets to rational decision-making, for they can doubly insure that what one agency neglects, another will not; they specialize personnel to distinct points of view. The claim is valid that effective rational coordination of the federal administration, if possible to achieve at all, would require an agreed set of values—if "rational" is defined as the practice of the root method of decision-making. But a high degree of administrative coordination occurs as each agency adjusts its policies to the concerns of the other agencies in the process of fragmented decision-making I have just described.

. . .

Succession of Comparisons (5b)

The final distinctive element in the branch method is that the comparisons, together with the policy choice, proceed in a chronological series. Policy is not made once and for all; it is made and re-made endlessly. Policy-making is a process of successive approximation to some desired objectives in which what is desired itself continues to change under reconsideration.

Making policy is at best a very rough process. Neither social scientists, nor politicians, nor public administrators yet know enough about the social world to avoid repeated error in predicting the consequences of policy moves. A wise policy-maker consequently expects that his policies will achieve only part of what he hopes and at the same time will produce unanticipated consequences he would have preferred to avoid. If he proceeds through a *succession* of incremental changes, he avoids serious lasting mistakes in several ways.

In the first place, past sequences of policy steps have given him knowledge about the probable consequences of further similar steps. Second, he need not attempt big jumps toward his goals that would require predictions beyond his or anyone else's knowledge, because he never expects his policy to be a final resolution of a problem. His decision is only one step, one that if successful can quickly be followed by another. Third, he is in effect able to test his previous predictions as he moves on to each further step. Lastly, he often can remedy a past error fairly quickly—more quickly than if policy proceeded through more distinct steps widely spaced in time.

Compare this comparative analysis of incremental changes with the aspiration to employ theory in the root method. Man cannot think without classifying, without subsuming one experience under a more general category of experiences. The attempt to push categorization as far as possible and to find general propositions which can be applied to specific situations is what I refer to with the word "theory." Where root analysis often leans heavily on theory in this sense, the branch method does not.

The assumption of root analysts is that theory is the most systematic and economical way to bring relevant knowledge to bear on a specific problem. Granting the assumption, an unhappy fact is that we do not have adequate theory to apply to problems in any policy area, although theory is more adequate in some areas—monetary policy, for example—than in others. Comparative analysis, as in the branch method, is sometimes a systematic alternative to theory.

Suppose an administrator must choose among a small group of policies that differ only incrementally from each other and from present policy. He might aspire to "understand" each of the alternatives—for example, to know all the consequences of each aspect of each policy. If so, he would indeed require theory. In fact, however, he would usually decide that, *for policy-making purposes,* he need know, as explained above, only the consequences of each of those aspects of the policies in which they differed from one another. For this much more modest aspiration, he requires no theory (although it might be helpful, if available), for he can proceed to isolate probable differences by examining the differences in consequences associated with past differences in policies, a feasible program because he can take his observations from a long sequence of incremental changes.

For example, without a more comprehensive social theory about juvenile delinquency than scholars have yet produced, one cannot possibly understand the ways in which a variety of public policies—say on education, housing, recreation, employment, race relations, and policing—might encourage or discourage delinquency. And one needs such an understanding if he undertakes the comprehensive overview of the problem prescribed in the models of the root method. If, however, one merely wants to mobilize knowledge sufficient to assist in a choice among a small group of similar policies—alternative policies on juvenile court procedures, for example—he can do so by comparative analysis of the results of similar past policy moves.

. . .

Successive Comparisons as a System

Successive limited comparisons is, then, indeed a method or system; it is not a failure of method for which administrators ought to apologize. None the less, its imperfections, which have not been explored in this paper, are many. For example, the method is without a built-in safeguard for all relevant values, and it also may lead the decision-maker to overlook excellent policies for no other reason than that they are not suggested by the chain of successive policy steps leading up to the present. Hence, it ought to be said that under this method, as well as under some of the most sophisticated variants of the root method—operations research, for example—policies will continue to be as foolish as they are wise.

Why then bother to describe the method in all the above detail? Because it is in fact a common method of policy formulation, and is, for complex problems, the principal reliance of administrators as well as of other policy analysts. And because it will be superior to any other decision-making method available for complex problems in many circumstances, certainly superior to a futile attempt at superhuman comprehensiveness. . . .

. . .

The Administrative System as Symbol

17

Murray Edelman

Administrative agencies are to be understood as economic and political instruments of the parties they regulate and benefit, not of a reified "society," "general will," or "public interest." At the same time they perform this instrumental function, they perform an equally important expressive function for the polity as a whole: to create and sustain an impression that induces acquiescence of the public in the face of private tactics that might otherwise be expected to produce resentment, protest, and resistance. The instrumental function of administrative agencies, as defined here, has been observed, demonstrated, and documented by every careful observer of regulatory agencies. This literature has nonetheless never successfully been used to challenge the widely held view and remains an esoteric facet of the study of economics and political science. The expressive function has received less attention from scholars, though the quiescence of masses in the face of demonstrable denial of what is promised them clearly calls for explanation.
. . .

Few if any norms are more deeply embedded in our culture, as verbal abstractions, than the two repeatedly cited as guiding administrative refereeing of conflict: that the weak should be protected from the strong and that conflict should be settled peacefully. Yet administrative surveillance over rival groupings commonly facilitates one of two quite different results: (a) aggrandizement by an organized group in the wake of symbolic reassurance of the unorganized . . . ; or (b) an alliance of the ostensibly rival groupings at the expense of "outside" groups. In neither case does the regulatory agency restrict claims backed by sanctions or referee a conflict. In both cases it becomes a psychologically and organizationally effective *part* of a political constellation which possesses potent private weapons already. Specifically, it becomes that instrument of the constellation whose function it is to allay outside political protest: to provide a setting of stability and predictability within which the organized groups involved can use their weapons with minimal anxiety about counterattack. It can perform this function better than any "private" group can do it because, as a public agency, it inevitably manipulates and evokes the myths, rituals, and other symbols attaching to "the state" in our culture.

Implicit in this formulation is the view that the creation of an administrative agency in a policy area signals the emergence of a changed relationship between the groups labeled as adversaries. The agency, the regulated groups, and the ostensible beneficiaries become necessary instruments for each other while continuing to play the role of rivals and combatants. Careful examination of the nature of the change in their strategic positions clarifies the sense in which this proposition holds true. The establishment of a National Labor Relations Board, Interstate Commerce Commission, Federal Communications Commission, Office of Price Administration, or utilities commission constitutes assurance that none of the groups directly involved can push any temporary or permanent bargaining advantage to the point of eliminating the other. Certain messages are implicitly but clearly conveyed by the very creation and continued functioning of the agency, and the messages are solace for very anxious people. Unions will continue to exist as part of the American economic scene. Radio stations, railroads, airlines, and utilities will not be nationalized. Negroes will be protected in their use of economic and other weapons. Consumers are assured that the majesty of the state will protect them from the threat posed by powerful economic concentrations and sellers. In short, existing institutions are legitimized, permitting them to utilize their bargaining weapons to the full, if they have any, and to survive and comfort themselves if they have not.

To see vividly this function of an administrative agency it is helpful to consider the alternative: the situation prevailing before any agency is established in a policy area, or the situation that would prevail if an existing agency were magically abolished. We have had enough case studies of the political origins of regulatory agencies to be well aware of what is involved. A group with oligopolistic or other economic weapons at its disposal maximizes its gain, testing to learn how much the traffic will bear. This strategy creates adverse interests and anxieties: tensions and a need for their resolution on the part of both the predatory group and of its victims. Both need a definition of the situation: a legitimizing act which will remove uncertainty and the more serious anxieties in precisely the fashion I have just posited that administrative agencies do.

If the Interstate Commerce Commission, for example, were suddenly abolished, its function of maintaining and raising rates and legitimizing mergers and abandonments of service would have to be performed by the private carriers themselves. Potential customers would fear sudden and substantial changes; and the carriers themselves would fear strong public protest. Anxieties on both sides and anticipatory protest would create a degree of instability and tension that would have to be eliminated, very likely by the creation of an agency much like the ICC.

The assurance that all involved groups are legitimate and can participate at will in a joint ritual (more of administrative action as ritual shortly) constitutes a demonstration of symbiosis rather than bitter-end rivalry or parasitism. If one of the groups involved is unorganized, this is as far as the symbiosis goes. For the unorganized group the benefits are partly psychic and partly a guarantee of survival. . . .

For the unorganized the administrative activity brings a change from the role of potential victims to the role of the protected: ostensible sharers with the regulated industry in the economic benefits together with a powerful showering of symbols suggesting that the new role is secure.

For those not immediately involved the same meaning is conveyed. Once it is assumed that an agency assures service and fair rates for consumers, protection of the industry against loss or destruction becomes a tactic in the protection of the industry's clients as well. A rate increase that would be rather obvious exploitation of these clients in a setting of economic infighting unrestrained by government is magically converted into help for the customers as well as the industry. Where the agency's functioning constitutes legitimizing of a claim on the national product, the same functioning symbolically involves both adversary parties as supporters of the claim. The commuter or airline passenger needs his transportation, and, by definition, the industry cannot now exploit him.

A rather more interesting symbiosis takes place where both adversary parties are organized, as in labor-management relations. Here the blood and thunder of battle, the charges and countercharges that the other group is behaving unfairly, the more or less incessant invocations of stereotyped images of the others' great strength and predatory habits, the occasional well-publicized resort to boycotts, sit-ins, and other economic and social weapons all serve to underline in the public mind the reality of the rivalry and the incompatibility of the rival interest.

It is true that there was a real effort by each adversary to crush the other for the first several decades after the industrial revolution came to the United States. Labor created such syndicalist or socialist organizations as the IWW and the Knights of Labor. Management used terrorism, espionage, its incomparably greater economic strength, and its psychological controls over judges and other public officials to break unions. This history of all-out warfare remains symbolically a part of the relationship between labor and management; but rivalry between management and labor in the go-for-broke sense disappeared at about the time administrative agencies were established in the field and was replaced by a common interest in a larger share of the national product to split between them. The new institutions did not neatly or completely replace the old ones everywhere, and the continued skirmishing effectively blinded practically everybody to the significance of the change for a long time. No group was more thoroughly blinded than those labor economists of the postwar years who had been drawn to the field in the first place by the picturesque and ideologically clean-cut infighting of the thirties and therefore had a large emotional stake in the thesis that the battle was real.

A major function of much union-management bargaining in the late fifties and sixties has been to provide a ritual which must be acted out as a prerequisite for the quiescent acceptance of higher prices and higher wages by those not directly involved. Nor is it surprising that the rite is most formalized precisely in the industries in which the bargaining and the speculation about the likelihood of a strike are most widely publicized: steel, autos, meat packing, heavy machinery, electronics. In these cases union-management bargaining has come close to joining such foreign institutions as codetermination and national economic councils or such domestic ones as the agreed bill process as virtual giveaways both of the game and of the gross national income. The symbiosis could hardly be clearer.

. . .

Administrative activity is effective in inducing a measure of wide acceptance of all the objectives symbolized by the agencies only because the mass public that does the accepting is ambivalent about these objectives. Its responses to events and speeches manifests both a recognition of the value of each function and anxiety about the self-seeking and predatory intentions of the economic groups profiting from them. The personification of the elements in such psychic tension, and resolution of the tension through an acting out of the contending hopes and fears, has always been a common practice in both primitive and advanced societies. To let the adversary groups oppose each other through the workings of an administrative agency continuously resolving the conflicts in "decisions" and policies replaces tension and uncertainty with a measure of clarity, meaning, confidence, and security. This is precisely the function performed in more primitive societies by the rain dance, the victory dance, and the peace pipe ceremony, each of which amounts to an acting out of contending forces that occasion widespread anxiety and a resolution that is acceptable and accepted.

. . .

The administrative system is in fact a rather sensitive instrument for highlighting those political functions that are widely, if ambivalently, supported. It has time and again been necessary to change the hierarchical locus of a function precisely to facilitate such highlighting, even though there was no reason to suppose that the locational change meant a shift in policy direction or in the relative influence of interested groups. The intense lobbying in the nineteenth century by farm, business, and labor groups for their "own" cabinet departments is one expression of this phenomenon, even though in each instance the new departments at first did little or nothing not done by the bureau before, and there was even a bit of scrambling to find things for them to do. . . .

Establishment of a function at the highest hierarchical level is symbolically important only where there is genuine doubt about its high valuation or political support, as in the instances just cited. Where the support is assured, as in the cases of the FBI or the Army Corps of Engineers, a shift to the highest vertical location is unnecessary and might even be impolitic in that activities of the agencies inconsistent with their symbolic claims might become conspicuous.

The creation in 1947 of a single Department of Defense is a revealing example of a shift in the name and conspicuousness of an established function without any significant corresponding change in policy or group influence. The name "defense," the single department, and the publicity accorded the activities of the Secretary of Defense and his staff highlight a function that is universally supported, as distinct from the image of rival service imperialism that had been prevalent. Larger claims on the national product are thus more easily legitimized, while the game of service imperialism need not be disturbed.

The forms benefits take also focus attention on a widely approved function rather than on the distribution of benefits to organized economic groupings. The administrative proceeding is so structured that benefits are perceived in relation to a symbolically potent and widely shared abstract objective and not in relation to their very material recipients. What we have here is a fascinating application of a well-known psychological phenomenon: that we screen percepts and interpret them in relation to a preconceived organization of reality. In administrative activity the organizing conception is very plainly presented and reiterated. It is given first in the very name of the agency. More important, it is reiterated and continuously emphasized as both proponents and opponents of specific policies justify their positions in the name of the same objective or organizing principle: a smoothly functioning transportation system or power system or communications system, rendering maximum service; the most effective defense posture; equality of management-labor bargaining power; fair trade practices; and so on.

Finally, the structure of the administrative system eliminates practically every opportunity to consider these various symbolic objectives at the same time, as rival claimants on the national product. As policy questions arise within each agency, decisions are justified in relation to the objective or organizing concept of that agency. An attack on the value of that organizing concept could come only from outside: from a different interest cluster. But this never happens in a setting in which any significant public attention to the attack could occur. It can happen only in congressional appropriation committee considerations, and there only to a slight degree and in a setting guaranteeing minimal weighing of the comparative values of alternatives even by the committee members, let alone the uninvolved public. The organizing principle retains its pristine potency.

The most valuable tangible benefits distributed by the federal government of the United States are certainly defense contracts. The form in which these become conspicuous to the uninvolved public is in defense appropriations, which highlight the universally approved defense function. That the appropriations mean high profits for the contractors is rendered inconspicuous by the political structures and modes of communication utilized. Administrative form both serves to confer an important benefit and legitimizes it through its presentation as a means of meeting a universal popular demand. There is no necessary implication here that the appropriations are not really needed for defense; only that the mode of structuring the benefit legitimizes it and makes its continuation probable whether or not it serves its ostensible instrumental function.

This form of benefit is probably feasible only if the instrumental objective to be served is potent and widely shared: defense, postal service, airmail service, road construction, and so on. Where the objective is less widely shared, the form of benefit characteristically changes. A classic example is agricultural subsidies, which are so structured as to highlight a virtuous abstraction: parity. The formula by which parity payments are computed is a periodically manipulated resultant of group bargaining, and the payoffs have disproportionately gone to large and commercial farming establishments; but the administrative organization symbolizes the creation of parity.

Though parity is practically a household word to newspaper readers, its dynamics are a mystery. Congress has required at one or another time that interest, taxes, freight rates, and wages be added to the formula for computing the index of prices paid by farmers. Before 1950 there were 170 items in the index; since 1950 there have been 337. It includes forty-eight agricultural commodities, each given its own weight. This weighting, inclusion, and exclusion is of course the real determinant of the benefit, not the abstraction "parity."

Another example of subsidies hidden under the guise of a popular objective are the large federal payments to publishers and advertisers in the form of second-class mail rates far lower than is necessary to cover the costs of delivering magazines and hard-sell blurbs. Again, the subsidy may or may not be justified, depending on the observer's values, but administrative structuring has a continuing influence on the process.

Where the benefits are not to come from the public treasury at all, but rather from a grant of official permission to charge higher rates for goods or services, the administrative form is still different; but it again amounts to a ritual emphasis upon a symbolically potent objective. Benefits are still offered so that they are perceived in relation to the abstract objective and not in relation to their material recipients. Thus administrative decision-makers on the regulatory commissions function in a setting in which they become in effect part of the management of the industry they are to regulate. They are forcefully and regularly bombarded with statements of the various costs confronting the industry and with its business problems; they associate formally and often informally with its top officers, learning their perspectives and their values. At the same time they are kept intensely aware of the sanctions that await them and the agency if these business and organizational considerations are ignored: congressional displeasure, public attacks, probable displacement at the end of their terms of office. Even more obviously, their careers and prestige are now tied to the industry. As the industry grows, so does their function and importance; if the industry dies, so does the agency. Symbiosis ripens into osmosis and digestion. There is no significant difference between this situation and that of the corporation officers themselves.

The organizational and psychological embrace of the industry around the regulatory commissioners go hand in hand. To be part of the organization in the sense of incessant exposure to its problems and decisional premises is to come to share its perspectives and values. This is not "pressure"; it is absorption. It explains the inevitability of a bias in choosing value premises: a bias which has been consistently observed by students of administrative regulation. The grant of benefits in these instances has the form of elaborate due process, involving complicated and drawn out inspection of data, both in the agency's offices and in formal hearings. But the screening apparatus through which decisional premises must pass is supplied by the organizational setting and can be counted on to grind out its foreordained result regardless of the awesomeness of the procedures. The latter serve quite another function: not so much to build rational calculations of the consequences of alternative decisions, as to legitimize what finally is announced by emphasizing the care with which it is related to the agency's symbolic objective. Occasional decisions slapping the industry but not altering the major trend further bolster the symbolism, for the commissioners themselves as much as for the mass public.

One type of procedural requirement is especially revealing. The legislature has flatly proscribed the gathering of particular kinds of data by some agencies. A rather flagrant example of this occurs in the Taft-Hartley Act, which forbids the National Labor Relations Board to employ staff members for economic analysis, forbids the hearing examiner from making recommendations in representation cases, and forbids the trial examiner in unfair labor practice cases from being present when the board considers the case at which he presided. Such provisions quite explicitly bar the board from paying overt attention to certain types of data or points of view, particularly facts and values growing out of observation of what occurred, or allegedly occurred, in the plant. The board is thus encouraged to behave less like an investigating administrative agency and more like a court, confining its attention chiefly to past interpretations of the law. Such ignoring of actual behavior in the plant is practically certain to mean overlooking much of the evidence that an employer charged with an unfair labor practice did things which indicate he has an anti-union bias. It is therefore not hard to understand why employer groups favored these procedural innovations in the Taft-Hartley law and unions opposed them.

Another example of this device appeared in a rider attached to the law appropriating Federal Trade Commission funds for 1954. In this instance Congress stipulated that "no part of the foregoing appropriation shall be available for a statistical analysis of the consumer's dollar."

While the pro-employer bias of the Taft-Hartley provisions is clear, they could not very often prevent the board from learning about significant anti-union behavior in the plant or other relevant information. Their effect, rather, is exactly what they purport to provide: to limit the publicizing of certain kinds of information *as part of the formal record and proceedings.* They thereby keep the rite unsullied when the NLRB or the FTC makes decisions of the kind pro-business congressmen hope for. To keep it unsullied is to preserve its sanctifying power in fuller potency.

The administrative system, as symbol and ritual, thus serves as legitimizer of elite objectives, as reassurance against threats, and sometimes as catalyst of symbiotic ties between adversaries. It should not be surprising that we find these larger social functions of the administrative system mirrored inside each of the agencies as well, in the gathering and choice of premises upon which decisions are based.

Simon and others have demonstrated that complete rationality in decision-making is never possible in any case: because knowledge of the consequences of any course of action is always fragmentary, because future values cannot be anticipated perfectly, and because only a very few of the possible alternative courses of action ever come to mind. By observing how administrative staff members are themselves guided in their work by the compelling symbols the system serves, we can go a considerable way toward defining the particular biases or policy directions which these limits upon rationality take. We can, that is, hope to observe some systematic patterns in departures from administrative rationality. . . .

The Budgetary Process

18

Aaron Wildavsky

The mind of man is an elusive substance. It cannot be directly observed for most purposes, and inferences about it are notoriously tricky. No wonder our attention is more readily caught by the clash of wills in the exercise of influence and the confrontation of rival strategies in the pursuit of funds. Yet the ways in which the human mind goes about making calculations in the process of arriving at decisions have a fascination for anyone concerned with how men attempt to solve problems. More important, perhaps, for our purposes, one cannot hope to understand why men behave as they do unless one has some idea about how they make their calculations. And, most important, methods of calculation are not neutral; the ways in which calculations are made affect the outcomes of the political system: the distribution of shares in policy among the participants, the "who gets what and how much" of politics. Different methods of calculation often result in different decisions. Otherwise, it would make no difference what kinds of calculations were made and there would be much less reason to pursue the topic.

Budgeting is complex, largely because of the complexity of modern life. Suppose that you were a Congressman or a Budget Bureau official interested in the leukemia research program and you wondered how the money was being spent. By looking at the National Cancer Institute's budgetary presentation you would discover that $42,012 is being spent on a project studying "factors and mechanisms concerned in hemopoiesis," and that $5,095 is being spent for "a study of the relationship of neutralizing antibodies for the Rous sarcoma virus to resistance and susceptibility for visceral lymphomatosis." Could you tell whether too much money is being spent on hemopoiesis in comparison to lymphomatosis or whether either project is relevant for any useful purpose? You might sympathize with Congressman Laird's plaintive cry, "A lot of things go on in this subcommittee that I cannot understand." It is not surprising, therefore, that one runs across expressions of dismay at the difficulties of understanding technical subjects. Representative Jensen has a granddaughter who is mentioned in hearings more often than most people, and who is reputed by him to have read "all the stuff she can get on nuclear science. She never reads a story book. . . . And she will ask me questions and she just stumps me. I say, 'Jennifer, for Heaven's sake. I can't answer that.' 'Well,' she says, 'You are on the Atomic Energy Commission Committee, Grandpa.' 'Yes,' he replies, 'But I am not schooled in the art.'" A cry goes up for simplification. "I just want this presentation made more simple and easy to grasp," a Representative says to an administrative official. Even those nominally "in the know" may be nonplussed. "That is a budget device," said

185

an agency budget officer, "which is difficult for me to understand, and I have been in this business for over 20 years."

In our personal lives we are used to discovering that things rarely turn out quite as we had expected. Somehow when it comes to political activities we seem to expect a much greater degree of foresight. Yet life is incredibly complicated and there is very little theory that would enable people to predict how programs will turn out if they are at all new. When Representative Preston says "I cannot recall any project of any size that has ever been presented to this committee—that came out in the end like the witnesses testified it would be at the outset," the problem is less one of always estimating on the low side than of not having sufficient knowledge to do better.

There are cases in which one might do better if one had endless time, and unlimited ability to calculate. But time is in terribly short supply, the human mind is drastically limited in what it can encompass, and the number of budgetary items may be huge, so that the trite phrase "A man can only do so much" takes on real meaning. "We might as well be frank," Representative Mahan stated, "that no human being regardless of his position and . . . capacity could possibly be completely familiar with all the items of appropriations contained in this defense bill. . . ." But decisions have to be made. "There is a saying around the Pentagon," McNeil [former defense comptroller] informs us, "that . . . there is only one person in the United States who can force a decision, and that is the Government Printer [when the budget must go to the press]."

Aside from the complexity of individual budgetary programs, there remains the imposing problem of making comparisons among different programs that have different values for different people. This involves deciding such questions as how much highways are worth as compared to recreation facilities, national defense, schools, and so on down the range of governmental functions. No common denominator among these functions has been developed. No matter how hard they try, therefore, officials in places like the Bureau of the Budget discover that they cannot find any objective method of judging priorities among programs. How, then, do budget officials go about meeting their staggering burden of calculation?

Aids to Calculation

Some officials do not deal with complexity at all; they are just overwhelmed and never quite recover. Others work terribly hard at mastering their subjects. "This [House Appropriations] Committee is no place for a man who doesn't work," a member said. "They have to be hardworking. It isn't just a job; it's a way of life." But sheer effort is not enough. It has become necessary to develop mechanisms, however imperfect, for helping men make decisions that are in some sense meaningful in a complicated world.

Budgeting is experiential. One way of dealing with a problem of huge magnitude is to make only the roughest guesses while letting experience accumulate. Then, when the consequences of the various actions become apparent, it is possible to make modifications to avoid the difficulties. This is the rationale implicit in former defense comptroller McNeil's statement justifying the absence of a ceiling on expenditures at the beginning of the Korean War.

There was no long background in the United States, with 150 years of peak and valley experience, as to what carrying on a high level of defense year in and year out for a long period would cost, or what was involved. I think a very good start was made in listing everything that anyone could think they needed . . . knowing full well, however . . . that if you overbought certain engines or trucks, it could be balanced out the following year. That method was used for a year or two and then sufficient experience had been gained . . . to know that . . . defense would cost in the neighborhood of $35 to $40 billion.

Budgeting is simplified.   Another way of handling complexity is to use actions on simpler items as indices of more complicated ones. Instead of dealing directly with the cost of a huge atomic installation, for example, Congressmen may seek to discover how personnel and administrative costs or real estate transactions with which they have some familiarity are handled. If these items are handled properly then they may feel better able to trust the administrators with the larger ones. The reader has probably heard of this practice under some such title as "straining at gnats." And no doubt this is just what it is in many cases; unable to handle the more complex problems the Congressmen abdicate by retreating to the simpler ones. Here I am concerned to point out that this practice may at times have greater validity than appears on the surface if it is used as a testing device, and if there is a reasonable connection between the competence shown in handling simple and complex items.

A related method calls for directing one's observations to the responsible administrative officials rather than to the subject matter, if one is aware that the subject is so difficult and the operations so huge that the people in charge have to be trusted. They are questioned on a point here and there, a difficulty in this and that, in an effort to see whether or not they are competent and reliable. A senior Congressman reported that he followed an administrator's testimony looking for "strain in voice or manner," "covert glances" and other such indications and later followed them up probing for weaknesses.

Budgeting officials "satisfice."   Calculations may be simplified by lowering one's sights. Although they do not use Herbert Simon's vocabulary, budget officials do not try to maximize but, instead, they "satisfice" (satisfy and suffice). Which is to say that they do not try for the best of all possible worlds, whatever that might be, but, in their words, they try to "get by," to "come out all right," to "avoid trouble," to "avoid the worst," and so on. If he can get others to go along, if too many others do not complain too long and too loud, then the official may take the fact of agreement on something as the measure of success. And since the budget comes up every year, and deals largely with piecemeal adjustment, it is possible to correct glaring weaknesses as they arise.

It is against a background of the enormous burden of calculation that the ensuing description of the major aid for calculating budgets—the incremental method—should be understood.

Budgeting is incremental. The largest determining factor of the size and content of this year's budget is last year's budget. Most of the budget is a product of previous decisions. As former Budget Director Stans put it, "There is very little flexibility in the budget because of the tremendous number of commitments that are made years ahead." The budget may be conceived of as an iceberg with by far the largest part below the surface, outside the control of anyone. Many items in the budget are standard and are simply reenacted every year unless there is a special reason to challenge them. Long-range commitments have been made and this year's share is scooped out of the total and included as part of the annual budget. There are mandatory programs such as price supports or veterans' pensions whose expenses must be met. The defense budget accounts for about half of the total and it is rarely decreased. There are programs which appear to be satisfactory and which no one challenges any more. Powerful political support makes the inclusion of other activities inevitable. The convergence of expectations on what must be included is indicated in Representative Flood's comments on the census of business, which had been in trouble in previous years. "I guess this is a sacred cow, is it not . . . ?" Flood said. "This has been generated by . . . the manufacturing industry community of the nation, for its particular benefit and the general welfare. . . . There is no longer any doubt that this is built right into our system any more. . . . " Agencies are going concerns and a minimum must be spent on housekeeping (though this item is particularly vulnerable to attack because it does not appear to involve program issues). At any one time, after past policies are paid for, a rather small percentage—seldom larger than 30 per cent, often smaller than 5—is within the realm of anybody's (including Congressional and Budget Bureau) discretion as a practical matter.

In order to be more precise, it is desirable to discover the range of variation of the percentage of increase or decrease of appropriations as compared to the previous year. Table 1 shows the results for 37 domestic agencies over a 12 year period. Almost exactly one-third of the cases (149 out of 444) fall within the 5 per cent range. A little more than half the cases (233) are in the 10 per cent bracket. Just under three-quarters of the cases (326) occur within 30 per cent. Less than 10 per cent (31) are in the extreme range of 50 per cent or more. And many of these are accounted for by agenices with extreme, built-in cyclical fluctuations, such as those of the Census Bureau.

Table 1* Budgeting is incremental.**

0- 5%	6- 10%	11- 20%	21- 30%	31- 40%	41- 50%	51- 100%	101 + %
149	84	93	51	21	15	24	7

*Figures recalculated from those supplied by Richard Fenno.
**Table shows the number of cases of 37 domestic bureaus over a 12 year period that fall into various percentages of increase over the past year (444 cases in all).

Budgeting is incremental, not comprehensive. The beginning of wisdom about an agency budget is that it is almost never actively reviewed as a whole every year in the sense of reconsidering the value of all existing programs as compared to all possible alternatives. Instead, it is based on last year's budget with special attention given to a narrow range of increases or decreases. Thus the men who make the budget are concerned with relatively small increments to an existing base. Their attention is focused on a small number of items over which the budgetary battle is fought. As Representative Norrel declared in testifying before the House Rules Committee, "If you will read the hearings of the subcommittees you will find that most of our time is spent in talking about the changes in the bill which we will have next year from the one we had this year, the reductions made, and the increases made. That which is not changed has very little, if anything, said about it." Most appropriations committee members, like Senator Hayden in dismissing an item brought up by the Bureau of Indian Affairs, "do not think it is necessary to go into details of the estimate, as the committee has had this appropriation before it for many years." Asked to defend this procedure, a budget officer (or his counterparts in the Budget Bureau and Congress) will say that it is a waste of time to go back to the beginning as if every year were a blank slate. "No need to build the car over again." No one was born yesterday; past experience with these programs is so great that total reconsideration would be superfluous unless there is a special demand in regard to a specific activity on the part of one or more strategically placed Congressmen, a new Administration, interest groups, or the agency itself. Programs are reconsidered but not all together and generally in regard to small changes. The political realities, budget officials say, restrict their attention to items they can do something about—a few new programs and possible cuts in a few old ones.

Senate practice is undoubtedly incremental. "It has been the policy of our [appropriations] committee," Senator Thomas reported, "to consider only items that are in controversy. When the House has included an item, and no question has been raised about it, the Senate Committee passes it over on the theory that it is satisfactory, and for that reason the hearings as a rule do not include testimony for or against items contained in the House bill."

Fair Share and Base

Time and again participants in the budgetary process speak of having arrived at an estimate of what was the "fair share" of the total budget for an agency. "None of this happened suddenly," a man who helps make the budget informed me. "We never go from $500 to $800 million or anything like that. This [the agency's] total is a product of many years of negotiations in order to work out a fair share of the budget for the agency."

At this point it is necessary to distinguish "fair share" from another concept, "the base." The base is the general expectation among the participants that programs will be carried on at close to the going level of expenditures but it does not necessarily include all activities. Having a project included in the agency's base thus means more than just getting it in the budget for a particular year. It means establishing the expectation that the expenditure will continue, that it is accepted as part of what will be done, and, therefore, that it will not normally be subjected to intensive scrutiny. (The word "base," incidentally, is part of the common parlance of officials engaged in budgeting and it would make no sense if their experience led them to expect wide fluctuations from year to year rather than additions to or subtractions from some relatively steady point.) "Fair share" means not only the base an agency has established but also the expectation that it will receive some proportion of funds, if any, which are to be increased over or decreased below the base of the various governmental agencies. "Fair share," then, reflects a convergence of expectations on roughly how much the agency is to receive in comparison to others.

The absence of a base or an agreement upon fair shares makes the calculation of what the agency or program should get much more difficult. That happens when an agency or program is new or when rapid shifts of sentiment toward it take place. A Senate Appropriations Committee report on the United States Information Agency demonstrates the problem. "Unlike the State Department," the report reads, "the USIA does not have a fixed, historic structure which sets a floor or ceiling on the amount of money which should be expended. Furthermore, its role must necessarily vary with the times. Therefore the issue of how much should be spent is not a matter of fixed obligations but a matter of judgment. . . . "

19

Rebuke
At
HEW

Morton Mintz

Twice in ten days, during the autumn of 1969, Robert H. Finch, Secretary of Health, Education, and Welfare, publicly criticized Dr. Jacqueline Verrett, a Food and Drug Administration research scientist. Dr. Verrett is the FDA staff member who discovered that artificial sweeteners called cyclamates cause severe deformities in chicken embryos. The first criticism came on October 8 in an interview Finch gave Gilbert C. Thelen, Jr., of the Associated Press. The second came on October 18 at a press conference at which Finch announced a surprise order halting production of cyclamate-sweetened foods for general consumption.

On the latter occasion, Finch, in response to questions, explained his "unhappiness" about Dr. Verrett. She had, he said, chosen "to go directly to the media without having consulted" her superior or the Secretary's office. Thus, she had not acted "in a very ethical way," he said.

A condemnation such as this would have been almost inconceivable in the reign of the last Republican Secretary of HEW before Finch, John W. Gardner. Shortly before President Johnson asked him to take over at HEW, Gardner, while president of the Carnegie Corporation, wrote a piece for the October, 1965, *Harper's* entitled "How to Prevent Organizational Dry Rot." Organizations of all kinds—"U.S. Steel, Yale University, the U.S. Navy, a government agency, or your local bank"—need not stagnate, Gardner said. If they do, it is "because the arts of organizational renewal are not yet widely understood." Saying that some of the rules for such renewal are known, he listed nine. Some, of course, are irrelevant to Finch's handling of the Verrett case. But it is interesting to note that Finch followed none of Gardner's rules for organizational renewal, and violated others.

Specifically, in chastising Dr. Verrett, the Secretary was hardly implementing "an effective program for the recruitment and development of able and highly motivated individuals." He was not providing "a hospitable environment for the individual," and he was not making any ascertainable contribution to "morale." Finally, as will be seen, the case exposed the lack of the "adequate system of internal communication" that Gardner also had listed as a requirement.

It should be emphasized that, once in office at HEW, Gardner applied his rules to the FDA. At the time he inherited it, the agency was all but universally recognized to be a disaster—a captive of the industries it was supposed to be regulating, and a poorly managed backwater with a police-inspector mentality at the top that repelled good scientists. To change all of this, Gardner brought in a reform commissioner, the bright, vigorous Dr. James

L. Goddard. In January, 1968, after Dr. Goddard had been in office for two years, I asked Gardner about the nature of his relationship with the then highly controversial commissioner. Considering how the FDA subsequently fell back into its old ways, what Gardner told me is especially instructive now:

I have backed Dr. Goddard very strongly and have never faltered in that, even when I thought he had done something not fully wise. I have looked at a lot of regulatory operations, including the Federal Communications Commission and the Federal Aviation Administration. I know what I want in a man to head such an operation. I want a man with driving determination to get the job done. In any regulatory activity, the forces tending to produce inaction are overwhelming. Interested parties can produce a thousand reasons why you should do nothing. You need a man who has a real bite to him, and a zest for action. You pray that he has impeccable judgment, but very few of us have that. I'd rather have a man I have to slow down than a man I have to wake up.

In the case of Jacqueline Verrett, there was, apparently, no one either to slow down or wake up Robert Finch.

Working in the FDA's Bureau of Science, Dr. Verrett had undertaken studies in which she injected cyclamates and a derivative created by body metabolism into some thirteen thousand chick embryos. She established a cause-effect relationship, with severe deformities of the legs, wings, and backs resulting in a rate of about 15 per cent for cyclamates and nearly 100 per cent for the derivative. By December, 1968, her data were substantial, if not as extensive as they would become over the next several months. Already, she had reached a "very firm" conclusion that there was a cause-effect relationship, and she had reported this in a memo to Dr. Herbert L. Ley, Jr., Commissioner of the FDA. Later, Dr. Ley said that, because of serious communications and related internal difficulties in the agency, he did not see the memo.

Meanwhile, Dr. Jack Shubert, a professor of radiation chemistry at the University of Pittsburgh Graduate School of Public Health, came to the FDA to participate in a seminar. While there, he learned of Dr. Verrett's work and informally discussed it with her. In May, 1969, Dr. Shubert wrote about Dr. Verrett's work in a dental society bulletin. Then, on September 4, he talked about it on a television show carried by KDKA in Pittsburgh.

In late September, Jean Carper, who writes a syndicated consumer column in collaboration with Senator Warren G. Magnuson (D–Wash.), Chairman of the Senate Commerce Committee, interviewed Dr. Verrett about the chick-embryo studies. On September 30, before most client newspapers printed the column, an NBC television crew came to the Bureau of Science to interview Dr. Verrett. She had notified her boss, Dr. Keith Lewis, and two FDA press officers that the interview had been requested. In addition, Deputy Commissioner Winton B. Rankin also was notified. It is true that the officials had relatively brief notice of the interview. But it is also true that the FDA officially knew about the Pittsburgh disclosures and had not concerned itself with them, and it is also true that no one objected to the NBC interview. Thus, Dr. Verrett had agency clearance to tell her story.

NBC carried the interview the next day, October 1. Dr. Verrett displayed malformed chicks and discussed the nature and results of her research. She did not extrapolate the results to humans—no one knows if they are, or are not, relevant. In response to a question, she advised women who might be pregnant to consult a physician before ingesting cyclamates, or, for that matter, any chemical that could be avoided.

Scientifically, this advice is not controversial—at least not since the revelation in 1962 that a sedative called thalidomide caused babies to be born without limbs. And through the years, warnings about unnecessary use of drugs or chemicals have been given by the Public Health Service, the American Medical Association, and the National Foundation, among others. Indeed, on the KDKA program in September, Dr. Claire Dick of Abbott Laboratories, the leading producer of cyclamates, was asked if she would use the sweeteners during pregnancy. "I don't think I would," she said. And, she added, most doctors would concur. Certainly, however, it can be seen that the appearance of Dr. Verrett and the hideous, malformed chicks on nationwide television would not be appreciatively received by soft-drink bottlers and food suppliers whose production of cyclamate-sweetened products yielded sales exceeding $1 billion (at retail) in 1968.

The Secretary and, for that matter, the Commissioner of the FDA, said later that the first they knew about the chick studies was when they watched NBC news on October 1. Two days later, Donald M. Kendall, President of PepsiCo, Inc., the parent company of Pepsi-Cola, then a leading buyer of cyclamates for diet soft drinks, appeared in the office of Secretary Finch. Kendall, who is a close friend of President Nixon and whose company was a client of Mr. Nixon's former law firm, told me that the purpose of the meeting was to discuss the December White House Conference on Food, Nutrition, and Health. Independently, Finch concurred with this statement, saying that he and Kendall, who was chairman of the Conference Panel on Food Safety and the Appropriateness of Food Additives, discussed whether it would be "proper or inappropriate" for the food industry to pay part of the cost of the conference. However, Finch and Kendall had different recollections of whether the discussion touched on the FDA and its handling of cyclamates. Kendall denied that the subject had even come up; Finch said that he himself had brought it up.

The matter lay dormant for a few days. Then came the surprise discovery, by a laboratory retained by the Abbott firm, that cyclamates caused bladder cancer in rats. After the National Cancer Institute confirmed the finding the data were referred to a special committee of the National Academy of Sciences's National Research Council. By coincidence, the committee was meeting in Washington at the time in response to a request from FDA Commissioner Ley. He had called the committee together to review both Dr. Verrett's findings, which had been virtually ignored in the top echelon of the agency until her television appearance, and studies by a fellow agency scientist, Dr. Marvin S. Legator, who had found chromosome breakage in rat tissue treated in the test tube with the cyclamate derivative. On the basis of the discovery of bladder cancer, the committee unanimously recommended to Finch that he halt sales of cyclamate-sweetened products.

Then, on October 18, the Secretary called a press conference to announce that the production of cyclamate-sweetened foods for general consumption would henceforth be prohibited. During the course of this session, Dr. Jesse L. Steinfeld, Deputy Assistant Secretary of HEW for Health and Scientific Affairs, joined Finch in publicly condemning Dr. Verrett. It was "unfortunate," said Dr. Steinfeld, that findings such as hers should be aired "in general news media, along with interpretations which at this moment certainly are far from justified."

It would not seem unfair to say that both officials, possibly because they were either inadequately informed or misinformed, were wrong on the facts. Dr. Verrett *did not,* as Finch asserted, violate a proper chain of command by going "directly to the media." Dr. Steinfeld was in error if he was imputing "unjustified interpretations" to her.

Dr. Steinfeld was careful to say that it is "absolutely essential" that tentative experimental data should be published "in the scientific literature" so that they can be communicated to "other scientists working in the field who do have the ability to interpret them and relate them to other ongoing research." To be sure, this is a laudable declaration, but it fails to deal adequately with two major points.

First, the thrust of the Finch-Steinfeld position on publication is, even if unintentionally, surely probusiness, but not surely propublic. It must be remembered that a great many food additives, drugs, and pesticides have come into massive use, with vast enterprises being built upon them, not after they have been proven safe, but merely because they have not been proven unsafe. What Finch and Dr. Steinfeld seem to have implied is that, in the face of troubling evidence such as that developed by Dr. Verrett and Dr. Legator, rather than subjecting businesses to risks with their economic health, millions or tens of millions of people should go on in ignorance taking avoidable risks with their physical health. This concept is especially difficult to accept because testing of the kind that can with certainty establish, for example, that a given substance causes cancer *in humans* can take a decade or longer. By the time the results are known, it could be too late for millions of possible victims to do anything about it. This is precisely the situation with oral contraceptives. They are being used by an estimated 8.5 million American women, even though the FDA acknowledges that it does not know whether the pills do or do not cause cancer.

The second point will be clearer if, for the sake of argument, we make the incorrect assumption that the attacks on Dr. Verrett were factually based, i.e., that she *had* gone "directly to the media without having consulted" her superior of the Secretary's office. Bearing in mind that she had fulfilled her obligation to keep her supervisor informed of her findings, was it the right of Robert Finch to decide if and when information developed by a public employee in his jurisdiction should be made available to the public? Was it the duty of Dr. Verrett to withhold findings of possibly great significance to the public health if Finch were to withhold permission to disclose? Why shouldn't the public know about the effects of cyclamates and their derivatives on chick embryos? Of course, such questions go far beyond the FDA and HEW. Why shouldn't the public know about all governmental discoveries directly affecting their welfare?

In the Verrett case, a Cabinet officer, slashing away at a relatively low-level subordinate, displayed no awareness of such concerns. I believe that Finch's two attacks on Dr. Verrett must have had an intimidating effect—not merely on scientists in the FDA and even elsewhere in HEW, but on all government employees who have data that the public should have but that could have an adverse effect on major economic interests. There is no reason why any dedicated public servant like Dr. Verrett should, as Senator Magnuson put it, be made into "a whipping post."

THE PRESIDENCY AND POLICY ANALYSIS

PART FIVE

Woodrow Wilson once said that "the President is at liberty, both in law and conscience, to be as big a man as he can." Wilson was defending an activist conception of the role of the President in the policy-making process. This perception has been shared by many antipluralists who see the presidency as the one office in the political system that embodies and can carry out the "general interest." For this idealized view to be valid, two assumptions must be correct. The first is that the President can effectively infuse the fragmented legislative and administrative policy-making process with dynamic political leadership. The second is that the President's policy preferences are responsive to the needs and interests of the general public. The purpose of Part Five is to examine the validity of these two assumptions in the context of the way in which any President must win public office and implement his policy preferences.

In a number of basic ways this idealized picture of the American presidency is misleading. First, the President obtains his political party's nomination by a process of coalition formation among the organized interest groups that form the core supporters of each major political party. Pluralism is pervasive in the process of selecting the candidate. The policy preferences of the active and influential core groups within each party form the bases of electoral platforms designed to reinforce habitual supporters and to activate marginal voters rather than to reach all citizens or social groups. Since the New Deal, the Democratic party has attempted to weld a loose activist coalition of organized labor, liberal intellectuals, black civil-rights organizations, white ethnic groups, and Southern party regulars. The corresponding activist groups for the Republican party consist of representatives of corporate management, conservative congressional Republicans, and the suburban middle class. When nominating conventions are politically successful, party platforms develop policy planks designed to reassure these core groups that their policy preferences will be embodied in the President's program. This process of policy development, whatever else may be said for or against it, is clearly not primarily designed to be responsive to an inactive and amorphous general public.

A second difficulty with the idealized picture of the presidency is that once a President has been elected, his capacity to act, even on behalf of the interest groups that comprise his winning coalition, is limited by the multiplicity of power centers in Congress and by the bureaucracy with which he must deal if he is to obtain his policy objectives. This fragmented decision-making context is especially problematic in domestic matters. To be sure, even in the domestic arena, the personal intervention of the President may infuse a deadlocked legislative process with energy and a wider policy perspective (similar personal initiatives have been known to mobilize unresponsive administrative agencies to support presidential program goals). But, as we have seen, public bureaucracies are characteristically unresponsive to hierarchical executive direction, and cabinet members often respond more quickly to the immediate demands of a single powerful Congressman than to remote presidential program goals.

The President's extensive powers in the areas of foreign and military policy raise still different challenges to the idealized concept of presidential leadership. In a formal sense, the President is clearly far less encumbered in these two areas by traditional legal and institutional checks on his behavior. Any President can draw upon his extensive constitutional authority as commander in chief and his near monopoly of institutional channels of information to supplement his personal resources of influence and the symbolic trappings of his office. He defines the issues and establishes the framework of options within which public dialogue takes place. But the very absence of competing information channels from Congress and other outside sources has made the formal and informal presidential advisory system a potent force in shaping the factual information and the decisional premises on which the President acts in foreign and defense matters.

The recent growth in the size and functions of the White House staff has led to what some have termed the "institutionalized presidency." This increased bureaucratization of the presidential staff poses a serious practical obstacle to the democratic norm of electoral control and accountability. So too, does the tendency of recent Presidents to rely on informal advice from trusted but unaccountable personal friends in matters of foreign policy. If knowledge is power, and if the information on which a President makes decisions is screened and structured for him by politically unaccountable sources, then it is fair to ask, Who is really making the far-reaching decisions for which we hold the President responsible? To ask the question is not to prejudge the answer but merely to indicate the flaws in the simplistic conception of the presidency—even in the areas of foreign policy and the making of military decisions.

The selections that follow attempt to clarify some of the difficulties raised in the foregoing discussion of presidential leadership. The selection from Norman Mailer's book *Miami and the Siege of Chicago* is an artist's view of the failure of the 1968 Democratic Convention to build a viable electoral coalition. By failing to recognize the antiwar movement as a legitimate political interest to be rewarded with a strong antiwar platform plank, presidential candidate Hubert Humphrey was demonstrating his excessive dependence on the interest-group blocks controlled by other major political actors—George Meany, Mayor Richard Daley, Governor John Connally, and President Lyndon Johnson. This coalition was simply not broad enough to win a national election in the face of growing public disillusionment and opposition to the war in Indo-China.

The second selection is drawn from Richard Neustadt's book *Presidential Power.* The Machiavellian maxims that structure Neustadt's analysis offer advice on how a President can maximize his personal influence by persuading others that it is in their self-interest to cooperate with him. Underlying Neustadt's argument is the assumption that the President's formal powers of command are inadequate for bringing coordination to the large and complex administrative apparatus that he heads. In persuading others, the President has numerous bargaining advantages, the most impressive of which is the symbolic status and authority of his office. In "The Power to Persuade," Neustadt discusses the strengths and weaknesses of the President in bargaining with others whose behavior he seeks to influence: cabinet secretaries, Congressmen, members of his political party, allied governments, administrative agency heads, and even members of the White House staff.

Norton Long's "Reflections on Presidential Power" raises several fundamental questions concerning the role of the President in the political system. His article attacks several myths that have permeated discussions of the presidency. Among these are the belief that the President suffers from deficient resources of power in the areas of foreign and defense policy and the belief that fragmentation of the executive branch is always harmful. Long's analysis of presidential power in crisis overlooks the danger of presidential overselling of external threats in the making of foreign-policy decisions. In part, so does his closing plea for a resurgence of presidential pedagogy. Nonetheless, his vision of the President as teacher and as patron of research and knowledge is, in the final analysis, a plea for meaningful moral leadership. The citizen's problem remains one of recognizing the fine line between moral leadership and symbolic manipulation.

In "The White House Staff Bureaucracy," Alex B. Lacy, Jr., traces the dramatic growth of the professional advisory staff in the White House since 1939. Lacy's analysis illustrates the widely divergent styles by which each of the Presidents since Franklin Roosevelt has attempted to coordinate his executive office. Styles have varied from the highly personalized relationship between Roosevelt and his staff to the highly specialized and bureaucratized Eisenhower office under the direction of Sherman Adams. The article concludes that the growth of the White House staff has not caused serious problems for Presidents wishing to exert their personality or created an institutional barrier to effective presidential action. Lacy's thorough assessment of past trends overlooks some possible future problems resulting from the ever increasing size and specialization of the President's staff. For example, in the Kennedy administration, national security advisor McGeorge Bundy directed a constantly changing staff that never exceeded ten men. In contrast, Henry Kissinger's staff in the Nixon White House numbers over one hundred. This growth may increase the influence of politically unaccountable technical specialists in shaping foreign policy.

In the same vein, Lacy's study suggests that frustration with his staff prompted Lyndon Johnson to rely heavily on informal advisors such as James Rowe, Clark Clifford, and Abe Fortas. Informal advisors such as Dean Acheson and Robert Lovette were granted access to President Kennedy's inner circle during the Cuban missile crisis. It is quite understandable that a President might wish to consult with persons whose judgment he respects. But in the larger context of democratic theory, this possibility raises the question of how such men can be held accountable for their role in policy making.

In times of real or imagined crisis in international affairs, the President seems to dominate the decision-making process. Yet his role is less initiator than judge of the range of options presented to him by those advisors whom he chooses to consult. In "The Missile Crisis," Elie Abel describes one day in the life of President Kennedy during the installation of Soviet missiles in Cuba. The selection illustrates the narrow scope of the persons and ideological perspectives included in the decision; the imperfect information on which decisions are made when an atmosphere of crisis prevails; and the narrow range and tactical nature of the options considered seriously in the debate—an air strike as opposed to a naval blockade of Cuba.

In situations of limited time and perceived threat, these limitations seem almost inevitable. The difficulty is that the ease with which a President can act in times of real crisis tends to encourage unnecessary "crisis mongering" in more problematic contexts by executives who feel hemmed in by institutional and political constraints on their behavior. The development of America's "cold war" global posture frequently has been compounded by this kind of presidential overselling of a perceived external threat. As Theodore Lowi has said, Presidents desiring a freer hand in foreign affairs often have been driven to convert "interactions into incidents, incidents into challenges, challenges into threats and threats into crises for the purpose of imposing . . . cohesion upon the members of the foreign policy establishment."

If this diagnosis of the roots of the oversell of America's anti-Communist impulse is correct, it constitutes an unfortunate conversion of means into ends. As the lesson of Vietnam suggests, it is not intuitively obvious that a unified foreign-policy establishment will propose wise policy alternatives. In fact, it is plausible to argue that a multiplicity of political perceptions and value perspectives should be introduced into the policy process. This would increase the chances for a wider range of policy options, including systematic review of the goals of a foreign policy, to be available to a President. If the members of the foreign-policy establishment all share the same mental map of international reality, their limited consciousness may severely narrow presidential options.

20

The Siege
of
Chicago

Norman Mailer

"Politics is property," said Murray Kempton, delegate from New York, over the epiphanies of a drink, and never was a new science comprehended better by a young delegate. Lyndon Johnson was first preceptor of the key that politics-is-property so you never give something away for nothing. Convention politics is therefore not the art of the possible so much as the art of what is possible when you are dealing with property holders. A delegate's vote is his holding—he will give it up without return no more than a man will sign over his house entire to a worthy cause.

The true property-holder is never ambivalent about his land, he does not mock it, or see adjacent estates as more deserving than his own—so a professional in politics without pride in his holding is a defector. The meanest ward-heeler in the cheapest block of Chicago has his piece—he cannot be dislodged without leaving his curse nor the knotty untangling of his relations with a hundred job-holders in the area; he gives up tithes in the umbilical act of loyalty to his boss, he receives protection for his holding in return.

Such property relations are to be witnessed for every political sinecure in the land—judgeships, jobs, contracts, promises—it comes down to chairs in offices, and words negotiable like bonds: all of that is politics as simple property. Everybody in the game has a piece, and that piece is workable, it is equivalent to capital, it can be used to accrue interest by being invested in such sound conservative enterprises as decades of loyalty to the same Machine. So long as the system progresses, so will one's property be blessed with dividends. But such property can also be used as outright risk capital —one can support an insurgent movement in one's party, even risk the loss of one's primary holding in return for the possibility of acquiring much more.

This, of course, is still politics at city hall, county or state house, this is the politics of the party regular, politics as simple property, which is to say politics as concrete negotiable power—the value of their engagement in politics is at any moment just about directly convertible to cash.

Politics at national level can still be comprehended by politics-as-property provided one remembers that moral integrity (or the public impression of such) in a high politician is also property, since it brings power and/or emoluments to him. Indeed a very high politician—which is to say a statesman or leader—has no political substance unless he is the servant of ideological institutions or interests and the available moral passions of the electorate, so serving, he is the agent of the political power they bestow on him, which power is certainly a property. Being a leading anti-Communist used to be an

203

invaluable property for which there was much competition—Richard Nixon had once gotten in early on the equivalent of an Oklahoma landgrab by staking out whole territories of that property. "End the war in Vietnam," is a property to some, "Let no American blood be shed in vain," is obviously another. A politician picks and chooses among moral properties. If he is quick-witted, unscrupulous, and does not mind a life of constant anxiety, he will hasten—there is a great competition for things valuable in politics—to pick up properties wherever he can, even if they are rival holdings. To the extent a politician is his own man, attached to his own search for his own spiritual truth—which is to say willing to end in any unpalatable position to which the character of his truth could lead him—then he is ill-equipped for the game of politics. Politics is property. You pick up as much as you can, pay the minimum for the holding, extract the maximum, and combine where you may—small geniuses like Humphrey saw, for example, that devout trade-unionism and devout anti-Communism might once have faced each other across no-man's-land but right after the second world war were ready to enrich each other into the tenfold of national respectability.

There is no need to underline Lyndon Johnson's ability to comprehend these matters. (For the higher game of international politics-is-property he was about as well-equipped as William F. Buckley, Eleanor Roosevelt, Barry Goldwater, George Patton, J. Edgar Hoover, Ronald Reagan, and Averill Harriman, but that is another matter.) Johnson understood that so far as a man was a political animal (and therefore not searching for some private truth which might be independent of politics) he was then, if deprived of his properties, close to being a dead man. So the true political animal is cautious —he never, except in the most revolutionary times, permits himself to get into a position where he will have to dare his political stake on one issue, one bet, no, to avoid that, he will even give up small pieces of his stuff for nothing, he will pay tribute, which is how raids are sometimes made, and how Barry Goldwater won his nomination. (For his followers promised political extermination with all dispatch to those marginal delegates not quite ready to come along.)

The pearl in the oyster of this proposition is that there is only one political job in America which has no real property attached to it, except for the fantastical property of promotion by tragedy, and that, of course, is the Vice Presidency. It is the only high office to which all the secondary characteristics of political property may adhere—comprehensive public awareness of the name, attention in the press to one's speeches, honory emoluments in the Senate, intimacy (of varying degree) with the President, junkets abroad. If you are very active as Vice President, everyone in America knows your name. But that is your only property. It is not the same thing as real power—more like being a movie star. Taken in proportion to the size of the office, the Vice President has less real holding than the ward-heeler in his anteroom chair. The Vice President can promise many things, but can be certain of delivering on nothing. So he can never be certain of getting anything back. It is not a job for a politician but a philosopher.

Mark it: politics is the hard dealing of hard men over properties; their strength is in dealing and their virility. Back of each negotiator is the magic of his collected properties—the real contention of the negotiation is: whose properties possess the more potent magic? A good politician then can deal with every kind of property holder but a fanatic, because the fanatic is disembodied from his property. He conceives of his property—his noble ideal!—as existing just as well without him. His magic partakes of the surreal. That is why Lyndon Johnson could never deal with Ho Chi Minh, and why he could manipulate Hubert Humphrey with absolute confidence. Humphrey had had to live for four years with no basic property, and nobody knew better than the President what that could do to an animal as drenched in politics as Hubert. Humphrey could never make his move. Deprived for four years of his seat as Senator, deprived of constituency, and the power to trade votes, the small intricate nourishing marrow of being able to measure the profit or loss of concrete favors traded for concrete favors, the exchange of political affections based on solid property-giving, property-acquiring negotiations, forced to offer influence he now might or might not possess, Humphrey never knew where to locate himself in negotiations spoken or unspoken with Lyndon Johnson. So his feet kept slipping. Against the crusades of law and order building on the Right, his hope was to build a crusade on the Left, not to divide the Left. But to do that, he would have had to dare the enmity of Lyndon Johnson, have had to dare the real chance that he might lose the nomination, and that was the one chance he could not take for that would be the hollowest death of them all. He would be lost in retirement, his idle flesh would witness with horror the decomposition of his ego. A politician in such trouble can give away the last of his soul in order not to be forced to witness how much he has given away already.

Hubert Humphrey was the small genius of American politics—his horror was that he was wed to Lyndon Johnson, the domestic genius of us all. Humphrey could not find sufficient pride in his liver to ask for divorce. His liver turned to dread. He came to Chicago with nobody to greet him at the airport except a handful of the faithful—the Vice President's own poor property—those men whose salary he paid, and they were not many. Later, a group of a few hundred met him at the Sherman House, the boys and the Humphrey girls were out. . . . Humphrey money was there in Chicago for convention frolics, and a special nightclub or cabaret in the Hilton called the Hubaret where you needed a scorecard to separate the trade-union leaders from the Maf, and the women—let us not insult women. Suffice it that the beehives were out, and every girl named Marie had a coif like Marie Antoinette. Every Negro on the take was there as well—some of the slickest, roundest, blackest swingers ever to have contacts in with everyone from Mayor Daley to the Blackstone Rangers. There was action at the Hubaret, and cheer for every late-night drinker. If Hubie got in, the after-hours joints would prosper; the politics of joy would never demand that all the bars be dead by four—who could argue with that?

Negroes in general had never been charmed with McCarthy. If he was the epitome of Whitey at his best, that meant Whitey at ten removes, dry wit, stiff back, two-and-a-half centuries of Augustan culture and their distillate

—the ironic manners of the tightest country gentry; the Blacks did not want Whitey at his best and boniest in a year when they were out to find every justification (they were not hard to find) to hate the Honkie. But if the Black militant and the Black workingman would find no comfort or attraction in McCarthy, think then of how the Black mixer-dixer was going to look on Clean Gene. He wasn't about to make a pilgrimage up to some Catholic rectory in the Minnesota North woods where they passed one bean through the hot water for bean soup, no, he wanted some fatback in his hand. You couldn't take the kind of hard and sanctified little goat turds McCarthy was passing out for political marbles back to the Black homefolk when they were looking for you to spread the gravy around. So Hubie Humphrey came into Chicago with nine-tenths of the organized Democratic Party—Black support, labor support, Mafia support, Southern delegates support, and you could find it all at the Hubaret if you were looking. . . .

There were 1,400–1,500 delegates secured for Hubert Humphrey on the day he came to town—such was the hard estimate of the hardest heads on his staff, Larry O'Brien, Norman Sherman, Bill Connell; the figure was low, they were not counting on the favorite sons of the South, nor on the small reserve of uncommitted delegates. Still there were rumors up of gale warnings, and much anxiety—Mayor Daley had led the Illinois delegation into caucus on Sunday, and led them out again without committing a single one of the state's 118 votes to a single delegate and there were stories Daley wanted Teddy Kennedy. John Connally of Texas, furious that the unit rule was about to be abolished in this convention, gave threats on Sunday of nominating Lyndon Johnson.

Either the convention was sewed up for Humphrey or the convention was soft. No one really knew. Usually it was enough to come to conventions with less than a first ballot victory, even two hundred votes less, and you were certain of winning. The panic among delegates to get on the winning side at the last minute is always a stampede. It is as though your land will double in value. Humphrey came in with one hundred to two hundred votes more than he needed, yet he was not without his own panic; he took care to announce on "Meet the Press" before taking the plane to Chicago that he supported President Johnson's Vietnam policies because they were "basically sound." For two months he had been vacillating, giving hints one day that he was not far from the doves, rushing back the next to be close in tone to the Administration. It could be said, of course, that it was part of his political skill to keep the McCarthyites uncertain of his position; once convinced that he would take a line close to Lyndon Johnson on the war in Vietnam, they might look—McCarthy included—to induce Teddy Kennedy to run. So Humphrey played at being a dove as a way of holding the youngest Kennedy in Hyannis. But what was he to gain besides the approval of Lyndon Johnson? A liaison with McCarthy could even give him a chance for victory in November. Yet Humphrey engaged in massive safe play after massive safe play, paying court to the South, paying court to LBJ, to Daley, to Meany, to Connally; even then, he came to Chicago with his nomination insecure. He had 1,500 votes, but if something went wrong he did not know if he could count on a single one of them—they could all wash away in the night.

Humphrey was staying at the Conrad Hilton, but his first act after landing at O'Hare was to proceed to the Sherman House to visit the Illinois delegation. Daley was working to induce Teddy Kennedy to run—once Teddy Kennedy ran and lost, he might have to accept a draft as Vice President. At the same time, once running, he might show huge strength—Daley would then be able to claim he stole the nomination from Humphrey and got it over to Kennedy. Daley could not lose. All the while he was encouraging Kennedy to run, Humphrey was promising Daley more and more treasures, obliged—since he had no political property of his own just yet—to mortgage future property. He was assigning future and double substance to Daley, to the unions, to the South, to business interests. His holding operations, his safe plays to guarantee the nomination once the nomination was already secure, became exorbitantly expensive. A joke made the rounds of the convention:

"What was Hubert able to keep?"

"Well, he was able to keep Muriel."

His dangers were absurdly small. McCarthy, three times unpopular with the delegates, for being right, for being proud that he was right, and for dealing only in moral property, had no chance whatsoever. Moreover, he was disliked intensely by the Kennedyites. If Bobby Kennedy and Gene McCarthy had been in the Sinn Fein together they would have carried their guns in holsters under opposite shoulders—they embodied the ultimate war of the Irish. McCarthy was reputed to carry volumes of Augustine and Aquinas in his suitcase; it is possible Bobby Kennedy thought one of the penalties of being Irish is that you could get lost in the *Summa Theologica*.

But Hubert Humphrey carried no gun and no tome.

The Power to Persuade

21

Richard E. Neustadt

The limits on command suggest the structure of our government. The constitutional convention of 1787 is supposed to have created a government of "separated powers." It did nothing of the sort. Rather, it created a government of separated institutions *sharing* powers. "I am part of the legislative process," Eisenhower often said in 1959 as a reminder of his veto. Congress, the dispenser of authority and funds, is no less part of the administrative process. Federalism adds another set of separated institutions. The Bill of Rights adds others. Many public purposes can only be achieved by voluntary acts of private institutions; the press, for one, in Douglass Cater's phrase, is a "fourth branch of government." And with the coming of alliances abroad, the separate institutions of a London, or a Bonn, share in the making of American public policy.

What the Constitution separates our political parties do not combine. The parties are themselves composed of separated organizations sharing public authority. The authority consists of nominating powers. Our national parties are confederations of state and local party institutions, with a headquarters that represents the White House, more or less, if the party has a President in office. These confederacies manage presidential nominations. All other public offices depend upon electorates confined within the states. All other nominations are controlled within the states. The President and congressmen who bear one party's label are divided by dependence upon different sets of voters. The differences are sharpest at the stage of nomination. The White House has too small a share in nominating congressmen, and Congress has too little weight in nominating Presidents for party to erase their constitutional separation. Party links are stronger than is frequently supposed, but nominating processes assure the separation.

The separateness of institutions and the sharing of authority prescribe the terms on which a President persuades. When one man shares authority with another, but does not gain or lose his job upon the other's whim, his willingness to act upon the urging of the other turns on whether he conceives the action right for him. The essence of a President's persuasive task is to convince such men that what the White House wants of them is what they ought to do for their sake and on their authority.

Persuasive power, thus defined, amounts to more than charm or reasoned argument. These have their uses for a President, but these are not the whole of his resources. For the men he would induce to do what he wants done on their own responsibility will need or fear some acts by him on his responsibility. If they share his authority, he has some share in theirs. Presidential "powers" may be inconclusive when a President commands, but always remain relevant as he persuades. The status and authority inherent in his office reinforce his logic and his charm.

. . .

A President's authority and status give him great advantages in dealing with the men he would persuade. Each "power" is a vantage point for him in the degree that other men have use for his authority. From the veto to appointments, from publicity to budgeting, and so down a long list, the White House now controls the most encompassing array of vantage points in the American political system. With hardly an exception, the men who share in governing this country are aware that at some time, in some degree, the doing of *their* jobs, the furthering of *their* ambitions, may depend upon the President of the United States. Their need for presidential action, or their fear of it, is bound to be recurrent if not actually continuous. Their need or fear is his advantage.

A President's advantages are greater than mere listing of his "powers" might suggest. The men with whom he deals must deal with him until the last day of his term. Because they have continuing relationships with him, his future, while it lasts, supports his present influence. Even though there is no need or fear of him today, what he could do tomorrow may supply today's advantage. Continuing relationships may convert any "power," any aspect of his status, into vantage points in almost any case. When he induces other men to do what he wants done, a President can trade on their dependence now *and* later.

The President's advantages are checked by the advantages of others. Continuing relationships will pull in both directions. These are relationships of mutual dependence. A President depends upon the men he would persuade; he has to reckon with his need or fear of them. They too will possess status, or authority, or both, else they would be of little use to him. Their vantage points confront his own; their power tempers his.

. . .

The power to persuade is the power to bargain. Status and authority yield bargaining advantages. But in a government of "separated institutions sharing powers," they yield them to all sides. With the array of vantage points at his disposal, a President may be far more persuasive than his logic or his charm could make him. But outcomes are not guaranteed by his advantages. There remain the counter pressures those whom he would influence can bring to bear on him from vantage points at their disposal. Command has limited utility; persuasion becomes give-and-take. It is well that the White House holds the vantage points it does. In such a business any President may need them all—and more.

[2]

This view of power as akin to bargaining is one we commonly accept in the sphere of congressional relations. Every textbook states and every legislative session demonstrates that save in times like the extraordinary Hundred Days of 1933—times virtually ruled out by definition at mid-century—a President will often be unable to obtain congressional action on his terms or even to halt action he opposes. The reverse is equally accepted: Congress often is frustrated by the President. Their formal powers are so intertwined that neither will accomplish very much, for very long, without the acquiescence of the other. By the same token, though, what one demands the other can resist. The stage is set for that great game, much like collective bargaining, in which each seeks to profit from the other's needs and fears. It is a game played catch-as-catch-can, case by case. And everybody knows the game, observers and participants alike.

. . .

In spheres of party politics the same thing follows, necessarily, from the confederal nature of our party organizations. Even in the case of national nominations a President's advantages are checked by those of others. In 1944 it is by no means clear that Roosevelt got his first choice as his running mate. In 1948 Truman, then the President, faced serious revolts against his nomination. In 1952 his intervention from the White House helped assure the choice of Adlai Stevenson, but it is far from clear that Truman could have done as much for any other candidate acceptable to him. In 1956 when Eisenhower was President, the record leaves obscure just who backed Harold Stassen's effort to block Richard Nixon's renomination as Vice-President. But evidently everything did not go quite as Eisenhower wanted, whatever his intentions may have been. The outcomes in these instances bear all the marks of limits on command and of power checked by power that characterize congressional relations. Both in and out of politics these checks and limits seem to be quite widely understood.

Influence becomes still more a matter of give-and-take when Presidents attempt to deal with allied governments. A classic illustration is the long unhappy wrangle over Suez policy in 1956. In dealing with the British and the French before their military intervention, Eisenhower had his share of bargaining advantages but no effective power of command. His allies had their share of counter pressures, and they finally tried the most extreme of all: action despite him. His pressure then was instrumental in reversing them. But had the British government been on safe ground *at home,* Eisenhower's wishes might have made as little difference after intervention as before. Behind the decorum of diplomacy—which was not very decorous in the Suez affair—relationships among allies are not unlike relationships among state delegations at a national convention. Power is persuasion and persuasion becomes bargaining. The concept is familiar to everyone who watches foreign policy.

In only one sphere is the concept unfamiliar: the sphere of executive relations. Perhaps because of civics textbooks and teaching in our schools, Americans instinctively resist the view that power in this sphere resembles power in all others. Even Washington reporters, White House aides, and congressmen are not immune to the illusion that administrative agencies comprise a single structure, "the" Executive Branch, where presidential word is law, or ought to be. . . .

Like our governmental structure as a whole, the executive establishment consists of separated institutions sharing power. The President heads one of these; Cabinet officers, agency administrators, and military commanders head others. Below the departmental level, virtually independent bureau chiefs head many more. Under mid-century conditions, Federal operations spill across dividing lines on organization charts; almost every policy entangles many agencies; almost every program calls for interagency collaboration. Everything somehow involves the President. But operating agencies owe their existence least of all to one another—and only in some part to him. Each has a separate statutory base; each has its statutes to administer; each deals with a different set of subcommittees at the Capitol. Each has its own peculiar set of clients, friends, and enemies outside the formal government. Each has a different set of specialized careerists inside its own bailiwick. Our Constitution gives the President the "take-care" clause and the appointive power. Our statutes give him central budgeting and a degree of personnel control. All agency administrators are responsible to him. But they *also* are responsible to Congress, to their clients, to their staffs, and to themselves. In short, they have five masters. Only after all of those do they owe any loyalty to each other.

"The members of the Cabinet," Charles G. Dawes used to remark, "are a President's natural enemies." Dawes had been Harding's Budget Director, Coolidge's Vice-President, and Hoover's Ambassador to London; he also had been General Pershing's chief assistant for supply in the First World War. The words are highly colored, but Dawes knew whereof he spoke. The men who have to serve so many masters cannot help but be somewhat the "enemy" of any one of them. By the same token, any master wanting service is in some degree the "enemy" of such a servant. A President is likely to want loyal support but not to relish trouble on his doorstep. Yet the more his Cabinet members cleave to him, the more they may need help from him in fending off the wrath of rival masters. Help, though, is synonymous with trouble. Many a Cabinet officer, with loyalty ill-rewarded by his lights and help withheld, has come to view the White House as innately hostile to department heads. Dawes's dictum can be turned around.

A senior presidential aide remarked to me in Eisenhower's time: "If some of these Cabinet members would just take time out to stop and ask themselves 'What would I want if I were President?,' they wouldn't give him all the trouble he's been having." But even if they asked themselves the question, such officials often could not act upon the answer. Their personal attachment to the President is all too often overwhelmed by duty to their other masters.

Executive officials are not equally advantaged in their dealings with a President. Nor are the same officials equally advantaged all the time. Not every officeholder can resist like a MacArthur, or like Arnall, Sawyer, Wilson, in a rough descending order of effective counter pressure. The vantage points conferred upon officials by their own authority and status vary enormously. The variance is heightened by particulars of time and circumstance. In mid-October 1950, Truman, at a press conference, remarked of the man he had considered firing in August and would fire the next April for intolerable insubordination:

> Let me tell you something that will be good for your souls. It's a pity that you . . . can't understand the ideas of two intellectually honest men when they meet. General MacArthur . . . is a member of the Government of the United States. He is loyal to that Government. He is loyal to the President. He is loyal to the President in his foreign policy. . . . There is no disagreement between General MacArthur and myself. . . .

MacArthur's status in and out of government was never higher than when Truman spoke those words. The words, once spoken, added to the General's credibility thereafter when he sought to use the press in his campaign against the President. And what had happened between August and October? Near-victory had happened, together with that premature conference on *post*-war plans, the meeting at Wake Island.

If the bargaining advantages of a MacArthur fluctuate with changing circumstances, this is bound to be so with subordinates who have at their disposal fewer "powers," lesser status, to fall back on. And when officials have no "powers" in their own right, or depend upon the President for status, their counter pressure may be limited indeed. White House aides, who fit both categories, are among the most responsive men of all, and for good reason. As a Director of the Budget once remarked to me, "Thank God I'm here and not across the street. If the President doesn't call me, I've got plenty I can do right here and plenty coming up to me, by rights, to justify my calling him. But those poor fellows over there, if the boss doesn't call them, doesn't ask them to do something, what *can* they do but sit?" Authority and status so conditional are frail reliances in resisting a President's own wants. Within the White House precincts, lifted eyebrows may suffice to set an aide in motion; command, coercion, even charm aside. But even in the White House a President does not monopolize effective power. Even there persuasion is akin to bargaining. A former Roosevelt aide once wrote of Cabinet officers:

> Half of a President's suggestions, which theoretically carry the weight of orders, can be safely forgotten by a Cabinet member. And if the President asks about a suggestion a second time, he can be told that it is being investigated. If he asks a third time, a wise Cabinet officer will give him at least part of what he suggests. But only occasionally, except about the most important matters, do Presidents ever get around to asking three times.

The rule applies to staff as well as to the Cabinet, and certainly has been applied *by* staff in Truman's time and Eisenhower's.

Some aides will have more vantage points than a selective memory. Sherman Adams, for example, as The Assistant to the President under Eisenhower, scarcely deserved the appellation "White House aide" in the meaning of the term before his time or as applied to other members of the Eisenhower entourage. Although Adams was by no means "chief of staff" in any sense so sweeping—or so simple—as press commentaries often took for granted, he apparently became no more dependent on the President than Eisenhower on him. "I need him," said the President when Adams turned out to have been remarkably imprudent in the Goldfine case, and delegated to him even the decision on his own departure. This instance is extreme, but the tendency it illustrates is common enough. Any aide who demonstrates to others that he has the President's consistent confidence and a consistent part in presidential business will acquire so much business on his own account that he becomes in some sense independent of his chief. Nothing in the Constitution keeps a well-placed aide from converting status into power of his own, usable in some degree even against the President—an outcome not unknown in Truman's regime or, by all accounts, in Eisenhower's.

The more an officeholder's status and his "powers" stem from sources independent of the President, the stronger will be his potential pressure *on* the President. Department heads in general have more bargaining power than do most members of the White House staff; but bureau chiefs may have still more, and specialists at upper levels of established career services may have almost unlimited reserves of the enormous power which consists of sitting still. . . .

. . .

A contemporary President may have to settle for a reputation short of the ideal. If so, what then should be his object? It should be to induce as much uncertainty as possible about the consequences of ignoring what he wants. If he cannot make men think him bound to win, his need is to keep them from thinking they can cross him without risk, or that they can be sure what risks they run. At the same time (no mean feat) he needs to keep them from fearing lest he leave them in the lurch if they support him. To maximize uncertainties in future opposition, to minimize the insecurities of possible support, and to avoid the opposite effect in either case—these together form the goal for any mid-century President who seeks a reputation that will serve his personal power.

. . .

Reflections on Presidential Power

22

Norton E. Long

Some 25 years ago there was a famous exchange . . . between Harold Laski and Don Price on the parliamentary and the presidential systems. Many of Laski's criticisms of the presidential system in this country are still standard in the conventional wisdom: the lack of disciplined, programmatic parties, the fragmentation of power, the strength of local and special interests, and, now clearly dated, the reactionary nature of the Supreme Court. England at the end of World War II was still, in Sir George Clark's term, "the pattern state" for many of the intellectuals of constitutional democracy. The writings of W. Y. Elliott, Thomas K. Finletter, and many others have celebrated the putative virtues of the British system. Indeed, so persuasive has been the English paradigm that the literature on parties and party reform, a central if not the central preoccupation of American political science, has been permeated with an idealized version of the British two-party system and its supposed beneficence. V. O. Key, Schattschneider, and the Committee on Political Parties of the American Political Science Association, till the recent stirrings of revisionism, provided the dominant and perhaps still dominant view of the two-party competitive model from whose British perfection we were deviant.

The Presidency as Fragile Mainspring

All, or nearly all, commentators, including self-styled conservatives such as Rossiter, see the American presidency as the mainspring of the polity. The generality of this opinion is recent. A few short years ago the Bricker Amendment had wide support and Eisenhower seemingly favored the Whig if not the errand boy conception of the President. Grant McConnell, an otherwise sober political scientist, now states, "To ask what is to become of the presidency is to ask what is to become of the entire American political order." This sense of the critical nature of the presidency raises some writers from the depths of pessimism to euphoria and perhaps down again. Thus James MacGregor Burns in short order moves from *The Deadlock of Democracy* to a *Presidential Government* with a concluding section titled "The Triumph of Presidential Government." Whether this triumph will withstand the retirement of Lyndon Johnson and the election of Richard Nixon or require yet another book remains to be seen. Neustadt, who is no Nervous Nelly, worries about the presidency along with others.

Regarding the presidency as a key if not the key institution, it is not surprising that Neustadt is alarmed by the fragility of presidential power he so keenly and sensitively depicted in his book. The President, in his view, in times of crisis "which a preponderance of his publics see or can be made to see as such," can break out of his limitations and convert the possibilities of his office into an adequate source of power. But since World War II we live in a world of crises which the publics either do not see as such or of which they have grown tired. Under these conditions the President may not be able to make of the opportunities of his office a sufficiently steady flow of power to master the urgent matters of which he but not his public is aware.

The alarm as to the adequacy of the President's powers springs from concern over foreign and domestic affairs. In the area of foreign concern it has frequently been contended that voter ignorance and prejudice in matters of foreign policy would seriously limit the President's freedom of action. Whether this is a fact or a fiction is open to serious question. Kenneth Waltz has examined this issue and finds the President quite capable, if he has a policy of his own, of getting the public to go along. At least they can be expected to go along until one might hope that even patient, reasonable men would question continuance in a manifestly losing game. As Waltz points out, Eisenhower was able after campaigning against the Democrats to adopt their policy and carry the public and his party with him. This scarcely indicates undue public resistance to a presidential lead. Indeed there is much to be said for Polsby and Wildavsky's view that "It would be pure fantasy to claim that our Presidents and their advisors have had wonderful ideas for making the world a better place only to have them frustrated by lack of ability to command support in Congress." The frustration seems to be as much or more with a Congress that feels incapable of moving without a presidential lead. If ever one might have expected presidential power to prove inadequate to meet a national crisis, it was in the case of the Marshall Plan. Here a President, already counted a lame duck, achieved an historic reversal of isolationism with the collaboration of the opposition party.

Conservatives have usually been concerned nevertheless over the adequacy of presidential power to direct foreign affairs and mobilize military might. Generally their concern over the latter has been the reverse of that affecting the liberals, though it was a conservative General Eisenhower who gave the liberals their current punch line. The American Tudor polity was designed to deal with foreign policy and defense, and its failures in these areas seem more attributable to cognitive deficiencies than deficiencies of power.

The usual concern with presidential power is on the left. The concern is with the attainment of social democratic objectives that the President, because of his peculiar constituency, can be expected to favor. They are objectives equally that many congressional power holders, because of their peculiar constituencies, are likely to view with little enthusiasm. Given these disparate perspectives, it is readily seen why those with a liberal orientation so frequently lament the lack of presidential power to secure requisite congressional action on presidential programs. The preferred means for bringing about the desired end is through disciplined, programmatic parties acting as instruments of the President, the national party leader. The means to the means, however, are far from clear. The gadgetry of reform has yet to produce reliable legal recipes for producing disciplined two-party systems. Many proposals to this end seem more likely to jeopardize the health of a reasonably functioning going concern than to improve upon it. Skepticism ranges from people like Clinton Rossiter to Nelson Polsby and Aaron Wildavsky.

British Model Questioned

The appeal of the disciplined two-party system, with the President cast as prime minister, stems from our "pattern state," Britain. It has a long line of apologists, including Wilson, and that eminent political scientist has been followed by many others. The competitive two-party system has been given high marks partly because of its supposed representative logic and even more because of its association in England and the United States with standards of living and other conditions it was thought to entail. The validity of this causal nexus is increasingly questioned. England is no longer regarded by some critics as showing a performance record that justifies its standing as a "pattern state." Disenchantment has mounted since World War II and has led to a reappraisal of prewar performance. For these critics the British two-party system failed to deal with the country's economy, stunted its education, mishandled its defense and burdened it with a costly empire. Max Nicholson has attempted to relate the outcomes in Britain to the political system that is at least in good part responsible for them. While his sharpest comments are reserved for the Treasury and the Administrative class, he recognizes that the "system" has been supported by the parties. Nicholson's attack on the mishandling of the economy is a reiteration of that made by Andrew Shonfield. Works on Suez have added reasons for skepticism about the British model in foreign and military affairs.

Critics of the British performance do not question the adequacy of political power, but the cognitive competence of the "system." The dialectic of Tories and Labour in the event seems less important than the continuity of Treasury control and the administrative class. The two parties, to survive, had to appeal to the same voters. Since they were interested in victory, their practice could hardly diverge too far over time. Despite the existence of two parties of principle, if the critics are right the top civil service is the real power in the British system. The lesson of British experience might be less that the President needs power over the legislature than that he needs power over the bureaucracy. At least since the Brownlow Committee, efforts have been made to reorganize the administration so that the President can control it. The Hoover Commission continued the effort to streamline the executive structure under the President. Recently Stephen Bailey has viewed with alarm the fragmentation of the Executive Branch and the lack of presidential power to manage it.

Much of the discussion of executive fragmentation is similar to the literature on metropolitan areas. It supposes an unstated common purpose and program in terms of which disparate entities and activies could be coordinated. The personal unity of the President, by being given authority, it is hoped, would unify the existing diversity. Many years ago Charles Hyneman challenged the dogmas of reorganization. The questions he raised have remained largely unanswered. The Hoover Commission doctrine, however, has remained. The allegations of economy and efficiency are now made with less confidence, as they are with respect to metropolitan reorganization. The esthetic attractions are among the most powerful factors giving this kind of proposal appeal. Very rarely are the political purposes avowed and argued. The contention is usually that the reorganization will provide an abstractly better government independent of any particular political purpose. A revisionist critique of the conventional wisdom that sees advantages in the present diversity and a value in the dialectic between . . . overall and partial views of the public interest is under way. The policy purposes of empowering the President need to be faced and argued. Structure does not exist for its own sake. As Rossiter well says, "The 'perfect pyramid' of administration is more a delusion than a panacea; rivalry and friction have virtues of their own."

The problems of presidential power involve the complex relations of legal authority, purpose, and power. Municipal reformers have discovered that conferring legal authority on a mayor by no means assures a corresponding increase in actual power sufficient to achieve the objectives desired. In fact the President's line authority frequently gives him less real power over those formally subordinate to him than his influence provides him with a formally independent agency. Legal authority may exist on the books but be a dead letter in fact. As Neustadt so well points out, "Rarely can he order, mostly must he persuade." And as Neustadt shows in the cases of MacArthur and the steel seizure, the necessity of ordering came as a last resort, a confession of weakness rather than a sign of strength. The problem of empowering the President with respect to Congress and the bureaucracy is one of tapping an adequate source of power. The passage of legislation can be no more than civic New Year's resolutions, evanescent and lacking in substance. Where it might be more, as in the case of the frequently proposed item veto for the President, one suspects it is because the public could and would back its use and hence increase the President's bargaining strength. Congressional reorganization has largely remained at the level of civil New Year's resolutions since leaders in it have been unable to tap sustained sources of public support.

It is frequently claimed that the President's responsibilities are fast outrunning his power to meet them, that public expectations of his performance far exceed his realistic capacity to meet them. Neustadt, who shares this concern, has pointed to the needs of others—Congress, bureaucracy, publics, domestic, and foreign—as major sources of presidential power; these are not automatic, legal powers of command but resources whose skillful use can turn them into major opportunities for influence and leadership. This "clerk-ship" of others' needs, as Neustadt perceptively shows, can routinize the meeting of these needs into a source of quite unclerkly power. Indeed for Congress, bureaucracy, and publics alike, the President dominates the content and timing of the agenda and the score card as well. Felt needs that turn public expectations toward the President can be turned into sources of presidential power. The expectations, even if they outrun actual legal authority, create the basis for its attainment or successful usurpation to the dismay of legalists.

Enough Power in Crisis?

The more serious matter, as Neustadt recognizes, is the situation of crisis in which the President is unable to get the public to recognize it as a crisis. A public grown tired, apathetic, bored, even escapist is an unpromising one from which to extract the sustained support the President is thought to require. In the past the President has been able to mobilize the public to meet crises. In an age of permanent crisis how is he to acquire enduring, steady sources of power sufficient to cope with the problems now thrust upon him?

The Vietnam War is a prime example of the problem. President Johnson, and now it would appear President Nixon, find their chief difficulty in maintaining public support for a policy combining unglamorous restraint with a costly application of a pressure whose dividends remain obscure. This is a classic case of the difficulty of mobilizing public support in a crisis to empower a President to continue a policy in which he believes. . . .

But what remedy would Neustadt or anyone else suggest? Much of the President's power depends on his standing on the Hill, and his standing on the Hill importantly depends on the Hill's view of his standing with the country. When the President's standing with the country ebbs, it necessarily affects his power. But the judgment of the Hill and other President-watchers does not merely reflect chance fluctuations in the Gallup applause meter. Veterans of politics are too well aware of presidential comebacks. In this sense the President need not court opinion from moment to moment. He must, however, carry most of his public with him over the long haul if he is making major demands on them for support. Is this bad? Does it too grievously hamper Presidents in undertaking momentarily unpopular but in the long run necessary and meritorious policies? It would help if we could examine an array of cases.

Suez, where a British prime minister, acting like a Churchill or a President, failed to consult, and with a desperate sense of Nasser being Hitler, plunged on, proved calamitous. One may question whether the power so to act was worth the risk of such an action.

The capacity to withdraw confidence which Neustadt sees in the subtle interaction of the Hill and the country with the President is an important means of forcing both responsiveness and responsibility. There is no having it both ways. If the President is to be free to follow a policy which he cannot persuade his publics, or most of them, to support, his power must for a time be rendered independent of opinion. That is, the Hill must at least for a span of time be his independently and perhaps in spite of the Hill's judgment of his standing with the country. To insure this is the purpose of those who opt for party government. Three questions need asking. First, are there really vital national needs that cannot be met with the existing system? Second, are there available means and mobilizable public demand for the creation of the parties required by the model? Third, does British or other relevant experience lend credibility to the hopes of the proponents of the change?

What Does the Country Want?

If one agrees with Rossiter that "much of the criticism [of the President's relations with Congress] is irrelevant, since it ignores the blunt truth that we long ago made our irrevocable choice of coordinate rather than unified government," that, except for minor improvements, is the end of the matter. It would not only leave party government an impossibility, it would also mean that presidential control of the bureaucracy would have to be shared with a coordinate Congress.

It is doubtful that we have made an irrevocable decision. Certainly if the American publics, or most of them, are persuaded that the achievement of many of their important purposes requires the revocation of the choice of a coordinate rather than unified government, that revocation is not beyond their power. Clearly only some of these publics have been so persuaded. Perhaps this is largely so because the case that has been made has been so theoretic. The danger in foreign affairs may seem to some less due to the President's lack of power than to the President's abuse of the abundance of power he now possessess. In domestic matters the main thrust of the criticism seems to be that the President cannot act as the head of a committed, powerful social democratic party. Perhaps in view of the level and distribution of income and the degree of social mobility in the country it should surprise neither that affluent liberals and their young should ardently criticize their failure nor that the failure should persist.

The country does indeed seem for the most part, despite rhetoric and anguish, to want a limited government with considerable freedom for the individual and his private life in the often contradictory confines of a mass economy and a mass culture. In such a situation we repair the ship at sea. Improvement is piecemeal and incremental rather than general and drastic. This accords with the situation in which for most of the society, domestically at all events, needs can be met by piecemeal, incremental improvement.

Incrementalism, however, is not enough for key and now aroused minorities. Their revolution of expectations feeds on both absolute and relative deprivation. They are joined by a youth radicalized by the impact of the draft destabilizing their lives at a normally unstable point. The draft is compounded by an unpopular, to them pointless and immoral, war. This is further exacerbated by a President raising hopes of inspiring leadership in the challenge of achieving the reality of civil rights and building a truly great society. The erosion of the promise of these goals in the ugliness of the war and the seeming hypocrisy of official rhetoric has aroused the violent hostility of some and the apathy, disaffection, and cynicism of others among the nation's youth. While a minority and not the base for positive presidential power under present and recent incumbents, the young, the young radicals, the Negro, and the Black militant are dangerously capable of fomenting a regressive reaction. This danger, our greatest within the country, requires no added presidential power. What it requires is something else.

Presidential Pedagogy

A role of the President that Neustadt discusses is that of teacher. In his book on *Presidential Power* Neustadt shows the unfortunate consequences of Truman's public pedagogy in the Korean War. In the context of his study the teaching is relatively narrowly related to the personal power of the President. The concept of the President's role as teacher has a broader application. Stalin, Mao, and the leaders of communism have given the role of teacher a bad name. Even the term "bully pulpit" has a smell of public relations evangelism. Yet Neustadt is right to point to the role of the President as teacher both for his own and more importantly for national power.

In his role as teacher the President develops and increases the cognitive competence of the government and the public. In his role as a teacher the President develops and sustains the sense of purpose in the government and in the public. In the matter of cognitive competence the nation's capacity to handle its economy has increased in a spectacular fashion. It took us a hundred years to put our understanding of small pox to effective use. It has taken vastly less to put Keynesian economics to effective use. In this increase in applied cognitive competence the President has played a critical role. The change from a nation that regarded depression as it once regarded disease, as caused by sin, to a nation that has the beginnings of a scientific understanding is a major advance in presidential and national power of a kind all too frequently reckoned with in political science.

Macro-Keynesianism has taken us a long way from the hopeless floundering of the '30's. Its own inadequacies to grapple with structural unemployment, insular poverty, and the hard core are becoming manifest. In addition, as Galbraith has pointed out, a satisfactory growth rate and a satisfactory GNP do not by any means equate with a socially desirable composition of these indicators. Macro-Keynesianism is doubtless an adequate theory for guiding the nation in the large. But it is incompetent to provide the basis for giving purpose and coordination to federal programs.

Here the fragmentation which Bailey laments is real enough. The theory at the disposal of the President is incompetent to provide the purpose and understanding in terms of which the unifunctional programs can be given coordinated direction. What is needed to provide common purpose is the common focus of a common territory, with a common population hopefully becoming a community whose common needs would provide the logic for coordinating government programs that now conflict or coexist. A national welfare state requires a local delivery system which means a system of local government appropriate to a nation. Such a system would give the President the structured local constituency for whose ends he could coordinate the bureaucracy.

Here too we need the President as teacher and promoter of research and knowledge. Moynihan has pointed to our cognitive deficiencies. *Newsweek's* issue of May 5, 1969, highlights this problem. "Such publicized ills as pollution and traffic congestion" [the President was told by the mayors], "are not deeply disturbing because they can be treated with money; instead the real crisis lies in the complex social problems that no one knows how to approach. Surprised and a bit skeptical, the President polled the table: was this true? Every one agreed. For example, said Stokes, most of the turmoil in Cleveland is being caused by 13- to 18-year-olds. 'What do you do," he asked. 'Send the National Guard into a high school?' "

Government is at bottom a moral enterprise. It is concerned with the legitimacy of the allocation of roles and access to the opportunity structure. The President's major job, like the Confucian emperor and the Communist leader, is the maintenance and renewal of the normative structure. When the old legitimacy wears thin, when official values lose credibility with the young, he is in the spotlight. His credibility renews the nation's. Church and state are only formally separate. The government and its President can lose or gain heaven's mandate.

The
White House
Staff Bureaucracy

23

Alex B. Lacy, Jr.

. . .

Early Presidents had to make do with very little professional staff. When Thomas Jefferson entered the White House in 1801, he had one messenger and an occasional secretary—the latter paid out of Jefferson's own pocket, and rarely even in Washington. President Ulysses S. Grant had two professional staffers; and Woodrow Wilson conducted World War I and a major diplomatic effort with seven. When President William McKinley asked a certain J. A. Porter to become his secretary, he was refused—because of "the low recognition value of the job."

Franklin D. Roosevelt, entering the White House in 1933, found that, despite such grave emergencies as the depression and the rise of fascism, things had not changed much. Throughout his first term, he operated with only three professional staff members, three secretaries—(press, appointments, corresponding)—and a small clerical staff. He frequently had to borrow staff members from other departments and agencies, sometimes even moving them to the White House. He also relied on old friends, like Judge Samuel I. Rosenman.

Obviously something had to be done, and in 1936 Roosevelt called upon three political scientists for aid. In 1937, the resulting President's Committee on Administrative Management, under the leadership of Louis Brownlow, submitted a report that led to a major reorganization and expansion of the Presidential staff.

"Where . . .," the committee asked, "can there be found an executive in any way comparable upon whom so much petty work is thrown? Or who is forced to see so many people on related matters and to make so many decisions on . . . incomplete information? How is it humanly possible to know fully the affairs and problems of over 100 separate major agencies . . .?"

Since the passage of the Reorganization Act of 1939, the total executive office of the President has rapidly grown to match the increased workload. It has now overflowed the old State, War, and Navy building that a few years earlier had housed three major departments. When the Brownlow Committee delivered its report, Roosevelt had 37 White House Office employees, and a budget of about $200,000. By 1967 the budget had increased to nearly $3 million, to support a staff of several hundred.

After 1939, the first big budget jump came in 1947 (from $250,996 in 1946 to $772,122), when President Truman insisted that all White House borrow-

222

ing of personnel from agencies and departments had to cease. The 1947 budget was therefore the first "honest" White House Office budget. The increase since then has been—with minor exceptions—a steady one. Roosevelt after 1939 operated with an average of eight professional staffers, while Eisenhower and Kennedy both began the Presidency with 21.

Now, nearly three decades after the great change, what, precisely, has been the impact of an expanded staff upon the Presidency? Is the President, as Woodrow Wilson described him in a famous lecture, still free "both in law and conscience to be as big a man as he can"? Or has the Presidential office, as Edward S. Corwin feared, become rigidly bureaucratized and institutionalized?

. . .

Staffs Vary with the President

The characteristics of the staffs varied, as the Presidents and the times themselves varied. Let us examine them one by one.

Roosevelt dominated every activity of his staff—this is its most impressive characteristic. The staff was an extension of FDR, personally as well as officially. Assignments might seem without reason or purpose, the staff might seem on the brink of chaos—but no one raised a question. Roosevelt initiated the assignments in detail, and personally checked to see that all were carried out (staff members say he never forgot one). All reports were made directly to him. And he was available to all staff members whenever they needed his attention—there was no chain of command.

FDR's relations with his staff were motivated, as Richard Neustadt observed, by "a concern for his position as *the* man in the White House." He believed in action, with "a strong feeling for a cardinal fact in government: that presidents . . . act in the concrete as they meet deadlines set by due dates." His staff members had to be jacks-of-all-trades. None was chosen as a specialist, and none developed pre-emptive influence in any area.

Roosevelt liked to hear differing points of view, and frequently gave two or more staff members the same assignment, and then delighted at their rivalry. Apparently this did not produce permanent hard feelings.

The reorganization plan of 1939 did not radically change the Roosevelt staff. The big change had taken place in 1933–34, because the Presidency and the personality of the President had themselves changed radically. As one staff member said, FDR suddenly needed additional staff in 1933 "because the people began to look to the President as . . . never before—writing to him, calling him."

Even after reorganization, White House Office activity continued to center on the three secretaries. Stephen Early (followed by Jonathan Daniels) was in charge of press relations; Marvin H. McIntyre handled appointments and made arrangements for trips, public appearances, and meetings; Brigadier-General Edwin M. "Pa" Watson was special legman and confidant.

The first three staffmen—James H. Rowe, William H. McReynolds, and Lauchlin Currie—handled whatever tasks were at hand. But the great task of all was to serve as eyes and ears for the President, and be available for anything.

During World War II, the White House Office changed considerably. Judge Samuel I. Rosenman became special counsel to the President. He drafted speeches and messages to Congress, and was responsible for reviewing bills and executive orders. Harry L. Hopkins moved into the White House as special assistant, and was involved in almost every activity during the war years. He actually lived in the President's personal quarters on the second floor. Although his position was a very special one, neither he, nor Judge Rosenman, was ever a chief of staff. Hopkins was never a Sherman Adams.

The schedule of FDR's staff was determined by FDR's schedule. The day began with a brief conference with several staff members while he had breakfast. FDR never had regular staff meetings, and the only other time members regularly met with him in groups was just before press conferences, when briefings were completed and strategy discussed. After breakfast, the staff was on its own, although called as needed and readily available.

The evenings were for drafting speeches, policy statements, and decision-making, which usually involved Rosenman, playwright Robert E. Sherwood, Hopkins, and borrowed staffers like Benjamin Cohen and Thomas Corcoran. After FDR went to bed, the drafting team frequently worked well into the morning.

Roosevelt was very close to his staffers, and probably socialized with them more than other Presidents did with theirs. Despite its apparent disorder, this may explain why the staff was so effective.

The Roosevelt-Truman transition was traumatic. Truman was unprepared to take over, and unfamiliar with the Roosevelt staff; he had only two of his own men, Matthew Connelly and Harry Vaughan. And the FDR staff was not sure whether he wanted them to stay.

While they hesitated, a number of old Truman friends, mostly from Missouri, turned up and without Truman's authorization tried to take over. One staffer reported, "We wondered if we had a Democratic Harding on our hands." Truman later completely cleared out the newcomers and asked several Roosevelt staff men to stay on.

In a year the staff was decisively reorganized. They continued to be generalists, but fell into fixed areas of assignment from politics to national resources.

Throughout, Truman followed Roosevelt's example by using the three secretaries to handle most recurrent duties. Charles G. Ross was press secretary until his death in December 1950. Matthew Connelly served as appointment's secretary and main political troubleshooter. William D. Hassett continued as corresponding secretary.

Staff work on policy centered on the assistant to the President, and the special counsel to the President. John R. Steelman, persuaded to return to government service by Truman, was the assistant to the President. He served as mediator and coordinator, handling executive family fights and working very closely with the Bureau of the Budget.

Rosenman stayed as special counsel until late 1945. Six months after he left, in June 1946, Clark Clifford took his place—and served four years. He was responsible for writing speeches, and checking bills and executive orders from a legal and policy point of view. Under him and his successor, Charles Murphy, it was the key staff position for policy.

Truman relied on his Cabinet and departments much more than Roosevelt had, keeping his White House staff small. Seldom did more than 11 men report to him directly.

With two exceptions, the administrative assistants were not front-line men in the Truman Administration. In fact, they served primarily as assistants to Murphy, Clifford, and Steelman. In my interviews with Truman men, I soon discovered that most felt that the President should not have more than a dozen reporting to him. Asked "Did you need more men on the staff?" the respondents unanimously replied No.

Like Roosevelt, Truman found that war necessitated special services. In 1950, he appointed W. Averell Harriman as a special assistant to keep the President informed about the Korean conflict. But Harriman never really functioned as a White House Office staff member.

The staff day began with a formal conference—meetings were so regular that everyone sat in the same place. Truman presided, and began by discussing previous reports and handing out new assignments. Then he went around the circle, permitting each member to be heard. The staff was convinced that these meetings were especially important: One said, "Every staff man could hear what his colleagues were doing—be informed, know what was going on."

The President was generally not available to the staff again until 3 P.M.; but 3 to 5 were set aside exclusively for staff and Cabinet, and basic policy matters were discussed.

Truman's staff was made up of very able men, who came to be devoted to him. They were not as intellectual as the Kennedy staff, but Truman probably could not have gotten maximum mileage out of intellectuals; he did get it out of his own group. As one told me, "He had a good concept of staff work. He could delegate. Once he got confidence in a man, he used him to his advantage."

Unlike his immediate predecessors, President Eisenhower had very definite ideas about staff, derived partly from his military experience. He believed in tight organization, efficiency, and keeping as much work as possible off the President. Responding to some critics who felt that the creative chaos of the Roosevelt staff might be better, he noted: "I have been astonished to read some contentions which seem to suggest that smooth organization guarantees that nothing is happening, whereas ferment and disorder indicate progress."

Ike Was Chief of Staff

Organization was the heart of the Eisenhower White House Office, and Sherman Adams the heart of the organization. He was a real chief of staff.

To quote one staffer, "He was the key to the whole thing and he managed everything with a firm hand." In his own book his publisher bills him as "the man who probably exercised more power as a President's confidential adviser and co-ordinator than any other individual in modern times."

The staff was highly structured, with a rigid chain of command and new titles to match. Each man was a specialist.

The basic staff job was to reduce the President's load. Nothing was supposed to go to Ike if it could be handled elsewhere. If it did go to him, it was supposed to be reduced to a one-page memo with firm recommendations, and none went without an "O.K., S.A." fixed on it.

Most respondents believed that Adam's reputation as a "hard boss" and "a difficult man to get along with" was well earned. Relations with him were strictly business. Nevertheless, the staff respected him and his ability to make decisions and get work done.

One Eisenhower innovation was a special office to manage the clerical staff, handle correspondence, and—most important—handle national-security and intelligence communications.

Eisenhower formalized the work that had been handled by Clark Clifford for Truman. He had two assistants who were primarily responsible for coordination of national-security policy matters, in addition to the staff secretary who handled communications. They reported directly to Eisenhower and received their assignments directly from him. They worked closely with the staff secretary, and these three usually saw the President daily. As one said: "I seldom saw Adams except in the White House Mess at lunchtime. He may have been 'Assistant President' for domestic affairs, but he had no influence over national-security matters."

Eisenhower made more use of the Cabinet than others had and used the National Security Council "regularly and seriously." It was an important apparatus of coordination for him. He developed and announced all of his national-security and foreign-policy decisions at its meetings so that each department and agency involved knew "how he made the decision, why, and what the rationale was." Working closely with Dulles, for whom he had great respect, Eisenhower exerted his greatest influence as President in the national-security and foreign-policy areas.

Unfortunately, Eisenhower had much less interest in domestic politics, and this made the congressional-liaison unit within the White House Office a very important one. The relatively modest operation of Murphy and his team in the Truman Administration gave way to a very elaborate system under General Wilton B. Persons with the able assistance of Bryce Harlow who will undoubtedly be a mainstay of the new Nixon staff. All who worked in legislative liaison for Eisenhower agreed that, especially in the early years, it "was like pulling eye teeth" to get the Republicans in Congress to support the President's program.

The work of the legislative-liaison team was also greatly complicated by Eisenhower's aversion to party politics. One Republican Congressman, asked about partonage under the new Republican administration, complained that not only had he not gotten additional jobs, but that he had lost one that he had under Truman.

The daily schedule of the White House Office under Adams centered on Adams' schedule, in sharp contrast to the Democratic years when the President's schedule ruled. The typical staff day ran from 7 A.M. to 7 P.M., and the week might include Saturday and Sunday meetings. Adams always wanted the staff there when he came, and he was an "early to bed, early to rise" man —much to their dismay. The staff was grateful that he liked to play golf on Saturdays.

In 1953, Adams held staff meetings every morning; after 1953, usually three a week. Eisenhower rarely attended. In these meetings, Adams gave assignments and outlined the day's work. Those who attended felt that these conferences were very important. General Persons, after he replaced Adams, held very few staff meetings, however. (Adams left in 1958, after he was accused of accepting gifts from industrialist Bernard Goldfine.)

When John F. Kennedy came into office, he had been the recipient of more expert advice about White House organization than any of his predecessors. He immediately decided that he could not operate on the Eisenhower pattern, and his staff organization represented a return to the basic Roosevelt-Truman model. It could not, of course, be a replica of either—because government in the 1960s was very different. And those elements of the Eisenhower experience that proved useful Kennedy did preserve.

From Campaign Staff to White House

Like Nixon in this respect, Kennedy had another advantage over his predecessors: he had already been operating for many months with a very elaborate campaign-staff organization. Most of the appointees to the White House Office staff had already developed work patterns as assistants to Kennedy. He knew what to expect from them, and they knew his expectations, abilities and needs.

President Kennedy was his own chief of staff. He initiated assignments; received all reports from his top aides; and, as Sorensen has written, "decided what it is he need *not* decide." He much preferred the burdens of close supervision to "being merely a clerk in his own office."

The workload centered on several key offices. The office of special counsel, under Theodore Sorensen, was restored to its former status. Sorensen was primary staff adviser on domestic policy, and speech-writer par excellence.

In foreign policy and national security, Sorensen's counterpart was McGeorge Bundy. Where Eisenhower's national-security advisers had been concerned with organization and coordination of vast and complex activities involving Defense, State, and a dozen other departments and agencies, the Bundy team was primarily concerned with advising Kennedy on policy matters; the President was his own coordinator.

Bundy was assisted by a group of very able men—an average of ten, called by Kennedy his "little State Department." Bundy held the only meetings that even resembled staff conferences in the Kennedy White House—a briefing each morning for key staffers. None of Kennedy's advisers were ever out of touch with foreign policy, and they could shift from domestic assignments to assist in a foreign-policy crisis with relative ease.

Appointments Secretary Kenneth O'Donnell occupied the third office of major importance. He was a political troubleshooter, handled liaison with the Secret Service and F.B.I. and made arrangements for the President's trips. He also kept watch over the White House Office services. Pierre Salinger, in his memoirs, ranks O'Donnell as the most important member of the staff.

Lawrence O'Brien, a first-class political strategist who became Humphrey's campaign manager was in charge of Kennedy's legislative liaison. Press relations, particularly crucial for Kennedy after his narrow victory of 1960, were handled by another campaign veteran, Pierre Salinger. Authur Schlesinger Jr.'s position was unique: he was the White House's liaison with intellectuals in general and with Adlai Stevenson in particular. He was not active in the day-to-day work of the White House, he was the idea man, and kept up a steady stream of memoranda.

There was no hierarchy in the Kennedy staff: He reacted against the abundance of titles under Eisenhower. Most staffers were simply "special assistant to the President," and Kennedy remarked that he wished all had that title.

In sharp contrast to most of their predecessors, the Kennedy men were constantly in the news. They made speeches and public appearances; there were detailed and often romantic stories about them in the press; and already three have written memoirs—behavior considered "unheard of" and "not proper" in the Truman and Eisenhower days.

The Johnson staff kept changing all through the time of this study. Until after the 1964 election, President Johnson was not really free to develop his own staff. He kept on as many of the Kennedy people as possible until 1964 —and it was this "let us continue" spirit that made the very smooth transition (contrasted to the Roosevelt-Truman trauma) possible. He was also plagued by departures of the key men he did have. Walter Jenkins had been his chief assistant for 20 years; undoubtedly he would have been the key staff member if he had not collapsed after a scandal in 1964. Then, after the election, Jack Valenti and Bill Moyers departed for outside high-pay and high-prestige jobs. During these same three years, most of the Kennedy men were also leaving the staff.

Some preliminary observations can, however, be made about the Johnson style. The President kept firm personal control over the work of the White House Office. More than any President since Roosevelt, he needed a staff that was intensely personal and absolutely attuned to him.

Perhaps because of his difficulties in fitting his staff to his needs, President Johnson has turned to outside advisers more than any other President since Roosevelt. The most important were three Washington lawyers: James Rowe (a Roosevelt administrative assistant), Abe Fortas (now a Supreme Court Justice), and Clark Clifford (who became Secretary of Defense last year).

What trends and conclusions can we distill from this detailed analysis of the various White House staffs?

Each President since 1939 has had a distinctly different White House operation, and we can expect the same from Richard Nixon. However, each also learned from and built upon his predecessors' work. Thus, Truman rejected the disorder of the Roosevelt staff, but followed its most salient characteristics as he gathered a group of generalists around him and personally supervised them. And although Kennedy rejected the basic tenets of the Eisenhower staff organization, he incorporated the particular aspects that were useful to him.

Despite the differences, there is a strong thread of continuity. Titles and the approaches to work have been different from one administration to the next; but such functions as appointments, press relations, and patronage have steadily formed the spine of the Office.

Each administration has also contributed an increased workload to the next. The Roosevelt staffers worked hard, but between crises had moments to relax; the Kennedy-Johnson staffers have had few such moments, and neither—most likely—will Nixon's. Every assignment is urgent, each mistake costly, every day high-pressure. The workload has increased enormously since 1930; even when measured by such simple criteria as numbers of phone calls and pieces of mail, the present workload is staggering.

The size of the staff—especially in the numbers of assistants backing up the front-line men—has also increased, but not as rapidly as the work. Moreover, to be effective, the President's personal staff must be small. Eisenhower had the largest staff—but even that was only 25; and respondents agree that more would not be useful.

Each choice of a staff member, therefore, has been crucial. In fact, the standards the staffer must meet are often more restrictive than those for Cabinet members. The choice often demands subtle and difficult judgments by the President. The 169 staffers studied were an able and well-trained group. There have been very few abject failures among them.

During the past three decades, then, an expanded personal staff in the White House Office has not prevented the President from being, to quote Woodrow Wilson, "both in law and conscience . . . as big a man as he can." In fact, the White House Office staff actually helps him exert his personality as fully as possible, by overcoming the limitations of the office. The staff has helped make the responsibility bearable, the chain of decisions easier, and the consequences a bit more certain. It will be interesting to see if the same holds true for Richard Nixon's staff.

From
The Missile
Crisis

24

Elie Abel

Thursday, October 18
This is the week when I had better earn my salary.
—John F. Kennedy to Dean Acheson, October 18, 1962

That Thursday, the President invited Dean Acheson to the White House. The tall, elegant, sharp-tongued former Secretary of State found Kennedy sitting alone in his study. They talked about forty-five minutes, considering the choices open to the President—blockade versus air strike. Kennedy had been fully briefed on Wednesday's discussion in the Executive Committee. He mentioned the Cuba–Pearl Harbor analogy, which Acheson had scorned when Robert Kennedy raised it the previous day. The President reviewed the bidding. Either way it would be a painful decision. Acheson looked ahead beyond the Presidential decision, to the day when the Allies and the world at large would have to be informed. "Talking to de Gaulle," he said, "will be a problem. We have no ambassador in Paris. Chip Bohlen will be at sea for several days. It's not the kind of thing that should be left to a chargé d'affaires." Acheson suggested sending Vice President Johnson to Paris. Letting the suggestion drop, Kennedy got up from his rocking chair and gazed out the French windows for a long time in silence.

"This is the week," the President said at last, "when I had better earn my salary."

Acheson reflected gratefully that Kennedy, not he, carried the burden of decision.

The Executive Committee was to meet twice with the President that day, at 11 A.M. and again at 10 P.M. At five o'clock he would be receiving Gromyko. The newspapers Thursday morning carried a report that the Defense Department had started a build-up of American air power in the Southeastern states, nearest to Cuba. It happened to be true. Somewhat defensively, the Pentagon confirmed the deployment of certain air units to the Southeast, calling it "an ordinary thing to do" in the light of the fact that Castro now possessed modern MIG jet fighters. There was no mention of missiles. To maintain the outward appearance that all was well, the President at 9:30 that morning handed out various aviation trophies. At ten o'clock he held a routine Cabinet meeting on various domestic matters. Kennedy did not once mention Cuba to his Cabinet. Those Cabinet officers who were privy to the unseen crisis—Rusk, McNamara, Dillon, and Robert Kennedy—had little to

230

say to their colleagues. The Attorney General looked around for Edward R. Murrow, director of the United States Information Agency. He found instead Murrow's deputy, Donald Wilson.

"Where is Ed?" he inquired.

"He is ill at home in Pawling [New York]," Wilson replied.

"Will he be back in a few days?"

"Not a chance."

The Attorney General looked vaguely troubled. "You'd better keep in touch," he said. Wilson had been planning to visit his mother in New Jersey that week end. "I think you'd better stick around over the week end," Robert Kennedy said. "We may need you." Although Don Wilson was an old friend and touch-football teammate of the Kennedy brothers, Bobby told him nothing that day.

In Rusk's conference room at the State Department that morning, the discussion had to do chiefly with tactics: whether the President should tell the world about the missiles in Cuba before acting to remove them. Dean Rusk had been careful not to identify himself with one school or the other —hawks or doves, as they later came to be known. He felt it was important to reserve his own position. When the final recommendation was ready he would have to urge it on the President, whichever way the decision went. That morning, however, Rusk spoke out against a surprise attack. Quite apart from the risk of provoking a spasm reaction in the Kremlin, he felt it would be costly in terms of political support. If the President acted without first consulting the Organization of American States, or the United Nations, or without any prior effort to approach the Russians, he would forfeit support round the world. It later developed that the Secretary of State was not so much recommending prior consultation as thinking aloud. In the afternoon session he seemed to turn the proposition around. Starting from the assumption that the United States could not tolerate the continued presence of Russian missiles in Cuba, he suggested Tuesday, October 23, as the deadline. If by that date the missile sites were still under construction, the United States should then inform its chief allies—he mentioned Britain, France, West Germany, Italy and Turkey—that it would use force to remove them. About Wednesday, October 24, the United States Air Force would strike the missile bases, the attack to be simultaneous with a public statement and a message to Khrushchev, warning him in plain language that Soviet counteraction would mean war. Taking the missiles out would not be the end of the matter, Rusk predicted. "If we don't do this," he said, "we go down with a whimper. Maybe it's better to go down with a bang."

Rusk's apparent turnabout illustrates the futility of trying to sort out the hawks from the doves. The fact is that nearly every man in the room changed his position at least once—and some more than once—during that anxious week of brainstorming. Rusk's two-part soliloquy—as he saw it—had nothing to do with advocating one course or the other; his purpose was to state each proposition as persuasively as he could in order that both might then be critically examined and debated. This left him open to the charge of straddling. Other participants called his views "opaque." In a *Saturday Evening Post* article, published after the crisis, Stewart Alsop and Charles Bartlett wrote: "Secretary Rusk's position does not come through loud and clear—he appears to have been a dawk or a hove from the start." As for McGeorge Bundy, treated far more gently by the same authors, other Executive Committee members agree that he changed position twice. Bundy started out talking of a diplomatic approach, next argued for doing nothing, and then became an air-strike advocate.

All this retrospective pigeonholing loses sight of the essential point. The President alone, as Commander in Chief, had the power to decide and did in fact give the orders. The President's was the controlling intelligence. He ran the operation, one official recalls, "like a lieutenant runs a platoon in combat." Bundy, Rusk, Stevenson, and the rest were there to advise him. He listened, then made his own decisions.

Each meeting opened with McCone's intelligence briefing. There was no agenda, only a checklist of topics which Bundy would have typed up a few minutes beforehand. The President would then call, in turn, on Rusk and McNamara, leading to a general discussion. Kennedy did a lot of listening. He was careful to give each of the secondary figures—Gilpatric, Nitze or Ball —his opportunity to be heard. When the time came he would state his own conclusion, often understating it. There were no scenes of high drama. Sometimes he would signal his decision by a nod of the head. Bundy would then distill the essence of the discussion in the form of a National Security Action Memorandum (NSAM), showing where the matter stood. At all times the President was in control of himself. Those who knew him best could sense that he was impatient or irritated when, on occasion, he would tap his front teeth with his forefinger. Long after the meeting had adjourned, back in the White House living quarters, the President would work off his tensions in solitude. Sitting in his rocker with a yellow legal-sized pad in his lap, he would cover page after page with notes of all kinds in that quirky scrawl of his, littering the floor with sheets of paper. Then the President's secretary, Mrs. Evelyn Lincoln, would scoop them up. One of the few who could decipher Kennedy's penmanship, Mrs. Lincoln would edit the notes, then type them neatly for his use the following day.

At the morning session with the President on Thursday, the Intelligence Board reported that the first Soviet medium-range missile in Cuba could be ready for launching in eighteen hours. The Joint Chiefs of Staff had started ordering precautionary troop movements. It began to appear that the decision-making machinery was racing the clock. There were now two elements of urgency: first, the danger that more missiles would soon be operational; second, the possibility that in spite of all the elaborate security measures, a leak might alert the Kremlin to the preparations under way in Washington. It was at least conceivable that if Khrushchev discovered what was going on, he would seize the initiative by serving an ultimatum before Kennedy was ready to serve his own.

There was talk that morning of ultimate policy goals. Should the President limit his objective to the simple removal of Soviet missiles, or use the occasion to get rid of Castro at the same time? The first alternative could perhaps be accomplished by the naval blockade. The second certainly would demand a full-scale invasion.

The President listened more than he spoke. Though, when he put questions, the others felt they could discern his trend of thought. For Kennedy the talk of invading Cuba inevitably brought up memories of the Bay of Pigs, his most humiliating failure. It was clear to everyone in the room that there must never be another such disaster.

Then came the turn of the lawyers present—Ball and Acheson most prominent among them—to consider the legality of each alternative. Acheson took the position that legal niceties were so much pompous foolishness in a situation where the essential security of the United States, its prestige, its pledged word to defend the Americas, was threatened. Although Fidel Castro had recently declared himself a Marxist-Leninist, Cuba did not belong to the Warsaw Pact. Thus an attack on Cuba would not necessarily bring the Soviet Union into a state of war with the United States, whereas an attack on Poland, for example, most assuredly would. Ball argued that a naval blockade, though traditionally regarded as an act of war, would have more "color of legality." Abram J. Chayes, Legal Adviser to the Secretary of State, was away in Paris for a series of meetings aimed at persuading the Western Allies to stop trading with Cuba. In his absence, Chayes' deputy, Leonard C. Meeker, presented a legal analysis suggesting, for the first time, that the blockade might better be called a defensive quarantine. He borrowed the phrase, with due acknowledgment, from Franklin D. Roosevelt's "quarantine-the-aggressor" speech. By noon, as Kennedy left to receive the Japanese Finance Minister, Eifaku Sato, it began to appear that the blockade advocates might prevail. Legalities had less to do with this than the practical argument that a naval blockade would avoid killing Russians and give the Kremlin time to reflect.

. . .

With the hour of decision fast approaching, Kennedy had called on a man he greatly admired—Robert A. Lovett, once Harry Truman's Secretary of Defense—to provide a fresh judgment. While the President fenced with Gromyko, Bundy briefed Lovett on the details and then led him upstairs to see Kennedy. Lovett was to join the Executive Committee for its climactic sessions just ahead. Apart from Acheson and McCloy, he was the only private citizen to be called in by the President.

The same day, Kennedy also notified former Presidents Truman and Eisenhower. John McCone, a California Republican, volunteered to tell Eisenhower. Although McCone has refused to divulge what passed between them at Gettysburg, there is reason to believe that Eisenhower took a skeptical view, suspecting perhaps that Kennedy might be playing politics with Cuba on the eve of Congressional elections. McCone enjoyed Eisenhower's confidence, having served in his Administration as chairman of the Atomic Energy Commission. But Ike evidently found it hard to forget or forgive Kennedy's dismissal of the speeches by Senator Keating, warning of the Soviet arms build-up.

Rusk's dinner for Gromyko at eight o'clock that night added nothing to the Administration's understanding of Soviet actions or motives. The two became embroiled in a long colloquy over Berlin and whether it was the

Russians or the Americans who had started the cold war. The dinner did, however, produce a comic by-product when McNamara and McCone strode into the State Department lobby just as Gromyko had gone up to the eighth floor dining room. Reporters and cameramen, out in force to record Gromyko's arrival, wrongly assumed that the Secretary of Defense and the CIA chief were going to the dinner. To make certain, one reporter asked if that was their destination. He accepted McNamara's "Yes" at face value. In fact they were on their way to the "think tank" in George Ball's conference room one floor below. A more cynical reporter might have boggled at the notion of McCone's breaking bread with Gromyko. This one did not. There were other narrow scrapes that day as the Administration nervously clutched its secrets. One sharp-eyed middle-level official said to his boss: "I know there is something going on that you don't want to talk about. But if security is all that tight, maybe you'd better tell all those big wheels from across the river to get their cars off the street." The boss looked out the window, saw for himself that the diplomatic entrance was jammed with long black official limousines bearing easily identified license plates. Thereafter, all but one of the limousines disappeared into the basement garage.

That evening in Ball's conference room—while Rusk and Gromyko were refighting the cold-war battles of the Forties and Fifties a floor above them —the Executive Committee members found a consensus developing against an air strike. They had divided into two groups, George Ball heading the blockade team, and McGeorge Bundy the air-strike team. They had been split almost evenly at the start: McCone, Dillon, Taylor, Acheson, Nitze, and eventually Bundy on the side of using American air power to "take out" the Russian missile sites; McNamara, Gilpatric, Robert Kennedy, Thompson, Ball, and now also Lovett for a naval blockade. (Adlai Stevenson had returned to New York for the conclusion of the general debate in the United Nations General Assembly.) Each team put its case as forcefully as it could in an exercise of comparative persuasiveness, similar to the war games played at military schools. At one stage the air-strike team suggested asking the Swiss Government, which looks after American interests in Cuba, to warn Castro in advance of the projected air attack, parallel with a warning to the Russians that they should evacuate their people from the missile sites. Tommy Thompson dealt with that suggestion. He argued that not much was to be gained by dealing with Castro, through the Swiss or otherwise. It was the Russians who had put missiles into Cuba. This was a major departure from Soviet policy and must have been fully considered in the Kremlin. Hence the Russians alone could take them out.

The air-strike team countered with the argument that a naval blockade could prove more dangerous than an air attack. The Russians, for example, might retaliate for the sinking of one of their ships by calling on their submarines in the area to sink an American ship. Then, inescapably, it would be up the ladder of escalating war, rung by rung.

Dean Rusk's impression was that, after hearing the pros and cons, the protagonists on both sides persuaded themselves that either course was difficult, far more difficult than they had imagined before examining the pitfalls and complexities. The overriding consideration was the President's own belief that an air strike by itself would accomplish little and would inevitably have to be followed by an invasion of Cuba. Ambassador Thompson had reinforced the President's own caution, arguing that, of all possible courses, a surprise attack on the missile sites was by far the most hazardous. It meant killing Russians, and Khrushchev, he warned, was notoriously impulsive.

That evening, Douglas Dillon changed his position. "I had wanted an air strike," he recalls. "I had assumed the Russians would deceive us. I expected nothing else. Nor did I believe that the Russians would necessarily send their missiles against the United States if we attacked their Cuban bases. What changed my mind was Bobby Kennedy's argument that we ought to be true to ourselves as Americans, that surprise attack was not in our tradition. Frankly, these considerations had not occurred to me until Bobby raised them so eloquently."

There is general agreement that McNamara helped the Attorney General mightily with his now-celebrated argument on "maintaining the options." He contended the decision confronting the President was not of the either-or variety. Let blockade be his first option, the contraband list limited at the start to offensive weapons. If that failed, the President would then have a choice of responses. He could decide to deny the Cubans other kinds of cargo —petroleum—for example—or he could move up the scale to an air strike, or even, at the far end, to an invasion. If one form of pressure failed in its purpose, then another, more severe, pressure could be applied. Nothing would be lost by starting from the bottom of the scale. Bundy credits Dillon with the refinement that brought about his own conversion. The Secretary of the Treasury's clinching argument in favour of the blockade was that it could be applied without losing the option to launch an air strike later. If, however, the air strike was to be the first step, other options would be closed.

At ten o'clock, the exhausted committee members were asked to rejoin the President. Nine of them piled into a single limousine to avoid attracting attention by the sudden arrival of a whole cavalcade at that late hour. Edwin Martin chose to walk the ten blocks to the White House. In the crush of bodies, someone remarked: "What if we get into a collision?"

The meeting with the President, which ran on past midnight, confirmed the trend toward a naval blockade. Kennedy promptly assigned Sorensen to start drafting the speech in which he would disclose the presence of Soviet missiles in Cuba and proclaim measures for their removal. Roswell Gilpatric handed General Taylor a batch of assignments for the Pentagon planners. He asked the Chairman of the Joint Chiefs to supply: 1) a list of riot-control equipment that the United States could provide to Latin-American governments should any of them need help in maintaining internal security; 2) a list of offensive weapons to be barred from Cuba by the blockade; 3) a study showing which of the Latin-American countries could assist in blockading Cuba; 4) another study, citing the pros and cons of extending the blockade to cover airplanes bound for Cuba, as well as ships at sea; 5) a report on the ramifications of working with Alpha 66 and other Cuban exile groups.

That night, Robert Kennedy telephoned his deputy, Katzenbach, at home and asked him to get started on a brief establishing the legal basis for a blockade of Cuba. George Ball's assistant, George Springsteen, called Abram Chayes away from his shipping discussions in Paris. It was a conversation remarkable for its brevity and for what was left unsaid.

"Come on home," Springsteen said to the State Department's Legal Adviser.

"What do you mean? What's going on? Is it important?"

"Sure, it's important. Come on home."

"What is it, Cuba?"

"Just shut up and come on home."

Abe Chayes came on home.

POLITICS AND THE SUPREME COURT

The belief that the Supreme Court is a nonpolitical institution has been described as "the most potent myth in American political life." Despite the Supreme Court's mystical halo, it is quite clear that in terms of its recruitment criteria, its decision-making process, and its impact, the Court is a political body. The purpose of Part Six is to examine the political significance of these three dimensions of the Court's policy-making role.

Because of its status as the final interpreter of American constitutionalism, the Court was able in the 1950s and 1960s to take public policy positions in the areas of civil rights and civil liberties that the other branches of government were either unable or unwilling to take. By the same token, the less libertarian decisions rendered by a majority of the Burger Court, particularly in the area of criminal procedure, are also symbolically enhanced by the rituals, trappings, and setting surrounding the publicly visible aspects of Supreme Court decision making.

These symbolic embellishments are usually justified by those who hold them to be a necessary shield that enables the Court to defend individuals and minority groups against infringement of their constitutional rights by temporary shifts in majority opinion. But those who have focused on the policy positions enunciated by the Supreme Court throughout our history have found scant evidence to support this libertarian image of the Court's impact. The fact that the Warren Court acted consistently in ways that upheld individual rights has caused some to forget that Supreme Court decisions in other periods have sanctioned public policies that defined people as property, promoted racial segregation, and defended child-labor practices on the ground that to do otherwise would violate the "property rights" of private industry. These positions were taken by Courts whose internal majorities were reflecting the political philosophies and policy preferences shaped by the dominant political-elite coalitions of their time— for example, Southern slaveholding interests under Roger Taney and laissez-faire capitalist interests in the late-nineteenth- and early-twentieth-century Courts.

The opening selection by Robert Dahl begins with an abstract dialogue between a proponent and a critic of the practice of judicial review in a democratic society. Dahl then explores the validity of the image of the Supreme Court as a staunch defender of individual rights against the encroachments of "majority tyranny." Using the entire history of the Supreme Court as a point of departure, he finds that the Court has only infrequently overruled the will of a determined lawmaking majority in Congress. Furthermore, because the selection of judges is based on political and ideological criteria rather than on strictly technical grounds, newly appointed justices are likely to reflect the dominant currents of political opinion in their time. If Dahl's analysis is correct, recent decisions of the Burger Court reversing the extension of defendant's rights can be interpreted as an attempt to symbolically confer legitimacy on Richard Nixon's "law and order" electoral coalition.

In "Recruiting Judges," Jack W. Peltason identifies the political factors considered important in the selection of members of the federal judiciary.

His article illustrates that interest conflict is at the very heart of judicial selection. Men are named to the federal bench because of assumptions made about the values they are likely to reflect once appointed. In seeking cues as to the political values of a future Supreme or Appellate Court judge, the President and the Senate look to such factors as his party identification, his past positions on constitutional questions, and the opinions of state and local officials personally familiar with his political views. In the case of appointments to lower federal courts, judgeships have become important sources of senatorial patronage. The Senate has evolved a practice of deferring to the choices of the individual Senators in the President's party who represent the state in which the judge will serve.

Anthony Lewis's book *Gideon's Trumpet* is an incisive portrait of the evolution of a single landmark Supreme Court decision. The case in question, *Gideon vs. Wainwright,* extended to indigent defendants in state criminal cases a right to counsel that was already guaranteed to defendants in federal cases. The third selection in Part Six, drawn from Lewis's book, illustrates the way in which the Court organizes its heavy workload, as well as the nature of its internal workings. The Court is a highly individualistic institution with little division of labor. Personal influence patterns among the judges depend mainly on the persuasive powers of each justice. However, the formal weekly conferences are structured in ways that symbolically enhance the expressed views of the Chief Justice and the senior members. Lewis also discusses the role of law clerks in decision making and the log-rolling agreements by which the Court's agenda is established.

25

The
Supreme
Court

Robert Dahl

Democracy and Judicial Review: A Dialogue

Does the power of judicial review entail a nondemocratic, an aristocratic, even an oligarchic principle of government? The defenders and critics of judicial review have wrestled with this question ever since *Marbury* v. *Madison*. Jefferson may have had *Marbury* v. *Madison* in mind when in his old age he wrote to a friend that "the judiciary in the United States is the subtle corps of sappers and miners constantly working underground to undermine the foundations of our confederated republic. . . . A judiciary independent of a king or executive alone is a good thing; but independence of the will of the nation is a solecism, at least in a republican government."

The controversy can perhaps be summarized best in a dialogue between a critic and an advocate of judicial review:

CRITIC: I am quite willing to concede that a tradition of constitutionality may convey a measure of legitimacy to judicial review. I contend, nonetheless, that judicial review is undemocratic. After all, most of the people in eighteenth-century Britain no doubt regarded their constitutional system —kings, lords, and all—as legitimate. Yet you would not argue, I'm sure, that eighteenth-century Britain was a democracy. Aristocracies, monarchies, even dictatorships, I suppose, might acquire legitimacy in the eyes of the people they rule; yet they would not be democratic. In different times and places, all sorts of political institutions have acquired a certain degree of legitimacy; yet I would not want many of these institutions in this country, nor, I imagine, would you. I wonder if judicial review hasn't generated a conflict between two different principles of legitimacy accepted by Americans—a conflict between our tradition of constitutionality and our commitment to democracy.

ADVOCATE: I do not think so. As Hamilton and Marshall said, ours is a *limited* government; I prefer to call it a libertarian democracy. I don't contend, as Marshall did, that judicial review is inherent in a written constitution; I know as well as you do that a number of other democracies that were not in existence when Marshall wrote his famous opinion now have written constitutions, and yet do not give their courts the power of judicial review. I would contend, however, that the *limited* character of our government is an absolutely essential characteristic. Stripped of its constitutional limitations, ours would be a totally different system. Moreover, we Americans continue to believe strongly in limited government. And judicial review helps to preserve limited government by protecting the Constitution from violations by state governments, by the federal government, or by particular parts of the federal government, such as the Congress. This is why Americans overwhelmingly believe in judicial review. Do you contend that democracy requires *unlimited* government?

CRITIC: You misunderstand me. I know full well that we possess a written Constitution. I realize that someone has to interpret the meaning of what is written in that Constitution. I can see that in the course of events cases come to the courts which depend on what the Constitution means. So, in deciding the cases before them, the courts must interpret the Constitution. Let me remind you, however, that the United States is not the only country in the world with a written constitution. In fact, I believe that every modern democracy in the world except Britain now has a written constitution: Switzerland, Sweden, Norway, The Netherlands, France, Canada, Ireland, Australia, to name a few well-known democratic countries. And the same is true of all the more recent democracies: West Germany, Austria, Italy, India, Japan. . . . Yet many of them do not have judicial review—and I think it fair to say that not one has a supreme court as powerful as ours.

ADVOCATE: I do not quite see how we could function without judicial review!

CRITIC: What are you afraid of—the American people? But if the American people wanted unlimited government, do you really think that a few men on our Supreme Court could prevent it? Why, the voters would elect a President and a Congress who would impeach and convict the Justices one day and appoint new ones the next! Limited government exists in this country not because the Supreme Court wants it but because, as you said yourself, we Americans want it. And limited government will cease the day Americans cease to want it, no matter what nine men on a court may say or do. So long as the bulk of the American people want limited government, they will elect representatives to Congress and the Presidency who adhere to this commitment. If Americans should stop wanting limited government, they will elect revolutionaries, and our Constitution will be as dead as the Articles of Confederation. So here is my answer: The best protection for limited government in a democracy, in fact the only protection, consists of the people and their elected representatives. What I am saying is this: Democracy depends on the self-restraint of the people. If they don't exercise self-restraint, you won't have a democracy and no Court can keep it for them. If they do exercise self-restraint, then you don't need to have judicial review.

ADVOCATE: What you say is all very well in the abstract. But remember, ours is also a federal system. Suppose a state government violates the Constitution—for example, by depriving some of its citizens of their right to assemble or to speak freely? A majority of the voters in the United States might oppose the state action, but even if they knew about it—which they probably would not—what could they do?

CRITIC: I admit that federalism complicates matters. Most federal republics, I notice, do have some form of judicial review; in this respect Canada, Australia, and more recently India have all rejected the British pattern. Another federal republic, West Germany, also has judicial review. I am quite willing to endorse the principle, on purely democratic grounds, that national majorities should prevail over state majorities. Even so, I do not see why you couldn't adopt the Swiss pattern; the federal judiciary could review the constitutionality of state laws but not federal laws.

ADVOCATE: If you need judicial review in order to keep the states from invading the powers of the federal government, doesn't the logic of your argument cut the other way, too? What if the federal government invades the powers of the states?

CRITIC: That might once have been a forceful argument. But is it not true that today the federal government can constitutionally regulate almost anything through its powers over taxation and interstate commerce? If the federal government does not regulate everything, that is only because the President and Congress do not want to do so. Again, you see, restraints depend on the people and their elected representatives, not on the courts.

ADVOCATE: You ignore the possibility that a demagogic President or a large congressional majority, or both together, might pass laws that would deprive some particular minority of important constitutional rights.

CRITIC: Don't we have periodic elections? If we Americans really believed in these rights, we would vote out such a Congress at the next election. If we did not, I do not see how the Supreme Court could maintain our rights, at least in the long run.

ADVOCATE: In the long run, no. But do we have to forget about the short run? A majority of voters, or a majority of their representatives, might act under the transitory pressures of impulse, passion, hysteria, crisis. Politicians might not be steadily anti-libertarian; yet they might be temporarily so. In such cases the Court could void laws passed during short-run aberrations.

CRITIC: Isn't this the heart of the matter? You assume that a majority of Americans and their elected representatives cannot always be trusted to act within the spirit of limited government or, as you say, libertarian democracy. You believe that when they are misguided, the Supreme Court can maintain the essential conditions of a libertarian democracy by nulli-

fying federal laws contrary to a Constitution designed for limited government. I admit that your argument is persuasive. But it raises two problems.
First, will the Supreme Court really stand up against a majority in order
to protect some embattled minority that is threatened by a federal law, or
will it not be moved by much the same passions and prejudices as the
majority of people and their representatives? Second, even assuming now
that the Court does stand against majorities, will it uphold general and
abstract principles of right or justice, or will it instead strike down laws
it disapproves on grounds of *policy?* Judges are human. As Jefferson said
in 1820: "Our judges are as honest as other men, and not more so. They
have, with others, the same passions for party, for power, and the privilege
of their corps." Even when judges are not swayed by the same passions
and prejudices as a majority, they may be moved by the passions and
prejudices of a particular minority. If they use judicial review and the claim
of 'constitutionality' simply to impose their own views about good and
bad laws, have they not contrived to evolve into exactly the kind of body
that your Constitutional Convention thought it was preventing?

ADVOCATE: Well, we both seem to agree on one thing anyway: Americans
seem to want judicial review. But if, as you say, they can sweep it aside
when they do not want it, how in the world can you argue that there is
anything undemocratic about judicial review?

The Supreme Court and Majority Control

What does the record of the Supreme Court reveal? In the course of its one
hundred and sixty-seven years, in eighty-five cases, the Court has struck
down ninety-four different provisions of federal law as unconstitutional, and
by interpretation it has significantly modified a good many more. It might
be argued, then, that in all or in a very large number of these cases the Court
was, in fact, defending the legitimate constitutional rights of some minority
against a 'tyrannical' majority. There are, however, some exceedingly serious
difficulties with this interpretation of the Court's activities.

To begin with, it is difficult to determine when any particular Court
decision has been at odds with the preferences of a national majority. Adequate evidence is not available, for scientific opinion polls are of relatively
recent origin; and, strictly speaking, national elections cannot be interpreted
as more than an indication of the first choice of about 40 to 60 per cent of
the adult population for certain candidates for public office The connection
between preferences among candidates and preferences among alternative
public policies is highly tenuous. On the basis of an election, it is almost
never possible to adduce whether a majority does or does not support one
of two or more *policy* alternatives about which candidates are divided. For
the greater part of the Court's history, then, there is simply no way of
establishing with any high degree of confidence whether a given alternative
was or was not supported by a majority or a minority of adults or even of
voters.

In the absence of relatively direct information, we are thrown back on indirect tests. The ninety-four provisions of federal law that have been declared unconstitutional were, of course, initially passed by majorities of those voting in the Senate and in the House. They also had the President's formal approval. One could, therefore, speak of a majority of those voting in the House and Senate, together with the President, as a 'law-making majority.' It is not easy to determine whether a law-making majority actually coincides with the preferences of a majority of American adults, or even with the preferences of a majority of that half of the adult population which, on the average, votes in congressional elections. Such evidence as we have from opinion polls suggests that Congress is not markedly out of line with public opinion, or at any rate with such public opinion as there is after one discards the answers of people who fall into the category, often large, labelled "no response" or "don't know." If we may, on these somewhat uncertain grounds, take a law-making majority as equivalent to a 'national majority,' then it is possible to test the hypothesis that the Supreme Court is shield and buckler for minorities against tyrannical national majorities.

Under any reasonable assumptions about the nature of the political process, it would appear to be somewhat naive to assume that the Supreme Court either would or could play the role of Galahad. Over the whole history of the Court, one new Justice has been appointed on the average of every twenty-three months. Thus a President can expect to appoint two new Justices during one term of office; and if this were not enough to tip the balance on a normally divided Court, he would be almost certain to succeed in two terms. For example, Hoover made three appointments; Roosevelt, nine; Truman, four; Eisenhower, five; Kennedy in his brief tenure, two. Presidents are not famous for appointing Justices hostile to their own views on public policy; nor could they expect to secure confirmation of a man whose stance on key questions was flagrantly at odds with that of the dominant majority in the Senate. Typically, Justices are men who, prior to appointment, have engaged in public life and have committed themselves publicly on the great questions of the day. As the late Mr. Justice Frankfurter pointed out, a surprisingly large proportion of the Justices, particularly of the great Justices who have left their stamp upon the decisions of the Court, have had little or no prior judicial experience. Nor have the Justices—certainly not the great Justices—been timid men with a passion for anonymity. Indeed, it is not too much to say that if Justices were appointed primarily for their 'judicial' qualities without regard to their basic attitudes on fundamental questions of public policy, the Court could not play the influential role in the American political system that it does in reality play.

It is reasonable to conclude, then, that the policy views dominant on the Court will never be out of line for very long with the policy views dominant among the law-making majorities of the United States. And it would be most unrealistic to suppose that the Court would, for more than a few years at most, stand against any major alternatives sought by a law-making majority. The judicial agonies of the New Deal will, of course, come quickly to mind; but President Franklin D. Roosevelt's difficulties with the Court were truly exceptional. Generalizing over the whole history of the Court, one can say that the chances are about two out of five that a President will make one appointment to the Court in less than a year, two out of three that he will make one within two years, and three out of four that he will make one within three years. President Roosevelt had unusually bad luck; he had to wait four years for his first appointment; the odds against this long interval are about five to one. With average luck, his battle with the Court would never have occurred; even as it was, although his 'court-packing' proposal did formally fail, by the end of his second term in 1940 Roosevelt had appointed five new Justices and he gained three more the following year: Thus by the end of 1941, Mr. Justice Roberts was the only remaining hold-over from the pre-Roosevelt era.

It is to be expected, then, that the Court would be least successful in blocking a determined and persistent law-making majority on a major policy. Conversely, the Court is most likely to succeed against 'weak' law-making majorities: transient majorities in Congress, fragile coalitions, coalitions weakly united upon a policy of subordinate importance or congressional coalitions no longer in existence, as might be the case when a law struck down by the Court had been passed several years earlier.

The Record

An examination of the cases in which the Court has held federal legislation unconstitutional confirms these expectations. Over the whole history of the Court, about half the decisions have been rendered more than four years after the legislation was passed. Thus the congressional majorities that passed these laws went through at least two elections before the decision was handed down and may well have weakened or disappeared in the interval. In these cases, then, the Court was probably not directly challenging current law-making majorities.

Of the twenty-four laws held unconstitutional within two years, eleven were measures enacted in the early years of the New Deal. Indeed, New Deal measures comprise nearly a third of all the legislation that has ever been declared unconstitutional within four years of enactment.

It is illuminating to examine the cases where the Court has acted on legislation within four years of enactment—where the presumption is, that is to say, that the law-making majority is not a dead one. Of the twelve New Deal cases, two were, from a policy point of view, trivial; and two, although perhaps not trivial, were of minor importance to the New Deal Program. A fifth involved the NRA, which was to expire within three weeks of the decision. Insofar as the unconstitutional provisions allowed "codes of fair competition" to be established by industrial groups, it is fair to say that President Roosevelt and his advisers were relieved by the Court's decision of a policy that they had come to find increasingly embarrassing. In view of the tenacity with which FDR held to his major program, there can hardly be any doubt that, had he wanted to pursue the policy objective involved in the NRA codes, as he did for example with the labor provisions, he would not have been stopped by the Court's special theory of the Constitution. As to the seven other cases, it is entirely correct to say, I think, that whatever some of the eminent Justices might have thought during their fleeting moments of glory, they did not succeed in interposing a barrier to the achievement of the objectives of the legislation; and in a few years most of the constitutional dogma on which they rested their opposition to the New Deal had been unceremoniously swept under the rug.

The remainder of the thirty-eight cases where the Court has declared legislation unconstitutional within four years of enactment tend to fall into two rather distinct groups: those involving legislation that could reasonably be regarded as important *from the point of view of the law-making majority* and those involving minor legislation. Although the one category merges into the other, so that some legislation must be classified rather arbitrarily, probably there will be little disagreement with classifying the specific legislative provisions involved in eleven cases as essentially minor from the point of view of the law-making majority (however important they may have been as constitutional interpretations). The specific legislative provisions involved in the remaining fifteen cases are by no means of uniform importance, but with one or two possible exceptions it seems reasonable to classify them as major policy issues from the point of view of the law-making majority. We would expect that cases involving major legislative policy would be propelled to the Court much more rapidly than cases involving minor policy, and, as the table above shows, this is in fact what happens (Table 1).

Table 1 Number of Cases Involving Legislative Policy Other than Those Arising Under New Deal Legislation Holding Legislation Unconstitutional Within Four Years After Enactment

Interval in Years	Major Policy	Minor Policy	Total
2 or less	11	2	13
3 to 4	4	9	13
Total	15	11	26

Thus a law-making majority with major policy objectives in mind usually has an opportunity to seek ways of overcoming the Court's veto. It is an interesting and highly significant fact that Congress and the President do generally succeed in overcoming a hostile Court on major policy issues (Table 2). It is particularly instructive to examine the cases involving major policy. In two cases involving legislation enacted by radical Republican Congresses to punish supporters of the Confederacy during the Civil War, the Court faced a rapidly crumbling majority whose death knell as an effective national force was sounded after the election of 1876. Three cases are difficult to classify and I have labelled them "unclear." Of these, two were decisions made in 1921 involving a 1919 amendment to the Lever Act to control prices. The legislation was important, and the provision in question was clearly struck down, but the Lever Act terminated three days after the decision and

Congress did not return to the subject of price control until the Second World War, when it experienced no constitutional difficulties arising from these cases (which were primarily concerned with the lack of an ascertainable standard of guilt). The third case in this category successfully eliminated stock dividends from the scope of the Sixteenth Amendment, although a year later Congress enacted legislation taxing the actual income from such stocks.

Table 2 Type of Congressional Action Following Supreme Court Decisions Holding Legislation Unconstitutional Within Four Years After Enactment (Other than New Deal Legislation)

Congressional Action	Major Policy	Minor Policy	Total
Reverses Court's Policy	10	2	12
Changes Own Policy	2	0	2
None	0	8	8
Unclear	3	1	4
Total	15	11	26

The remaining ten cases were ultimately followed by a reversal of the actual policy results of the Court's action, although not necessarily of the specific constitutional interpretation. In four cases, the policy consequences of the Court's decision were overcome in less than a year. The other six required a long struggle. Workmen's compensation for longshoremen and harbor workers was invalidated by the Court in 1920; in 1922 Congress passed a new law which was, in its turn, knocked down by the Court in 1924; in 1927 Congress passed a third law, which was finally upheld in 1932. The notorious income tax cases of 1895 were first somewhat narrowed by the Court itself; the Sixteenth Amendment was recommended by President Taft in 1909 and was ratified in 1913, some eighteen years after the Court's decisions. The two child labor cases represent the most effective battle ever waged by the Court against legislative policy-makers. The original legislation outlawing child labor, based on the commerce clause, was passed in 1916 as part of Wilson's New Freedom. Like Franklin Roosevelt later, Wilson was somewhat unlucky in his Supreme Court appointments; he made only three appointments during his eight years, and one of these was wasted, from a policy point of view, on Mr. Justice McReynolds. Had McReynolds voted 'right,' the subsequent struggle over the problem of child labor need not have occurred, for the decision in 1918 was by a Court divided five to four, McReynolds voting with the majority. Congress moved at once to circumvent the decision by means of the tax power, but in 1922 the Court blocked that approach. In 1924, Congress returned to the engagement with a constitutional amendment that was rapidly endorsed by a number of state legislatures before it began to meet so much resistance in the states remaining that the enterprise miscarried. In 1938, under a second reformist President, new legislation was passed twenty-two years after the first; this a Court with a New Deal majority finally accepted in 1941, and thereby brought to an end a battle that had lasted a full quarter-century.

The entire record of the duel between the Court and the law-making majority, in cases where the Court has held legislation unconstitutional within four years after enactment, is summarized in Table 3.

Table 3 Type of Congressional Action After Supreme Court Decisions Holding Legislation Unconstitutional Within Four Years After Enactment (Including New Deal Legislation)

Congressional Action	Major Policy	Minor Policy	Total
Reverses Court's Policy	17	2	19
None	0	12	12
Other	6*	1	7
Total	23	15	38

*In addition to the actions in Table 2 under "Changes Own Policy" and "Unclear," this figure includes the NRA legislation affected by the *Schechter Poultry* case.

A consideration of the role of the Court as defender of minorities, then, suggests the following conclusions:

First, judicial review is surely inconsistent with democracy to the extent that the Court simply protects the policies of minorities from reversal or regulation by national majorities acting through regular law-making procedures.

Second, however, the frequency and nature of appointments to the Court inhibit it from playing this role, or otherwise protecting minorities against national law-making majorities. National law-making majorities—i.e., coalitions of the President and a majority of each house of Congress—generally have their way.

Third, although the Court evidently cannot hold out indefinitely against a persistent law-making majority, in a very small number of important cases it has succeeded in delaying the application of a policy for as long as twenty-five years.

Judges as Policy-Makers

How can we appraise decisions of the third kind just mentioned? It might be argued that the one function of the Court is to protect rights that are in some sense basic or fundamental. Thus (the argument might run), in a country where basic rights are, on the whole, respected, one would expect only a small number of cases where the Court has had to plant itself firmly against a law-making majority. But majorities may, on rare occasions, become 'tyrannical'; when they do, the Court intervenes; and although the constitutional issue may, strictly speaking, be technically open, the Constitution assumes an underlying fundamental body of rights and liberties which the Court guarantees by its decisions.

Even without examining the actual cases, however, it is somewhat unrealistic to suppose that a Court whose members are recruited in the fashion of Supreme Court Justices would long adhere to norms of abstract Right or Justice substantially at odds with those of a majority of elected leaders. Moreover, in an earlier day it was perhaps easier to believe that certain rights are so natural and self-evident that their fundamental validity is as much a matter of definite knowledge, at least to all reasonable creatures, as the color of a ripe cherry.

But today we know that the line between abstract Right and policy is extremely hard to draw. A policy decision might be defined as an effective choice among alternatives about which there is, at least initially, some uncertainty. This uncertainty may arise because of inadequate information as to (a) the alternatives that are thought to be 'open'; (b) the consequences that will probably ensue from choosing a given alternative; (c) the level of probability that these consequences will actually ensue; and (d) the relative value of the different alternatives.

No one, I imagine, will quarrel with the proposition that the Supreme Court, or indeed any court, must make and does make policy decisions in this sense. But such a proposition is not really useful to the question before us. What is critical is the extent to which a court can and does make policy decisions by going outside established 'legal' criteria found in precedent, statute, and Constitution. Now in this respect the Supreme Court occupies a most peculiar position, for it is an essential characteristic of the institution that from time to time its members decide cases where legal criteria are not in any realistic sense adequate to the task. The distinguished legal scholar and member of the Court, the late Mr. Justice Frankfurter, once described the business of the Supreme Court in these words:

It is essentially accurate to say that the Court's preoccupation today is with the application of rather fundamental aspirations and what Judge Learned Hand calls "moods," embodied in provisions like the due process clauses, which were designed not to be precise and positive directions for rules of action. The judicial process in applying them involves a judgment . . . that is, on the views of the direct representatives of the people in meeting the needs of society, on the views of Presidents and Governors, and by their construction of the will of legislatures the Court breathes life, feeble or strong, into the inert pages of the Constitution and the statute books.

Very often, then, the cases before the Court involve alternatives about which there is severe disagreement in the society, as in the case of segregation or economic regulation; the very setting of the case is, then, political. Moreover, these are usually cases where competent students of constitutional law, including the learned Justices of the Supreme Court themselves, disagree; where the words of the Constitution are general, vague, ambiguous, or not clearly applicable; where precedent may be found on both sides; and where experts differ in predicting the consequences of the various alternatives or the degree of probability that the possible consequences will actually ensue. Typically, in other words, although there may be considerable agreement as to the alternatives thought to be open, there is very serious disagreement— both as to questions of fact bearing on consequences and probabilities and as to questions of value.

If the Court were assumed to be a 'political' institution, no particular problems would arise, for it would be taken for granted that the members of the Court would resolve questions of fact and value by introducing assumptions derived from their own predispositions or those of influential clienteles and constituents. However, since much of the legitimacy of the Court's decisions rests upon the belief that it is not a political institution but exclusively a legal one, to accept the Court as a political institution would solve one set of problems at the price of creating another. Nonetheless, if it is true that the nature of the cases arriving before the Court is sometimes of the kind I have described, then the Court cannot act strictly as a legal institution. It must, that is to say, choose among controversial alternatives of public policy by appealing to at least some criteria of acceptability on questions of fact and value that cannot be found in or deduced from precedent, statute, and Constitution.

In making these choices does the Court rise to a level of abstract Right or Justice above the level of mere policy? The best rebuttal to this view of the Court will be found in the record of the Court's decisions. Surely the six cases referred to a moment ago, where the policy consequences of the Court's decisions were overcome only after long battles, will scarcely appeal to many contemporary minds as evidence for the proposition under examination. A natural right to employ child labor in mills and mines? To be free of income taxes by the federal government? To employ longshoremen and harbor workers without the protection of workmen's compensation? The Court itself did not rely upon such arguments in these cases, and it would do no credit to their opinions to reconstruct them along such lines.

So far, however, our evidence has been drawn from cases in which the Court has held legislation unconstitutional within four years after enactment. What of the other forty cases? Do we have evidence in these that the Court has protected fundamental or natural rights and liberties against the dead hand of some past tyranny by the lawmakers? The evidence is not impressive. In the history of the Court there has never been a single case arising under the First Amendment in which the Court has held federal legislation unconstitutional. If we turn from these fundamental liberties of religion, speech, press, and assembly, we do find a handful of cases—something less than ten—arising under Amendments Four to Seven in which the Court has declared acts unconstitutional that might properly be regarded as involving rather basic liberties. An inspection of these cases leaves the impression that, in all of them, the lawmakers and the Court were not very far apart; moreover, it is doubtful that the fundamental conditions of liberty in this country have been altered by more than a hair's breadth as a result of these decisions.

Over against these decisions we must put the fifteen or so cases in which the Court used the protections of the Fifth, Thirteenth, Fourteenth, and

Fifteenth Amendments to preserve the rights and liberties of a relatively privileged group at the expense of the rights and liberties of a submerged group: chiefly slaveholders at the expense of slaves, white people at the expense of colored people, and property holders at the expense of wage earners and other groups. These cases, unlike the relatively innocuous ones of the preceding set all involved liberties of genuinely fundamental importance, where an opposite policy would have meant thoroughly basic shifts in the distribution of rights, liberties, and opportunities in the United States —where, moreover, the policies sustained by the Court's action have since been repudiated in every civilized nation of the Western world, including our own. Yet, if our earlier argument is correct, it is futile—precisely because the basic distribution of privilege *was* at issue—to suppose that the Court could have acted much differently in these areas of policy from the way in which it did in fact act.

Some Conclusions

Thus the role of the Court is not simple; and it is an error to suppose that its functions can be either described or appraised by means of simple concepts drawn from democratic or moral theory. It is possible, nonetheless, to derive a few general conclusions about the Court's role as a policy-making institution.

National politics in the United States, as in other stable democracies, is dominated by relatively cohesive alliances that endure for long periods of time. One recalls the Jeffersonian alliance, the Jacksonian, the extraordinarily long-lived Republican dominance of the post-Civil-War years, and the New Deal alliance shaped by Franklin Roosevelt. Each is marked by a break with past policies, a period of intense struggle, followed by consolidation, and finally decay and disintegration of the alliance.

Except for short-lived transitional periods when the old alliance is disintegrating and the new one is struggling to take control of political institutions, the Supreme Court is inevitably a part of the dominant national alliance. As an element in the political leadership of the dominant alliance, the Court of course supports the major policies of the alliance. Acting solely by itself with no support from the President and Congress, the Court is almost powerless to affect the course of national policy.

The Supreme Court is not, however, simply an *agent* of the alliance. It is an essential part of the political leadership and possesses some bases of power of its own, the most important of which is the unique legitimacy attributed to its interpretations of the Constitution. This legitimacy the Court jeopardizes if it flagrantly opposes the major policies of the dominant alliance; such a course of action, as we have seen, is one in which the Court will not normally be tempted to engage.

It follows that within the somewhat narrow limits set by the basic policy goals of the dominant alliance, the Court *can* make national policy. Its discretion, then, is not unlike that of a powerful committee chairman in Congress who cannot, generally speaking, nullify the basic policies substantially agreed on by the rest of the dominant leadership, but who can, within these limits, often determine important questions of timing, effectiveness, and subordinate policy. Thus the Court is least effective against a current law-making majority—and evidently least inclined to act. It is most effective when it sets the bounds of policy for officials, agencies, state governments, or even regions, a task that has come to occupy a very large part of the Court's business.

Few of the Court's policy decisions can be interpreted sensibly in terms of a 'majority' versus a 'minority.' In this respect the Court is no different from the rest of the political leadership. Generally speaking, policy at the national level is the outcome of conflict, bargaining, and agreement among minorities; the process is neither minority rule nor majority rule but what might better be called *minorities* rule, where one aggregation of minorities achieves policies opposed by another aggregation.

The main objective of presidential leadership is to build a stable and dominant aggregation of minorities with a high probability of winning the Presidency and one or both houses of Congress. Ordinarily the main contribution of the Court is to confer legitimacy on the fundamental policies of the successful coalition.

But if this were the only function of the Supreme Court, would it have acquired the standing it has among Americans? In fact, at its best—and the Court is not always at its best—the Court does more than merely confer legitimacy on the dominant national coalition. For one thing, by the way it interprets and modifies national laws, perhaps but not necessarily by holding them unconstitutional, the Supreme Court sometimes serves as a guide and even a pioneer in arriving at different standards of fair play and individual right than have resulted, or are likely to result, from the interplay of the other political forces. Thus in recent years the Court has modified by interpretation or declared unconstitutional provisions of federal law restricting the rights of unpopular and even widely detested minorities—military deserters, Communists, and alleged bootleggers, for example. The judges, after all, inherit an ancient tradition and an acknowledged role in setting higher standards of justice and right than the majority of citizens or their representatives might otherwise demand. If the standards of justice propounded by the Court are to prevail, for reasons we have already examined they cannot be too remote from general standards of fairness and individual right among Americans; but, though some citizens may protest, most Americans are too attached to the Court to want it stripped of its power.

There are times, too, when the other political forces are too divided to arrive at decisions on certain key questions. At very great risk, the Court can intervene in such cases; and sometimes it may even succeed in establishing policy where President and Congress are unable to do so. Probably in such cases it can succeed only if its action conforms to a widespread set of explicit or implicit norms held by the political leadership: norms which are not strong enough or are not distributed in such a way as to insure the existence of an effective law-making majority but are nonetheless sufficiently powerful to prevent any successful attack on the legitimacy and power of the Court. . . .

. . .

Yet in order to *confer* legitimacy, the Court must itself *possess* legitimacy. For in a political society thoroughly permeated by the democratic ethos, where the legitimacy of every political institution depends finally on its consistency with democracy, the legitimacy of judicial review and the Court's exercise of that power must stem from the presumption that the Court is ultimately subject to popular control. The more the Court exercises self-restraint and the less it challenges the policies of law-making majorities, the less the need or the impulse to subject it to popular controls. The more active the Court is in contesting the policies of law-making majorities, the more visible becomes the slender basis of its legitimacy in a democratic system, and the greater the efforts will be to bring the Court's policies into conformity with those enacted by law-making majorities.

To the extent that the Supreme Court accepts the policies of law-making majorities, then, it retains its own legitimacy and its power to confer legitimacy on policies; yet to that extent it fails to protect minorities from control or regulation by national majorities. To the extent that it opposes the policies of national law-making majorities in order to protect minorities, it threatens its own legitimacy. This is the inescapable paradox of judicial review in a democratic political order.

26

Recruiting
Judges

Jack W. Peltason

Thousands of interest conflicts involve the federal courts. They can be conveniently discussed in terms of three general categories. First, there are the struggles to determine which men shall be the judges. Second, there are the conflicts over the judges' decision-making and opinion-writing. Finally, there are battles to implement decisions, to maximize or minimize their usefulness, and to make these decisions mean what each interest wants them to mean. The first kind of conflict is the subject of this chapter.

The decision as to *who* will make the decisions affects what decisions will be made. Although this appears obvious, during a considerable portion of our national history the fiction of judges as automatic dispensers of decisions was so strongly supported that men talked as though it made no difference who the judges were so long as they were competent legal technicians. People talked that way, but they did not act that way. There have always been struggles to secure the selection of the judge who any given group thinks is most likely to support its values.

Even today the official theory of the judiciary tends to conceal the interests conflict and makes it appear that the problem of judicial selection can best be described in terms of selection of technicians rather than policy-makers. The stress is on the necessity of "keeping the judges out of politics."

Politics and Judicial Selection

What is meant by the statement that judges should be selected without regard to politics? Some apparently mean that party politicians should have no voice in choosing judges. Others mean that Presidents, in nominating judges, should consider only the desirability of the particular candidates and exclude any consideration of paying off political obligations or building support for other programs.

The third meaning given to the demand that politics should not affect the selection of judges is that those who do the appointing should not consider whether the candidates belong to a particular political party and should not consider the values the candidate is likely to support. Rather the appointing or electing authorities should select a man with judicial temperament and sound legal knowledge. A man with a judicial temperament is defined as a man who is not committed to any particular interests and who will decide cases without respect to the consequences of his decisions.

Regardless of which meaning is intended, politics has been important in the selection of federal judges. Politicians participate, obligations are paid and alliances built by passing out federal judicial positions, and great care has

255

been taken to select men in terms of the values which they are most likely to defend on the bench. Furthermore, the accusation that the opposition is selecting judges on the basis of politics whereas one's own side selects the best men stems from the confusion as to the criteria to determine who are the best men. Beyond the obvious requirements of finding a man who is honest, has a fair degree of emotional stability, can write, and is willing to comply with the community mores, the best judge is one most likely to make the best decisions. Which are the best decisions? That is what politics is about.

John Marshall, for example, was a brilliant jurist to the Federalists but a violent and biased partisan to the Jeffersonians. Spencer Roane, Jefferson's candidate for Chief Justice, was to Jefferson an able and impartial dispenser of justice, but to the Federalists he was a prejudiced judge. In the judgment of most historians, Marshall was the better man, but the historians' judgment is based upon general approval of the interests which Marshall supported, not on Marshall's lack of partisanship or his technical knowledge of the rules of the common law. Similarly, prior to 1937 those who objected to the conservative majority on the Supreme Court accused these judges of being intemperate partisans who wrote their own views into the law. Since 1937 those who dislike the values supported by the justices have charged the judges with being politicians.

Despite the political nature of the selection process, despite the fact that judges, especially those of our higher federal courts, have as much to say about the group struggles as do legislators, the entire selection process is surrounded by conventions which make it difficult to discuss openly the conflict of values. A candidate for Congress seeks group support, makes pledges and discusses how he will vote if elected. Various organizations endorse or oppose legislative candidates without apology. But when it comes to selecting judges, the candidates are not supposed to discuss publicly how they will decide cases or indicate the interests they will represent if chosen for the bench. It is even considered inappropriate for Senators who must approve the nominations to question the candidates too closely about their position on constitutional or legal questions. Rather, the hearings are in terms of bar association endorsements and testimonials by various individuals dealing with the integrity and honesty of the candidates. . . . Yet the actual contests turn on anticipations as to the interests which the candidate is most likely to represent.

Appointing Judges

The Constitution calls for the President to select federal judges with the consent of the Senate. But the Constitution does not give an accurate description of the selecting process, especially of district judges. It would be more accurate to say that federal district judges are selected by the individual Senator or local party organization in the area which they are to serve, subject to presidential veto. Judgeships are important senatorial patronage and the Senate seldom fails to confirm any man acceptable to the individual Senator from the state in which the judge is to serve. It always fails to confirm if the man is unacceptable to the individual Senator, provided the Senator belongs to the same political party as the President. If the judge is to serve in a state in which there is no Senator who belongs to the same party as the President, the President has greater freedom in picking the judge, but he usually does so in consultation with local party officials.

Factors Considered

Party considerations are most important. Since 1885 over 90 per cent of all federal judges have been filled by members—in most cases active members —of the same party as the President who chose them and most have been supporters of the Senators who nominated them. . . .

As the low men in the judicial hierarchy district judges are not as important in the final disposition of interest conflict as are their superiors. On the other hand, there are a large number of district judgeships which function in particular states so that they are useful to reward faithful service, gain support from various factions, even to get rid of possible political antagonists. Thus in the selection of district judges Presidents have paid somewhat more attention to party and less attention to values likely to be supported than has been the case in the selection of circuit and Supreme Court judges. In addition individual Senators have more voice in selecting district judges than they do in choosing those higher up the ladder.

Promotion from district to circuit judge is not uncommon, but promotion from circuit judge to the Supreme Court is unusual. Furthermore, the importance of Supreme Court justices in determining which interests shall get their way has made it less likely that these positions will be filled in order to build support. Rather, care has been taken to select men who will promote the same concepts of the public interest as are held by the President. Some Presidents have been more successful in predicting how the men they select will act as judges than have others. Theodore Roosevelt took unusual pains to be sure that he was getting men who could be "counted upon," even going so far as to seek assurances that his nominees would vote right if chosen.

The Senate does not take lightly its responsibility to confirm nominees. The procedure normally followed in selecting district and circuit judges is for the Attorney General, the Senator from the state in which the judge is to function, provided he belongs to the President's party, and the American Bar Association's Committee on the Federal Judiciary to consult with one another. The President then nominates a candidate who is given a full Federal Bureau of Investigation check, the file being made available only to the Chairman of the Senate Committee on the Judiciary. Routinely the Senators from the state in which the judge is to sit are notified and wires are sent to the representatives of the state and local bar associations asking for their views on the nominee. In the event that any objections are heard a public hearing is likely to be held.

Lawyers play a leading role in the selection of federal judges. The Canons of Legal Ethics stipulate that since "lawyers are better able than laymen to appraise accurately the qualifications of candidates for judicial office," the lawyers have a positive duty to speak out. Since knowledge of the law is thought to be important in determining the judge's decisions, only lawyers are chosen, although there is no constitutional requirement to this effect. Furthermore, the spokesmen for the bar are deferred to by laymen in the selection of candidates. The Senate Judiciary Committee is composed solely of lawyers. Senators are hesitant to recommend men whom the leaders of the bar would condemn as unfit and such action by the bar associations reduces the nominees' chances of getting confirmed. Recently the Attorney General has gone so far as to submit the names of all candidates, except for the Supreme Court, to the appropriate committee of the American Bar Association before sending the nominations to the Senate. The Senate Judiciary Committee always asks for the Bar Association's opinion.

Despite the important position of the bar, the present system does not give the leaders of the American Bar Association as much authority as some would like. Mr. Loyd Wright, a member of the American Bar Association Committee, for example, is quite disturbed by the fact that the Committee's recommendations are sometimes not followed and he charged that to have politicians select the judges destroys the independence of the courts. He told the Senate Judiciary Committee, "This great arm of government is being prostituted by the politicians who have the right of the appointing power." Professor Joseph P. Harris is another who believes that the bar should be given more of a voice. He has written that under the present system "it is not uncommon for nominations to be given to politician-lawyers of little standing at the bar, who have secured the necessary political support." Apparently instead of the support of politicians, Professor Harris would prefer to require the support of the leaders of the bar. However, it is doubtful if the Senators and the interests they represent would be willing to give up their present patronage. If they did, it would transfer to the bar association the struggles to select the "right" men and would alter the nature of the interests represented by judges, probably in the direction of the interests supported by the *American Bar Association Journal.*

Two Case Studies

In 1916 the Supreme Court was participating without apology or restraint in the major clashes among interests. Groups whose interests were defeated in the legislature carried the battle before federal judges and discovered that the judges could be counted upon to label some of the unwanted legislation unconstitutional or at least interpret it in such a way as to leave the maximum area of conduct unregulated. The balance among the justices was close. Then in 1916 President Wilson nominated Louis D. Brandeis to fill the vacancy created by the death of Justice Lamar.

By 1916 Brandeis was a well-known campaigner for vigorous governmental regulation of utilities, for savings-bank insurance, against bigness, and for conservation. He had been active before the Supreme Court and had successfully persuaded the judges to sustain laws limiting hours of work. Quite clearly Brandeis's nomination presented a threat to those interests that had been most successful in securing judicial representation from the 1890s.

Opposition to Brandeis was phrased not in terms of his views but of his supposed lack of judicial temperament. On the other hand Brandeis's supporters also played down his values since they did not want to lose the support of the southern Democrats on the Judiciary Committee. Each side sought testimonials from distinguished members of the bar. Each side accused the other of representing a selfish special interest.

The Senate Judiciary Committee held public hearings. Leading the opponents were some distinguished attorneys, including five former presidents of the American Bar Association. President Lowell of Harvard, heading a list of fifty-five Bostonians—where Brandeis lived—wrote: "We do not believe that Mr. Brandeis has the judicial temperament and capacity which should be required in a judge of the Supreme Court. His reputation as a lawyer is such that he does not have the confidence of the people." Bishop Cannon, leader of the prohibition groups, also testified against Brandeis. On the other side, supporting him, were representatives of trade unions, some distinguished Bostonians, Harvard President-Emeritus Eliot for example, and, most important, the President of the United States.

Brandeis himself, although careful to comply with the conventions that require the nominee not to seek confirmation openly, was "accidentally" brought into contact with two doubtful Senators and was able to win their support. The election of 1916 was approaching and President Wilson was able to rally the members of his own party. Finally, on the vote to confirm, although all the Republicans opposed, all the Democrats plus three Progressives voted for Brandeis.

The opponents of John J. Parker who was nominated to the Supreme Court in the spring of 1930 were more successful. At the time of his nomination Judge Parker had served for five years on the Court of Appeals for the Fourth Circuit. Prior to this, he had been active in North Carolina Republican politics. Parker's nomination was opposed by the leaders of the American Federation of Labor and the National Association for the Advancement of Colored People. Spokesmen for the NAACP emphasized that when campaigning for governor in 1920, Parker had responded to the charges that the Republican Party intended to enfranchise the Negro by saying, "The participation of the Negro in politics is a source of evil and danger to both races and is not desired by the wise men in either race or by the Republican Party of North Carolina."

The American Federation of Labor based its opposition on an opinion Parker had written for the circuit court in the Red Jacket case. A lower court had issued an injunction against a union for trying to persuade workers who had signed yellow-dog contracts to join the union. Parker voted to sustain the lower court on the ground that the Supreme Court's decision in the Hitchman case required him to do so. The leaders of the American Federation of Labor thought otherwise. Other members of the anti-Parker interest included Progressive Republicans, Republican Senators from states with large Negro and labor votes, and a majority of the Democratic Senators. There were enough of these to block the nomination.

The bitter debates over Brandeis and Parker were unusual. Presidents normally are careful to choose men who have not aroused any major group and [are] therefore likely to be confirmed readily. The most "available" man is one who has had noncontroversial public service.

. . .

From Gideon's Trumpet

27

Anthony Lewis

Justice Brandeis is credited with the comment that "however much one could criticize the Supreme Court of the United States, it endured and deserved its place in our political structure because it did its own work." That is no small claim in the city of Washington, where few high officials write their own speeches or even their own letters. Alone among the great institutions in Washington the Court seems to have escaped Parkinson's Law—the thesis that the number of employees in any office continually increases and the work expands to occupy the new hands. The work at the Supreme Court is still done by nine men, assisted by eighteen young law clerks. Nothing is delegated to committees or task forces.

Indeed, what the Court turns out is not an institutional product in the sense that the work of Executive Departments is. In the Justice Department, for example, a legislative proposal would be drafted in rough by junior lawyers, worked over by more experienced hands, scrutinized by section chiefs, approved by one or more assistant attorneys general and the deputy attorney general, and finally put before the Attorney General for his approval. It is a hierarchical system, necessarily and appropriately.

At the Supreme Court there is no hierarchy. Even the Chief Justice is only, as has been said, "first among equals." He has symbolic and administrative pre-eminence, for example presiding over the sessions of the Court and over the Judicial Conference of the United States, which includes representatives of all the federal courts. But in the business of the Supreme Court his influence depends entirely on his moral and intellectual power to persuade. Each justice has one vote, and it is in the keeping of his own mind and conscience. Each works largely on his own, with his law clerks when he chooses, and the result is that there really are nine separate law offices—different in work habits as well as in philosophy. Justice Jackson said: "The fact is that the Court functions less as one deliberative body than as nine, each justice working largely in isolation except as he chooses to seek consultation with others. These working methods tend to cultivate a highly individualistic rather than a group viewpoint."

Each justice is responsible for every case that comes before the Supreme Court. There is no division of labor among committees or panels. This is a fact that has long escaped public understanding. Even some lawyers seem to think the petitions for certiorari are divided up among the justices. Chief Justice Hughes complained of this misconception as long ago as 1934: "I find that some think that applications for certiorari are distributed among the justices ratably, that is, one-ninth to each justice. . . . Now the fact is that all matters calling for action by the Court in the disposition of cases are dealt with by all the members of the Court. . . . All the justices pass upon all the applications for certiorari."

As a mechanical matter, petitions for certiorari in the ordinary case are handled as follows. The party seeking review is required to file forty printed copies of its petition. (The Court's rules are most particular about printing: All printed documents filed in the Court must be 6 1/8 inches by 9 1/4 in size, with type no smaller than 11-point, "adequately leaded," and the paper "opaque and unglazed.") The other side has thirty days to file a brief in opposition to the grant of review. To prevent the justices from forming any views on a case before both sides are available, the practice is to have the Clerk's Office hold each petition for thirty days and then distribute it together with the brief in opposition if one has been received. One copy goes to each of the nine offices. There individual practices set in.

Most justices, but not all, have their law clerks look over each petition (and the opposing response) and prepare a brief memorandum summarizing the issues. This fact led to an inflated view of the law clerk's role. Justice Jackson joked about it, saying he detected a suspicion at the Bar that "the law clerks constitute a kind of junior court which decides the fate of certiorari petitions." More recently Justice Tom C. Clark remarked that he had been "asked by prominent lawyers, who should know better, to please speak to my law clerks about their petitions."

The law clerks to the individual justices are not to be confused with the permanent employees in the office of the Clerk of the Supreme Court. The former assist a justice for a year or two, working for him personally—not for the Court as a whole. They are bright young men who are at most a few years out of law school, where they stood near the top of the class and probably were on the law review. Almost all federal and many state judges now have law clerks, and the competition is intense for the honor of a clerkship, especially in the Supreme Court. There each justice selects his clerks by his own method, one delegating the job to a professor at his old law school, another to a committee, others making the choice themselves after interviewing applicants. Many Supreme Court law clerks have gone into teaching, and they are among the country's most respected legal scholars. Others have become prominent in public office (Secretary of State Dean Acheson was clerk to Brandeis), in business (the late Irving S. Olds of United States Steel clerked for Holmes), and on the bench (Justice Byron R. White was clerk to Chief Justice Vinson).

Some of today's right-wing critics of the Supreme Court have picked on the law clerks as a convenient target, attributing to them Svengali-like powers over the justices. The truth is less interesting. Law clerks assist in research and may write drafts of material for the justice. They also perform the function of keeping him in touch with current trends of legal scholarship, especially the often critical views of the law schools about the Supreme Court. That is an important role in a Court which could so easily get isolated in its ivory tower. But the law clerks do not judge. They can only suggest. As a practical matter, a young man who is there only briefly is unlikely to make any significant change in the actual votes cast on cases by a judge who has been considering these problems for years.

The procedure for handling certiorari petitions, as described so far, is that used for the printed petitions on the regular appellate docket. *Gideon v. Cochran* was, of course, an *in forma pauperis* petition, and the Court has had to devise special methods of handling such cases because of the special difficulties they present.

The paupers' petitions, Justice Frankfurter once wrote, are often "almost unintelligible and certainly do not present a clear statement of issues necessary for our understanding." Their meager content can be contrasted with the information that the man of means is required to supply when he files a petition for certiorari. The rules require him to show the jurisdictional basis for Supreme Court review, including the time when he raised his federal questions. He must print the text of the lower court's opinions in the case, and he must supply at least one typewritten copy of the transcript of the trial-court proceedings. Prisoners rarely supply any of this material in their *in forma pauperis* petitions. The result is that there is often great difficulty even figuring out what happened to the prisoner—what the case is all about. Lower-court opinions would be informative, but in the prisoners' case the lower courts rarely bother to write any. That was true with Gideon. The Florida Supreme Court had turned him down in a stereotype order making no reference to the facts of his case. All it said was: "The above-named petitioner has filed a petition for writ of habeas corpus in the above cause, and upon consideration thereof, it is ordered that said petition be and the same is hereby denied." Not very helpful to a justice in Washington trying to find out what was decided in Florida.

The burden of the paupers' cases has been steadily growing heavier in the Supreme Court. In recent years their number has increased much more sharply than the volume of business on the regular docket. Twenty-five years ago fewer than one hundred *in forma pauperis* cases were filed each term. The number passed one thousand in the 1949 term and for the first time exceeded the volume of prepaid appellate cases. Now there are about fifteen hundred each term. The Court itself has taken a broad view of the statute allowing poor persons to file without formalities. It said in 1948 that one need not be "absolutely destitute" to qualify. In that case Justice Hugo L. Black wrote: "We think an affidavit is sufficient which states that one cannot because of poverty pay or give security for the costs and still be able to provide himself and dependents with the necessities of life." Otherwise an impoverished man would have to choose between his family and his cause —perhaps abandoning "what may be a meritorious claim in order to spare himself complete destitution." As a practical matter the Court seldom second-guesses a man's own declaration of poverty in an *in forma pauperis* affidavit.

. . .

The Chief Justice's three law clerks have the special duty of scrutinizing the *in forma pauperis* applications. (He has three instead of the two clerks allotted to other justices so that this arduous job can be done.) One of the clerks prepares a typewritten memorandum on each case, stating what the claim appears to be and any relevant legal framework. The memorandum is then circulated among the nine justices. If the claim seems to be a serious one, and in all cases of prisoners under death sentence, the original red envelope containing the application is attached to the law clerk's memorandum when it is circulated; in any case a justice can call for the file. If a case raises a question that the law clerk examining the file thinks may interest the Court, he may suggest to the Chief Justice even before the papers are circulated that the state authorities be asked to file a response. The hope is that a response may clarify the legal issues, fill in the factual background, and bring out any obstacles to the Court's taking jurisdiction of the case.

. . .

The nine justices meet in a formal conference every Friday during or preceding a week in which cases are argued or opinions announced—about three Fridays out of four during the October-to-June term. The conference room is an oak-paneled chamber adjoining the Chief Justice's office in the rear of the Court building. Book shelves lining the walls are filled with law reports, and there is a long massive table in the center of the room. A single portrait, of Chief Justice John Marshall, looks down at the justices seated around the table.

The conference has a record for secrecy probably unrivaled in official Washington. So far as is known, no one not a justice of the Supreme Court has ever been allowed into the conference room during one of the sessions. No secretaries, no law clerks, no librarians, no messengers. If a message arrives, the junior justice—the one most recently appointed—goes to the door to get it. The purpose of this absolute secrecy is twofold. It ensures against premature disclosure of the Court's decisions, and it protects the privacy of the justices' discussion. The latter may be the more important reason. Genuine intellectual exchange among men of strong views is not always easy at best; it would be the more difficult if each justice had to fear public recriminations about some argument he advanced in the heat of debate. The justices must be free to argue to the hilt, without fear of reading in some popular journal that "Justice X wanted another Munich."

Members of the Court have disclosed, however, the general way the conference is conducted. It begins at ten A.M. and usually runs on until late in the afternoon. At the start each justice, when he enters the room, shakes hands with all the others there (thirty-six handshakes altogether). The custom, dating back generations, is evidently designed to begin the meeting at a friendly level, no matter how heated the intellectual differences may be. The conference takes up, first, the applications for review—a few appeals, many more petitions for certiorari. Those on the Appellate Docket, the regular paid cases, are considered first, then the paupers' applications on the Miscellaneous Docket. (If any of these are granted, they are then transferred to the Appellate Docket.) After this the justices consider, and vote on, all the cases argued during the preceding Monday through Thursday. These are tentative votes, which may be and quite often are changed as the opinion is written and the problem thought through more deeply. There may be further discussion at later conferences before the opinion is finally handed down.

Because so many men are involved, with the resulting risk of chaos, the discussion follows a quite formal procedure. The Chief Justice begins the consideration of each case by stating the issue and his views. The senior associate, now Justice Black, speaks next, and so on down the line. As presiding officer the Chief Justice shapes the character of the conference, not only by the way he first formulates the issues but by deciding, for example, how long to let debate continue before calling for a vote. Chief Justice Hughes was regarded by some as the greatest master of the conference. "To see him preside," wrote Justice Frankfurter, "was like witnessing Toscanini lead an orchestra." But during the Hughes years Justice Harlan F. Stone complained that the Chief was too firm, too controlling. Then Stone became Chief Justice, and his colleagues protested that the conferences dragged because he was not firm enough.

At the typical conference these days the justices pass on nearly one hundred matters, a formidable number. A little arithmetic will quickly indicate how impossible a burden that would impose if every justice were to talk on every case. Ten years ago, when the docket was significantly shorter than today's, Justice Jackson figured that the average conference list would permit "five minutes of deliberation per item, or about thirty-three seconds of discussion per item by each of the nine justices. . . . All that saves the Court from being hopelessly bogged down," Jackson added, "is that many of these items are so frivolous on mere inspection that no one finds them worthy of discussion, and they are disposed of by unanimous consent." Each justice, before the weekly conference, sends to the Chief's Office a list of cases he considers not worthy of discussion; the cases on which all nine are agreed are thereupon passed over at the conference.

Voting in the conference is in inverse order to discussion: the junior justice first. It takes only four votes to grant certiorari or to put an appeal down for oral argument. The theory of having less than a majority grant review is that a case deemed important by as many as four justices is at least worthy of the Court's consideration; the majority is always free to work its will later, on the merits of the issue presented. (Justice Frankfurter argued that a majority of five should be free, indeed, to dismiss the writ of certiorari as "improvidently granted," but this view was rejected as inconsistent with the integrity of the so-called Rule of Four for granting review.) Even when there are fewer than four justices who personally want to take on a case, the necessary four votes may well be obtained by judicial log-rolling. (You vote for my case and I'll vote for yours.) The outside world does not know how the Court reaches the decision to grant or deny review of a case—or how it reaches any decision at conference, although some of these secrets have been disclosed by the publication of justices' papers. Most thoughtful persons have concluded that there should be no such publication at least until all participants in the events described have left the Court, lest freedom of discussion at conference be inhibited by the fear of premature disclosure. One member of the present Court was so distressed by the gossip retailed in one judicial biography that he ordered all his own papers burned—to prevent their misuse in the event of his death.

At the conference of June 1, 1962, the Court had before it two jurisdictional statements asking the Court to hear appeals, twenty-six petitions for certiorari on the Appellate Docket, ten paupers' applications on the Miscellaneous Docket, and three petitions for rehearing. (The last are almost never granted.) There were some important cases among these. One was a challenge to the constitutionality of New York's legislative districts; the justices decided to send this back to a federal court in New York for reconsideration in light of their recent decision, in a Tennessee case, that federal courts could scrutinize state legislative apportionments. Another case arose from the Freedom Rides. Six Negroes had been convicted of breach of the peace for their effort to desegregate a Shreveport, Louisiana, bus terminal. The Court, having read the printed petition and response in this case, decided to grant the petition for review and then summarily to reverse the convictions for lack of any supporting evidence except the constitutionally impermissible fact that they had violated the custom of segregation. The Kohler Company of Wisconsin was asking the Court to review the finding of the National Labor Relations Board that it had committed unfair labor practices in the bitter dispute, dating back to 1954, with the United Automobile Workers. The justices also considered some of the cases that had been argued earlier in the term and that now were ready for disposition. They discussed some draft opinions. They decided to put down for re-argument next fall the great dispute between Arizona and California over the water of the Colorado River. And, finally, they passed on the handwritten petition for certiorari filed by Clarence Earl Gideon, prisoner No. 003826, Florida State Penitentiary, Raiford, Florida.

The results of the deliberations at this conference were made known to the world shortly after ten A.M. the following Monday, June 4th, when a clerk posted on a bulletin board the mimeographed list of the Supreme Court's orders for that day. One order read:

890 Misc. GIDEON v. COCHRAN

The motion for leave to proceed *in forma pauperis* and the petition for writ of certiorari are granted. The case is transferred to the appellate docket. In addition to other questions presented by this case, counsel are requested to discuss the following in their briefs and oral argument:

"Should this Court's holding in *Betts v. Brady*, 316 U.S. 455, be reconsidered?"

THE
POLITICS
OF
PROTEST

Protest politics is an inevitable by-product of incremental pluralism. Confronted with political institutions designed to facilitate bargaining and compromise, groups that lack the money and organization necessary to participate effectively in the pressure system have often been forced to resort to unconventional methods of political participation to call attention to their plight. In the main, the picture of protest politics drawn by pluralist political analysts is distorting and reflects a conservative, system-oriented bias. Mistrust of the mass public has led many pluralists to present an incomplete analysis of political protest movements throughout our history. According to the pluralists, interest-group bargaining by political elites promotes political stability, because established group leaders, pursuing short-range economic objectives, can be accommodated through a process of rational discussion. In contrast, the pluralist picture of political protest focuses not on the possible "reasonableness" of the substantive grievances expressed in protest activities, but rather on the "irrational" political style and the invitations to conflict embodied in the crusading rhetoric of emerging political movements. The pluralists claim that such appeals are irrational in the "utopianism" of their expectations and in the sense that they are self-defeating—that is, that they employ means inappropriate to their ends. Part Seven will examine the validity of these two claims.

Establishing a dichotomy between "rational" interest politics and "irrational" protest politics is conceptually misleading; by doing so, pluralists avoid distinguishing between protest leaders who can and those who cannot simultaneously bargain quietly with political elites and communicate successfully with their mass followings.* Thus pluralists fail to acknowledge that protest may be a rational choice of means available to obtain a seat at the bargaining table when the more conventional resources used by corporate pressure groups—money and bureaucratic organization—are not available. The choice of a protest posture may also appear to be an instrumentally rational means to mobilize members of a movement when potential recruits have such a low sense of political efficacy that appeals to mass solidarity are necessary to get them to act on behalf of their own interests.

Political protest and the threat or resort to mass action—strikes, boycotts, picketing, etc.—have played a far greater and more persistent role in our past than might be guessed from reading the pluralist writers. Much of the history of political protest in America has been a history of collective action by otherwise powerless groups followed by attempts by dominant elites to incorporate the goals of the protesters within the accepted value structure. For example, in the 1930s the labor movement employed confrontationist tactics that eventually led to labor representatives obtaining political

---

*For example, the decline of the white radical student movement on college campuses has been cited by some pluralists as evidence of both the utopianism and the self-defeating behavior of protest politics. Their very choice of evidence illustrates a lack of conceptual clarity. One might just as easily point to the relative success of black student movements on college campuses in obtaining concrete objectives as evidence that protest can be used as a tool in a rational strategy rather than as an end in itself.

legitimacy and recognized bargaining power. The overwhelming success of this use of direct action is ironically underlined by the fact that today organized labor is so well-entrenched a political force that the president of the United Auto Workers recently crossed a picket line to oppose the unionization of secretaries within his own bureaucratized corporate headquarters.

The point is that the group theory, as a descriptive theory of politics, needs revision to include the threat and the use of direct action as a political resource by groups that lack other bargaining resources. Such actions may be designed to force dominant elites to extend political access or material benefits to disadvantaged groups. Or they may be designed to call public attention to felt grievances and deprivations so as to expand the arena of conflict and recruit potential allies from among other groups.

The first selection in Part Seven, Jewel L. Prestage's "Black Politics and the Kerner Report: Concerns and Direction," assesses the significance of the *Report of the National Advisory Commission on Civil Disorders* in the context of black political socialization, normative democratic theory, and contemporary black politics. Prestage's analysis of the political socialization of American blacks indicates that blacks relate far less favorably to the political system than do similarly situated whites. She regards the commission's finding that black men have been systematically excluded from meaningful participation in the American political system as a factor that weakens the black man's bonds of political obligation to the system. Her selection includes a discussion of future political strategies designed to enhance the economic well-being, the self-respect, and the identity of black people. She calls for a flexible strategy that gives serious consideration to the possibility of indigenous control of the ghetto and that recognizes both the economic and the psychological needs of black people.

Over the past two decades many unorganized black and white low-income neighborhoods have benefitted from the community-organizing efforts of the late Saul Alinsky. Alinsky, a professional organizer, believed that no group could maintain a high level of political effectiveness as long as it was dependent on outside sources of support. He advocated the development of indigenous or "native" leadership as a prerequisite to the success of any protest movement. The brief extract from his interview with Marion Sanders, "The Professional Radical, 1970," illustrates some of the amusing tactics by which Alinsky himself was able to create indigenous resources.

Michael Lipsky's "Rent Strikes: Poor Man's Weapon" is a case study and analysis of protest by low-income blacks in five urban centers in the context of the theory of conflict expansion. Lipsky depicts the organizer of rent strikes as having to maintain political momentum in the face of four potentially imcompatible constituencies—his own membership, the mass media, sympathetic third parties, and the direct targets of protest. Trying to juggle the conflicting expectations of each of these groups often saps the energy of even the most skillful protest leader. In order to satisfy the psychological needs of members and to capture access to the media, group leaders must engage in denunciations of the power structure. This often alienates potential external sources of support, as well as the public officials who are the direct protest targets. Lipsky's case study supports Alinsky's claim that unless protest groups are able to develop indigenous political resources, their chances of sustained success are slight.

Black Politics
and the Kerner Report:
Concerns and Direction

28

Jewel L. Prestage

Reactions to the report of the *National Advisory Commission on Civil Disorders* have been widespread and varied, both in terms of their sources and their content. This discussion is essentially an effort to relate the *Report* to some of the theories and research findings in three areas of political science; namely, political socialization, democratic theory, and black political strategy. Any value accruing from this effort will probably be the results of the questions raised rather than directions or answers given.

Political Socialization

One of the comparatively new and rapidly developing fields of inquiry for political scientists is political socialization. Greenstein defines political socialization as ". . . all political learning formal and informal, deliberate and unplanned, at every stage of the life cycle, including not only explicitly political learning but also nominally nonpolitical learning which affects political behavior. . . ."

Because political socialization has been interpreted as involving "all political learning at every stage of the life cycle" the dimensions of research possibilities are indeterminable. It has been suggested that a full-blown characterization of political socialization would include classifications of: (1) who learns, (2) what is learned, (3) the agents of political socialization, (4) the circumstances of political socialization, and (5) the effects of political learning.

An understanding of the political socialization function is essential to the understanding and analysis of any political system, and the stability and continued existence of a political system depend, in no small measure, on the extent to which the citizenry internalizes political norms and attitudes supportive of the system. Political socialization, then, is induction into the political culture, the means by which an individual "comes to terms" with his political system. The *Report* would seem to suggest that "coming to terms" is an especially traumatic experience for black people in America.

Examined in the context of current findings of political socialization research, the *Report* gives rise to several crucial concerns. The nature of these concerns is implicit in the observations which follow.

First, the political world of American blacks is so radically different from the political world of American whites that it might well constitute a "subculture" within a dominant or major culture. Even though there has been a

272

great volume of writing and research on political socialization, very little has been directed to political socialization of American blacks. The studies suggest that black people tend to relate rather differently to the political system and have a far greater sense of personal alienation and political futility than do similarly located whites. Ghetto residents, like other citizens, tend to formulate their attitudes toward the political system largely on the basis of their contact with the system. For example, ghetto blacks believe that police brutality and harassment occur in their neighborhood to a much greater extent than whites believe that violations occur in white areas. In Detroit, for example, 91 per cent of the rioters believed anger at police had something to do with causing the riots. It is not surprising that the policeman, primarily a symbol of law and order in white neighborhoods, is for ghetto people a symbol of injustice, inhumanity and of a society from which they are alien as well as alienated. Studies of white policemen assigned to ghetto areas indicate that black fears and reservations about the police may not be entirely imaginary. Bobby Richardson, writing about police brutality in New Orleans, states ". . . brutality, man, is a state of mind, not just a whipping with a billy, although plenty of the brothers get beat up on. They know that brutality is the way you are treated and the way a policeman will arrest one man and not another. And the way he will talk to you and treat you. Brutality is just an extension of prejudice, and it is easier to brutalize one man than it is another."

Similarly, blacks tend to be less trusting of their political system (local and national) than do their white counterparts. Surveys done in Newark reveal that both "rioters" and "non-involved" blacks have a high distrust of local government with 44.2 per cent and 33.9 per cent, respectively, reporting they could "almost never" trust the Newark government to do what is right. In Detroit, 75 per cent of the rioters and 58.7 per cent of the non-involved felt that "anger with politicians" had a "great deal" or "something" to do with causing riots.

Especially crucial for students of political socialization is the proportion of blacks, rioters and non-involved, who indicated that the country was not worth fighting for in a major world war. In Detroit the percentages were 39.4 for rioters and 15.5 for the non-involved, while the Newark survey revealed these sentiments on the part of 52.8 per cent of the rioters and 27.8 per cent of the non-involved. These figures are striking, especially those related to the non-involved blacks, and would seem to indicate substantial disaffection among blacks. Similar results were ascertained in a recent study of black youth in Atlanta where 49 per cent took a negative stance on the proposition, "Black Americans should be proud to be fighting in Viet Nam."

Given the above data, it is interesting to note the Commission's contrasting finding that rioters were not seeking to change the American system, but merely to gain full participation in it. However, the deep disaffection from the system by blacks and the continued reluctance of the system to accept blacks as full participants might lead one to question the Commission's conclusion. Could it be that black rioters were attempting to change the system and to gain full participation simultaneously? Or, more directly, would not full participation by blacks in itself represent a fundamental change in the system? Such reservations regarding the goals of rioters receive some support from the recent report of Mayor Richard Daley's committee to study Chicago's riots of April, 1968. This committee reported a growing feeling among blacks that "the existing system must be toppled by violent means." This feeling was said to have its strongest expression among black teenagers, where there is "an alarming hatred for whites." Such feelings were found to be based on the attitude that "the entire-existing political-economic-educational structure is anti-black."

Assuming the blacks of the ghetto have internalized the American dream of freedom, equality and justice, there is small wonder that "coming to terms" with the system has produced deep alienation, frustration and despair. Throughout the history of this country, blacks have, for the most part, been excluded from full benefits of this society. The fact that the rest of the country has experienced progressive affluence (flagrantly paraded before blacks through mass media) while blacks became poorer is a story much too familiar to belabor here. In the face of "the American dream" of equal opportunity and abundance, blacks have been forced to live "the American nightmare" of poverty, discrimination and deprivation. Despite some progress, American blacks continue to live in this "credibility gap" and part of the results are distrust, estrangement and violence.

Data from the Detroit survey indicate that all blacks included in the survey were not equally alienated and distrusting. Least alienated were the "counter-rioters," a major portion of whom (86.9 per cent) regarded the country as worth fighting for. Of this group, 88.9 per cent felt that getting what you want out of life is a matter of "ability" rather than "being in the right place" as compared to 76.9 per cent of the rioters and 76.1 per cent of the non-involved. The typical counter-rioter was described as an active supporter of existing social institutions and considerably better educated and more affluent than either the rioter or the non-involved. This would lead one to speculate that black attitudes or perceptions may be changed when "reality" changes.

Finally, the *Report* attributes responsibility for the present civil disorders to "white racism" in America, "the racial attitude and behavior of white Americans toward black Americans." The fact that a political system theoretically committed to democratic values finds itself embroiled in a major crisis resulting from undemocratic practices raises some fundamental questions regarding the real operative values of the system. How do white Americans reconcile theory and reality? What are the special problems which this situation suggests relative to political socialization of white Americans? Is resocialization of American whites a prerequisite for the fundamental policy changes recommended by the Commission? A number of scholars and writers, some black and some white, have long maintained that the race problem in America is essentially a white problem, created and perpetuated by whites. If the problem is to be solved it must be solved by whites. As Myrdal stated many years ago, "all our attempts to reach scientific explanations of why the Negroes are what they are and why they live as they do have regularly led to determinants on the white side of the race line."

Coming to grips with the fundamental cause of the riots, white racism, is more a task for American whites than for blacks. The process will no doubt necessitate an admission on the part of white Americans that the American dream remains a dream, that full democracy in America is yet to be realized. In short, it will entail alteration of the American political culture, a re-examination of basic values and possibly a rewriting of American history to revise the image of blacks in the minds of whites and blacks. More funda-mentally, it will possibly require a restructuring of the socialization process for blacks and whites if our commitments to democratic values are to be translated into actual practices. The question for which the *Report* provides no answer is "how can this be done?" It is in the delineation of the broad outlines of such a process that political science and other social science research can possibly make its most significant contribution.

Democratic Theory

"Democracy is . . . characterized by the fact that power over significant authoritative decisions in a society is distributed among the population. The ordinary man is expected to take an active part in governmental affairs, to be aware of how decisions are made and to make his views known."

Any attempt to view the *Report* in the context of democratic theory would seem to raise an array of tantalizing questions, one of which is the relation-ship between *political obligation* and *consent.*

In a democracy the basis of political obligation is consent. Such consent implies a high level of citizen participation in the political process of at least the unrestricted right of the interested citizen to participate. Consequently, democratic political systems have traditionally institutionalized certain structures and practices that allow for the orderly and periodic involvement of citizens in decision-making. A brief examination of the record tends to substantiate the Commission's contention that throughout the course of American history, black men have been essentially "subjects" rather than "participants" in the political process.

. . . Since 1900, blacks have staged an uphill battle in quest of full partici-pation in the body politic. Most significant among legal victories for blacks have been the outlawing of white primaries in 1944, the passage of Civil Rights acts in 1957, 1960, and 1964, the Anti-Poll Tax Amendment in 1963 and finally the Federal Voting Rights Act of 1965.

Perhaps the most reliable source of information on current black registra-tion and voting in the South is the Voter Education Project of the Southern Regional Council. According to its director, Vernon Jordan, the 1965 Voting Rights Act has had a marked impact on voter registration among southern Negroes. He states that significant gains have come in Alabama, Louisiana, Georgia, South Carolina, Virginia, and Mississippi. In Mississippi, Negro registration jumped from 8 per cent to nearly 60 per cent in just two and a half years.

. . .

Also noteworthy is the election of over 200 blacks to public office in the South since the Voting Rights Act was passed. There are presently 50 blacks holding local, parish and state offices in Louisiana, all elected since 1965.

These accelerated advances in black registration and election are indeed impressive, but they do not eradicate the voting problem. With the exception of Texas, black registration percentages are still below white percentages in all the states included in the Voter Education Project survey, and in many areas blacks still experience substantial difficulties in gaining the franchise. Also, the number of blacks holding statewide positions in government and political parties is in no way proportionate to the number of blacks in the population.

Wilson observes that "The political participation of the Negro in the North is significantly higher than in the South but even so is lower than that of most other Northern population groups." It ought to be pointed out that low participation in the North cannot be attributed to the type of legal restrictions historically operative in the South. Social science surveys have indicated that persons with low socioeconomic status tend to vote less than persons of high socioeconomic status. In addition, Negroes in the urban North are more geographically mobile than whites and are less likely to be able to satisfy residence requirements for voting. Non-partisan elections, candidates running at-large and weak party organization also contribute to low turnout among low income voters. And it could well be that "the extent to which an individual feels effective as part of the institutionalized process may well determine the degree to which he participates in those processes. In sum, the individual's perception of his personal effectiveness should be supportive to the values he places on participation." Thus, while there are no legal deterrents to Negro voting in the North, the cultural deterrents (income, education, occupation) are attributable to the system. That is, the prevailing social, economic and educational arrangements operate in a manner which relegates Negroes to this status, and as long as Negroes face these artificial barriers it is reasonable to assume that their level of political participation will not change.

The extent of constraints on black participation, North and South, would seem to suggest an absence of consent by blacks and thus possible relief from obligations traditionally incumbent upon citizens in a democracy. Of interest in this connection is a recent re-examination of the principles of obligation and consent and related problems rendered by Pitkin.

Pitkin, in a highly provocative treatise, holds that obligation depends not on any actual act of consenting, past or present, but on the character of the government. If it is just government, doing what a government should, then you must obey it. If it is unjust, then you have no such obligation. Or, your obligation depends not on whether you have consented but on whether the government is such that you ought to consent to it. Are its actions consistent with the type of government men in a hypothetical state of nature would have consented to establish and obey? Pitkin's study would suggest that any assessment of the riots and the rioters would of necessity involve grappling with these kinds of concerns.

The propensity among blacks to disobey certain basic canons of the political system has produced strains in the system which threaten to destroy its very foundation. Could this propensity derive fundamentally from the unwillingness of the system to incorporate blacks as full partners in the political process? Cook has projected that "on the empirical level, a tradition of exclusion from participation in the political system breeds disrespect for, and disloyalty to, that system." "Men rarely question the legitimacy of an established order when all is going well; the problem of political obligation is urgent when the state is sick. . . ."

Does exclusion from participation, coupled with exclusion from benefits of "the good life" of the system, not only remove the obligation to obey, but also give rise to the obligation to disobey or revolt? These queries are relevant, but they are also difficult in as much as they solicit precise guidance in specific and varied kinds of situations. Pitkin underscores the inadequacy of classical democratic theory as well as her own theory on consent by noting that both provide insufficient cues for determining what authority to resist and under what conditions. In the same way, both provide only imperfect guidelines for assessing and evaluating the consistency between civil disorder of the magnitude of riots and the obligation of citizens to obey the authority of society invested with the duty of enforcing the law.

Black Political Strategy

. . . The crucial problem of the black man in the American political arena seems to revolve around the magnitude of the needs of the black people (as set forth in the *Report* and elsewhere), in relationship to the limited potential of politics as a vehicle for ministering to those needs. More succinctly put, it now seems incumbent upon black men to decide if politics, in the traditional sense, is now more of an irrelevancy rather than an imperative in the search for solutions to their problems. If politics is relevant, then what types of strategies will best serve the needs of the black community, North and South? If irrelevant, what are the alternatives?

Questions of strategy are significant and there are those who feel that this aspect of the black protest movement has not received sufficient attention from leaders in that movement. In fact, the alleged absence of a programmatic element in radical politics in America today, especially the black protest movement, provoked Lasch to state, "the very gravity of the crisis makes it all the more imperative that radicals try to formulate at least a provisional theory which will serve them as a guide to tactics in the immediate future as well as to long range questions of strategy." Along the same general lines, Crozier points out that America is now committed to the omnipotence of reason and the black protest movements are out of step with that development. Very pointedly, he reflects that "it is no longer possible to make good through mere numbers, through the vote or through manual labor, but only through the ability to play the game of modern calculation. And in that area the Negro is still fundamentally disadvantaged. The more rational the society becomes, the more he loses his foothold." Could it be that traditional politics characterizes the black subculture while a more rational-calculating variety of politics has long been the pattern in the dominant political culture?

The literature of the discipline and popular periodicals are replete with suggestions of appropriate strategies and/or programs for solving the race problem. Some of the more popularly suggested and researched strategies include black-liberal white coalitions, black-conservative white coalitions, fluctuating or *ad hoc* coalitions, separate black political parties, Black Power, ghetto power. No examination of this proliferation of literature can be made in this limited commentary. Nor will any full-blown theory or strategy be offered. However, it does seem reasonable to submit that any strategy designed to redefine the status of black people in America must of necessity be devised with certain considerations.

First, political strategy for blacks must take into account the difficulties inherent in being a numerical minority. Minority strategy must be highly flexibly based, to a large degree, on the fluctuating attitudes and actions of the white majority in any given setting. It must also be directed toward overcoming traditional constraints on the exertion of effective power by Negroes endemic to the black community itself. Second, any therapeutic strategy must acknowledge the reality that blacks in the ghetto already constitute a "separate society," and must address itself seriously to black charges of control by "alien, outside" agents. Indigenous control of the ghetto and similar demands cannot be summarily dismissed as, for example, "old wine in new bottles." Third, given the general apathy and insensitivity of whites toward problems of blacks, it seems reasonable to suggest that any meaningful gains for blacks will come as a result of *demands,* supported by evidence of black willingness to cause great inconvenience to the community at large if these legitimate demands are ignored. Fourth, it might be that the Commission placed too much emphasis on the material aspects of the black man's problem (and the material aspects are indeed important) and did not devote enough attention to such psychological needs as dignity, self-respect and identity and to the relationship between the latter and any corrective actions, political or otherwise. Taking these psychological dimensions into account will probably necessitate innovations in and restatements of traditional concepts and theories regarding democracy, civil disobedience, protest, and other forms of political activity. New tactics, new rhetoric and new sources of leadership will most probably emerge and must be accommodated by the system. Fifth, and in a similar view, it would seem that black strategy and black strategists ought not be constrained to political alternatives if these alternatives prove to be mostly dysfunctional for blacks, and there is a growing body of opinion which holds that they may well be. Finally, the magnitude of the problems faced by blacks is such that the correctives must be radical. If radical programs are not adopted, the Kerner Report may be more a prelude to, rather than a summation of, the worst race riots in the history of this nation, for there seems to be little reason to believe that black rioters will be satisfied with anything less than radical corrective action.

29

The Professional Radical, 1970

Saul Alinsky/ a Conversation with Marion K. Sanders

The whole concept of organizing people on an altruistic basis, the way white liberals tried to do something for the blacks, is a lot of crap. This just isn't the way life is. Invariably, the right things get done for the wrong reasons. So the organizer looks for wrong reasons to get right things done.

. . .

Suppose one of our men is trying to organize a community on the issue of water pollution—that's got a lot of people very upset in the suburbs where you turn on a faucet and nothing comes out but foam from detergents. It's a good issue but I can't tell you what tactics he'd use because in organization you are always improvising. For instance, The Woodlawn Organization— TWO—in Chicago got Mayor Daley to deal with them after they threatened to tie up all the rest rooms at O'Hare—keeping all the booths occupied. O'Hare is one of Daley's sacred cows. Another time TWO people piled rats on the steps of City Hall. Daley got that message too. The Northwest Community organizations in Chicago filled an old truck with garbage and dumped it on an alderman's lawn. They got better garbage pickups after that.

The only thing the poor have as far as power goes is their bodies. When TWO has a bunch of housing complaints they don't forward them to the building inspector. They drive forty or fifty of their members—the blackest ones they can find—to the nice suburb where the slumlord lives and they picket his home. Now we know a picket line isn't going to convert the slumlord. But we also know what happens when his white neighbors get after him and say, "We don't care what you do for a living—all we're telling you is to get those niggers out of here or you get out." That's the kind of jujitsu operation that forces the slumlord to surrender and gets repairs made in the slums.

. . . We'll be taking on some more of Mayor Daley's sacred cows—the corporations . . . that are mainly responsible for pollution—which really should be spelled pollootion because it amounts to looting the public. If Commonwealth Edison complains that it will take a long, long time to get rid of their coal-burning, air-polluting generators, then I say—the hell with them. Let's take the company over in public ownership. . . . Of course, I expect people to start yelling "socialism" when they hear this. This is a word with a lot of different definitions according to who's talking about what. The characters who live in swanky Lake Forest call it socialism when the government's welfare programs give money to the poor. But you don't hear them bellyaching when they ride along freeways built 90 per cent with federal money or when they latch onto a nice fat defense contract. When the other guy gets money, it's socialism; but when you get it, that's "cooperation between the private and public sectors."

Rent Strikes: Poor Man's Weapon

30

Michael Lipsky

The poor lack not only money, but power. Low-income political groups may be thought of as politically impoverished. In the bargaining arena of city politics the poor have little to trade.

Protest has come to be an important part of the politics of low-income minorities. By attempting to enlarge the conflict, and bring outside pressures to bear on their concerns, protest has developed as one tactic the poor can use to exert power and gain greater control over their lives. Since the sit-in movement of 1960, Negro civil-rights strategists have used protest to bring about political change, and so have groups associated with the war on poverty. Saul Alinsky's Industrial Areas Foundation continues to receive invitations to help organize low-income communities because it has demonstrated that it can mobilize poor people around the tactics of protest.

The Harlem rent strikes of 1963 and 1964, organized by Jesse Gray, a dynamic black leader who has been agitating about slum housing for more than 15 years, affected some tenants in approximately 150 Harlem tenements. Following the March on Washington in August, 1963, the rent strikes played on the liberal sympathies of New Yorkers who were just beginning to re-examine the conditions of New York City slums. Through a combination of appeal and threat, Jesse Gray mounted a movement that succeeded in changing the orientation of some city services, obtained greater *legal* rights for organized tenants, and resulted in obtaining repairs in a minority of the buildings in which tenants struck. Along with rent strikes conducted by Mobilization for Youth, a pre-war poverty program, the rent strikes managed to project images of thousands of aroused tenants to a concerned public, and to somewhat anxious reform-oriented city officials.

The rent strikes did not succeed in obtaining fundamental goals. Most buildings in which tenants struck remained in disrepair, or deteriorated even further. City housing officials became more responsive to housing problems, but general programs to repair slum housing remained as remote as ever. Perhaps most significant, the rent strike movement, after a hectic initial winter, quickly petered out when cold weather again swept the Harlem streets. Focusing upon the rent strikes may help explain why this protest failed, and why protest in general is not a reliable political weapon.

Protest Has Long-Range Limits

Protest as a political tactic is limited because protest leaders must appeal to four constituencies at the same time. A protest leader must:

281

1. Nurture and sustain an organization composed of people who may not always agree with his program or style;
2. Adapt to the mass media—choose strategies and voice goals that will give him as much favorable exposure as possible;
3. Try to develop and sustain the protest's impact on third parties—the general public, sympathetic liberals, or anyone who can put pressure on those with power; and
4. Try to influence directly the targets of the protest—those who have the power to give him what he wants.

The tensions that result from the leader's need to manipulate four constituencies at once are the basic reason why protest is an unreliable political tactic, unlikely to prove successful in the long run.

Protest activity may be defined as a political activity designed to dramatize an objection to some policies or conditions, using unconventional showmanship or display and aimed at obtaining rewards from the political system while working within that system. The problem of the powerless is that they have little to bargain with, and must acquire resources. Fifteen people sitting in the Mayor's Office cannot, of themselves, hope to move City Hall. But through the publicity they get, or the reaction they evoke, they may politically activate a wider public to which the city administration is sensitive.

The tactic of activating third parties to enter the political process is most important to relatively powerless groups, although it is available to all. Obviously any organization which can call upon a large membership to engage in political activity—a trade union on strike, for example—has some degree of power. But the poor in individual neighborhoods frequently cannot exert such power. Neighborhood political groups may not have mass followings, or may not be able to rely on membership participation in political struggles. In such cases they may be able to activate other political forces in the city to enter the conflict on their behalf. However, the contradictions of the protest process suggest that even this tactic—now widely employed by various low-income groups—cannot be relied upon.

Take, for example, the problem of protest leaders and their constituents. If poor people are to be organized for protest activities, their involvement must be sustained by the symbolic and intangible rewards of participation in protest action, and by the promises of material rewards that protest leaders extend. Yet a leadership style suited to providing protesters with the intangible rewards of participating in rebellious political movements is sometimes incompatible with a style designed to secure tangible benefits for protest group members.

Furthermore, the need of protest leaders to develop a distinctive style in order to overcome the lack of involvement of potential group members diffuses as well as consolidates support. People who want psychological gratification (such as revenge or public notice and acknowledgment), but have little hope of material rewards, will be attracted to a militant leader. They want angry rhetoric and denunciation. On the other hand, those people who depend on the political system for tangible benefits, and therefore believe in it and cooperate with it to some extent, are likely to want moderate leadership. Groups that materially profit from participation in the system will not accept men who question the whole system. Yet the cohesion of relatively powerless groups may be strengthened by militant, ideological leadership that questions the rules of the game, that challenges their morality and legitimacy.

On the other hand, the fact that the sympathies and support of third parties are essential to the success of protesters may make the protesters' fear of retribution, where justified, an asset. For when people put themselves in danger by complaining, they are more likely to gain widespread sympathy. The cattle-prod and police-dog tactics of Alabama police in breaking up demonstrations a few years ago brought immediate response and support from around the country.

In short, the nature of protesters curtails the flexibility of protest leadership. Leaders must limit their public actions to preserve their basis of support. They must also limit protest in line with what they can reasonably expect of their followers. The poor cannot be expected to engage in activities that require much money. The anxieties developed throughout their lives—such as loss of job, fear of police, or danger of eviction—also limit the scope of protest. Negro protest in the South was limited by such retributions or anxieties about facing reprisals.

Jesse Gray was able to gain sympathy for the rent strikers because he was able to project an image of people willing to risk eviction in order to protest against the (rarely identified) slumlords, who exploited them, or the city, whose iceberg pace aided landlords rather than forced them to make repairs. In fact, Gray used an underutilized provision of the law which protected tenants against eviction if they paid their rent to court. It was one of the great strengths of the rent strikes that the image of danger to tenants was projected, while the tenants remained somewhat secure and within the legal process. This fortunate combination is not readily transferable to other cases in which protest activity is contemplated.

Apart from problems relating to manipulation of protest group members, protest leaders must command at least some resources. For instance, skilled professionals must be made available to protest organizations. Lawyers are needed to help protesters use the judicial process, and to handle court cases. The effectiveness of a protest organization may depend upon a combination of an ability to threaten the political system and an ability to exercise legal rights. The organization may either pay lawyers or depend on volunteers. In the case of the rent strikes, dependence on volunteer lawyers was finally abandoned—there were not enough available, and those who were willing could not survive long without payment.

Other professionals may be needed in other protest circumstances. A group trying to protest against an urban-renewal project, for example, will need architects and city planners to present a viable alternative to the city's plan.

Financial resources not only pay lawyers, but allow a minimum program of political activity. In the Harlem rent strikes, dues assessed against the protesters were low and were not collected systematically. Lawyers often complained that tenants were unwilling to pay incidental and minor fees, such as the $2 charge to subpoena departmental records. Obtaining money for mimeo flyers, supplies, rent, telephones, and a small payroll became major problems. The fact that Jesse Gray spent a great deal of time trying to organize new groups, and speaking all over the city, prevented him from paying attention to organizational details. Furthermore, he did not or could not develop assistants who could assume the organizational burden.

Lack of money can sometimes be made up for by passionate support. Lawyers, office help, and block organizers did come forth to work voluntarily for the rent strike. But such help is unreliable and usually transient. When spring came, volunteers vanished rapidly and did not return the following winter. Volunteer assistance usually comes from the more educated and skilled who can get other jobs, at good salaries. The diehards of *ad hoc* political groups are usually those who have no place to go, nothing else to do.

Lack of money also can be overcome with skilled nonprofessionals; but usually they are scarce. The college students, Negro and white, who staffed the rent-strike offices, handled paper work and press releases, and served as neighborhood organizers, were vital to the strike's success. Not only could they communicate with tenants, but they were relatively sophisticated about the operations of the city government and the communications media. They could help tenants with city agencies, and tell reporters what they wanted to hear. They also maintained contacts with other civil-rights and liberal organizations. Other workers might have eventually acquired these skills and contacts, but these student organizers allowed the movement to go into action quickly, on a city-wide scale, and with a large volume of cases. One of the casualties of "black power" has been the exclusion of skilled white college students from potentially useful roles of this kind.

Like the proverbial tree that falls unheard in the forest, protest, politically speaking, does not exist unless it is projected and perceived. To the extent that a successful protest depends on appealing to, or perhaps also threatening, other groups in the community, publicity through the public media will set the limits of how far that protest activity will go toward success. (A number of writers, in fact, have noticed that the success of a protest seems directly related to publicity outside the immediate protest area.) If the communications media either ignore the protest or play it down, it will not succeed.

When the protest *is* covered, the way it is given publicity will influence all participants including the protesters themselves. Therefore, it is vital that a leader know what the media consider newsworthy, and be familiar with the prejudices and desires of those who determine what is to be covered and how much.

Media's Demands May Be Destructive

But media requirements are often contradictory and hard to meet. TV wants spot news, perhaps 30 seconds' worth; newspapers want somewhat more than that, and long stories may appear only in weekly neighborhood or ethnic papers. Reporters want topical newsworthiness in the short run—the more exciting the better. They will even stretch to get it. But after that they want evidence, accuracy, and reliability. The leader who was too accommodating in the beginning may come to be portrayed as an irresponsible liar.

This conflict was well illustrated in the rent strike. Jesse Gray and the reporters developed an almost symbiotic relationship. They wanted fresh, dramatic news on the growth of the strike—and Gray was happy to give them progress reports he did not, and could not, substantiate.

Actually, just keeping the strikes going in a limited number of buildings would have been a considerable feat. Yet reporters wanted more than that —they wanted growth. Gray, of course, had other reasons for reporting that the strike was spreading—he knew that such reports, if believed, would help pressure city officials. In misrepresenting the facts, Gray was encouraged by sympathetic reporters—in the long run actually undermining his case. As a *New York Times* reporter explained, "We had an interest in keeping it going."

Having encouraged Gray to go out on a limb and overstate the support he had, the reporters later were just as eager for documentation. It was not forthcoming. Gray consistently failed to produce a reliable list of rent-strike buildings that could withstand independent verification. He took the reporters only to those buildings he considered "safe." And the newspapers that had themselves strongly contributed to the inflation of Gray's claims then helped deflate them and denied him press coverage.

The clash between the needs of these two constituencies—the media and the protesters—often puts great strain on leaders. The old-line leader who appeals to his followers because of his apparent responsibility, integrity, and restraint will not capture the necessary headlines. On the other hand, the leader who finds militant rhetoric a useful weapon for organizing some people will find the media only too eager to carry his more inflammatory statements. But this portrayal of him as an uncompromising firebrand (often meant for a limited audience and as a limited tactic) will alienate him from people he may need for broad support, and may work toward excluding him from bargaining with city officials.

If a leader takes strong or extreme positions, he may win followers and newspaper space, but alienate the protest's target. Exclusion from the councils of bargaining or decision-making can have serious consequences for protest leaders, since the targets can then concentrate on satisfying the aroused public and civic groups, while ignoring the demands of the protesters.

What a protest leader must do to get support from third parties will also often conflict with what he must do to retain the interest and support of his followers. For instance, when Negro leaders actually engage in direct bargaining with politicians, they may find their supporters outraged or discouraged, and slipping away. They need militancy to arouse support; they need support to bargain; but if they bargain, they may seem to betray that militancy, and lose support. Yet bargaining at some point may be necessary to obtain objectives from city politicians. These tensions can be minimized to some extent by a protest organization's having divided leadership. One leader may bargain with city officials, while another continues rhetorical guerilla warfare.

Divided leadership may also prove useful in solving the problem that James Q. Wilson has noted: "The militant displays an unwillingness to perform those administrative tasks which are necessary to operate an organization." The nuts and bolts of administrative detail are vital. If protest depends primarily on a leader's charisma, as the rent strikes did to some extent, allocating responsibility (already difficult because of lack of skilled personnel) can become a major problem. In the rent strike, somebody had to coordinate court appearances for tenants and lawyers; somebody had to subpoena Building and Health Department records and collect money to pay for them; and somebody had to be alert to the fact that, through landlord duplicity or tenant neglect, tenants might face immediate eviction and require emergency legal assistance. Jesse Gray was often unable, or unwilling, to concentrate on these details. In part failures of these kinds are forced on the protest leader, who must give higher priority to publicity and arousing support than to administrative detail. However, divided leadership can help separate responsibility for administration from responsibility for mobilization.

Strain between militancy to gain and maintain support and reasonableness to obtain concessions can also be diminished by successful "public relations." Protest groups may understand the same words differently than city officials. Imperatives to march or burn are usually not the commands frightened whites sometimes think they are.

Bargaining Is for Insiders

Protest success depends partly upon enlarging the number of groups and individuals who are concerned about the issues. It also depends upon ability to influence the shape of the decision, not merely whether or not there will be a decision. This is one reason why protest is more likely to succeed when groups are trying to veto a decision (say, to stop construction of an expressway), than when they try to initiate projects (say, to establish low-cost transportation systems for a neighborhood).

Protest groups are often excluded from the bargaining arena because the civic groups and city officials who make decisions in various policy areas have developed relationships over long periods of time, for mutual benefit. Interlopers are not admitted to these councils easily. Men in power do not like to sit down with people they consider rogues. They do not seek the dubious pleasure of being denounced, and are uneasy in the presence of people whose class, race, or manners are unfamiliar. They may make opportunities available for "consultation," or even "confrontation," but decisions will be made behind closed doors where the nature of the decision is not open to discussion by "outsiders."

As noted before, relatively powerless protest groups seldom have enough people of high status to work for their proposals. Good causes sometimes attract such people, but seldom for long. Therefore protest groups hardly ever have the expertise and experience they need, including professionals in such fields as law, architecture, accounting, education, and how to get government money. This is one area in which the "political impoverishment" of low-income groups is most clearly observed. Protest groups may learn how to dramatize issues, but they cannot present data or proposals that public officials consider "objective" or "reasonable." Few men can be both passionate advocate and persuasive arbiter at the same time.

Ultimately the success of a protest depends on the targets.

Many of the forces that inhibit protest leaders from influencing target groups have already been mentioned: the protesters' lack of status, experience, and resources in bargaining; the conflict between the rhetoric that will inspire and hold supporters, and what will open the door to meaningful bargaining; conflicting press demands, and so on.

But there is an additional factor that constrains protest organizations that deal with public agencies. As many students of organizations have pointed out, public agencies and the men who run them are concerned with maintaining and enhancing the agency's position. This means protecting the agency from criticism and budget cuts, and attempting to increase the agency's status and scope. This piece of conventional wisdom has great importance for a protest group which can only succeed by getting others to apply pressure on public policy. Public agencies are most responsive to their regular critics and immediate organizational allies. Thus if they can deflect pressure from these, their reference groups, they can ease the pressure brought by protest *without meeting any of the protest demands.*

At least six tactics are available to targets that are inclined to respond in some way to protests. They may respond with symbolic satisfactions. Typical, in city politics, is the ribbon-cutting, street-corner ceremony, or the Mayor's walking press conference. When tension builds up in Harlem, Mayor Lindsay walks the streets and talks to the people. Such occasions are not only used to build support, but to persuade the residents that attention is being directed to their problems.

City agencies establish special machinery and procedures to prepare symbolic means for handling protest crises. For instance, in those New York departments having to do with housing, top officials, a press secretary, and one or two others will devote whatever time is necessary to collecting information and responding quickly to reporters' inquiries about a developing crisis. This is useful for tenants: It means that if they can create enough concern, they can cut through red tape. It is also useful for officials who want to appear ready to take action.

During the New York rent strikes, city officials responded by: initiating an anti-rat campaign; proposing ways to "legalize" rent strikes (already legal under certain conditions); starting a program to permit the city to make repairs; and contracting for a costly university study to review housing code enforcement procedures. Some of these steps were of distinct advantage to tenants, although none was directed at the overall slum problem. It is important to note, however, that the announcement of these programs served to deflect pressure by reassuring civic groups and a liberal public that something was being done. Regardless of how well-meaning public officials are, real changes in conditions are secondary to the general agency need to develop a response to protest that will "take the heat off."

■ Another tactic available to public officials is to give token satisfactions. When city officials respond, with much publicity, to a few cases brought to them, they can appear to be meeting protest demands, while actually meeting only those few cases. If a child is bitten by a rat, and enough hue and cry is raised, the rats in that apartment or building may be exterminated, with much fanfare. The building next door remains infested.

Such tokenism may give the appearance of great improvement, while actually impeding real overall progress by alleviating public concern. Tokenism is particularly attractive to reporters and television news directors, who are able to dramatize individual cases convincingly. General situations are notoriously hard to dramatize.

■ To blunt protest drives, protest targets may also work to change their internal procedures and organization. This tactic is similar to the preceding one. By developing means to concentrate on those cases that are most dramatic, or seem to pose the greatest threats, city officials can effectively wear down the cutting-edge of protest.

As noted, all New York City agencies have informal arrangements to deal with such crisis cases. During the rent strikes two new programs were developed by the city whereby officials could enter buildings to make repairs and exterminate rats on an emergency basis. Previously, officials had been confined by trying to find the landlords and to taking them to court (a time-consuming, ineffective process that has been almost universally criticized by knowledgeable observers). These new programs were highly significant developments because they expanded the scope of governmental responsibility. They acknowledged, in a sense, that slum conditions are a social disease requiring public intervention.

At the same time, these innovations served the purposes of administrators who needed the power to make repairs in the worst housing cases. If public officials can act quickly in the most desperate situations that come to their attention, pressure for more general attacks on housing problems can be deflected.

The new programs could never significantly affect the 800,000 deteriorating apartments in New York City. The new programs can operate only so long as the number of crises are relatively limited. Crisis treatment for everyone would mean shifting resources from routine services. If all cases receive priority, then none can.

The new programs, however welcomed by some individual tenants, help agencies to "cool off" crises quicker. This also may be the function of police review boards and internal complaint bureaus. Problems can be handled more expeditiously with such mechanisms while agency personnel behavior remains unaffected.

■ Target groups may plead that their hands are tied—because of laws or stubborn superiors, or lack of resources or authority. They may be sympathetic, but what can they do? Besides, "If-I-give-it-to-you-I-have-to-give-it-to-everyone."

Illustratively, at various times during the rent strike, city officials claimed they did not have funds for emergency repairs (although they found funds later), and lacked authority to enter buildings to make emergency repairs (although the city later acted to make emergency repairs under provisions of a law available for over 60 years). This tactic is persuasive; everyone knows that cities are broke, and limited by state law. But if pressure rises, funds for specific, relatively inexpensive programs, or expansion of existing programs, can often be found.

■ Targets may use their extensive resources and contacts to discredit protest leaders and organizations: "They don't really have the people behind them"; they are acting "criminally"; they are "left-wing." These allegations can cool the sympathies of the vital third parties, whether or not there is any truth behind them. City officials, especially, can use this device in their contacts with civic groups and communication media, with which they are mutually dependent for support and assistance. Some city officials can downgrade protesters while others appear sympathetic to the protesters' demands.

■ Finally, target groups may postpone action—time is on their side. Public sympathy cools quickly, and issues are soon forgotten. Moreover, because low-income protest groups have difficulty sustaining organization (for reasons suggested above), they are particularly affected by delays. The threat represented by protest dissipates with time, the difficulty of managing for constituencies increases as more and more information circulates, and the inherent instability of protest groups makes it unlikely that they will be able to take effective action when decisions are finally announced.

Survey Research as Procrastination

The best way to procrastinate is to commit the subject to "study." By the time the study is ready, if ever, the protest group will probably not be around to criticize or press for implementation of proposals. The higher the status of the study group, the less capable low-status protest groups will be able to effectively challenge the final product. Furthermore, officials retain the option of rejecting or failing to accept the reports of study groups, a practice developed to an art by the Johnson administration.

This is not to say that surveys, research and study groups are to be identified solely as delaying tactics. They are often desirable, even necessary, to document need and mobilize public and pressure group support. But postponement, for whatever reason, will always change the pressures on policy-makers, usually in directions unfavorable to protest results.

Groups without power can attempt to gain influence through protest. I have argued that protest will be successful to the extent that the protesters can get third parties to put pressure on the targets. But protest leaders have severe problems in trying to meet the needs and desires of four separate and often conflicting constituencies—their supporters, the mass media, the interested and vital third parties, and the targets of the protest.

By definition, relatively powerless groups have few resources, and therefore little probability of success. But to survive at all and to arouse the third parties, they need at least some resources. Even to get these minimal resources, conflicting demands limit the leader's effectiveness. And when, finally, public officials are forced to recognize protest activity, it is not to meet the demands, but to satisfy other groups that have influence.

Edelman has written that, in practice, regulatory policy consists of reassuring mass publics symbolically while at the same time dispensing tangible concessions only to narrow interest groups. Complementing Edelman, I have suggested that public officials give symbolic reassurances to protest groups, rather than real concessions, because those on whom they most depend will be satisfied with appearances of action. Rent strikers wanted to see repairs in their apartments and dramatic improvements in slum housing; but the wider publics that most influence city officials could be satisfied simply by the appearance of reform. And when city officials had satisfied the publics this way, they could then resist or ignore the protesters' demands for other or more profound changes.

Kenneth Clark, in *Dark Ghetto,* has observed that the illusion of having power, when unaccompanied by material rewards, leads to feelings of helplessness and reinforces political apathy in the ghetto. If the poor and politically weak protest to acquire influence that will help change their lives and conditions, only to find that little comes from all that risk and trouble, then apathy or hostility toward conventional political methods may result.

If the arguments presented in this article are convincing, then those militant civil-rights leaders who insist that protest is a shallow foundation on which to build long-term, concrete gains are essentially correct. But their accompanying arguments—the fickleness of the white liberal, the difficulty of changing discriminatory institutions as opposed to discriminatory laws—are only part of the explanation for the essential failure of protest. An analysis of the politics involved strongly suggests that protest is best understood by concentrating on problems of managing diverse protest constituencies.

It may be, therefore, that Saul Alinsky is on soundest ground when he recommends protest as a tactic to build an organization, which can then command its own power. Protest also may be recommended to increase or change the political consciousness of people, or to gain short-run goals in a potentially sympathetic political environment. This may be the most significant contribution of the black power movement—the development of group consciousness which provides a more cohesive political base. But ultimately relatively powerless groups cannot rely on the protest process alone to help them obtain long-run goals, or general improvements in conditions. What they need for long-run success are stable political resources—in a word, power. The American political system is theoretically open; but it is closed, for many reasons suggested here, to politically impoverished groups. While politicians continue to affirm the right to dissent or protest within reason, the political process in which protest takes place remains highly restricted.

DEMOCRACY AND MASS SOCIETY

Alexis de Tocqueville's *Democracy in America,* written in 1835, depicted active participation by citizens as the chief bulwark of democracy. De Tocqueville characterized the growth of "voluntary associations" and the accessibility of a fledgling American press "within every man's reach" as the best methods available for effective political participation by even the weakest citizen. Despite these observations, he expressed concern over the perceptible trend toward economic inequality resulting from the rising power of a new political elite—an "aristocracy of manufacturers."

De Tocqueville saw that mass production might have a debilitating effect on the capacity for political participation by the working class. As the task of the worker became ever more narrow and specialized, the worker became increasingly proficient at performing his one small and repetitive part of the production process. This added to the efficiency of mass production and to the profits of the manufacturing class. At the same time, it rendered the worker ever more dependent upon his job and his place of work. In de Tocqueville's words, "in the midst of universal movement it has rendered him stationary." The fragmented production process alienated the worker from his work and from the products of his labor and also deadened the critical faculties so necessary for effective political participation.

Unlike the worker, the manufacturer's faculties and his capacity to influence political life tended to expand in proportion as his interests surveyed a "more extensive whole." In contrast to the old aristocracy, the manufacturing elite lived apart from their men. They lacked any sense of obligation to the worker or to the community at large. De Tocqueville predicted that if workers did not yield a sufficient profit, the new aristocracy would cast them aside "to be supported by the charity of the public." Thus, the masses who worked would become alienated from their work and from the political process. Those who did not, the multitude of "wretchedly poor," would be even more powerless and more estranged, having "few means of escaping from their position."

The five articles that conclude this book deal with key contemporary implications of de Tocqueville's vision of democracy in mass society. We have already seen that de Tocqueville's "voluntary associations" have given way to bureaucratized private-interest groups. His confidence in a decentralized press accessible to the politically weak also has little place in the contemporary American context where the media of mass communication have become increasingly centralized, concentrated, and inaccessible to the average citizen. This tendency has important implications for democratic theory and practice.

Any group seeking a reordering of our national priorities or a fundamental social change confronts the significant obstacle of obtaining access to the mass media to present its policy positions. In an age of instant communications, access to the "soapbox," the mimeograph machine, or the neighborhood newspaper no longer provides a meaningful opportunity to persuade the public of the wisdom of one's political position. Full access to the mass media by people of all political persuasions is the only means by which a weak political minority can hope to mobilize political support on an issue and overcome the conservative impact of organized private power. This is especially difficult in view of the increasing concentration of ownership of the media, its pervasive commercialization, and the instant access given to public officials already in power. The first selection in Part Eight, Jerome A. Barron's "An Emerging First Amendment Right of Access to the Media?" discusses the prospects for opening up radio and television to a wider diversity of political ideas and values. In theory, the "fairness" doctrine requires the communications industry "to afford reasonable opportunity for the discussion of conflicting views." In practice, this regulation has discouraged radio and television stations from devoting significant portions of their programming to the discussion of any controversial issues. More vigorous regulation by the Federal Communications Commission might combat this persistent evasion of the spirit of the "fairness" doctrine. As we have already seen, however, vigilant regulation by public authority has become increasingly difficult. The low public visibility of the regulatory decision-making process, the growth of private power, and the cultural inhibitions against the use of public power have conspired in the development of a tendency toward mutual cooperation between regulator and regulated. If left unchecked, this trend will pose serious obstacles to effective citizen participation in the political life of mass society.

Alexis de Tocqueville's vision of democracy in mass society was considerably closer to the mark when he predicted that America's growing economic inequality undermined constitutional guarantees of political equality. The technological changes and the mass production process unleashed by de Tocqueville's "manufacturing aristocracy" have dramatically altered the social structure, raising the standard of living for many Americans, but leaving others poor, unhappy, and alienated. The contemporary American economic system is really three economies in one. The poor are completely left out of the benefits generated by technological change. They live in *preindustrial* conditions, lacking the basic necessities of life and the power even to enter the industrial economy. Blue-collar workers and even many white-collar technocrats are presently participating in an *industrial* economy. As their tasks become increasingly specialized, their intellectual horizons are diminished; they confront the persistent prospect of falling by the wayside if their specialties become technologically obsolete. Only those who have acquired the capacity to adapt easily to new roles and contexts—those who, with de Tocqueville, are in a position to survey the "more extensive whole"—are the full beneficiaries of the *postindustrial* economy of affluence. The two selections that follow deal with the problems of preindustrial poverty and industrial alienation in contemporary America.

In the early 1960s Michael Harrington's book *The Other America* painted a dismal picture of the plight of the "invisible poor." The poor are no longer invisible, but their problems are much the same today as they were a decade ago. In "The Other America Revisited," Harrington indicts American society for callousness in the face of its increased knowledge of
294

the reality of poverty. His essay discusses the vast scope of underemployment in black urban ghettos and the relationship between the humiliating experiences of the subemployed and their resort to urban violence. Although Harrington is encouraged by the growing political activism among the poor, he believes that fundamental economic redistribution can only come about if the poor recruit a majority of the nonpoor into a cohesive new national political coalition. This would require a nearly superhuman effort to overcome the insecurity rampant in the industrial economy and to tap the sense of obligation of the new aristocracy of postindustrial America.

The scope of this task is emphasized by the fact that the most intense opposition to domestic social welfare programs designed to benefit poor people has come from the lower-middle-class white worker. The tragic irony is that the so-called hardhat suffers from many of the same deprivations that affect black people and the poor—political powerlessness, social isolation, and lack of respect. Despite our Jacksonian myths, the technologically marginal worker in contemporary America gets few social benefits and even less respect. In "The Forgotten American," Peter Schrag explores the pervasive alienation found among America's blue- and white-collar working class. He poignantly traces their feelings of anger and frustration to confusion in the face of rapidly changing social standards, estrangement from unresponsive public and private bureaucracies, and frustrated aspirations for upward mobility. He then analyzes the possibilities of left- and right-wing populistic revolt by the forgotten American.

The third and foremost obstacle to a reordering of national priorities in order to respond to human needs is the fact that the national economy is linked very closely to public spending for national defense. Despite the scope and importance of the problems of poverty and alienation in our three-tiered economy, the largest single output of the American political system remains the massive annual appropriation for national defense. Since the Korean War, annual military expenditures have consistently amounted to between 7 and 10 percent of the nation's entire Gross National Product. In the fourth selection, "The Price of War," Bruce M. Russett asks the question, "Who pays for defense?" He finds that the segment of society most heavily burdened by rises in defense expenditures is the individual consumer. Despite the rhetoric of "guns and butter," personal consumption drops sharply as taxes to pay for defense spending rise. Other key casualties of increases in military expenditures are public expenditures for welfare, education, and health, especially at the state and local levels of government. The impact of defense spending is even greater than Russett's findings suggest, because his study only measures the effect of military spending on already existing programs. To these must be added the lack of spending for programs designed to meet emerging needs. Mass transportation and financial aid to the decaying cities are good examples.

What, then, is to be done to reorder national priorities? If we take seriously Peter Odegard's warning, expressed at the beginning of this volume, in "The Alienation of Political Science," public expenditures have grown so massively in the realm of national defense precisely because private power holders have limited the use of public power in the domestic arena to that of an umpire among contending private power systems. Unlike domestic expenditures for programs to feed the hungry and house the poor, defense expenditures do not generate goods and services that compete with private markets. Indeed, such expenditures actually serve to undergird the market economy by generating defense contracts that produce jobs. Thus, trade union leaders whose members work in defense industries provide support for increased defense expenditures as a dependable means to job security in a rapidly changing technological environment. If measured by its share of public expenditures, the coalition consisting of the defense industry, organized labor, and the military doubtless represents the most politically potent interest group in American politics today.

The final selection in this book was written by Harold Lasswell in 1941. It is intended as a prophetic vision of where we may be heading as a nation if we are unable to build a viable peacetime political economy. In "The Garrison State," Lasswell predicted the development of a world of superstates, each dominated by an elite of specialists on war and violence. His essay analyzes the prospects for the survival of democratic societies in the face of the growing influence of military modes of organization and behavior in realms once thought to be strictly civilian. The skills of the emerging elite are not those of the traditional soldier—strength, boldness, and charisma. Rather they are the technological skills of the managers of large scale organizations—expertise, symbolic manipulation, and efficient administration. The elite seeks to boost morale by improving the economic conditions of all but the technologically unskilled lower social strata. In return they expect docile acceptance of their vision of the political future. Lasswell's theory should serve as a warning to those who see little to lose in the decline of active political participation by the individual citizen. The obstacles are great, but de Tocqueville's ideal of an informed and active citizenry may still be the best safeguard against the development of a world oligarchy of managers who manipulate the symbol of "external threat" to undergird an economy that ignores the poor and the technologically obsolete.

An Emerging First Amendment Right of Access to the Media?

31

Jerome A. Barron

... The relationship of the "fairness" and "equal time" concepts to the first amendment objective of the widest possible dissemination of controversial ideas has been insufficiently appreciated. The merit of programming standards should not depend upon whether radio is no longer a limited access medium or whether television still is. Diversity of ideas, not multiplicity of forums, is the primary objective of the first amendment. To be sure, it is hoped that a greater number of forums will create a more diverse opinion process. A flick of the radio dial should be sufficient to dispel that illusion, however. Since the sameness of programming has come to be the dominant characteristic of American radio, the mere abundance of radio stations should not be sufficient for first amendment compliance. An abundance of radio stations no more guarantees diversity of opinion than the scarcity of television stations assures one-sidedness.

A positive approach to free expression in broadcasting requires less new legal architecture than is the case with the printed media. Some affirmative obligations already exist—for example, the "equal time rule" and the "fairness" doctrine, both found in section 315 of the Federal Communications Act. To be sure, since their inception these efforts to assure debate have been unceasingly attacked by the industry and their allies in the press who realize that their own lack of legally imposed responsibility to the communications process stands in direct contrast to the situation in broadcasting. What is needed is not more legislation, but a wider appreciation of the relationship of the section 315 responsibilities to basic first amendment goals. If meaningful interchange of ideas is to be anything but an oratorical term, the constitutional underpinning—the decisiveness of opportunity of access to the public —must be stressed in order to obtain wider industry understanding and cooperation. As it is, the communications industry, by creating in the public's mind an identity between itself and the first amendment, has achieved the public relations triumph of the twentieth century over the eighteenth.

Some background on the development of the "fairness" doctrine is useful in order to understand the controversy which has arisen concerning it and broadcast regulations generally. The language of section 315 defines the basic outline of the doctrine: Broadcast licensees are required "to operate in the public interest and to afford reasonable opportunity for the discussion of conflicting views on issues of public importance." It is instructive to note that the language of the statute itself goes a long way toward the goal of imposing an affirmative duty of access for controversial issues. Of course, it has not been so broadly interpreted. Rather, it has been viewed by the FCC as merely giving statutory force to the "fairness" doctrine. The FCC administratively promulgated the doctrine in 1949, and it imposed upon station licensees an affirmative obligation to provide an opportunity for counter-attack on controversial public issues—assuming, of course, that one side of the controversy has already been presented by the station licensee.

It would seem, however, that a statutory duty "to afford reasonable opportunity for the discussion of conflicting views" is a command to do more than merely provide an opportunity for response once the station has decided to give time to a particular issue. If the statute were administered to require licensees to provide access for significant public issues, one of the most important means for evasion of the "fairness" principle would be weakened. At the present time, dislike of a particular side of an issue or unwillingness to be required to give free time for reply are frequently sufficient reason for a licensee to decide to avoid a particular issue altogether. An access approach to the language of section 315 would make the road to evasion of the fairness doctrine a little steeper. If section 315 were read as a command requiring access for controversial public issues as well as a restatement of the "fairness" principle, then we would have a structure to stimulate access to ideas in broadcasting similar to that advocated above for the press.

In broadcasting, however, access would necessarily have more teeth. The fact that station licenses must be renewed every three years means, at least in theory, that the extent of a licensee's performance in the public interest is evaluated by the FCC when it decides whether to renew the license for another term. If persistent evasion of the principles of access and fairness has been a routine feature of a licensee's programming, then there is no reason why another applicant should not be licensed in its stead. But the remedy need not be that drastic. Informal agency rulings, cease and desist orders, and renewals for one year terms rather than the normal three year term are all milder ways of dealing with the problem of enforcement.

What this illustrates is that the existing structure of broadcast regulation permits an understanding of the problem of access which can be inclusive enough to reach failure to recognize or seek out dominant public issues. These issues, of intense concern to the vitality and stability of the public order, are given minimal attention in broadcasting as a routine matter. The area of race relations is a prime example of an issue where access is not so much denied as underplayed.

The portrayal of the races on the mass media effectively illustrates the defects of an approach to freedom of expression which is entirely concerned with protecting expression only after it has satisfied admission criteria formulated by managers of the mass media with no analysis of how these criteria work. A solution to the problem of access in terms of black-white relationships is more subtle and intractable than merely structuring the law so that if a Negro group seeks a reply to an anti-Negro or anti-civil rights editorial, or wishes space for a political advertisement, the mass media will have an obligation to take it. Moreover, the underrepresentation of the

Negro as a normal citizen on television and in the daily press is more than an access problem. The mass media not unsurprisingly reflect the society which they mirror. It is no accident that one of the most distinguished Negro novels is called the *Invisible Man.* That certainly is the image of the Negro in mass communications. Until recently, the Negro simply did not exist in the world of television advertising, and he is only barely present now. Political and constitutional theorists have speculated over definitions of speech— speech which is protected and speech which is unprotected—but every communication, whatever its primary purpose, also doubles as an idea. Professor Charles Black has explained that commercial advertising itself, with its insistence on acquisitiveness, is an idea from which he at least would like to shield his children. Similarly, the white word of television advertising reflects the idea that normality is white—the reality of twenty million Negroes simply is not visible in mass communications as a matter of routine presentation. It is, of course, true that the Negro is presented, but most often he is presented as a social irritant and disturber of the peace.

How can a more representative presentation of the Negro be secured? Presumably as a response to the death of Martin Luther King and also to deal with the problem of understanding or ignoring the Negro in broadcasting, a questionnaire recently was circulated by FCC Commissioners Kenneth Cox and Nicholas Johnson. This action is extremely instructive in terms of illustrating what can be done under existing authority. The inquiry was directed to broadcasters in a single state, Oklahoma, and asked how many members of minority groups the broadcasters employed in their stations and how much programming they devoted to problems of the Negro community and to problems of race relations generally. Such inquiries have more potential, at least in the long run, than elaborate procedures for governing television or radio during riots. Certainly the dilemma of the electronic media in a time of violence is how to inform the public without inflaming it. But, as noted in the Kerner Commission chapter on mass media, the failure of the mass media is not in riot reporting but in the day-to-day portrayal or non-portrayal of Negro life:

[T]he communications media, ironically, have failed to communicate. They have not communicated to the majority of their audience—which is white—a sense of the degradation, misery, and hopelessness of living in the ghetto. They have not communicated to whites a feeling for the difficulties and frustrations of being a Negro in the United States. They have not shown understanding or appreciation of—and thus, have not communicated—a sense of Negro culture, thought, or history.

The absence of Negro faces and activities from the media has an effect on white audiences as well as black. If what the white American reads in the newspapers or sees on television conditions his expectation of what is ordinary and normal in the larger society, he will neither understand nor accept the black American. By failing to portray the Negro as a matter of routine and in the context of the total society, the news media have, we believe, contributed to the black-white schism in this country.

Commissioners Cox and Johnson have been attacked within the broadcasting industry merely for inquiring into the number of Negro personnel employed by broadcasters and the amount of race-connected programming performed by them in a single state. The industry's attack is based on allegations of restraint upon freedom of expression. But would a requirement that the conventional means of communication give some coverage to the nation's largest racial minority as a part of their day-to-day programming thwart the industry's effort to secure freedom of expression? Of course, the first amendment shields the communications industry and all others from government censorship. But is this in any way inconsistent with requiring the industry as a matter of its internal practice to make some attempt to represent the major social components in our national life, particularly when dialogue between the races is so urgently needed?

The "Fairness" Doctrine and the First Amendment: The Significance of the Constitutional Question

What I have called the public relations triumph, the exploitation of a romantic theory of the first amendment for completely commercial and non-ideological ends, is presently being utilized in a renewed attack on the "fairness" doctrine—particularly the so-called "personal attack" provision. In July 1967 the FCC adopted a provision which requires that when licensees attack the "honesty, character, integrity or like personal qualities" of a person or group, the licensee must furnish a tape or script to whomever is attacked and offer him—free of charge in most cases—air time for reply. The Commission defended its rule on the ground that it embodied the first amendment goal stated in *New York Times v. Sullivan* that "debate on public issues should be uninhibited, robust, and . . . may well include vehement, caustic, and sometimes unpleasantly sharp attacks on government and public officials."

Recently, in the context of the libel field, the Supreme Court in an 8–1 decision has emphasized the wide ranging scope afforded to newspapers to make "unpleasantly sharp attacks." But the Court has yet to focus on the most important aspect of the constitutional principle enunciated in *New York Times v. Sullivan*—that the underlying goal is debate. Affording newspapers relative immunity from libel actions without imposing some obligation that they provide space for reply is not constitutionally encouraged debate but judicially supported monologue or, worse, harangue. The application of the "fairness" principle to the "personal attack" situation in broadcasting is a well considered response to the first amendment goals stated by the Supreme Court and stands in sharp contrast to judicial silence on the affirmative obligation of newspapers to allow their quarry some measure of response.

The FCC's performance in the "fairness" area has always been fairly uneven. One reason is that the broadcasting industry has exhibited a tendency to overreact to the "fairness" principles. Moreover, until quite recently the constitutional position of the "fairness" doctrine really had not received direct judicial consideration. Recently, however, the Court of Appeals for the District of Columbia, in *Red Lion Broadcasting Co. v. FCC,* squarely upheld the constitutionality of the "fairness" doctrine as entirely consistent with the first amendment.

The Supreme Court accepted review in *Red Lion* but deferred decision until resolution of a similar case in the Seventh Circuit that has just recently been decided. In considering the personal attack and political editorial rules issued by the FCC subsequent to *Red Lion,* which presented issues similar to those in *Red Lion,* the Seventh Circuit disagreed with the District of Columbia Circuit. Although it did not consider the constitutionality of the "fairness" doctrine, the court held that "In view of the vagueness of the Commission's rules, the burden they impose on licensees, and the possibility they raise of both Commission censorship and licensee self-censorship, we conclude that the personal attack and political editorial rules would contravene the first amendment."

The facts of *Red Lion* are illustrative both of the operation of the "personal attack" aspect of the "fairness" doctrine and of the manner in which the "fairness" doctrine implements debate instead of retarding the objectives of free expression. In November 1964 a Pennsylvania broadcaster carried a program by the Rev. Billy James Hargis, who attacked a book by Fred Cook which had been critical of Barry Goldwater, the Republican candidate for President. Cook requested an opportunity to reply to Hargis, but the radio station said that the "personal attack" aspect of the "fairness" doctrine required it to supply free time for reply only if no paid sponsorship could be found. The station wished Cook to affirm that he could not obtain such sponsorship. Cook complained to the FCC, which replied essentially that the station had the duty to make reply time available, paid or not. The FCC stated that it was not necessary for Cook to show that he could neither afford nor find sponsored time before the station's duty to provide reply time went into effect. The Commission reasoned that the public interest required that the public be given an opportunity to learn the other side and that this duty stood even if the expense of the reply time had to be sustained by the station. A formal order to that effect was entered and the station appealed to the United States court of appeals.

Judge Tamm for the court of appeals pointed out that federal courts have continuously held that regulatory action by the FCC does not violate the first amendment because broadcasting is a limited access medium. He reasoned that fairness does not restrict "free speech" but implements it:

After having independently selected the controversial issue and having selected the spokesman for the presentation of the issue in accord with their unrestricted programming, the Doctrine, rather than limiting the petitioners' right of free speech, recognizes and enforces the free speech right of the victim of any personal attack made during the broadcast.

Judge Tamm approved the FCC's use of the limited access idea to justify fairness by holding that the purpose of the Federal Communications Act is to permit the Government to license frequencies without interfering with free speech—licensing which is, after all, supposed to be in the public interest. However, the irony of allowing such licensees to "themselves make radio unavailable as a medium of free speech" was at last pointed out by a court. Hopefully, this kind of analysis will be extended as a matter of constitutional doctrine to all components of the communications industry. The economic interdependence of the media and the fact that the one or two newspapers which presently exist in our large cities usually also own one of the important radio and television stations in the community give the media enormous power for private censorship. What is necessary is not to point to the lack of a "fairness" principle with regard to the legal responsibilities of newspapers but rather to point to the "fairness" principle as a standard which should have some analogue in the press as well.

Another useful perspective on this problem arises from Judge Tamm's refusal to hold that the "fairness" principle infringes upon the political rights of the people, justifying the Commission's rule that when a licensee has chosen to sponsor a program which presents one side of an issue and has been unable to obtain "paid sponsorship for the appropriate presentations of the contrasting viewpoint or viewpoints, he cannot reject a presentation otherwise suitable to the licensee—and *thus leave the public uninformed*—on the ground that he cannot obtain paid sponsorship for that presentation." Again, for government to require some observance to the informing function of the first amendment seems entirely in order. The broadcasters contended that the "fairness" doctrine operated as a prior restraint, *i.e.*, that they were forced to become the "first censors" of all public interest broadcasting because if a licensee might have to broadcast an opposing view, indeed give free time to it, it might not broadcast the particular matter at all. Judge Tamm rejected this argument:

I do not find in the operation of the Fairness Doctrine any restriction upon the rights of the people to engage in political activities. . . . Broadcasters alone determine the programs they will carry, the format to be followed, and the personnel to be utilized in these broadcasts.

Moreover, he pointed out that no broadcast material is required to be first submitted to the FCC, and that the licensees' latitude "in the selection of program material, program substance, and identity of program personnel is bounded only by their own determination of the public interest of their end product." To the spectre the industry is fond of raising that the FCC's disapproval of a licensee's responsiveness to the "fairness" doctrine may result in loss of the license at renewal time, Judge Tamm observed that the Commission had made it clear that no sanction would be invoked "against any broadcaster for an honest mistake in judgment."

Judge Tamm has taken what may be called a "problem-solving" approach to constitutional law and the first amendment; he has given some consideration to making the first amendment work, to analyzing its practice as well as stating its theory. He concluded:

there is no abrogation of the petitioners' free speech right. On the contrary, I find that the conduct of the petitioners absent the remedial procedures afforded the complainant Cook would, in fact, constitute a serious abridgment of his free speech rights. I find in the Fairness Doctrine a vehicle completely legal in its origin which implements by the use of modern technology the "free and general discussion of public matters [which] seems absolutely essential to prepare the people for an intelligent exercise of their rights as citizens."

The *Red Lion* determination that the duty of the broadcaster to furnish an unpaid reply to a personal attack was not violative of the first amendment is an important step in the evolution of a constitutional theory that will be sensitive to the unanticipated power which the marriage of technology and capital has placed in the relatively few hands which dominate mass communications. *Red Lion* suggests the method by which to build a constitutionally rooted opinion-making structure. If the Supreme Court affirms *Red Lion,* it will augur well for the beginnings of a first amendment theory which will have contemporary relevance. Otherwise the prospects for constructing a public forum model, within the context of privately owned mass media, will be quite dim. And so, ironically, will be the entire future of private broadcasting. Oddly enough, the ultimate role of public television is to a considerable extent contingent upon whether private broadcasting legally can be required to assume some measure of public and social responsibility. Perhaps when *Red Lion* is finally reviewed by the Supreme Court the centrality of the concept of access to the problem of protecting freedom of expression will be considered. The presentation of such an issue could not help but expose the incomplete nature of the present law in the area where the law of libel and the first amendment intersect. Hopefully, the Court will reflect on the new reading of section 315 suggested earlier insofar as it reveals the necessity to promote access for ideas as well as protection of ideas once they have been admitted to the forum.

In conclusion, *Red Lion* is a critical case in many ways. The importance the broadcasting industry attaches to the case is illustrated by the substantial briefs amici curiae filed by the major networks in support of the station and against the "fairness" doctrine. The case may settle the future of program regulation generally, not merely for public issue programming. At the least, it raises the question of whether the first amendment should receive a different interpretation when the new mass media, radio and television, rather than the press, are involved. Another and broader approach would be to review the impact of the new technology on all the media when viewed against a background of economic combinations continuously concentrating the ownership of the media. Such a review by the Supreme Court might result in an urgently needed inquiry into whether traditional first amendment theory should be rethought so that it can meet the challenge posed by the alliance of modern capital and technology.

The previous defense of "fairness" is undertaken without being unmindful of the problems in the enforcement of the "fairness" doctrine. Of course these problems exist, but seen from a constitutional perspective, many of these difficulties are soluble. Recently a group attacked the free use of broadcast time to advertise the Peace Corps. Should this and similar problems be solved by hunting about for some group opposed to the purposes of the Peace Corps and giving that group free time? Or is it wiser to keep government out of the business of propaganda? For broadcasting to identify with and echo governmentally sponsored positions would be most unfortunate. This is particularly so since the executive branch often holds a single view on a variety of controversial issues and is in a strong position to exert pressure both on the FCC and on the licensed station holders.

The experience of the mass media in totalitarian countries, as well as the experience of French television in a presumably democratic country, illustrates the dangers to free discussion of controversial issues inherent in a close connection between the media and government. An illustration of this danger is provided by a recent case in which a student newspaper editor at a state university refused to follow a college rule that the paper could print praise of the state government but not criticism. The college expelled the editor. A federal court reinstated him, and the case is now on appeal. There is an important and fundamental difference—a difference which must be stressed —between a positive role for the first amendment which is achieved through a governmentally sponsored *process* for stimulating the interchange of ideas and a positive role for the first amendment in which the government contributes substantively to the information process in any institutionalized way. If the new experiment in public television can be sufficiently separated from direct political pressures so that it is a governmentally sponsored structure for infusing a new and non-commercial approach to programming, it will be successful. But at all costs broadcasting, whether private or public, must be prevented from becoming a mere conduit for the views espoused by the particular political administration in power.

"Equal Time" and the McCarthy Case: A Problem of Access

Reference to another recent case illustrates both the limitations of the present approach to the affirmative obligations of broadcasting and at the same time indicates that the constitutional dimension of the problem is at last being dimly perceived. The case, *McCarthy v. FCC,* involves the request of Senator Eugene McCarthy for "equal time" to answer the hour-long interview of President Johnson carried by the three major television networks on December 19, 1967. Senator McCarthy contended that President Johnson was a "legally qualified candidate" within the meaning of section 315 of the Communications Act. The FCC denied the Senator's request on the ground that section 315 only applies to legally qualified persons who, among other things, had previously announced their candidacies, and that Lyndon Johnson had not announced his candidacy. As it turned out the FCC was a reasonably good prophet, but at the time it did not seem so. Moreover, the FCC refused even to give Senator McCarthy a chance to show that President Johnson was acting as a candidate in fact. But suppose an incumbent President did not announce his candidacy until his party's national convention? Would section 315 be unavailable to provide "equal time" for announced candidates in the President's party to answer the incumbent President's "non-political" speeches? What of the opposition candidates? Is it not difficult to think of a more efficient way to maximize the already significant institutional aura of an incumbent President and to further minimize the chances for unseating him?

The court of appeals did give a little encouragement to those who think that political change can be achieved through conventional means of communications, however. The court indicated that the question of the right to "equal time" is a sensitive problem which requires more than a simple-minded inquiry into whether the previous speaker is an "announced" candidate. The court therefore suggested that the approach to the problem could not be mechanical. Moreover, the court provided some guide to a definition: "program content, and perhaps other criteria, may provide a guide to reality where a public figure allowed television or radio time has not announced for public office."

But the court nevertheless declared, in an understatement which is perhaps a disservice to the gravity of the problem, that "no rule in this sensitive area can be applied mechanically without, in some instances at least, resulting in unfairness and possible constitutional implications." This use of governmentally licensed facilities to aid an incumbent President suggests a kind of media-government alliance or implicit endorsement which seems contrary to the basic purposes of the first amendment. If the central meaning of the first amendment is to allow criticism of government, as some have said, then unimpeded praise of the government would itself seem to present a first amendment violation. But the constitutional dimension of the problem of access to the major communications media is just beginning to be understood.

Conclusion

It would be misleading to ask what the affirmative role of government should be in implementation of first amendment goals if that suggests that the halo which private managers of the media have long assumed is now, somewhat threadbare, to be placed intact on government. What must be emphasized is the positive dimension of the first amendment: The first amendment must be read to require opportunity for expression as well as protection for expression once secured. Provision of opportunity for expression is, under an affirmative approach to the first amendment, the responsibility of both governmentally controlled as well as privately controlled means of communication. No illusions are entertained about government power as compared with private power. The need is to build counter-balances into each sector to stimulate them to develop a responsiveness to the longing for an information process which is truly participatory. Moreover, any dichotomy which suggests that government is the ally or that private power is the enemy, or vice versa, of contemporary civil liberties is overly simplistic, particularly when the determination of what is public and what is private becomes an increasingly difficult task.

In the area of communications we are on the verge of a more comprehensive and sensitive idea of what freedom of expression should mean in a technological age. The rise of an affirmative approach in broadcasting indicates that the eighteenth century associations which still insulate the press are not present in broadcasting, making possible a more realistic appraisal of the electronic media. But there is a need for such an appraisal of other forums as well—forums such as the press and public facilities, whose capacities for censorship have received little attention until recently. Similarly, attempts to identify procedures created to assure debate with the suppression of ideas must be understood for what they are: the unreflecting use of hallowed symbols for purposes which are antithetical to debate and discussion.

The Other America Revisited

32

Michael Harrington

The Other America was published in March, 1962. Now . . . the condition that book described is objectively not quite as evil as it was; politically and morally, it is worse than ever. For despite a long, federally induced boom and an "unconditional" war on poverty, tens of millions of Americans still live in a social underworld and an even larger number are only one recession, one illness, one accident removed from it.

Ironically, perhaps the most dramatic single breakthrough of the government's anti-poverty effort is the increase in our official knowledge of the needless suffering that we tolerate. President Johnson's program did not achieve full employment for all nor provide impoverished children and aging people with an income but it did generate a tremendous amount of research, seminars, discussions, and even mass-media reports. So, since the poor have become less invisible, for we know they are there, the society has become even more guilty; now it knows its callousness.

Revisiting the other America in 1969 is easier than going there in the late fifties and early sixties. Now Washington has produced some revealing maps of misery. In general, the official figures show some progress in eliminating poverty, but the accomplishment is so modest that one economic downturn would annul it—and the powerful voices urging a calculated increase in unemployment so that the price stability of the affluent can be protected would bring just such a downturn. Even if that does not come to pass, there is a disturbing potential in the other America of 1969 that particularly menaces both the young and the black poor. In looking at these trends statistically, one must remember that, even though the definitions and the percentages are much more precise than in 1962, there is an enormous margin of error which usually favors understatement and over-optimism. Not very long ago, the government triumphantly announced that there had been a major decrease in deteriorated housing. Then in the summer of 1967 it turned out that the gains had actually been negligible or even nonexistent; and in the 1968 Report of the Council of Economic Advisers the Administration admitted that housing deterioration in big-city slums had actually increased. These inaccuracies were not the result of a conscious attempt to delude. They were honest mistakes—but they were often seized upon by those who want to minimize the problem of poverty in America.

More generally there is a real invisibility of the poor. The Bureau of the Census has only recently discovered that it had not counted a significant minority of the adult Negro males in the ghetto. Some years before this acknowledgment, Bayard Rustin had told me that there were more blacks in

America than the government figured. He pointed out that there were special problems in a place like Harlem—for instance, people doubling-up in apartments, a fair number of individuals who feared any contact with The Man, even with the census-taker—which could lead the professionals to err. I thought that Rustin had created an amateur's fantasy until the hard data began to come in (for instance, the 1967 Manpower Report of the Department of Labor found an "undercount" of twenty per cent of the adult men in the slums). This means that there are several million Americans whose conditions of life are so mercurial that they do not even qualify to be a statistic.

With this understanding that the government's numbers are too sanguine, we should take a closer look at them. One of the most imaginative students of the "poverty line" is Mollie Orshansky of the Department of Health, Education, and Welfare. . . . She takes the Department of Agriculture's low-cost diet plan ($5.90 a week for a four-person family in January, 1964) and the "economy" plan (for "temporary or emergency use when funds are low" at $4.60 a week, or twenty-two cents per meal per person, in January, 1964) and puts them at the center of an imagined budget. Neither diet guarantees adequacy, but if a family falls below them it is certain that they will miss important nutrients.

Miss Orshansky then worked out the rest of the poverty budgets in relation to these food costs. In this way, anyone who falls below the poverty line will have less than a minimum diet for health or, more generally, will have to choose between necessities. (The 1968 Report of the Citizens' Board of Inquiry into Hunger and Malnutrition in the United States concluded that "malnutrition among the poor has risen sharply over the past decade.") Using the Orshansky approach, the Social Security Administration came up with a figure of $3,130 for an urban family of four as the upper limit of impoverishment.

By 1966, the poverty line had risen to $3,335. (While this index went up by nine per cent, the average income of four-person families in America had increased by thirty-seven per cent, so the new criterion meant that the poor had even less of a share of affluence.) As a result, 17.8 per cent of the people were under the line in 1966 as compared to twenty-four per cent in 1959. This statistic allows the celebrators of America to claim that the other America is disappearing at a reasonable rate. It is that claim which I want to challenge here.

. . .

. . . The poverty line, is, after all, an artificial, if extremely useful, construct. Miss Orshansky herself has pointed out that millions hover just above the definition (Daniel Patrick Moynihan calls them the "at risk" population). In 1966, there were more than three million families with incomes between $3,000 and $4,000; most of them were not officially classified as poor but all of them were in danger of becoming so with one bad break in the national economy or in their private lives.

Indeed, as Robert C. Wood . . . has pointed out, the "average" American who works and earns between $5,000 and $10,000 a year "owes plenty in installment debts on his car and appliances. He finds his tax burden heavy, his neighborhood services poor, his national image tarnished, and his political clout diminishing. This, too, is alienation." And the Bureau of Labor Statistics said that, in late 1966, it took $9,191 a year for a four-person urban family to maintain a "moderate standard of living." If life for the organized, theoretically well-paid working class is still this precarious, one is probably justified in including as well all Americans in 1969 with family incomes (for four, in a city) of less than $5,000 within the magnetic field of poverty. This has explosive implications if the proposal of the top corporate executives to "trade off" an unemployment increase for an inflation decrease are put into action. It also means that the ambiance, if not the precise dimensions, of the other America has changed little since 1962 even though the society has produced unprecedented wealth.

In two particularly tragic cases it is not necessary to speculate about the numbers. The children and the blacks among the poor are worse off than when the war on poverty began. "All told," writes Mollie Orshansky, "even in 1966, after a continued run of prosperity and steadily rising family income, one-fourth of the nation's children were in families living in poverty or hovering just above the poverty line." This fact, of course, has the most disturbing and dangerous implications for the future. On the one hand, poverty more and more becomes a fate because the educational, economic, and social disadvantages of life at the bottom become progressively more damaging; and, on the other hand, the poor still have more children than any other group. Present evidence points to the melancholy conclusion that the twenty-five per cent of the young who are poor, or near-poor, will have large families very much like the ones of which they are now members. If this is true, the current incidence of poverty among children will guarantee that, short of radical political decisions, the next generation in the other America will be even more numerous than this one.

With Negroes, the problem is more a relative position than an absolute increase in indignity, but this is still a politically explosive fact. In 1959 the Social Security Administration fixed the black percentage of the other Americans at twenty-five per cent; by 1966, the proportion had risen to thirty-three per cent. This, of course, still shows that the scandal of poverty actually afflicts more whites than blacks, but it also indicates that discrimination even applies to the rate at which people escape from beneath the poverty line. During these years of prosperity even the worst off of the white Americans have had a special advantage, compared to the Negroes.

It is important to add to this brief survey of the federally certified dimensions of needless economic and social suffering in this country the remarkable "sub-employment" index of the Department of Labor. The index was developed in order to get a more accurate picture of the working—and non-working—lives of people in the slums. Whereas the official definition of unemployment . . . only counts those who are out of work and looking for work, the notion of sub-employment is much more comprehensive. It gives weight to part-time unemployment, to the fact that many people have to toil for poverty wages, to the twenty per cent of the "invisibles" in the slums, and to those who do not look for a job because they are sure they will not find one.

On this basis, the Labor Department discovered sub-employment rates in November, 1966, that ranged from around thirty per cent in the New York ghettos to near fifty per cent in New Orleans. The full significance of this analysis did not become apparent until the winter of 1967 and the report of the National Commission on Civil Disorders. For it was then that the nation learned that the typical rioter was not the least educated, most impoverished, and chronically unemployed citizen of the ghetto. Rather, he was a high-school dropout and a teen-ager and he had worked—but at a menial job. In other words, the frustrations of sub-employment—most particularly of laboring long hard hours without any real hope of advancement—are perhaps more likely to incite a man to violence than the simple despair of having no job at all.

To sum up—by courtesy of the government's card file (and computer tapes) on outrages in this nation—there has been modest progress in the official figures: a drop in the poverty population from twenty-five per cent to around eighteen per cent. Nevertheless, those who crossed the line are still very close to the world of hunger and hovels. There are signs that the present-day children of the poor will become the parents of even poorer children in the immediate future. Black Americans are falling further and further behind the whites. And the sub-employment statistics indicate a depression while the official jobless rates are cited to show that there is full employment.

What of the quality of life among the poor? Here, I think, the reality is more optimistic, but it is very easy to visualize a reversal of the positive trends.

The war on poverty was never more than a skirmish and the provisions for "maximum feasible participation of the poor" were quickly subverted by hysterical mayors. In theory, the country wants the disadvantaged to stand up and fight for their rights as all the immigrant groups did; in practice, we have knocked people down for taking that pious myth seriously. And yet, there has been a significant growth in local insurgency. It was given an impetus, a public legitimacy, by the anti-poverty efforts of recent years. To a degree, then, the other America has become less passive and defeated, more assertive. This is an enormous gain, for it is the psychological precondition for political and economic advance.

In saying this, I do not wish to suggest for a moment that the poor constitute a latter-day proletariat in the socialist sense of the term (a group goaded to solidarity and struggle by the common conditions of working life). Romantics who held such a theory have been shocked by the seemingly low rates of participation in various community elections. The industrial plant, which assembles large groups of people under a single discipline and with similar grievances about wages and working conditions, is very different from a slum. The company and its assembly line provide an institutional spine for union organizers, but in the world of the tenements there is no such unifying experience and people turn upon one another more than they join together. As the President's Crime Commission reported, the main victims of violence by the black poor were the black poor.

Once this crucial point is understood, the militancy of recent years becomes important. In the South, the dramatic struggles of a mass movement in the street have led to the registration of more than a million new black voters. In the ghettos of the North, where the enemies of Negro freedom are more subtle than Governor Wallace and the disintegrative power of poverty more compelling, there have been urban *Jacqueries,* spontaneous, unplanned riots, and the emergence among the ghetto young of a new pride of race. No one knows how deep these organizational efforts go (my impression is that the black militants have still to reach the majority of the black poor in any systematic fashion) and yet there is no doubt that there is more movement and thought and less despairing acceptance of social wrongs.

The Negroes are not alone in their insurgency. In California, some Mexican-Americans have organized economically in unions and exercised powerful political impact during the 1968 Democratic primary. In New York, Puerto Ricans have provided a mass base for unions in hospitals and public employment, and so have Negroes. Throughout the country, there are organizations of mothers on welfare demanding an end to the bureaucratic humiliations that are carefully structured into public assistance in America. And in Appalachia, poor whites have even had some limited success in the struggle against strip mining.

Yet, as I argued at some length in the book *Toward a Democratic Left,* even if these rebellious movements grow in size and cohesion, even if they reach out to a majority of the poor, they will not be able to transform the society by themselves. Therefore the future of activism in the other America depends, in a considerable measure, upon what the non-poor do. This is certainly true if one thinks in terms of the need to create a vast majority coalition, for only such a movement would be capable of initiating the radical changes that are required if poverty is to be abolished in America. Paradoxically, the more fundamental and thoroughgoing an economic and social program, the more heterogeneous and inclusive must its supporters be. This is a truth not always appreciated by some of the sincerely self-righteous on the American Left. Even more immediately, insurgency among the poor is profoundly affected by the movement of the national economy. This leads to some larger generalizations about the dynamic of the other America in 1969.

When the Kennedy Administration began, the poor, with the exception of some Southern Negroes, were largely passive and pessimistic. This was partly a reflection of the daily life of the Eisenhower years: chronic unemployment and recession, official indifference, the invisibility of forty to fifty million people. The blacks made the first breakthrough below the Mason-Dixon line, and under the leadership of Martin Luther King, Jr., a general climate of hope developed. There was even the governmental policy of having the poor participate in the anti-poverty program. The economic and political upswing and the success of the black freedom movement in the South created the base for the beginning of a new spirit in the other America

But, as that spirit expressed itself in various forms of militant protest, a new period began in 1965. The war in Vietnam began to dominate American domestic politics and the thirty billion dollars or more invested annually in that tragedy precluded any serious attempt at an "unconditional" war on poverty. The modest impact of the new economics was felt at the bottom of the American economy but in every way the tax cut was inversely—and perversely—related to need; the rich got the most benefit and profit, the poor the least. So the demands for change did not end. There was a great danger in this situation and it came to the fore in the Wallace campaign of 1968. When the struggle against poverty was part of a broad strategy of domestic economic expansion, white workers and members of the lower middle class had a certain common interest with blacks and the rest of the other America, even if they did not lose their prejudices. But when, because of Vietnam, the fight against want seemed to take on the aspect of a competition between the have-nots and the have-littles for scarce private and public goods, there were backlashers who feared that their own jobs, homes, and public places were being threatened.

. . . If the talk of "trading off" a little unemployment in return for increased price stability becomes more than talk, and joblessness, as a result, rises to five or six per cent, the extremely modest employment gains of our recent efforts would be abolished and the nation would return to the *status quo ante,* or worse. Up to now, when the private sector has hired marginal workers, even with federal inducements, it has done so only because a relatively tight labor market had made it economically feasible to take a few—a very few —risks on the hard-core jobless; the moment the official unemployment rate hits five per cent it will become economically imperative for corporations to fire those men and women.

This would drastically affect the quality of life in the other America. It would deprive the poor of part of their already meager economic resources (the richer a union, or a community organization, the longer it can strike). It would confirm the suspicion, which is never dispelled in the minds of the poor, that the political order of the larger society is systematically rigged against those in it who are the worst off. And most terrible of all, it would teach those who had dared to be hopeful that America was only kidding and that cynicism is the better part of valor. Under such circumstances, a few would become even more militant; the many would sink back into apathy.

Sometimes, when I contemplate this possibility, I think the leaders of the United States have acted as Trotsky said the German Communists did before the rise of Hitler: they have infuriated all classes and won none. The poor were given promises that were not fulfilled, but the rhetoric made many workers and middle-class people fearful that they were being slighted, and the resulting political standoff alienated many of the most idealistic and active among the young. Politically, the entire society moved to the Right, and in the other America the fifth anniversary of the declaration of the war on poverty was a mockery.

. . . Looking back to the other America of 1962, it may be that in the years that have passed since then we have raised up the hopes of the most abused people of this land only in order to knock them down.

The Forgotten American

33

Peter Schrag

"You better pay attention to the son of a bitch before he burns the country down."

There is hardly a language to describe him, or even a set of social statistics. Just names: racist-bigot-redneck-ethnic-Irish-Italian-Pole-Hunkie-Yahoo. The lower middle class. A blank. The man under whose hat lies the great American desert. Who watches the tube, plays the horses, and keeps the niggers out of his union and his neighborhood. Who might vote for Wallace (but didn't). Who cheers when the cops beat up on demonstrators. Who is free, white, and twenty-one, has a job, a home, a family, and is up to his eyeballs in credit. In the guise of the working class—or the American yeoman or John Smith—he was once the hero of the civics book, the man that Andrew Jackson called "the bone and sinew of the country." Now he is "the forgotten man," perhaps the most alienated person in America.

Nothing quite fits, except perhaps omission and semi-invisibility. America is supposed to be divided between affluence and poverty, between slums and suburbs. John Kenneth Galbraith begins the foreword to *The Affluent Society* with the phrase, "Since I sailed for Switzerland in the early summer of 1955 to begin work on this book. . . ." But *between* slums and suburbs, between Scarsdale and Harlem, between Wellesley and Roxbury, between Shaker Heights and Hough, there are some eighty million people (depending on how you count them) who didn't sail for Switzerland in the summer of 1955, or at any other time, and who never expect to. Between slums and suburbs: South Boston and South San Francisco, Bell and Parma, Astoria and Bay Ridge, Newark, Cicero, Downey, Daly City, Charlestown, Flatbush. Union halls, American Legion posts, neighborhood bars and bowling leagues, the Ukrainian Club and the Holy Name. Main Street. To try to describe all this is like trying to describe America itself. If you look for it, you find it everywhere: the rows of frame houses overlooking the belching steel mills in Bethlehem, Pennsylvania, two-family brick houses in Canarsie (where the most common slogan, even in the middle of a political campaign, is "Curb your dog"); the Fords and Chevies with a decal American flag on the rear window (usually a cut-out from the *Reader's Digest,* and displayed in counter-protest against peaceniks and "those bastards who carry Vietcong flags in demonstrations"); the bunting on the porch rail with the inscription, "Welcome Home, Pete." The gold star in the window.

312

When he was Under Secretary of Housing and Urban Development, Robert C. Wood tried a definition. It is not good, but it's the best we have:

He is a white employed male . . . earning between $5,000 and $10,000. He works regularly, steadily, dependably, wearing a blue collar or white collar. Yet the frontiers of his career expectations have been fixed since he reached the age of thirty-five, when he found that he had too many obligations, too much family, and too few skills to match opportunities with aspirations.

This definition of the "working American" involves almost 23-million American families.

The working American lives in the gray area fringes of a central city or in a close-in or very far-out cheaper suburban subdivision of a large metropolitan area. He is likely to own a home and a car, especially as his income begins to rise. Of those earning between $6,000 and $7,500, 70 percent own their own homes and 94 percent drive their own cars.

94 percent have no education beyond high school and 43 percent have only completed the eighth grade.

He does all the right things, obeys the law, goes to church and insists— usually—that his kids get a better education than he had. But the right things don't seem to be paying off. While he is making more than he ever made— perhaps more than he'd ever dreamed—he's still struggling while a lot of others—"them" (on welfare, in demonstrations, in the ghettos)—are getting most of the attention. "I'm working my ass off," a guy tells you on a stoop in South Boston. "My kids don't have a place to swim, my parks are full of glass, and I'm supposed to bleed for a bunch of people on relief." In New York a man who drives a Post Office trailer truck at night (4:00 P.M. to midnight) and a cab during the day (7:00 A.M. to 2:00 P.M.), and who hustles radios for his Post Office buddies on the side, is ready, as he says, to "knock somebody's ass." "The colored guys work when they feel like it. Sometimes they show up and sometimes they don't. One guy tore up all the time cards. I'd like to see a white guy do that and get away with it."

Nobody knows how many people in America moonlight (half of the eighteen million families in the $5,000 to $10,000 bracket have two or more wage earners) or how many have to hustle on the side. "I don't think anybody has a single job any more," said Nicholas Kisburg, the research director for a Teamsters Union Council in New York. "All the cops are moonlighting, and the teachers; and there's a million guys who are hustling, guys with phony social security numbers who are hiding part of what they make so they don't get kicked out of a housing project, or guys who work as guards at sports events and get free meals that they don't want to pay taxes on. Every one of them is cheating. They are underground people—*Untermenschen*. . . . We really have no systematic data on any of this. We have no ideas of the attitudes of the white worker. (We've been too busy studying the black worker.) And yet he's the source of most of the reaction in this country."

The reaction is directed at almost every visible target: at integration and welfare, taxes and sex education, at the rich and the poor, the foundations and students, at the "smart people in the suburbs." In New York State the legislature cuts the welfare budget; in Los Angeles, the voters reelect Yorty after a whispered racial campaign against the Negro favorite. In Minneapolis a police detective named Charles Stenvig, promising "to take the handcuffs off the police," is elected mayor by a margin stunning even to his supporters: in Massachusetts the voters mail tea bags to their representatives in protest against new taxes, and in state after state legislatures are passing bills to punish student demonstrators. ("We keep talking about permissiveness in training kids," said a Los Angeles labor official, "but we forget that these are our kids.")

And yet all these things are side manifestations of a malaise that lacks a language. Whatever law and order means, for example, to a man who feels his wife is unsafe on the street after dark or in the park at any time, or whose kids get shaken down in the school yard, it also means something like normality—the demand that everybody play it by the book, that cultural and social standards be somehow restored to their civics-book simplicity, that things shouldn't be as they are but as they were supposed to be. If there is a revolution in this country—a revolt in manners, standards of dress and obscenity, and, more important, in our official sense of what America is— there is also a counter-revolt. Sometimes it is inarticulate, and sometimes (perhaps most of the time) people are either too confused or apathetic—or simply too polite and too decent—to declare themselves. In Astoria, Queens, a white working-class district of New York, people who make $7,000 or $8,000 a year (sometimes in two jobs) call themselves affluent, even though the Bureau of Labor Statistics regards an income of less than $9,500 in New York inadequate to a moderate standard of living. And in a similar neighborhood in Brooklyn a truck driver who earns $151 a week tells you he's doing well, living in a two-story frame house separated by a narrow driveway from similar houses, thousands of them in block after block. This year, for the first time, he will go on a cruise—he and his wife and two other couples—two weeks in the Caribbean. He went to work after World War II ($57 a week) and he has lived in the same house for twenty years, accumulating two television sets, wall-to-wall carpeting in a small living room, and a basement that he recently remodeled into a recreation room with the help of two moonlighting firemen. "We get fairly good salaries, and this is a good neighborhood, one of the few good ones left. We have no smoked Irishmen around."

Stability is what counts, stability in job and home and neighborhood, stability in the church and in friends. At night you watch television and sometimes on a weekend you go to a nice place—maybe a downtown hotel —for dinner with another couple. (Or maybe your sister, or maybe bowling, or maybe, if you're defeated, a night at the track.) The wife has the necessary appliances, often still being paid off, and the money you save goes for your daughter's orthodontist, and later for her wedding. The smoked Irishmen— the colored (no one says black; few even say Negro)—represent change and instability, kids who cause trouble in school, who get treatment that your kids never got, that you never got. ("Those fucking kids," they tell you in South Boston, "raising hell, and not one of 'em paying his own way. Their

fucking mothers are all on welfare.") The black kids mean a change in the
rules, a double standard in grades and discipline, and—vaguely—a challenge
to all you believed right. Law and order is the stability and predictability of
established ways. Law and order is equal treatment—in school, in jobs, in the
courts—even if you're cheating a little yourself. The Forgotten Man is Jackson's man. He is the vestigial American democrat of 1840: "They all know
that their success depends upon their own industry and economy and that
they must not expect to become suddenly rich by the fruits of their toil." He
is also Franklin Roosevelt's man—the man whose vote (or whose father's
vote) sustained the New Deal.

There are other considerations, other styles, other problems. A postman
in a Charlestown (Boston) housing project: eight children and a ninth on the
way. Last year, by working overtime, his income went over $7,000. This year,
because he reported it, the Housing Authority is raising his rent from $78
to $106 a month, a catastrophe for a family that pays $2.20 a day for milk,
has never had a vacation, and for which an excursion is "going out for ice
cream." "You try and save for something better; we hope to get out of here
to someplace where the kids can play, where there's no broken glass, and
then something always comes along that knocks you right back. It's like
being at the bottom of the well waiting for a guy to throw you a rope." The
description becomes almost Chaplinesque. Life is humble but not simple; the
terrors of insolent bureaucracies and contemptuous officials produce a
demonology that loses little of its horror for being partly misunderstood. You
want to get a sink fixed but don't want to offend the manager; want to get
an eye operation that may (or may not) have been necessitated by a military
injury five years earlier, "but the Veterans Administration says I signed away
my benefits"; want to complain to someone about the teen-agers who run
around breaking windows and harassing women but get no response either
from the management or the police. "You're afraid to complain because if
they don't get you during the day they'll get you at night." Automobiles,
windows, children, all become hostages to the vague terrors of everyday life;
everything is vulnerable. Liabilities that began long ago cannot possibly be
liquidated: "I never learned anything in that school except how to fight. I got
tired of being caned by the teachers so at sixteen I quit and joined the
Marines. I still don't know anything."

American culture? Wealth is visible, and so, now, is poverty. Both have
become intimidating clichés. But the rest? A vast, complex, and disregarded
world that was once—in belief, and in fact—the American middle: Grey-
hound and Trailways bus terminals in little cities at midnight, each of them
with its neon lights and its cardboard hamburgers; acres of tar-paper beach
bungalows in places like Revere and Rockaway; the hair curlers in the super-
market on Saturday, and the little girls in the communion dresses the next
morning; pinball machines and the *Daily News,* the *Reader's Digest* and Ed
Sullivan; houses with tiny front lawns (or even large ones) adorned with
statues of the Virgin or of Sambo welcomin' de folks home; Clint Eastwood
or Julie Andrews at the Palace; the trotting tracks and the dog tracks—Aurora
Downs, Connaught Park, Roosevelt, Yonkers, Rockingham, and forty others

—where gray men come not for sport and beauty, but to read numbers, to study and dope. (If you win you have figured something, have in a small way controlled your world, have surmounted your impotence. If you lose, bad luck, shit. "I'll break his goddamned head.") Baseball is not the national pastime; racing is. For every man who goes to a major-league baseball game there are four who go to the track and probably four more who go to the candy store or the barbershop to make their bets. (Total track attendance in 1965: 62 million plus another 10 million who went to the dogs.)

There are places, and styles, and attitudes. If there are neighborhoods of aspiration, suburban enclaves for the mobile young executive and the aspiring worker, there are also places of limited expectation and dead-end districts where mobility is finished. But even there you can often find, however vestigial, a sense of place, the roots of old ethnic loyalties, and a passionate, if often futile, battle against intrusion and change. "Everybody around here," you are told, "pays his own way." In this world the problems are not the ABM or air pollution (have they heard of Biafra?) or the international population crisis; the problem is to get your street cleaned, your garbage collected, to get your husband home from Vietnam alive; to negotiate installment payments and to keep the schools orderly. Ask anyone in Scarsdale or Winnetka about the schools and they'll tell you about new programs, or about how many are getting into Harvard, or about the teachers. Ask in Oakland or the North Side of Chicago, and they'll tell you that they have (or haven't) had trouble; somewhere in his gut the man in those communities knows that mobility and choice in this society are limited. He cannot imagine any major change for the better; but he can imagine change for the worse. And yet for a decade he is the one who has been asked to carry the burden of social reform, to integrate his schools and his neighborhood, has been asked by comfortable people to pay the social debts due to the poor and the black. In Boston, in San Francisco, in Chicago (not to mention Newark or Oakland) he has been telling the reformers to go to hell. The Jewish schoolteachers of New York and the Irish parents of Dorchester have asked the same question: "What the hell did Lindsay (or the Beacon Hill Establishment) ever do for us?"

The ambiguities and changes in American life that occupy discussions in university seminars and policy debates in Washington, and that form the backbone of contemporary popular sociology, become increasingly the conditions of trauma and frustration in the middle. Although the New Frontier and Great Society contained some programs for those not already on the rolls of social pathology—federal aid for higher education, for example—the public priorities and the rhetoric contained little. The emphasis, properly, was on the poor, on the inner cities (*e.g.,* Negroes) and the unemployed. But in Chicago a widow with three children who earns $7,000 a year can't get them college loans because she makes too much; the money is reserved for people on relief. New schools are built in the ghetto but not in the white working-class neighborhoods where they are just as dilapidated. In Newark the head of a white vigilante group (now a city councilman) runs, among other things, on a platform opposing pro-Negro discrimination. "When pools are being built in the Central Ward—don't they think white kids have got frustration?

The white can't get a job; we have to hire Negroes first." The middle class, said Congressman Roman Pucinski of Illinois, who represents a lot of it, "is in revolt. Everyone has been generous in supporting anti-poverty. Now the middle-class American is disqualified from most of the programs."

The frustrated middle. The liberal wisdom about welfare, ghettos, student revolt, and Vietnam has only a marginal place, if any, for the values and life of the working man. It flies in the face of most of what he was taught to cherish and respect: hard work, order, authority, self-reliance. He fought, either alone or through labor organizations, to establish the precincts he now considers his own. Union seniority, the civil service bureaucracy, and the petty professionalism established by the merit system in the public schools become sinecures of particular ethnic groups or of those who have learned to negotiate and master the system. A man who worked all his life to accumulate the points and grades and paraphernalia to become an assistant school principal (no matter how silly the requirements) is not likely to relinquish his position with equanimity. Nor is a dock worker whose only estate is his longshoreman's card. The job, the points, the credits become property:

Some men leave their sons money [wrote a union member to the *New York Times*], some large investments, some business connections, and some a profession. I have only one worthwhile thing to give: my trade. I hope to follow a centuries-old tradition and sponsor my sons for an apprenticeship. For this simple father's wish it is said that I discriminate against Negroes. Don't all of us discriminate? Which of us . . . will not choose a son over all others?

Suddenly the rules are changing—all the rules. If you protect your job for your own you may be called a bigot. At the same time it's perfectly acceptable to shout black power and to endorse it. What does it take to be a good American? *Give the black man a position because he is black, not because he necessarily works harder or does the job better.* What does it take to be a good American? Dress nicely, hold a job, be clean-cut, don't judge a man by the color of his skin or the country of his origin. What about the demands of Negroes, the long hair of the students, the dirty movies, the people who burn draft cards and American flags? Do you have to go out in the street with picket signs, do you have to burn the place down to get what you want? What does it take to be a good American? *This is a sick society, a racist society, we are fighting an immoral war.* ("I'm against the Vietnam war, too," says the truck driver in Brooklyn. "I see a good kid come home with half an arm and a leg in a brace up to here, and what's it all for? I was glad to see *my kid* flunk the Army physical. Still, somebody has to say no to these demonstrators and enforce the law.") What does it take to be a good American?

The conditions of trauma and frustration in the middle. What does it take to be a good American? Suddenly there are demands for Italian power and Polish power and Ukrainian power. In Cleveland the Poles demand a seat on the school board, and get it, and in Pittsburgh John Pankuch, the seventy-three-year-old president of the National Slovak Society, demands "action, plenty of it to make up for lost time." Black power is supposed to be nothing but emulation of the ways in which other ethnic groups made it. But have they made it? In Reardon's Bar on East 8th Street in South Boston where the workmen come for their fish-chowder lunch and for their rye and ginger, they still identify themselves as Galway men and Kilkenny men; at the newsstand in Astoria you can buy *Il Progresso, El Tiempo,* the *Staats-Zeitung,* the *Irish World,* plus papers in Greek, Hungarian, and Polish. At the parish of Our Lady of Mount Carmel the priests hear confession in English, Italian, and Spanish and, nearby, the biggest attraction is not the stickball game, but the *bocce* court. Some of the poorest people in America are white, native, and have lived all of their lives in the same place as their fathers and grandfathers. The problems that were presumably solved in some distant past, in that prehistoric era before the textbooks were written—problems of assimilation, of upward mobility—now turn out to be very much unsolved. The melting pot and all: millions made it, millions moved to the affluent suburbs; several million—no one knows how many—did not. The median income in Irish South Boston is $5,100 a year but the community-action workers have a hard time convincing the local citizens that any white man who is not stupid or irresponsible can be poor. Pride still keeps them from applying for income supplements or Medicaid, but it does not keep them from resenting those who do. In Pittsburgh, where the members of Polish-American organizations earn an estimated $5,000 to $6,000 (and some fall below the poverty line), the Poverty Programs are nonetheless directed primarily to Negroes, and almost everywhere the thing called urban backlash associates itself in some fashion with ethnic groups whose members have themselves only a precarious hold on the security of affluence. Almost everywhere in the old cities, tribal neighborhoods and their styles are under assault by masscult. The Italian grocery gives way to the supermarket, the ma-and-pa store and the walk-up are attacked by urban renewal. And almost everywhere, that assault tends to depersonalize and to alienate. It has always been this way, but with time the brave new world that replaces old patterns becomes increasingly bureaucratized, distant, and hard to control.

Yet beyond the problems of ethnic identity, beyond the problems of Poles and Irishmen left behind, there are others more pervasive and more dangerous. For every Greek or Hungarian there are a dozen American-Americans who are past ethnic consciousness and who are as alienated, as confused, and as angry as the rest. The obvious manifestations are the same everywhere—race, taxes, welfare, students—but the threat seems invariably more cultural and psychological than economic or social. What upset the police at the Chicago convention most was not so much the politics of the demonstrators as their manners and their hair. (The barbershops in their neighborhoods don't advertise Beatle Cuts but the Flat Top and the Chicago Box.) The affront comes from middle-class people—and their children—who had been cast in the role of social exemplars (and from those cast as unfortunates worthy of public charity) who offend all the things on which working-class identity is built: "hippies [said a San Francisco longshoreman] who fart around the streets and don't work"; welfare recipients who strike and march for better treatment; "all those [said a California labor official] who challenge the precepts that these people live on." If ethnic groups are beginning to organize to get theirs, so are others: police and firemen ("The cop is the new nigger"); schoolteachers; lower-middle-class housewives fighting sex education and bussing; small property owners who have no ethnic communion but a passionate interest in lower taxes, more policemen, and stiffer penalties for criminals. In San Francisco the Teamsters, who had never been known for such interests before, recently demonstrated in support of the police and law enforcement and, on another occasion, joined a group called Mothers Support Neighborhood Schools at a school-board meeting to oppose—with their presence and later, apparently, with their fists—a proposal to integrate the schools through bussing. ("These people," someone said at the meeting, "do not look like mothers.")

Which is not to say that all is frustration and anger, that anybody is ready "to burn the country down." They are not even ready to elect standard-model demagogues. "A lot of labor people who thought of voting for Wallace were ashamed of themselves when they realized what they were about to do," said Morris Iushewitz, an officer of New York's Central Labor Council. Because of a massive last-minute union campaign, and perhaps for other reasons, the blue-collar vote for Wallace fell far below the figures predicted by the early polls last fall. Any number of people, moreover, who are not doing well by any set of official statistics, who are earning well below the national mean ($8,000 a year), or who hold two jobs to stay above it, think of themselves as affluent, and often use that word. It is almost as if not to be affluent is to be un-American. People who can't use the word tend to be angry; people who come too close to those who can't become frightened. The definition of affluence is generally pinned to what comes in, not the quality of life as it's lived. The $8,000 son of a man who never earned more than $4,500 may, for that reason alone, believe that he's "doing all right." If life is not all right, if he can't get his curbs fixed, or his streets patrolled, if the highways are crowded and the beaches polluted, if the schools are ineffectual, he is still able to call himself affluent, feels, perhaps, a social compulsion to do so. His anger, if he is angry, is not that of the wage earner resenting management—and certainly not that of the socialist ideologue asking for redistribution of wealth—but that of the consumer, the taxpayer, and the family man. (Inflation and taxes are wiping out most of the wage gains made in labor contracts signed during the past three years.) Thus he will vote for a Louise Day Hicks in Boston who promises to hold the color line in the schools or for a Charles Stenvig calling for law enforcement in Minneapolis but reject a George Wallace who seems to threaten his pocketbook. The danger is that he will identify with the politics of the Birchers and other middle-class reactionaries (who often pretend to speak for him) even though his income and style of life are far removed from theirs: that taxes, for example, will be identified with welfare rather than war, and that he will blame his limited means on the small slice of the poor rather than the fat slice of the rich.

If you sit and talk to people like Marjorie Lemlow, who heads Mothers Support Neighborhood Schools in San Francisco, or Joe Owens, a house painter who is president of a community-action organization in Boston, you quickly discover that the roots of reaction and the roots of reform are often identical, and that the response to particular situations is more often contingent on the programs of the politicians and leaders who appear to care than on the conditions of life or the ideology of the victims. Mrs. Lemlow wants to return the schools to some virtuous past; she worries about disintegration of the family and she speaks vaguely about something that she can't bring herself to call a conspiracy against Americanism. She has been accused of leading a bunch of Birchers, and she sometimes talks Birch language. But whatever the form, her sense of things comes from a small-town vision of national virtues and her unhappiness from the assaults of urban sophistication. It just so happens that a lot of reactionaries now sing that tune, and that the liberals are indifferent.

Joe Owens—probably because of his experience as a Head Start parent, and because of his association with an effective community-action program —talks a different language. He knows, somehow, that no simple past can be restored. In his world the villains are not conspirators but bureaucrats and politicians, and he is beginning to discover that in a struggle with officials the black man in the ghetto and the working man (black or white) have the same problems. "Every time you ask for something from the politicians they treat you like a beggar, like you ought to be grateful for what you have. They try to make you feel ashamed."

The imponderables are youth and tradition and change. The civics book and the institution it celebrates—however passé—still hold the world together. The revolt is in their name, not against them. And there is simple decency, the language and practice of the folksy cliché, the small town, the Boy Scout virtues, the neighborhood charity, the obligation to support the church, the rhetoric of open opportunity: "They can keep Wallace and they can keep Alabama. We didn't fight a dictator for four years so we could elect one over here." What happens when all that becomes Mickey Mouse? Is there an urban ethic to replace the values of the small town? Is there a coherent public philosophy, a consistent set of beliefs to replace family, home, and hard work? What happens when the hang-ups of upper-middle-class kids are in fashion and those of blue-collar kids are not? What happens when "do your own thing" becomes not the slogan of the solitary deviant but the norm? Is it possible that as the institutions and beliefs of tradition are fashionably denigrated a blue-collar generation gap will open to the Right as well as to the Left? (There is statistical evidence, for example, that Wallace's greatest support within the unions came from people who are between twenty-one and twenty-nine, those, that is, who have the most tenuous association with the liberalism of labor.) Most are politically silent; although SDS has been trying to organize blue-collar high school students, there are no Mario Savios or Mark Rudds—either of the Right or the Left —among them. At the same time the union leaders, some of them old hands from the Thirties, aren't sure that the kids are following them either. Who speaks for the son of the longshoreman or the Detroit auto worker? What happens if he doesn't get to college? What, indeed, happens when he does?

Vaguely but unmistakably the hopes that a youth-worshipping nation historically invested in its young are becoming threats. We have never been unequivocal about the symbolic patricide of Americanization and upward mobility, but if at one time mobility meant rejection of older (or European) styles it was, at least, done in the name of America. Now the labels are blurred and the objectives indistinct. Just at the moment when a tradition-bound Italian father is persuaded that he should send his sons to college—that education is the only future—the college blows up. At the moment when a parsimonious taxpayer begins to shell out for what he considers an extravagant state university system the students go on strike. Marijuana, sexual liberation, dress style, draft resistance, even the rhetoric of change become monsters and demons in a world that appears to turn old virtues upside down. The paranoia that fastened on Communism twenty years ago (and sometimes still does) is increasingly directed to vague conspiracies undermining the schools, the family, order, and discipline. "They're feeding the kids this generation-gap business," says a Chicago housewife who grinds out a campaign against sex education on a duplicating machine in her living room. "The kids are told to make their own decisions. They're all mixed up by situation ethics and open-ended questions. They're alienating children from their own parents." They? The churches, the schools, even the YMCA and the Girl Scouts, are implicated. But a major share of the villainy is now also attributed to "the social science centers," to the apostles of sensitivity training, and to what one California lady, with some embarrassment, called "nude therapy." "People with sane minds are being altered by psychological methods." The current major campaign of the John Birch Society is not directed against Communists in government or the Supreme Court, but against sex education.

(There is, of course, also sympathy with the young, especially in poorer areas where kids have no place to play. "Everybody's got to have a hobby," a South Boston adolescent told a youth worker. "Ours is throwing rocks." If people will join reactionary organizations to protect their children, they will also support others: community-action agencies which help kids get jobs, Head Start parent groups, Boys Clubs. "Getting this place cleaned up" sometimes refers to a fear of young hoods; sometimes it points to the day when there is a park or a playground or when the existing park can be used. "I want to see them grow up to have a little fun.")

Beneath it all there is a more fundamental ambivalence, not only about the young, but about institutions—the schools, the churches, the Establishment —and about the future itself. In the major cities of the East (though perhaps not in the West) there is a sense that time is against you, that one is living "in one of the few decent neighborhoods left," that "if I can get $125 a week upstate (or downstate) I'll move." The institutions that were supposed to mediate social change and which, more than ever, are becoming priesthoods of information and conglomerates of social engineers, are increasingly suspect. To attack the Ford Foundation (as Wright Patman has done) is not only to fan the embers of historic populism against concentrations of wealth and power, but also to arouse those who feel that they are trapped by an alliance of upper-class WASPs and lower-class Negroes. If the foundations have done anything for the blue-collar worker he doesn't seem to be aware of it. At the same time the distrust of professional educators that characterizes the black militants is becoming increasingly prevalent among a minority of lower-middle-class whites who are beginning to discover that the schools aren't working for them either. ("Are all those new programs just a cover-up for failure?") And if the Catholic Church is under attack from its liberal members (on birth control, for example) it is also alienating traditionalists who liked their minor saints (even if they didn't actually exist) and were perfectly content with the Latin Mass. For the alienated Catholic liberal there are other places to go; for the lower-middle-class parishioner in Chicago or Boston there are none.

Perhaps, in some measure, it has always been this way. Perhaps none of this is new. And perhaps it is also true that the American lower middle has never had it so good. And yet surely there is a difference, and that is that the common man has lost his visibility and, somehow, his claim on public attention. There are old liberals and socialists—men like Michael Harrington —who believe that a new alliance can be forged for progressive social action:

From Marx to Mills, the Left has regarded the middle class as a stratum of hypocritical, vacillating rear-guarders. There was often sound reason for this contempt. But is it not possible that a new class is coming into being? It is not the old middle class of small property owners and entrepreneurs, nor the new middle class of managers. It is composed of scientists, technicians, teachers, and professionals in the public sector of the society. By education and work experience it is predisposed toward planning. It could be an ally of the poor and the organized workers—or their sophisticated enemy. In other words, an unprecedented social and political variable seems to be taking shape in America.

The American worker, even when he waits on a table or holds open a door, is not servile; he does not carry himself like an inferior. The openness, frankness, and democratic manner which Tocqueville described in the last century persists to this very day. They have been a source of rudeness, contemptuous ignorance, violence—and of a creative self-confidence among great masses of people. It was in this latter spirit that the CIO was organized and the black freedom movement marched.

There are recent indications that the white lower-middle class is coming back on the roster of public priorities. Pucinski tells you that liberals in Congress are privately discussing the pressure from the middle class. There are proposals now to increase personal income-tax exemptions from $600 to $1000 (or $1,200) for each dependent, to protect all Americans with a national insurance system covering catastrophic medical expenses, and to put a floor under all incomes. Yet these things by themselves are insufficient. Nothing is sufficient without a national sense of restoration. What Pucinski means by the middle class has, in some measure, always been represented. A physician earning $75,000 a year is also a working man but he is hardly a victim of the welfare system. Nor, by and large, are the stockholders of the Standard Oil Company or U.S. Steel. The fact that American ideals have often been corrupted in the cause of self-aggrandizement does not make them any less important for the cause of social reform and justice. "As a movement with the conviction that there is more for people than greed and fear," Harrington said, "the Left must . . . also speak in the name of the historic idealism of the United States."

The issue, finally, is not *the program* but the vision, the angle of view. A huge constituency may be coming up for grabs, and there is considerable evidence that its political mobility is more sensitive than anyone can imagine, that all the sociological determinants are not as significant as the simple facts of concern and leadership. When Robert Kennedy was killed last year, thousands of working-class people who had expected to vote for him—if not hundreds of thousands—shifted their loyalties to Wallace. A man who can change from a progressive democrat into a bigot overnight deserves attention.

The
Price
of War

34

Bruce M. Russett

"Peace" stocks are up; "war" stocks are down; congressmen scrutinize Pentagon expenditures with newly-jaundiced eyes. Any (New Left) schoolboy can rattle off a list of the top ten defense contractors: General Electric, Boeing, General Dynamics, North American Aviation. . . . Scholars and journalists have worked hard lately, and now almost everyone knows who *profits* from defense spending. But who knows who *pays* for it?

Nothing comes free, and national defense is no exception. Yet curiously little attention has been paid to the question of which segments of American society and its economy are disproportionately sacrificed when defense spending rises. Despite some popular opinion to the contrary, our economy is a good deal less than infinitely expansible. Something has to give when military expenditures take larger bites out of the pie. But when this happens, what kinds of public and private expenditures are curtailed or fail to grow at previously established rates? What particular interests or pressure groups show up as relatively strong or relatively weak in maintaining their accustomed standards of living? And which of them are better able to seize the opportunities offered when international conflict cools off for a while?

The questions, of course, are implicitly political, and they are important. But the answers have to be sought within economic data. What we want, in a sense, is a "cost-benefit" analysis of war or the preparations for war, an analysis that will tell us not only who most profits from war, but who most bears its burden. Apart from the direct costs in taxation and changes in wages and prices, which I will not go into here, there are the equally significant costs in social benefits, in opportunities foregone or opportunities postponed.

What I want to do here is to examine *expenditures*—by categories of the Gross National Product, by their function and by governmental unit—to see what kinds of alternative spending suffer under the impact of heavy military spending. The necessary data are available for the period 1939–1968, and they allow us to see the effects of two earlier wars (World War II and the Korean War) as well as the burdens of the current Vietnam venture.

First, however, an overview of the changing level of defense expenditures may be helpful. For 1939, in what was in many ways the last peacetime year this nation experienced, defense expenditures were under $1.3 billion. With the coming of war they rose rapidly to a still unsurpassed peak of $87.4 billion in 1944. The 1968 figure was by contrast around $78.4 billion, reflecting a build-up, for the Vietnam war, from levels of about $50 billion in the first half of this decade. The raw dollar figures, however, are deceptive because they reflect neither inflation nor the steady growth in the economy's productive capacity that makes a constant defense budget, even in price-adjusted dollars, a diminishing burden.

The graph shows the trend of military expenditures as a percentage of Gross National Product over the past thirty years.

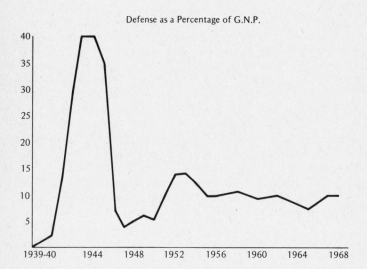

Defense as a Percentage of G.N.P.

We immediately see the great burdens of World War II, followed by a drop to a floor considerably above that of the 1930's. The Cold War and particularly the Korean action produced another upsurge in the early 1950's to a level that, while substantial, was by no means the equal of that in the Second World War. This too trailed downward after the immediate emergency was past, though again it did not retreat to the previous floor. In fact, not since the beginning of the Cold War has the military accounted for noticeably less than 5 percent of this country's G.N.P.; not since Korea has it had as little as 7 percent.

This repeated failure to shrink the military establishment back to its prewar level is a phenomenon of some interest to students of the dynamics of international arms races and/or Parkinson's Law. It shows up even more clearly in the data on military personnel, and goes back almost a century to demonstrate the virtual doubling of the armed forces after every war. From 1871 to 1898 the American armed forces numbered fewer than 50,000; after the Spanish-American War they never again dropped below 100,000. The aftermath of World War I saw a leveling off to about 250,000, but the World War II mobilization left 1,400,000 as the apparent permanent floor. Since the Korean War the United States military establishment has never numbered fewer than about 2,500,000 men. Should the post-Vietnam armed forces and/or defense portion of the G.N.P. prove to be higher than in the early and mid-1960's, that will represent another diversion from private or civil public resources and a major indirect but perhaps very real "cost" of the war.

Returning to the graph, we see the effect of the Vietnam build-up, moving from a recent low of 7.3 percent in 1965 to 9.2 percent in 1968. This last looks modest enough, and is, when compared to the effects of the nation's two previous major wars. At the same time, it also represents a real sacrifice by other portions of the economy. The 1968 G.N.P. of the United States was well in excess of $800 billion; if we were to assume that the current war effort accounts for about 2 percent of that (roughly the difference between the 7.3 percent of 1965 and the 9.2 percent of 1968) the dollar amount is approximately $16 billion. That is in fact too low a figure, since some billions were already being devoted to the war in 1965, and direct estimates of the war's cost are typically about $25 to $30 billion per year. The amounts in question, representing scarce resources which might be put to alternative uses, are not trivial.

I assume that defense spending has to come *at the expense* of something else. In the formal sense of G.N.P. proportions that is surely true, but it is usually true in a more interesting sense as well. Economics is said to be the study of the allocation of scarce resources; and, despite some periods of slack at the beginning of war-time periods (1940–41 and 1950), resources have generally been truly scarce during America's wars. Major civilian expenditures have not only lost ground proportionately (as would nevertheless happen from a military spending program financed entirely out of slack) but they have also failed to grow at their accustomed rates, they have lost ground in constant dollars as a result of inflation, or they have even declined absolutely in current dollars. During World War II, for example, such major categories as personal consumption of durable goods, all fixed investment, federal purchases of nonmilitary goods and services, and state and local expenditures all declined sharply in absolute dollar amounts despite an inflation of nearly 8 percent a year.

Some observers argue that high levels of military spending are introduced to take up the slack and maintain demand in an otherwise depression-prone economy. If this were the case, opportunity costs would be minimal. But there is little evidence for that proposition in the American experience of recent decades. Certainly the Vietnam experience does not support it. I assume, *pace* "Iron Mountain," that with the demonstrable public and private needs of this society, and with modern tools of economic analysis and manipulation, full or near-full employment of resources would be maintained even in the face of major cuts in military spending. Because of the skill with which economic systems are now managed in modern economies, defense expenditures are much more likely to force trade-offs than they were some thirty years ago. Hence the point of my original question, "Who pays for defense?"

I do not argue that defense expenditures are necessarily without broader social utility. Spending for military research and development produces important (if sometimes overrated) technological spill-overs into the civilian sector. The education, skills and physical conditioning that young men obtain during service in the armed forces are likely to benefit them and their society when they return to civilian life. Nevertheless the achievement of such benefits through spill-overs is rarely the most efficient way to obtain them. While scientific research may be serendipitous, the odds are far better that a new treatment for cancer will come from medical research than from work on missile systems. Therefore we must still consider as real costs the trade-offs that appear when defense cuts deep into the G.N.P., though they are not quite so heavy as a literal interpretation of the dollar amounts would imply.

One must also recognize that some civilian expenditures—for health, for education and for research—have been stimulated by Cold War and ultimately military requirements. Such were various programs of the 1950's, when a greater need was felt for a long-run girding of the loins than for more immediate military capabilities. Still, to concede this is far from undercutting the relevance of the kind of question we shall be asking. If civilian and military expenditures consistently compete for scarce resources, then the one will have a negative effect on the other; if both are driven by the same demands, they will be positively correlated. If they generally compete but are sometimes viewed as complementary, the negative correlation will be fairly low.

An evaluation of the relationship of defense and alternative kinds of spending in this country requires some explicit criteria. There is room for serious argument about what those criteria should be, but I will suggest the following:

(1) It is bad to sacrifice future productivity and resources for current preparation for war or war itself; insofar as possible such activities should be financed out of current consumption. Such an assumption might be easily challenged if it were offered as a universal, but for the developed countries of North America and Western Europe in recent years it seems defensible. All of them are now, relative to their own past and to other nations' present, extremely affluent, with a high proportion of their resources flowing into consumption in the private sector. Furthermore, for most of the years 1938–1968, the demands of defense have not been terribly great. Since the end of World War II, none of these countries has had to devote more than about 10 percent of its G.N.P. to military needs, save for the United States during the Korean War when the figure rose to just over 13 percent. It is surely arguable that such needs rarely require substantial mortgaging of a nation's future.

(a) By this criterion one would hope to see periodic upswings in defense requirements financed largely out of personal consumption, with capital formation and such social investment in the public sector as health and education being insensitive to military demands.

(b) Another aspect of this criterion, however, is that one would also anticipate that in periods of *declining* military needs the released resources would largely be *kept* for investment and education rather than returned to private consumption. In a strong form the criterion calls for a long-term increase in the proportion of G.N.P. devoted to various forms of investment, an increase that would show up on a graph as a fluctuating line made up of a series of upward slopes followed by plateaus, insensitive to rising defense needs but responsive to the opportunities provided by relaxations in the armament pace.

(2) Another point of view, partially in conflict with the last comment, would stress the need for a high degree of *insulation from political shocks*. A constant and enlarging commitment to the system's social resources is necessary for the most orderly and efficient growth of the system, avoiding the digestive problems produced by alternate feast and famine. Some spending, on capital expenditures for buildings for instance, may be only temporarily postponed in periods of fiscal stringency, and may bounce back to a higher level when the pressure of defense needs is eased. To that degree the damage would be reduced, but not eliminated. In the first place, school construction that is "merely" postponed four years will come in time to help some students, but for four years a great many students simply lose out. Secondly, boom and bust fluctuations, even if they do average out to the socially-desired dollar level, are likely to be inefficient and produce less real output than would a steadier effort.

Guns, Butter and Structures

Calculation of a nation's G.N.P. is an exercise in accounting; economists define the Gross National Product as the sum of expenditures for personal consumption, investment or capital formation, government purchases of goods and services and net foreign trade (exports minus imports). Each of these categories can be broken down. Private consumption is the sum of expenditures on durable goods (e.g., automobiles, furniture, appliances), nondurables (e.g., food, clothing, fuel) and services (airline tickets, haircuts, entertainment); investment includes fixed investment in nonresidential structures, producers' durable equipment (e.g., machinery), residential structures and the accumulation or drawing down of stocks (inventories); government purchases include both civil and military expenditures of the federal government and spending by state and local units of government. Except for inventories (which fluctuate widely in response to current conditions and are of little interest for this study) we shall look at all these, and later at a further breakdown of public expenditures by level and function.

In Table 1, the first column of figures—the percentage of variance explained—tells *how closely* defense spending and the alternate spending category vary together—how much of the changes in the latter can be "accounted for" by defense changes. The regression coefficient tells *the amount in dollars* by which the alternate spending category changes in response to a one dollar increase in defense. The proportionate reduction index shows the damage suffered by each category relative to its "normal" base. It assumes for illustration a total G.N.P. of $400 billion, an increase of $25 billion in defense spending from the previous period, and that the alternative expenditure category had previously been at that level represented by its mean percentage of G.N.P. over the 1946–67 period. This last measure is important for policy purposes, since the *impact* of the same dollar reduction will be far greater to a $100 billion investment program than to a $500 billion total for consumer spending.

Table 1 The Effect of Defense Spending on Civilian Activities in the United States, 1939–68

	% of Variation	Regression Coefficient	Index of Proportionate Reduction
Personal Consumption			
Total	84	−.420	−.041
Durable Goods	78	−.163	−.123
Nondurable Goods	04	−.071	−.014
Services	54	−.187	−.050
Fixed Investment			
Total	72	−.292	−.144
Nonresidential Structures	62	−.068	−.140
Producers' Durable Equipment	71	−.110	−.123
Residential Structures	60	−.114	−.176
Exports	67	−.097	−.115
Imports	19	−.025	−.037
Federal Civil Purchases	38	−.048	−.159
State and Local Government			
Consumption	38	−.128	−.105

Looking at Table 1, one can see that, in general, the American experience has been that the consumer pays most. Guns do come at the expense of butter. Changes in defense expenditure account for 84 percent of the ups and downs in total personal *consumption,* and the regression coefficient is a relatively high −.420. That is, a one dollar rise in defense expenditures will, all else being equal, result in a decline of $.42 in private consumption.

Of the subcategories, sales of consumer durables are most vulnerable, with 78 percent of their variations accounted for by defense. Spending on services is also fairly vulnerable to defense expenditures, with the latter accounting for 54 percent of the variance. But the negative effect of defense spending on nondurables is not nearly so high, with only 4 percent of the variance accounted for. This is not surprising, however, as needs for nondurables are almost by definition the least easily postponed. Moreover, during the World War II years new consumer durables such as automobiles and appliances were virtually unavailable, since the factories that normally produced them were then turning out war material. Similarly, due to manpower shortages almost all services were expensive and in short supply, and long-distance travel was particularly discouraged ("Is this trip necessary?"). Hence, to the degree that the consumers' spending power was not mopped up by taxes or saved, an unusually high proportion was likely to go into nondurables.

Investment (fixed capital formation) also is typically hard-hit by American war efforts and, because it means a smaller productive capacity in later years, diminished investment is a particularly costly loss. Defense accounted for 72 percent of the variations in investment, which is only a little less than that for defense on consumption, and the reduction of $.292 in investment for every $1.00 rise in defense is substantial. The coefficient is of course much lower than that for defense and consumption (with a coefficient of −.420) but that is very deceptive considering the "normal" base from which each starts. Over the thirty years for which we have the figures, consumption took a mean percentage of G.N.P. that was typically about five times as great as investment. Thus in our hypothetical illustration a $25 billion increase in defense costs in a G.N.P. of $400 billion would, *ceteris paribus,* result in a drop in consumption from approximately $256 billion to roughly $245 billion or only a little over 4 percent of total consumption. Investment, on the other hand, would typically fall from $51 billion to about $44 billion, or more than 14 percent. *Proportionately,* therefore, investment is much *harder* hit by an expansion of the armed services than is consumption. Since future production is dependent upon current investment, the economy's *future* resources and power base are thus much more severely damaged by the decision to build or employ current military power than is current indulgence. According to some rough estimates, the marginal productivity of capital in the United States is between 20 and 25 percent; that is, an additional dollar of investment in any single year will produce 20–25 cents of annual additional production in perpetuity. Hence if an extra billion dollars of defense in one year reduced investment by $292 million, thenceforth the level of output in the economy would be *permanently* diminished by a figure on the order of $65 million per year.

This position is modified slightly by the detailed breakdown of investment categories. Residential structures (housing) vary less closely with defense spending than do nonhousing structures or durable goods for producers, but its regression coefficient is the strongest and shows that it takes the greatest proportionate damage. Within the general category of investment, therefore, nonresidential structures and equipment usually hold up somewhat better proportionately than does housing. Doubtless this is the result of deliberate public policy, which raises home interest rates and limits the availability of mortgages while trying at the same time to maintain an adequate flow of capital to those firms needing to convert or expand into military production.

The nation's international *balance of payments* is often a major casualty of sharp increases in military expenditures; the present situation is not unusual. Some potential exports are diverted to satisfy internal demand, others are lost because domestic inflation raises costs to a point where the goods are priced out of the world market. Imports may rise directly to meet the armed forces' procurement needs—goods purchased abroad to fill local American military requirements show up as imports to the national economy—and other imports rise indirectly because of domestic demand. Some goods normally purchased from domestic suppliers are not available in sufficient quantities; others, because of inflation, become priced above imported goods. If the present situation is "typical," the Vietnam war's cost to the civilian economy would be responsible for a loss of more than $1.5 billion dollars in exports.

The import picture is more complicated. According to the sketch above, imports should *rise* with defense spending, but in Table 1 the percentage of variance explained is very low and the regression coefficient is actually *negative.* This, however, is deceptive. The four years of World War II show unusually low importation due to a combination of enemy occupation of normal sources of goods for the United States, surface and submarine combat in the sea lanes and the diversion of our allies' normal export industries to serve *their* war needs. To assess the impact of defense expenditures on imports in a less than global war one must omit the World War II data from the analysis. Doing so produces the expected rise in imports with higher defense spending, on the order of +.060. This suggests that the current effect of Vietnam may be to add, directly and indirectly, over $1 billion to the nation's annual import bill. Coupled with the loss of exports, the total damage to the balance of payments on current account (excluding capital transfers) is in the range $2.5–$3.0 billion. That still does not account for the entire balance of payments deficit that the United States is experiencing (recently as high as $3.4 billion annually) but it goes a long way to explain it.

The Public Sector

In the aggregate there is no very strong impact of defense on *civil public expenditures.* The amount of variation accounted for by defense is a comparatively low 38 percent; the regression coefficients are only –.048 for federal civil purchases and –.013 for state and local governments. During the four peak years of World War II changes in federal civil expenditures were essentially unrelated to changes in defense spending. Samuel P. Huntington, however, notes, "Many programs in agriculture, natural resources, labor and welfare dated back to the 1930's or middle 1940's. By the mid-1950's they had become accepted responsibilities of the government," and hence politically resistant to the arms squeeze. If so, the overall inverse relationship we do find may be masking sharper changes in some of the less well-entrenched subcategories of central government budgeting. Further masking of the impact on actual programs may stem from the inability of government agencies to reduce costs for building-maintenance and tenured employees, thus forcing them in dry times to cut other expenses disproportionately.

When relating state and local government expenditures to defense some restraint is required. There really is no relationship except *between* the points above and below the 15 percent mark for defense. During World War II state and local government units did have their spending activities curtailed, but overall they have not been noticeably affected by defense purchases. Quite to the contrary, spending by state and local political units has risen steadily, in an almost unbroken line, since 1944. The rise, from 3.6 percent of the G.N.P. to 11.2 percent in 1968, has continued essentially heedless of increases or diminution in the military's demands on the economy.

When we look at the breakdowns by function, however, it becomes clear that the effect of defense fluctuations is more serious, if less distinct than for G.N.P. categories. I have chosen three major items—education, health and welfare—for further analysis, on the grounds that one might reasonably hypothesize for each that expenditure levels would be sensitive to military needs, and, for the first two, that a neglect of them would do serious long-term damage to the economy and social system of the nation.

All three are sensitive to defense spending, with *welfare* somewhat more so than the others, which is not surprising. In most of this analysis reductions in expenditure levels that are forced by expanded defense activities represent a *cost* to the economic and social system, but welfare is different. Insofar as the *needs* for welfare, rather than simply the resources allocated to it, are reduced, one cannot properly speak of a cost to the economy. Rather, if one's social preferences are for work rather than welfare, the shift represents a *gain* to the system. Heavy increases in military pay and procurement do mean a reduction in unemployment, and military cutbacks are often associated with at least temporary or local unemployment. The effect seems strongest on state and local governments' welfare spending. In fact, the inverse relationship between defense and welfare at most spending levels is *understated* at 54 percent on Table 2. At all but the highest levels of defense spending achieved in World War II, the inverse relationship is very steep, with small increases in military needs having a very marked dampening effect on welfare costs. But manpower was quite fully employed during *all* the years of major effort in World War II, so ups and downs in defense needs during 1942–45 had little effect.

Table 2 The Effect of Defense Spending on Public Civil Activities in the U.S., Fiscal Years 1938–67

	% of Variation	Regression Coefficient	Index of Proportionate Reduction
Education—Total	*35*	*−.077*	*−.139*
Institutions of Higher Education	12	−.013	−.146
Local Schools	34	−.053	−.125
Other Education	19	−.014	−.265
Federal Direct to Education	16	−.013	−.309
Federal to State and Local Governments for Education	08	−.004	−.140
State and Local Government for Education	24	−.060	−.124
Health and Hospitals—Total	*32*	*−.017*	*−.113*
Total Hospitals	30	−.014	−.123
Federal for Hospitals	25	−.004	−.130
State and Local for Hospitals	29	−.011	−.120
Other Health—Total	*22*	*−.003*	*−.087*
Federal for Health	06	−.001	−.101
State and Local for Health	45	−.002	−.078
Welfare—Total	*54*	*.019*	*−.128*
Federal Direct for Welfare	13	.003	−.493
Federal to State and Local Governments for Welfare	17	−.005	−.087
State and Local for Welfare	30	−.011	−.134

Both for education and for health and hospitals, the relationship to the immediate requirements of national defense is less powerful (less variance is explained), but nonetheless important. Furthermore, the regression coefficient is quite high for education, and since the mean share of G.N.P. going to education is only 3.5 percent for the period under consideration, the proportionate impact of reductions is severe.

A widespread assumption holds that public expenditures on *education* have experienced a long-term secular growth in the United States. That assumption is correct only with modifications. The proportion of G.N.P. devoted to public education has increased by three quarters over the period, from 3.0 percent in 1938 to 5.3 percent in 1967. But it has by no means been a smooth and steady upward climb. World War II cut deeply into educational resources, dropping the educational percentage of G.N.P. to 1.4 in 1944; only in 1950 did it recover to a level (3.6 percent) notably above that of the 1930's. Just at that point the Korean War intervened, and education once more suffered, not again surpassing the 3.6 percent level before 1959. Since then, however, it has grown fairly steadily without being adversely affected by the relatively modest rises in defense spending. Actually, educational needs may have benefitted somewhat from the overall decline in the military proportion of the economy that took place between the late 1950's and mid-1960's. The sensitivity of educational expenditures to military needs is nevertheless much more marked on the latter's upswings than on its declines. Education usually suffers very immediately when the military needs to expand sharply; it recovers its share only slowly after defense spending has peaked. Surprisingly, *federal* educational expenditures are less related (less variance explained) than is spending by state and local units of government; also, local schools at the primary and secondary levels are more sensitive than are public institutions of higher education, whose share has grown in every year since 1953.

Public expenditures for *health* and hospitals are only a little less sensitive to the pressures of defense than are dollars for education. Here again the image of a long-term growth deceptively hides an equally significant pattern of swings. Health and hospitals accounted for a total of .77 percent of G.N.P. in 1938; as with education this was sharply cut by World War II and was not substantially surpassed (at 1 percent) until 1950. Once more they lost out to the exigencies of defense in the early 1950's, and bounced back slowly, at the same rate as did education, to recover the 1950 level in 1958. Since then they have continued growing slowly, with a peak of 1.23 in 1967. Thus, the pattern of health and hospitals is almost identical to that for education—some long-term growth, but great cutbacks in periods of heavy military need and only slow recovery thereafter. In detail by political unit the picture is also much the same—despite reasonable a priori expectation, federal spending for this item is less closely tied to the defense budget than is that by state and local governments. It should also be noted that the *impact* of defense on health and hospitals is slightly less severe than on education.

It seems fair to conclude from these data that America's most expensive wars have severely hampered the nation in its attempt to build a healthier and better-educated citizenry. (One analyst estimates that what *was* done to strengthen education accounted for nearly half of the United States per capita income growth between 1929 and 1957.) A long-term effort has been made, and with notable results, but typically it has been badly cut back whenever military needs pressed unusually hard.

It is too soon to know how damaging the Vietnam war will be, but in view of past patterns one would anticipate significant costs. The inability to make "investments" would leave Americans poorer, more ignorant and less healthy than would otherwise be the case. We have already seen the effect of the war on fixed capital formation. Consumption absorbed a larger *absolute* decline in its share of G.N.P. between 1965 and 1968 than did fiscal investment—from 63.3 to 62.1 percent in the first instance, from 14.3 to 13.8 percent in the second; but given the much smaller base of investment, the *proportionate* damage is about twice as great to investment as to consumption. In most of the major categories of public social "investment," nevertheless, the record is creditable. Despite a rise from 7.6 to 9.1 percent in the defense share between 1965 and 1967, the total public education and health and hospitals expenditure shares went up 4.5 to 5.3 percent and from 1.17 to 1.23 percent respectively. And even federal spending for education and health, though not hospitals, rose. There are of course other costs involved in the inability to *initiate* needed programs—massive aid to the cities is the obvious example. But on maintaining or expanding established patterns of expenditure the score is not bad at all.

The pattern of federal expenditures for *research and development* indicates some recent but partially hidden costs to education and medicine. From 1955 through 1966 R & D expenditures rose spectacularly and steadily from $3.3 billion to $14.9 billion. Obviously such a skyrocketing growth could not continue indefinitely; not even most of the beneficiary scientists expected it to do so, and in fact the rate of increase of expenditures fell sharply as early as 1966–the first year since 1961 when the defense share of G.N.P. showed any notable increase.

Finally, we must note a very important sense in which many of these cost estimates are substantially underestimated. My entire analysis has necessarily been done with expenditure data in current prices; that is, not adjusted for inflation. Since we have been dividing each expenditure category by G.N.P. in current dollars that would not matter *providing that price increases were uniform throughout the economy.* But if prices increased faster in, say, education or health than did prices across the board, the *real* level of expenditure would be exaggerated. And as anyone who has recently paid a hospital bill or college tuition bill knows, some prices have increased faster than others. From 1950 through 1967 the cost of medical care, as registered in the consumer price index, rose by 86.2 percent. Thus even though the health and hospital share of public expenditure rose in *current* prices, the *real share* of national production bought by that spending *fell* slightly, from one percent to about .99 percent. Presumably the difference has been made up in the private sector, and benefits have been heavily dependent upon ability to pay. Comparable data on educational expenses are less easy to obtain, but we do know that the average tuition in private colleges and universities rose 39 percent, and in public institutions 32 percent, over the years 1957–1967. This too is faster than the cost of living increase over those years (not more than 20 percent), but not enough to wipe out a gain for government education expenditures in their share of real G.N.P.

In evaluating the desirability of an expanded defense effort, policy-makers must bear in mind the opportunity costs of defense, the kinds and amounts of expenditures that will be foregone. The relationships we have discovered in past American experience suggest what the costs of future military efforts may be, although these relationships are not of course immutable. Should it be concluded that certain new defense needs must be met, it is possible by careful choice and control to distribute the burdens somewhat differently. If costs cannot be avoided, perhaps they can be borne in such a way as to better protect the nation's future.

The Garrison State

35

Harold D. Lasswell

The purpose of this article is to consider the possibility that we are moving toward a world of "garrison states"—a world in which the specialists on violence are the most powerful group in society. From this point of view the trend of our time is away from the dominance of the specialist on bargaining, who is the businessman, and toward the supremacy of the soldier. We may distinguish transitional forms, such as the party propaganda state, where the dominant figure is the propagandist, and the party bureaucratic state, in which the organization men of the party make the vital decisions. There are mixed forms in which predominance is shared by the monopolists of party and market power.

All men are deeply affected by their expectations as well as by their desires. We time our specific wants and efforts with some regard to what we reasonably hope to get. Hence, when we act rationally, we consider alternative versions of the future, making explicit those expectations about the future that are so often buried in the realm of hunch.

In the practice of social science, as of any skill in society, we are bound to be affected in some degree by our conceptions of future development. There are problems of timing in the prosecution of scientific work, timing in regard to availability of data and considerations of policy. In a world where primitive societies are melting away it is rational to act promptly to gather data about primitive forms of social organization. In a world in which the scientist may also be a democratic citizen, sharing democratic respect for human personality, it is rational for the scientist to give priority to problems connected with the survival of democratic society. There is no question here of a scientist deriving his values from science; values are *acquired* chiefly from personal experience of a given culture, *derived* from that branch of culture that is philosophy and theology, *implemented* by science and practice.

The picture of the garrison state that is offered here is no dogmatic forecast. Rather it is a picture of the probable. It is not inevitable. It may not even have the same probability as some other descriptions of the future course of development. What, then, is the function of this picture for scientists? It is to stimulate the individual specialist to clarify for himself his expectations about the future, as a guide to the timing of scientific work. Side by side with this "construct" of a garrison state there may be other constructs . . .

Expectations about the future may rest upon the extrapolation of past trends into the future. We may choose a number of specific items—like population and production curves—and draw them into the future according to some stated rule. This is an "itemistic" procedure. In contrast, we may set up a construct that is frankly imaginative though disciplined by careful consideration of the past. Since trend curves summarize many features of the past, they must be carefully considered in the preparation of every construct.

. . .

To speak of a garrison state is not to predict something wholly new under the sun. Certainly there is nothing novel to the student of political institutions about the idea that specialists on violence may run the state. On the contrary, some of the most influential discussions of political institutions have named the military state as one of the chief forms of organized society. Comte saw history as a succession (and a progression) that moved, as far as it concerned the state, through military, feudal, and industrial phases. Spencer divided all human societies into the military type, based on force, and the industrial type, based on contract and free consent.

What is important for our purposes is to envisage the possible emergence of the military state under present technical conditions. There are no examples of the military state combined with modern technology. During emergencies the great powers have given enormous scope to military authority, but temporary acquisitions of authority lack the elements of comparative permanence and acceptance that complete the garrison state. Military dictators in states marginal to the creative centers of Western civilization are not integrated with modern technology; they merely use some of its specific elements.

The military men who dominate a modern technical society will be very different from the officers of history and tradition. It is probable that the specialists on violence will include in their training a large degree of expertness in many of the skills that we have traditionally accepted as part of modern civilian management.

The distinctive frame of reference in a fighting society is fighting effectiveness. All social change is translated into battle potential. Now there can be no realistic calculation of fighting effectiveness without knowledge of the technical and psychological characteristics of modern production processes. The function of management in such a society is already known to us; it includes the exercise of skill in supervising technical operations, in administrative organization, in personnel management, in public relations. These skills are needed to translate the complicated operations of modern life into every relevant frame of reference—the frame of fighting effectiveness as well as of pecuniary profit.

This leads to the seeming paradox that, as modern states are militarized, specialists on violence are more preoccupied with the skills and attitudes judged characteristic of nonviolence. We anticipate the merging of skills, starting from the traditional accouterments of the professional soldier, moving toward the manager and promoter of large-scale civilian enterprise.

In the garrison state, at least in its introductory phases, problems of morale are destined to weigh heavily on the mind of management. It is easy to throw sand in the gears of the modern assembly line; hence, there must be a deep and general sense of participation in the total enterprise of the state if collective effort is to be sustained. When we call attention to the importance of the "human factor" in modern production, we sometimes fail to notice that it springs from the multiplicity of special environments that have been created by modern technology. Thousands of technical operations have sprung into existence where a few hundred were found before. To complicate the material environment in this way is to multiply the foci of attention of those who live in our society. Diversified foci of attention breed differences in outlook, preference, and loyalty. The labyrinth of specialized "material" environments generates profound ideological divergencies that cannot be abolished, though they can be mitigated, by the methods now available to leaders in our society. As long as modern technology prevails, society is honeycombed with cells of separate experience, of individuality, of partial freedom. Concerted action under such conditions depends upon skillfully guiding the minds of men; hence the enormous importance of symbolic manipulation in modern society.

The importance of the morale factor is emphasized by the universal fear which it is possible to maintain in large populations through modern instruments of warfare. The growth of aerial warfare in particular has tended to abolish the distinction between civilian and military functions. It is no longer possible to affirm that those who enter the military service take the physical risk while those who remain at home stay safe and contribute to the equipment and the comfort of the courageous heroes at the front. Indeed, in some periods of modern warfare, casualties among civilians may outnumber the casualties of the armed forces. With the socialization of danger as a permanent characteristic of modern violence the nation becomes one unified technical enterprise. Those who direct the violence operations are compelled to consider the entire gamut of problems that arise in living together under modern conditions.

. . .

In the garrison state there must be work—and the duty to work—for all. Since all work becomes public work, all who do not accept employment flout military discipline. For those who do not fit within the structure of the state there is but one alternative—to obey or die. Compulsion, therefore, is to be expected as a potent instrument for internal control of the garrison state.

The use of coercion can have an important effect upon many more people than it reaches directly; this is the propaganda component of any "propaganda of the deed." The spectacle of compulsory labor gangs in prisons or concentration camps is a negative means of conserving morale—negative since it arouses fear and guilt. Compulsory labor groups are suitable popular scapegoats in a military state. The duty to obey, to serve the state, to work —these are cardinal virtues in the garrison state. Unceasing emphasis upon duty is certain to arouse opposing tendencies within the personality structure of all who live under a garrison regime. Everyone must struggle to hold in check any tendencies, conscious or unconscious, to defy authority, to violate the code of work, to flout the incessant demand for sacrifice in the collective interest. From the earliest years youth will be trained to subdue—to disavow, to struggle against—any specific opposition to the ruling code of collective exactions.

. . .

The chief targets of compulsory labor service will be unskilled manual workers, together with counterélite elements who have come under suspicion. The position of the unskilled in our society has been deteriorating, since the machine society has less and less use for unskilled manual labor. The coming of the machine was a skill revolution, a broadening of the role of the skilled and semiskilled components of society. As the value of labor declines in production, it also declines in warfare; hence, it will be treated with less consideration. (When unskilled workers are relied upon as fighters, they must, of course, share the ideological exultation of the community as a whole and receive a steady flow of respect from the social environment.) Still another factor darkens the forecast for the bottom layers of the population in the future garrison state. If recent advances in pharmacology continue, as we may anticipate, physical means of controlling response can replace symbolic methods. This refers to the use of drugs not only for temporary orgies of energy on the part of front-line fighters but in order to deaden the critical function of all who are not held in esteem by the ruling elite.

For the immediate future, however, ruling élites must continue to put their chief reliance upon propaganda as an instrument of morale. But the manipulation of symbols, even in conjunction with coercive instruments of violence, is not sufficient to accomplish all the purposes of a ruling group. We have already spoken of the socialization of danger, and this will bring about some equalitarian adjustments in the distribution of income for the purpose of conserving the will to fight and to produce.

. . .

As legislatures and elections go out of use, the practice of petition will play a more prominent role. Lawmaking will be in the hands of the supreme authority and his council; and, as long as the state survives, this agency will exert effective control ("authority" is the term for formal expectations, "control" is the actual distribution of effective power).

This means that instrumental democracy will be in abeyance, although the symbols of mystic "democracy" will doubtless continue. Instrumental democracy is found wherever authority and control are widely dispersed among the members of a state. Mystic "democracy" is not, strictly speaking, democracy at all, because it may be found where authority and control are highly concentrated yet where part of the established practice is to speak in the name of the people as a whole. Thus, any dictatorship may celebrate its "democracy" and speak with contempt of such "mechanical" devices as majority rule at elections or in legislatures.

What part of the social structure would be drawn upon in recruiting the political rulers of the garrison state? . . . the process will not be by general election but by self-perpetuation through co-option. The foremost positions will be open to the officers corps, and the problem is to predict from what part of the social structure the officers will be recruited. Morale considerations justify a broad base of recruitment for ability rather than social standing. Although fighting effectiveness is a relatively impersonal test that favors ability over inherited status, the turnover in ruling families from generation to generation will probably be low. Any recurring crisis, however, will strengthen the tendency to favor ability. It seems clear that recruitment will be much more for bias and obedience than for objectivity and originality. Yet, as we shall presently see, modern machine society has introduced new factors in the military state—factors tending to strengthen objectivity and originality.

In the garrison state all organized social activity will be governmentalized ... Government will be highly centralized, though devolution may be practiced in order to mitigate "bureaucratism." There is so much outspoken resistance to bureaucratism in modern civilization that we may expect this attitude to carry over to the garrison state. Not only will the administrative structure be centralized, but at every level it will tend to integrate authority in a few hands. The leadership principle will be relied upon; responsibility as a rule will be focused upon individual "heads."

We have sketched some of the methods at the disposal of the ruling élites of the garrison state—the management of propaganda, violence, goods, practices. Let us consider the picture from a slightly different standpoint. How will various kinds of influence be distributed in the state? Power will be highly concentrated, as in any dictatorial regime. We have already suggested that there will be a strong tendency toward equalizing the distribution of safety throughout the community (that is, negative safety, the socialization of threat in modern war). In the interest of morale there will be some moderation of huge differences in individual income, flattening the pyramid at the top, bulging it out in the upper-middle and middle zones. In the garrison state the respect pyramid will probably resemble the income pyramid. (Those who are the targets of compulsory labor restrictions will be the principal recipients of negative respect and hence will occupy the bottom levels.) So great is the multiplicity of functions in modern processes of production that a simple scheme of military rank is flagrantly out of harmony with the facts. Even though a small number of ranks are retained in the military state, it will be recognized that the diversity of functions exercised by each rank is so great that the meaning of a specific classification will be obscure. Summarizing, the distribution of power will show the largest inequalities. The patterns of income and respect will fall between these two, showing a pronounced bulge in the upper-middle and middle strata. The lower strata of the community will be composed of those subject to compulsory labor, tending to constitute a permanent pariah caste.

What about the capacity of the garrison state to produce a large volume of material values? The élites of the garrison state, like the élites of recent business states, will confront the problem of holding in check the stupendous productive potentialities of modern science and engineering. We know that the ruling élites of the modern business state have not known how to control productive capacity; they have been unwilling to adopt necessary measures for the purpose of regularizing the tempo of economic development. Hence, modern society has been characterized by periods of orgiastic expansion, succeeded by periods of flagrant underutilization of the instruments of production.

The rulers of the garrison state will be able to regularize the rate of production, since they will be free from many of the conventions that have stood in the way of adopting measures suitable to this purpose in the business state. The business élite has been unwilling to revise institutional practices to the extent necessary to maintain a continually rising flow of investment. The institutional structure of the business state has called for flexible adjustment between governmental and private channels of activity and for strict measures to maintain price flexibility. Wherever the business élite has not supported such necessary arrangements, the business state itself has begun to disintegrate.

Although the rulers of the garrison state will be free to regularize the rate of production, they will most assuredly prevent full utilization of modern productive capacity for nonmilitary consumption purposes. The élite of the garrison state will have a professional interest in multiplying gadgets specialized to acts of violence. The rulers of the garrison state will depend upon war scares as a means of maintaining popular willingness to forego immediate consumption. War scares that fail to culminate in violence eventually lose their value; this is the point at which ruling classes will feel that bloodletting is needed in order to preserve those virtues of sturdy acquiescence in the regime which they so much admire and from which they so greatly benefit. We may be sure that if ever there is a rise in the production of nonmilitary consumption goods, despite the amount of energy directed toward the production of military equipment, the ruling class will feel itself endangered by the growing "frivolousness" of the community.

We need to consider the degree to which the volume of values produced in a garrison state will be affected by the tendency toward rigidity. Many factors in the garrison state justify the expectation that tendencies toward repetitiousness and ceremonialization will be prominent. To some extent this is a function of bureaucracy and dictatorship. But to some extent it springs also from the preoccupation of the military state with danger. Even where military operations are greatly respected, the fighter must steel himself against deep-lying tendencies to retreat from death and mutilation. One of the most rudimentary and potent means of relieving fear is some repetitive operation—some reiteration of the old and well-established. Hence the reliance on drill as a means of disciplining men to endure personal danger without giving in to fear of death. The tendency to repeat, as a means of diminishing timidity, is powerfully reinforced by successful repetition, since the individual is greatly attached to whatever has proved effective in maintaining self-control in previous trials. Even those who deny the fear of death to themselves may reveal the depth of their unconscious fear by their interest in ritual and ceremony. This is one of the subtlest ways by which the individual can keep his mind distracted from the discovery of his own timidity. It does not occur to the ceremonialist that in the spider web of ceremony he has found a moral equivalent of war—an unacknowledged substitute for personal danger.

The tendency to ceremonialize rather than to fight will be particularly prominent among the most influential elements in a garrison state. Those standing at the top of the military pyramid will doubtless occupy high positions in the income pyramid. During times of actual warfare it may be necessary to make concessions in the direction of moderating gross-income differences in the interest of preserving general morale. The prospect of such concessions may be expected to operate as a deterrent factor against war. A countervailing tendency, of course, is the threat to sluggish and well-established members of the upper crust from ambitious members of the lower officers' corps. This threat arises, too, when there are murmurs of disaffection with the established order of things on the part of broader components of the society.

It seems probable that the garrison state of the future will be far less rigid than the military states of antiquity. As long as modern technical society endures, there will be an enormous body of specialists whose focus of attention is entirely given over to the discovery of novel ways of utilizing nature. Above all, these are physical scientists and engineers. They are able to demonstrate by rather impersonal procedures the efficiency of many of their suggestions for the improvement of fighting effectiveness. We therefore anticipate further exploration of the technical potentialities of modern civilization within the general framework of the garrison state.

What are some of the implications of this picture for the research program of scientists who, in their capacity as citizens, desire to defend the dignity of human personality?

It is clear that the friend of democracy views the emergence of the garrison state with repugnance and apprehension. He will do whatever is within his power to defer it. Should the garrison state become unavoidable, however, the friend of democracy will seek to conserve as many values as possible within the general framework of the new society. What democratic values can be preserved, and how?

Our analysis has indicated that several elements in the pattern of the garrison state are compatible with democratic respect for human dignity. Thus, there will be some socialization of respect for all who participate in the garrison society (with the ever present exception of the lowest strata).

Will the human costs of a garrison state be reduced if we civilianize the ruling élite? Just how is it possible to promote the fusion of military and civilian skills? What are some of the devices capable of overcoming bureaucratism? To what extent is it possible to aid or to retard the ceremonializing tendencies of the garrison state?

It is plain that we need more adequate data from the past on each of these problems and that it is possible to plan to collect relevant data in the future. We need, for instance, to be better informed about the trends in the skill pattern of dominant élite groups in different parts of the world. In addition to trend data we need experimental and case data about successful and unsuccessful civilianizing of specialists on violence.

Many interesting questions arise in connection with the present sketch about transition to the garrison state. What is the probable order of appearance—Japan, Germany, Russia, United States of America? What are the probable combinations of bargaining, propaganda, organization, and violence skills in éites? Is it probable that the garrison state will appear with or without violent revolution? Will the garrison state appear first in a small number of huge Continental states (Russia, Germany, . . . United States) or in a single world-state dominated by one of these powers? With what symbol patterns will the transition to the garrison state be associated? . . .

The function of any developmental construct, such as the present one about the garrison state, is to clarify to the specialist the possible relevance of his research to impending events that concern the values of .which he approves as a citizen. Although they are neither scientific laws nor dogmatic forecasts, developmental constructs aid in the timing of scientific work, stimulating both planned observation of the future and renewed interest in whatever past events are of greatest probable pertinence to the emerging future. Within the general structure of the science of society there is place for many special sciences devoted to the study of all factors that condition the survival of selected values. This is the sense in which there can be a science of democracy, or a science of political psychiatry, within the framework of social science. If the garrison state is probable, the timing of special research is urgent.